APPROACHES
TO
SEMIOTICS

edited by

THOMAS A. SEBEOK

Research Center for the Language Sciences
Indiana University

36

THE SEMIOTICS OF HUMAN SOUND

by

PETER F. OSTWALD

1973

MOUTON

THE HAGUE · PARIS

LIBRARY OF CONGRESS CATALOG CARD NUMBER: 73-84551

Printed in The Netherlands by Zuid-Nederlandsche Drukkerij nv, 's-Hertogenbosch

FOREWORD

For anyone interested in sound, a book poses some delicate problems. First, there is the unmistakable fact that books are silent documents. Reading them can rarely give you the PRIMARY EXPERIENCE of sound which is obtainable by listening to a lecture, turning on the radio, or engaging in a conversation. Second, there is the problem of the cipher-system – in this instance printed language. When we hear language spoken, it becomes easier to relate the meaning of words to the people who are speaking, to the immediate purpose of the talk, and to the social context in which the speaker and listener are embedded. But as soon as something gets WRITTEN DOWN, especially in verbal form, a SECONDARY PROCESS of intellectualization has to take over. The sonic communicative experience becomes more abstract, and the meanings of messages – which were originally social interchanges – seem to assume a life-of-their-own, divorced from the immediate needs of people. Thus ideas, once committed to paper, run the risk of being taken out of context, of being overvalued, or of being ignored.

This is a particular danger with so-called 'papers' written as part of the scientific or scholarly pursuit of knowledge. One may feel himself to be 'on the right track', and after a certain amount of discussion be encouraged to 'put it in writing', only to find out later that this track went into a misleading or unwanted direction. By that time it is impossible to 'retract' very much, and an author is then faced with the prospect of either having to disown part of his past or of trying to amend it with additional writing.

The opportunity given me by the editors of Mouton and Company to publish those of my papers which deal with the Semiotics of Human Sound therefore led me to re-read what I have written (which cannot be exactly the same as what I have thought, felt, or said) in the course of some dozen-or-so years of professional affiliation with a Medical School and Neuropsychiatric Institute. Here we have different groups of students, earning degrees in medicine, psychiatry, psychology, physiology, and other fields. We also have different groups of patients some who speak too much, others who speak too little, and still others who are unable to form words properly, or to listen. In attempting to help the patients and train the students, my colleagues and I want to find better ways of UNDERSTANDING human behavior, and it is that goal which motivates our research.

One of the most interesting developments in psychiatric theory during the past quarter of a century has been the possibility of understanding nonverbal aspects of psychopathology. Whereas content of messages was the focus of diagnostic and therapeutic interest for such a long time, we can now deal much better with the FORMS of human expression – the bodily movements, the facial gestures, the vocal behavior, and the proxemic patterns. My own research fits best, I suppose, into the field which G. Trager (1958) so imaginatively christened PARALANGUAGE, and I hope that the present collection of papers may serve to review some of the important developments that have taken place in this field. But since sound and paralanguage cannot be analyzed without also paying attention to language, I will have to take the risk of offending those readers who are qualified linguists (my credentials are in psychiatry) by commenting from time to time on what I think language is all about.

Let me say a few words for example about the curious attitudes, or 'ambivalences', which so many members of my profession hold in regard to language. I do not know to what extent linguists or other scientists with a primary investment in the study of language might also be subject to these attitudes, but if they are this could partly account for some of the ways that paralinguistic research has been both stimulated and neglected during the past 15 years.

Psychiatry treats language[1] (and its collateral paralanguage) with a mixture of reverence and disdain. As practitioners we are of course quite fond of verbal behavior and do a lot of listening and speaking in our daily work with patients. The orderliness, logical structure, and symbolic richness of language tantalizes our intellectual curiosity. Every psychiatric

---

[1] An excellent definition of language was provided by John B. Carroll (1955): "A language is a structured system of arbitrary vocal sounds and sequences of sounds which is used, or can be used, in interpersonal communication by an aggregation of human beings, and which rather exhaustively catalogs the things, events, and processes in the human environment."

examination includes an analysis of language – not only what the patient says but also how he says it and what meanings he tries to convey. But on the other hand, we are deeply suspicious of language. Psychiatrists know that verbalization is only one of several modalities for human self-expression, and that when a patient relies on language too much he can be as seriously upset as when he doesn't use it at all. Linguistic symbols have to be patterned in linear sequences and tied to conventionalized meanings. This skill, once mastered, can be used to mislead as well as to inform and psychiatry has a toolshed filled with tests and special methods to go beyond the deliberate formulas of speech so as to understand who a patient really is, what he expects from life, and where he gets mixed up in his behavior with people.

When I went to medical school (1946-1950) linguistics was not yet a subject that could by any stretch of the imagination be considered 'relevant' to biology. Its sibling relationship to anthropology assured that only those students who looked beyond anatomy and physiology would be the slightest bit interested in language sciences. If these students needed encouragement, they could find it in the work of J. Ruesch and G. Bateson (1951), who put the field of communication on the map, so to speak, for the new generation of psychiatrists.

While an initial contact with the study of language might indicate to the physician that he will find here a degree of clarity which is a welcome relief from the uncertainty of clinical work, closer inspection of the field soon shatters that illusion. Notably within the last decade under the influence of N. Chomsky (1965), linguistics became passionately focused on the intrinsic structure of the language code, especially on 'deeper' levels of grammatical generation and transformation. This led temporarily to a lessening of interest in the actual or 'surface' appearance of the verbal stream of language behavior, except among those more phonologically-oriented researchers – for example P. Lieberman (1967) – for whom any consideration of language has to include the study of sentence-determining acoustical cues. Now in the 1970's the powerful beacon of psycholinguistic research is again swinging towards the relationships between language and speaking, or what is known as sociolinguistics (Fishman 1971).

There have also been important changes in the neighboring fields, for example in psychology. During the time that I wrote the papers collected in this book, stimulus-response theories by B. F. Skinner (1957) excited the imagination of investigators who wished to discover how precisely a given vocal sound might be able to control a specific behavioral sequence. For a while it almost seemed as if any kind of sound would have to be considered 'verbal' so long as one is able to demonstrate a behavioral response to it. This conception of sonic communication threatened to upset the possibility of ever again separating verbal from nonverbal stimuli. Fortunately we were protected from this quagmire by the tidal wave which is pressing psychology towards a biological orientation. This wave gained momentum slowly but surely during the many years that J. Piaget observed and wrote about psychological processes, but only relatively recently and thanks to thoughtful translations has its full impact been felt (Furth 1969). During the intervening period a cross-fertilization between ethology and social psychology also took place, as realized in E. Lenneberg's contribution (1967).

The interdisciplinary work of scholars and scientists who met together at conferences or worked together on projects of mutual interest should also be mentioned. This technique for transmitting scientific information was in fact very instrumental in shaping the evolution of what we know about human sound and paralanguage. One has to hear and emit the sonic variations which are paralinguistically meaningful – reading about them is simply not enough – in contrast to language which can be understood through words. Thus the Indiana University Conference on Paralinguistics and Kinesics that T. A. Sebeok organized in 1962 represents an important milestone in scientific progress, bringing together practitioners from the different contributing fields, including linguistics, psychology, medicine, education, anthropology, and sociology, and placing paralanguage into its proper relationship to the other sciences concerned with signs, i.e., the general field of Semiotics.

I was invited to review the 'state of the art' of diagnostic semiology in Indiana, and tried to indicate some of the remarkable changes which have taken place in this field since the turn-of-the-century (see article 20, this volume). During the 19th century psychiatry was more neurological and dealt largely with organic theories about psychopathology. For several decades after the turn of the century, psychodynamic relationships were emphasized and psychoanalysis had its golden age. Around World War II, anthropologists and social scientists began telling us to be more respectful of cultural differences and societal controls, with the result that we entered an era of community psychiatry. The hospital is being used much less as a place for treating emotionally disturbed people, and the socio-economics of medical practice are changing also. These developments all have an impact on the way clinical semioticians are trained for practice and research.

To compensate for the shifts in emphasis and changing attitudes taking place in the neighboring fields in my own research over the years, I have divided the material of this book into five sections. Each has an introduction to indicate how it is related to the others. In general, you may expect to find, between the covers of this book, an approach to semiotics that lies midway between the computer specialist's and the cultural anthropologist's. Computer specialists must translate every behavioral item into a codification so that a machine can comprehend. Anthropologists must be sensitive to every conceivable nuance of social experience so that mankind can comprehend. Psychiatrists have to work in various orbits between these two extremes, since our job is to improve the psychobiological functions of identified persons in families and other social groups.

ACKNOWLEDGEMENTS

The source of any republished article is noted on its first page, and I am very grateful to the original publishers for permission to include this material in the book. In preparing the present volume, Mrs. Ruth Prael has diligently and most ably assisted with secretarial help. I have received grants from several sources over the years: The United States Public Health Service, Foundation's Fund for Research in Psychiatry, American Fund for Psychiatry, National Fund for Medical Education, Research Committee of the University of California, and the California Department of Mental Hygiene. Some of my projects have involved co-workers who are individually named in the appropriate places. Professor Thomas A. Sebeok of Indiana University has given wise counsel and direction. Jurgen Ruesch, M.D., Professor of Psychiatry at the University of California, has been unstintingly generous with ideas and encouragement. To these and others whose assistance has been so important I want to express my deep-felt thanks and sincere gratitude.

Peter Ostwald

CONTENTS

III. LISTENING – THE PERCEPTUAL EXPERIENCE OF SOUND

IV. EMPATHIC COMMUNICATION WITH SOUNDS THAT HAVE
MEANING

V. FRONTIERS OF RESEARCH

SECTION I

SOUNDS AND HUMAN BEHAVIOR

INTRODUCTORY STATEMENT

Soundmaking is a universal biological phenomenon. I am interested in the various sounds made by people, how they are produced and perceived, and under what conditions they become meaningful.

The first two papers, both written at about the same time over ten years ago, deal with this subject-matter rather differently. "Human Sounds" was intended for an audience of clinicians, is more metaphorical, and has an informal style. The second paper, written for the journal *Logos*, shows a more systematic approach and calls attention to the pertinent literature about human sounds available in 1959.

These were some of the fundamental viewpoints:

- Sounds are identified as ENVIRONMENTAL PRESSURE CHANGES which humans can use for obtaining information about the world they occupy and for influencing each other.
- Anatomical and physiological characteristics of the HUMAN BODY set limits to the way sound is received and emitted.
- Meaningfulness of sounds depends on (1) the immediate CONTEXTS in which any given pattern is heard or made, (2) the temporal SEQUENCES into which sound patterns are organized, and (3) MEMORY.
- Each discipline of knowledge – psychology, medicine, linguistics, philosophy, musicology, etc. – casts its own 'net' of meaning over the FLUCTUATING MANIFESTATIONS OF NATURE, thereby providing reference points to its own theories.

The next two papers, numbers 3 and 4, are about primitive oral sounds, viz. whistling and humming. They bring us closer to the BASICALLY EMOTIONAL nature of human soundmaking. Both whistling and humming have to do with hedonistic pleasures, with self-stimulation, with arousal and sleep, and with the desire to be soothed. The importance of sound in primal mother-child socialization is discussed, and we begin to consider how the soundmaking of infancy is gradually transformed into speech. (This topic will be taken up again in several places, for example Section V, of the present volume.)

The analysis of humming and whistling focuses on certain crucial contrasts between preverbal and verbal soundmaking. Nonverbal sounds have an immediate and universal appeal and are closer to the bio-genetically determined aspects of behavior. Verbal sounds, by contrast, belong to the socio-cultural repertoire. They are meaningful primarily in the context of language, which is acquired from the experience of being with other people and adapting one's signal-and-sign behavior to the practices of the community.

I should call attention at this point to several research findings which were published subsequent to the appearance of papers 1 through 4, because the ideas contained therein are confluent with my own. Two articles by Busnel and co-workers (1962) described the linguistic uses of whistling. They show photographs of the French Pyrenees region, where the terrain is such as to make whistling an extremely helpful form of communication. A few portraits of whistlers are given; interestingly these are exclusively pictures of men. The articles also contain sonagrams of different whistle sounds. Busnel was impressed with the absence of correlation between phonemic patterns and meaning. He suggested that rhythmic elements of the whistle may be important carriers of information. "The difficulty of breaking the whistle language down is that we do not know whether there are elements involved related to a phonemic or suprasegmental system, or whether the whistle language operates as a symbolic system with no current relationships" (Busnel 1962 – translation by L. Gantzel).

The topic of humming has received attention from Applebaum (1968), a pediatrician in Florida who studied the sounds made by infants while suckling and bottle-feeding. Using a laryngeal contact microphone, he recorded definite humming sounds, especially prominent when the infant sucks at the breast, but not directly correlated with the sucking movements. The sounds are very similar to coos which infants produce under conditions of relaxed social interaction when engaged in visual eye-contact and smiling. A colleague, Dr. Marjorie Raskin, recently told me that she discovered hum-like sounds to be unusually soporific in experiments with bio-feedback. The patient is required to regulate his brain-wave rhythm (Lynch and Paskewitz 1971) in accordance with a tone stimulus, which, when it reaches a certain frequency, tends to put the experimenter to sleep.

The last paper about *Sounds and Human Behavior* reviews some of the linguistic contributions to this subject. It was written almost ten years after the earlier papers, during which time I had the good fortune to become better acquainted with research and theories about language. Whatever struck me as useful for teaching medical students, clinical psychologists, and residents in psychiatry has been included in different lectures or seminars. The paper (5) is based on notes made between 1969 and 1971.

1

HUMAN SOUNDS*

(1960)

This chapter is about the sounds that people make. Humans are noisy creatures, and their sounds have been studied from many points of view. Musicology, phonetics, acoustics, and psychology are but a few of the possible approaches to human sounds. In the twentieth century sounds are generally considered within the framework of communication; they are looked upon as signals used to relay messages between a sender and a receiver (Ruesch and Bateson 1951).

We will be concerned here with many kinds of human sound, differing in complexity all the way from the simple body noises to the elaborate sound patterns called words. The table on page 21 shows how these different sounds can be arranged according to the conditions under which they are used in communication. For communication with body organ noises like burps or wheezes, for example, all that is required of the sender is an involuntary contraction of smooth-muscles. Any listener within hearing distance can recognize this sound. For communication with specialized sounds like speeches or symphonies, on the other hand, much more is involved. The sender must have a great deal of skill, training, ambition, and endurance, and only listeners who are receptive and ready to get the message can appreciate such sounds. Between the two extremes lie sounds that, for communication, require various degrees of preparation, training, and tolerance on the part of sender and receiver. These sounds include informally spoken words, and many of the so-called noises made with tools, machines, and musical instruments.

At any level shown in the table, communication may break down. Treatment of such breakdowns in communication with sounds may have

---

* Reprinted from D. A. Barbara (ed.), *Psychological and Psychiatric Aspects of Speech and Hearing* (Springfield, Illinois: Charles C. Thomas, Publisher, 1960).

Tabulation of conditions for communication with sounds

Type of Sound	Smooth Muscle Activity	Striated Muscle Activity	Volitional Control of Behavior	Experience With People	Language Skills	Group Audience
Public Speaking	+	+	+	+	+	+
Conversation	+	+	+	+	+	
Songs and Instrumental Music	+	+	+	+	(+)	
Oral Noises	+	+	+	(+)		
Tool and Machine Noises	+	+	+			
Noisy Behavior	+	+	(+)			
Body Organ Noises	+	(+)				

to be directed towards repair of the physical components of the sound-equipment: ears, hands, mouth, throat, etc. Or treatment may involve attention to the connections inside the sender or receiver: brain, nerves, endocrines, etc., which link these components together and coordinate their use. In either case the clinician must know about the traditions that are behind communication and recognize that social and environmental factors determine how people use sounds. He must also tolerate individual differences and respect the uniquely personal styles whereby people communicate with sounds.

Historical facts about sounds

Early man was given to mystical speculation about natural phenomena, including sounds. It was thought that sound must be a powerful and indestructible substance which animated everything that moved. Thus according to ancient folklore, the noises made by a spear on impact contained deathdealing powers and the roar of the waterfall contained the energy that caused the earth to tremble. The Assyrians felt that evil deities, like *Ea* and *Ramman*, produced dreaded sounds and that these caused thunder, tides, and winds. Even the sounds from human activities were at first held to be of superhuman origin. In Mesopotamia the goddess *Ishtar* allegedly produced music of "the soft reed pipe," and her partner *Tammuz* rendered "the tender voice." (Wellesz 1957).

But as his control over natural forces increased, man gradually lost his fear of many of these sounds and used them for pleasurable and defensive ends. For one thing, people found they could imitate many noises and use them to attract or frighten each other. With the mouth and throat they learned to mimic roaring beasts and warbling birds. Louder noises, like those of fire, wind, or rainfall, were symbolized by words, called onomatopoeias, closely resembling the actual sounds associated with these phenomena. They could imitate these sounds directly by using the body and various crude implements. The sounds produced by stamping on the ground and rattling bones and stones might resemble a stampede of animals, for example. Thunder was imitated by beating hollow tree trunks or thudding on skins stretched over empty pots. The calls of animals were produced by blowing into shells or horns. Whining and whirring sounds resulted from reeds that were blown or strings that were plucked (Sachs 1940).

Soon it was recognized that sounds, since they produced certain predictable forms of human behavior, could be used to control individuals and groups of people. The Egyptians, for example, made cunning use of trumpets and drums to summon their troops and incite them to battle. Their flutes and pipes stirred the populace to rapture and excited erotic frenzy for the Festival of Osiris. Among the Jews, vocal sounds in the form of psalms and chants served to induce religious feeling in the temple, while harps, viols, and trumpets came to be reserved for politics and warfare. The Bible, for example, cites the soothing effects of music on Saul and other important personages, and gives accounts of battles, like that of Jericho, where victory was attributed to the noise of trumpets.

During the Greek era of Western civilization, the subject of sounds was approached scientifically. Combinations of sounds capable of evoking various states of feeling in the human listener were systematically described with the result, for instance, that a poet could learn exactly how many syllables to use, and in what order, so that his verses might resemble the rhythms of funeral processions, dances, combat, and similar events. Tones and harmonies were subjected to acoustical analysis by Pythagoras and other mathematicians who measured the vibration frequencies of strings. The relationship between sounds and symbols was recognized, and the nature of language and speech was hotly debated by Socrates and his friends.

The Romans exploited what was known about sounds and expanded many of their established uses. Musical instruments became more complicated; in fact, two organs were found in the ruins of Pompeii. Roman generals skillfully employed noises for warfare. They stationed musicians in empty camps or located buglers far away from the main body of the army for the specific purpose of confusing and deceiving the enemy. Nero, who was a trained singer and instrumentalist, boosted his own popularity and discredited his rivals by employing a claque of more than five thousand persons for public meetings. He instructed this mob in the art of applause, distinguishing *bombi*, like the buzzing of bees, *imbrices*, like the sounds of rain or hail on a roof, and *testae*, like the crashing of pots.

With the collapse of the Roman Empire much knowledge about sounds was lost and many of the arts of sound-making went into decline. Musical instruments were destroyed and performance of vocal music was hampered by religious rules and regulations. Some pre-Christian traditions, such as the Oriental pentatonic scale, survived in monasteries and ghettos. Until the eighth century A.D. when Pope Gregory the Great codified the modes, songs and chants were passed from one generation to the next by word of mouth and were thereby subject to continued modification.

The Arabs made use of sounds for healing and utilized music for entertainment and love. As the Arabian Nights tell us: "to some people music is like food; to others like medicine; and to others like a fan."

During the Middle Ages several crucial technical innovations affected the use of sounds. Guido d'Arezzo devised musical notation in the eleventh century. He placed notes on different horizontal lines to indicate their pitch and gave names – *do*, *re*, *mi*, etc. – to the different tones, a method called *solfeggio*. This meant that a composer could transmit rules for the performance of his music to singers and players without himself having to teach them. It also made performance easier because less memorizing was necessary. Two or more voices could be sung simultaneously, giving rise to *polyphonic* music of great richness and beauty. The printing press contributed to widespread dissemination of words, some of which, like Dante's depiction of the noises of hell, were onomatopoeic symbols.

The Renaissance saw a revival of interest in the sounds of nature (Lowinsky 1954). Songs, particularly those of France, specialized in programmatic description of street noises, battle scenes, and the warbling of birds. Rhythmical effects suggesting dancing, gallop, and other movements were denoted with the help of a mathematical system devised by Johannes de Muris. New types of musical instruments were built, and the old Pythagorean method of tuning them was overhauled, with the result that a greater range of tones could be exploited in performance. Leonardo da Vinci, an accomplished singer, accompanied himself on a lute constructed from the skull of a horse. He also studied acoustics and wrote about various sounds, ranging from words of poetry to the flatus of pregnant women.

In the seventeenth and eighteenth centuries sounds were produced with a previously unheard of virtuosity and freedom. The well-tempered scale gave Bach and other geniuses the means for combining voices and instruments in such a way as to produce patterns of harmony which are popular even today. Court comedies of the period made explicit use of suspicious bedroom noises, and audiences knew exactly what to expect when they heard the rustling of silks, a tinkle of keys, and someone knocking on the door. Swift, in his writings about fantastic people and places, invented names that suggested noises of the commode. Engineers even built models that could make sounds without the direct efforts of a human being. Abbe Mical constructed an orchestra of mechanical players, for example, and von Kempelen built the first talking robots (Pierce and David 1958).

In the nineteenth century, the pervasive spirit of violent revolt and romantic idealism was portrayed lucidly in sounds (Barzun 1956). Beethoven's stark melodic fragments suggested themes like the 'pounding of fate'. Enlarged symphony orchestras, with modernized and versatile instruments, produced music that resembled thunder and storms, or bucolic scenes with twittering birds. Oboes and English horns were used to provoke melancholy, and it is said that the "ranz des vaches", a mountain tune played on the Alpine horn, was so suggestive of depression that men of the Swiss Guard would inevitably desert or commit suicide on hearing it. Tchaikowsky used cannon blasts in the *1812 Overture* to evoke a martial atmosphere. The music-dramas of Richard Wagner played upon the primitive association between sound and magic. For example, the power of a sword was symbolized by a musical theme whose sounding invariably reminded the listener of the inanimate object and myths associated with it. Incoherent words, in the mouths of fantastically disguised stage apparitions, transcended specific meanings, thus further charging the emotional tension produced by dramatic harmonies, vivid orchestration, and theatrical hocus-pocus.

Sound-making in the twentieth century

Many of the traditional distinctions between music, poetry, speech, and noise-making have disappeared within the past fifty years. We see on one hand a revival of ancient and non-Western ideas about sounds, and on the other, the effects of the machine age on the human ear (C. Harris 1957).

Phonograph records have made medieval and oriental music newly accessible, with the result that many sounds hitherto considered strange and ugly are now acceptable to the listener. Certain composers have even deliberately tried to change the reaction of Western audiences to random noises. Cage and others instruct the performer to whack the body of a musical instrument, say by slamming the lid of the piano! Some go so far as to incorporate accidental sounds like the coughs of the audience, shuffling of feet, gurgling of the radiator and even silence itself into a formal musical composition. So-called popular music often uses shrillness, nonsense, and primitive rhythm to excite the listener. Poets have also experimented with medieval and oriental sounds. Pound, for example, used fragments of obscure language in his cantos.

Twentieth century ears have had to get accustomed to all kinds of disagreeable and annoying noises produced by engines, tools, rockets, and other mechanical devices. Gradually the boundary has blurred between sounds considered ugly and those traditionally called beautiful. Consider the music of our time. First of all, the idea of a tonal center around which a melody was constructed and harmonized went out of fashion. Schoenberg and his students began to write music in which all twelve tones of the scale were given equal importance. Varese, Antheil and others began to write music for orchestras that included the clatter of airplane motors and other noise-making machinery. Finally Stockhausen and the other composers of *musique concrete* tape-recorded various mechanical, electronic, and human noises for performance by high-fidelity radio equipment. Such music has an important psychological consequence for an audience. The listener is exposed to a disturbing and even painful auditory experience. But his distress is offset by the knowledge that what he hears is controlled by a machine and therefore not subject to the unpredictability or eccentricity of a human performance.

At the same time the expressive function of vocal sound has changed rapidly. Songs are now written that blend the abstractness of tones with the concreteness of words, using a kind of sing-song speech or words uttered at exaggerated pitch levels. In the theater, players are asked to utter nonsense, or even produce body organ noises. For example, in Beckett's *Waiting for Godot*, Lucky's long monologue of broken words and noises resembles nothing so much as a 'Vodor' or other mechanical talking machine, gone haywire.

Furthermore, in the twentieth century, electronic devices have greatly increased the range of distances over which we can communicate. The sixty-six million telephones in the U.S.A. enable people to have relationships with each other through the medium of sound alone. This has important consequences for speech and hearing: Two persons meeting each other for the first time over the telephone may establish ideas about each other based entirely on auditory perceptions. But because the frequency response of the telephone is only about three hundred to thirty-four hundred cycles per second, some of the vocal cues for the speaker's personality and the intelligibility of his words are lost in such a transaction. People who use the telephone a great deal learn how to modify their voices to compensate for the distortion of sound, thereby contributing to further changes in manners of speech, and to patterns of listening.

Radio is the other medium of long-distance communication which has affected our use of sounds (Turnbull 1951). Since 1920, when Conrad's shanty beamed the Harding-Cox election returns to an estimated five hundred listeners, the radio industry has expanded to the point where, in 1955, about one hundred and thirty-five million radios were in use throughout the United States. Not only the radio programs which he deliberately chooses influence the listener, but also those sounds that enter his ears accidentally from radios that are kept playing in homes, automobiles, and other places. To some extent everyone has been taught what to say and how to say it by radio and other media of mass communication: Radio voices have become so stereotyped that one does not need to listen to the words to find out whether the speaker refers to soap, news, or loneliness. Radio has also conditioned our reactions to noises. In 1921, Thomas Cowan introduced sound effects into radio programs, and now listeners associate various background sounds and action noises with certain moods, situations, and events.

The sound technician uses steady, sustained sounds to suggest continuous movement, directness, stability, and formality. Quiet sounds imply repose and tranquility. Undulating sounds that vary in pitch or rhythm suggest purposeful movement and insistence. With intermittent sounds, the technician alludes to indecision, disorder, and lack of leadership. With sounds that suddenly increase in volume, he gives the feeling of climax, aggressiveness, and definite action. When sounds gradually get louder, they create suspense or relentless progress. Sounds that suddenly fade indicate cowardice, fear, and defeat; those that gradually fade evoke dejection or temporary defeat. Sounds that increase in volume and then suddenly stop or continue at a specific level create the illusion of opposition, conflict, and frustration. High-pitched sounds set a gay mood, whereas low-pitched ones suggest sadness.

Scientists have made us aware of the presence of inaudible sounds (Griffin 1958). Griffin, Busnel, and other investigators found that certain animals such as bats, fish, and insects make noises which we rarely or never hear. Modern methods of tape recording and acoustic analysis enabled the investigators to study the physical properties of these sounds. Inaudible sounds also have human uses. While no evidence to date shows these sounds to be of any importance in communication, ultrasonic waves have been used in medical research and therapy, degassing of liquids, laundering, agglomeration of smoke and fog, and industrial testing.

Sounds which the human body produces

Like a piano, the human body consists basically of a hard case which acts as a resonator, numerous internal components whose movements cause sound vibrations, and several openings that allow these vibrations to escape in certain directions. But unlike the piano or any other musical instrument, the body contains its own power source, is driven by a built-in executor, and has ears to receive and a brain to evaluate its own performance. The human body is the most elegant and versatile sound-producer ever devised.

The versatility of the human sound-maker is apparent if one looks at the many component parts of the body and studies the way they are used to make different noises. The skull, for example, serves as a drum for angry children to beat with their fists or against the wall. Even adults use their heads for sound-making. They tap it when they are bored, or slap it when they try to remember something. Many persons produce sounds with their teeth. They grind, click, and crunch them; they may feel them chatter when chilly or scared; they may gnash them during states of anger or frustration. Inflated cheeks, like tom-toms, give off melodious sounds when smartly struck with pencils or fingers.

The sounds of the body would not carry very far without the boost or amplification given by resonating cavities like the chest. The chest and its contents are of course intrinsically involved in the production of the voice for speech and singing. But more primitive sounds also rely on the chest for sonority and power: hiccups, moans, wheezes, and other physiological sounds. Some persons, in imitation of our simian ancestors, thump the chest as a sign of courage. The heart-beat, probably medicine's most important diagnostic sound, originates in the chest.

Among the internal organs of the body which make noises, the digestive tract is probably the most musical, a sort of miniature band. The mouth, a kind of trumpet, can hiss, blare and chomp. The esophagus, like a bassoon, produces gulps, burps, and belches, which, when properly timed, can cause considerable hilarity. The stomach, akin to a French horn, gurgles, growls, and groans. The intestines, resembling nothing so much as a glockenspiel, tinkle during peristalsis. The trombone-like colon zooms as it leisurely churns away at semisolid gruel. Now and then its noises, especially the sudden, high-pitched beeps and bloops, embarrass the band director. Tuba-like 'brummps' indicate the deposit of feces in the rectum in anticipation of the final discharge to the accompaniment of a fanfare of noises.

The hands are largely under conscious control. Their gestures can communicate ideas, and their sounds may suggest definite feelings. There are many different forms of applause, for example. Cupped palms produce an explosive noise to express enthusiasm and glee; but a light pitter-patter with the extended fingers indicates restraint or polite tolerance. Various sounds are also made with the joints. Cracking the knuckles can be rather alarming. Then there is finger-snapping, which may be used as a signal to animals or other people. Tremors such as the pill-rolling manifestation of Parkinson's disease can be noisy. The closed fist is used to pound for attention and to punctuate oratory.

Whereas sounds from the hands can have protean meanings, those made by the feet tend to be stereotyped. They readily identify a person and indicate fairly well what he is doing. Single sharp stomps, for example, can only be made when one stands still, and they point to the sound-maker's whereabouts. Tapping with the feet signifies that the person is moving rapidly, running, dancing, or simply marking time. Shuffling indicates fatigue or weakness. A slurching gait characterizes the drunkard. Plodding steps mark the obese or lethargic individual. A flopping or flailing gait means that his legs are uncoordinated or crippled. Hobbling stigmatizes the lame walker or the amputee. Finally, there is the three-legged gait of a man who uses a cane.

The surface of the human body produces its own set of sounds. The skin and its appendages, for example, emit delicate lilting noises. Stroking or scraping the beard makes fuzzy or raspy sounds. Finger-nail clicking, an art superbly cultivated by Flamenco dancers, may indicate tension and excitement. The sounds of the skin are clearly associated with emotional release. Stroking the skin may tickle, whereas rubbing it arouses many sensuous feelings. We slap each other on the back to indicate friendliness, but punishment is inflicted by slapping someone's face, hands, or buttocks. Some persons slap the thigh or abdomen during fits of laughter.

But since all the skin surface cannot be exposed, we also produce sounds with the body covering of clothes, ornaments, and gadgets. Our shoes can squeak like kittens; and boots, belts, and other items of leather make a variety of squawking noises. Corsets, garters, and suspenders can be made to snap and crackle. Satins and silks swish; corduroys emit glissando sounds; woolens and cottons are soft and muffled; starched linens crunch. Top hats and bowlers, with their hollow echo sounds, complete the noisy wardrobe. Jewelry provides the body with audible as well as visible adornment. Beads and pearls jangle. Charm-bracelets, sequins, and wrist-watches are often very noisy. Some people even carry small alarm-clocks which always seem to go off during lectures or concerts. Pockets carry coins, pencils, and other loose sound-makers. And let us not forget that arch-enemy of silence, the hearing aid, which in the hands of certain people produces the most raucous electronic whines.

The effects of sounds

Sounds, like all other stimuli, have varied effects on human beings (C. Harris 1957). People come to enjoy some of these effects, calling the sounds that produce them pleasant and seeking them out. They learn to dislike the effects produced by certain sounds, label these sounds 'noises', and try to avoid them. To understand the effects of sounds, one must consider their physical properties, the conditions under which they are heard, and the personal characteristics of individual listeners.

Only the most intense sounds seem to directly affect the entire body of the listener. The energy of ultrasonic waves, if absorbed by the tissues of the body, produces heat. The skin may burn, especially where there is hair, and the underlying muscles become warmer. High intensity sounds can also cause vibrations in the listener's head which affect its internal organs. For example, the roar of a jet-engine may blur the subject's vision if the sound agitates his eyeballs. Or he may lose his sense of balance because of the effect of sound vibrations on his organs of equilibrium.

The more usual effects of sounds, however, result from the impact of vibrations on the sensitive structures of the ear. Very loud sounds produce feelings of pain, pressure, or tingling in addition to the so-called auditory sensations. Stimuli from the ear travel to the brain and spinal cord via sensory nerves. Although the exact neurophysiological mechanisms involved in the transmission of sound stimuli throughout the nervous system are not completely known, many of the effects of these stimuli have been recorded and studied. Several studies, for example, concern the acuity of vision. A faint light becomes more readily visible when sound accompanies it. Tasks which involve visual concentration are definitely affected by sudden and continuous sounds.

The effect of a loud sound, particularly a sudden, unexpected one, is to startle the listener. Startle reactions to sounds have characteristic physiological components. A reaction to the sound of a pistol shot, for example, includes elevation of the blood pressure; quickening of the heart beat; changes in breathing and sweating; and sharp muscular contractions over the entire body. Unexpected sounds may have far-reaching effects on the listener's overall behavior pattern if the startle reaction interferes with his current activities or prevents him from pursuing certain goals. To compensate for these effects of sounds, listeners either escape from the situation or learn to adapt to it.

Adaptation to sounds requires the listener to expand his energy. He must make an effort to accustom himself to sounds, to learn when to expect them and to interpret what he hears. In the face of inadequate reserves, the listener may begin to show fatigue, digestive disturbances, weight-loss, anxiety, and other symptoms of maladaptation to stress. Sounds also have a direct effect on the ear. Continued exposure causes a loss of acuity, followed by partial deafness.

Once a listener has learned to adapt to sounds and finds them familiar and tolerable, their effects upon him will be determined largely by the situation or conditions under which he listens. For example, the sound of a fire-engine will bring relief to persons trapped in a burning building who hope for rescue but will annoy pedestrians who must scamper out of the truck's way. Furthermore, the effects of familiar sounds depend on the personality of the listener – on his individual hopes, fears, and expectations. Thus the sound of the doorbell delights the friendly host but frightens the fugitive.

One of the most useful effects of sounds is to arouse people, to wake them from sleep, and alert them from drowsiness. Arousal follows stimulation with sounds that are loud, high-pitched, irregular, and of uncertain origin. Once aroused, the person may experience many things, and the after-effects of arousal, whether pleasant or unpleasant, are incorrectly attributed to the sound itself. Thus the sound of a jet aircraft boom is annoying to the store-owner whose plateglass windows are smashed to bits. His lawyer, on the other hand, may welcome such a sound because one after-effect could be a profitable law-suit.

Another effect of sounds that are loud, highpitched, irregular, and of uncertain origin is to obscure or mask less noticeable sounds. This pleases or annoys the listener, depending on what he wishes to hear. For instance, the masking effects of whispers during a symphony concert disconcerts the person who wants to listen to the music. But the person interested in gossip may find the effects of the masking whisper pleasant.

Sounds have effects on the social behavior of people. They control the rhythmic movements of persons in groups. Listeners feel compelled to synchronize their body movements with the rhythms of sounds they hear. A waltz, for instance, induces listeners to sway gently, and a march compels them to walk with a precise gait. Sounds also induce suspiciousness. From their point of origin they spread in all directions, through walls and around corners. Thus many sounds can be heard by people who were never intended to hear them. The innate curiosity of chance listeners may drive them towards the point of origin of the sound; they turn around, look searchingly, and may try to follow the sound in an effort to trace its meaning.

The effect of sounds in verbal communication is to convey coded information to the listener. Sounds transmit meanings when they make recognizable verbal patterns. The spoken word carries meaning because its component sounds, called phonemes, are long enough to be perceived and short enough to be remembered. For instance, the effect of the sound *sh* is to alert the listener and remind him of rushing water, warnings for silence, and other possibilities. The effect of *i* immediately after *sh* is to organize these possibilities. Since *shi* has definite linguistic potentials, the listener now expects to hear a word, but is uncertain what it will be. Could it be an obscenity? Then personal and social prejudices about taboo words contribute to his reaction to the sounds. Could it be a word not in the listener's vocabulary? If so, an entirely different set of responses would be called for. The effect of the sound *p* following *shi* is to remove all doubt, for *ship* gives an English-speaking listener the appropriate acoustic cue for a word signifying 'a large sea-going vessel'.

Control and regulation of sounds

The human ear is an incredibly sensitive sound receiver. It responds to pressure fluctuations so tiny as to displace the ear-drum only one-tenth the diameter of a hydrogen atom. A listener must be able to regulate the flow of stimuli that comes from such a responsive microphone. He must sift out those sounds that do not carry essential information so that more important messages can reach his brain. The neurophysiological basis for these processes is not yet fully understood (Galambos 1954). Experimental work with cats and other animals, however, suggests that between the ear and the cortical centers of the brain lie numerous relay points where sounds which are unnecessary or harmful to the organism can be filtered out. The existence of such internal controls over sound stimuli would help to explain how it is possible for people to sleep in a noisy place and yet wake at the sound of an alarm clock set the night before. It might also account for the selectivity of the ears which enables a listener to concentrate on a single voice amidst a din of conversation, or to recognize an unusual ping among the noises of an automobile engine.

Many factors external to the listener control and regulate the sounds that impinge on his ears and subsequently reach his brain. The first of these is the size and shape of the instrument that makes the sounds he hears. In the case of sounds of human origin, the body itself prevents the production of certain noises. The size and shape of the vocal tract regulates the sounds of the voice, and the overall physique of the sound-maker controls what noises he can make with tools, machines, and musical instruments. For example, there is a limit to the amount of air contained in the chest. Instruments larger than a tuba require other sources of air; hence the pipe-organ. Successful sound-making with pianos, violins, harps, and most other instruments requires careful attention to the physical limitations of the hands, the strength of the muscles, and the mobility of the various joints.

Another external limitation of the sounds we hear is the sound-maker's need to coordinate his activities. For instance, he cannot eat and speak concurrently, and during a meal grunting noises and gestures commonly displace spoken words. Certain sound-making processes interfere with each other. During elimination, for example, the larynx must be closed so that abdominal pressure can build up for expulsion of waste matter. This obviously puts the brake on speech.

Besides the physical limitations which regulate the sounds we make, various social restrictions control sound-production. Standards of conduct regarding sound-making are set up in each family. Children imitate their parents and adopt from them many ways of laughing, grunting, and mannerisms of speech like accents or stammering. Parents usually direct and control the noises of their children with slogans like "Speak Up", "Silence Is Golden", or "Children May be Seen But Not Heard". They may insist upon instruction in music, foreign languages, and other sound-making skills for their youngsters.

Teachers, schools, clubs, unions, professional societies, and numerous other social institutions further regulate and control the sounds we make. For example, Oxford training imprints a tell-tale accent on speech, one which may last a life-time. It is also possible to recognize violinists trained in the Russian School, due to characteristics of tone, vibrato, and glissando.

Professional and occupational groups tend to indoctrinate their membership in certain manners of sound-making. From voice alone, it is often possible to identify clergymen, lawyers, teachers, and other professionals. Few people would find it difficult to distinguish bootblacks, barbers, ditchdiggers, and other workers on the basis of the noises they make. Special privileges about sound-making are given to some occupations. Bell-ringers, organists, cantors, and priests have the right to intone the sounds of religious worship. Clowns and acrobats are permitted to entertain their audiences with raucous and impolite noises. Policemen carry big sticks and loud whistles. Singers and musicians who belong to the proper union can provide the noise for public meetings. Bandleaders and prompters can dictate the beginning and end of sound-making. Trumpeters, announcers, and hosts raise curtains with sounds. Interlocutors, referees, and masters-of-ceremony keep the noise from getting out of hand.

Even the law demands that sound-making be controlled so that we are not excessively disturbed by noises. City ordinances usually require that automobiles have mufflers on the exhausts, that honking with horns be minimized, and that loud and disorderly conduct be restricted to certain times and places. Many unwritten laws exert control upon human sounds through the pressure of public opinion. In Europe before the nineteenth century, for example, castration was performed on male sopranos so that princely courts and churches could have these highly desired voices. Sexual prejudices and taboos against noise-making by women may account for the fact of so few outstanding female musicians. Traditionally women are expected to be more contained and silent than men, and their instruction in music was limited to such lady-like instruments as lutes and harps. Times change, of course, and during World War II many noisy women were employed as boilermakers or riveters.

Written and unwritten rules about sound-making may differ markedly between various countries or regions of the world. Regional differences of spoken language are called dialects. More general mannerisms of expression also control the sounds human beings make. Stanislavski, for example, noted that Slavic people tend to speak in minor keys, and that their voices, as well as body gestures, music, and other expressive traits tend in general to be broad, moody, and intense. The French, on the other hand, tend to speak in major keys, with rippling sounds and melodies that match other aspects of their demeanor.

Sound-making customs are transmitted through the festivals and holiday celebrations of different countries. In Scotland there will be bagpipes and in China the noise of firecrackers. Anniversaries of military events generally call for the sounds of marching, drums, and speeches. Sundays and holidays may require churchbells and hymns. Indeed, many habits of human sound-making are linked to unique rituals and the legends that accompany them. For example, the noise produced by blowing into a ram's horn, the *Shofar*, is reserved for the Jewish holidays that solemnize the beginning of the year and require atonement for sins committed during the old one.

Above and beyond the many physical and social factors already mentioned, there are numerous general conditions of life, such as climate, weather, diet, and terrain that control and regulate the sounds we make and hear. The temperature of the air and the speed and direction of the wind affect the velocity whereby sounds travel from sender to receiver. Fog usually raises the overall sound-pressure in an area, necessitating somewhat increased effort for successful communication. Cold weather by causing people to shiver, sneeze, and sniffle adds to their repertoire of nonverbal noises. And they must wear overcoats and galoshes – additional sources of noise. In warm weather, sound travels more quickly. People make noises with motorboats, tennis rackets, croquet mallets, and other outdoor implements. Diet, through its effect on thea mount of gas in the digestive tract, regulates the production of gastrointestinal noises. Total food intake also directly affects the vigor and intensity of humans who make sounds.

In view of their physical characteristics, sound waves are immediately controlled by the space wherein they travel. The terrain, for example, provides inescapable limits to communication with sounds. From the top of a mountain there is little reverberation, and a message may travel undistorted for many miles. In a canyon sounds can echo, and the intelligibility of words is rapidly lost. Fences, bushes, trees, walls, and various other obstacles modify human sounds by reflection and absorption. Consequently noises made in the country differ from those made in the city, even though produced in an identical way. Both vocal and non-vocal sound-making is regulated by terrain: Where a soft, melodious voice would be appropriate in an urban living room, in a rural environment such as a farm it could scarcely compete with the noises of animals or carry across the greater distances between people. Such an environment requires accessory noise like yodeling, sirens or horns. Whistles are also used for outdoor communication, and a whistle-language characteristic of ancient hunting cultures can still be heard on mountainous Gomera Island, off the coast of Spain.

Architecture is the other essential environment that controls and regulates the sounds we hear. The modern science of acoustics is prominently concerned with the improvement of communication through modification of homes, auditoriums, and other buildings. Where rooms are small and crowded, the inhabitants have no difficulty hearing each others' noises. In a larger space, however, a single person may have to pant, sneeze, or wheeze to make himself heard. Intervening walls and floors require that the sound-maker shuffle, scrape, or pound to keep in touch with the listener. Across halls, floors, balconies, and gardens it would be necessary to shout and scream. Large buildings have speaking tubes or telephones for efficient communication. It must not be forgotten that architecture and social conventions constantly overlap. In some buildings silence is enforced, and noises are barricaded by draped booths, and sound-proofed cubicles, or cells. In libraries and chapels one soft-pedals the voice, retards the motion of limbs, and checks all nonessential sounds. Noise-making is actually encouraged in other buildings: in the stadium and assembly hall, voices are amplified by microphone and megaphone, and there is plenty of space for trampling, echoes, and applause. Whistles and shrieks tear through the air. Tooting horns and clanging bells add to the pandemonium. But the custom of the concert hall requires that one sit quietly, restricting himself to polite whispers, gentle rustles with the program, and accidental coughs.

Time might be looked upon as the ultimate regulator of sounds. The night is still. In the early morning sounds that arouse are permitted. The cock crows, milkmen rattle up steps, and alarms go off. Noises that keep us alert and on our toes are heard during the day. Typewriters clatter, people walk and talk, and produce many noises as byproducts of their labors. Toward evening sounds change in character. As people slow down there are yawns and sleepy voices. *Eine Kleine Nachtmusik* may provide distraction from the cares of the day. Jazz and rock 'n roll exhaust the keyed-up person. Croonings and soft music intoxicate the lover. Radio and phonograph may lull one to sleep.

The human voice

The term human voice refers to certain sounds that originate in the body, plus the effects of these sounds on listeners (Fletcher 1953). The voice originates in the chest, throat, and head. It provides listeners with acoustic stimulus patterns from which they select, on the basis of individual needs and training, significantly informative items. Phonemes carry information as to the words the speaker uses. The musical quality of the sound provides the listener with information about the age, sex, and health of the speaker. Those elements of the voice known as rhythm, flow, and inflection tell the listener how to interpret the words.

Persons differ regarding the information they consider necessary or desirable when listening to a voice. A speech therapist, for instance, needs facts about the speaker's vocal equipment. A teacher may require knowledge about the speaker's verbal and intellectual skills. Psychiatrists must evaluate the speaker's emotional reactions in personal relationships. A theater director wants to find out whether the speaker can communicate with an audience across the footlights.

The wealth of information contained in a voice together with the different needs of various listeners accounts for the fact that no standard descriptive scheme suffices for all voices. Nevertheless, several clinical workers have described human voices by focusing on the characteristics of the speaker. Sheldon, for example, tried to correlate voices with the speaker's body build; he described characteristic voices produced by people who are long and thin (ectomorphs), round and fat (endomorphs), or square and muscular (mesomorphs). Moses based his descriptions of voices on the emotions experienced by speakers. He wrote of the typical voices of people who are fearful, depressed, confused, or angry.

Another approach to the voice is to disregard the characteristics of the speaker and to focus on the sounds he produces. Acoustic analysis of the voice yields characteristic time-frequency-intensity patterns which can be represented visually and do not require descriptive words.

Few clinics as yet have the equipment or staff required for an analysis of the voice based on acoustical measurement of its component sounds. This means that the responses of trained listeners constitute the basis for voice analysis. Check sheets and rating scales are useful in the evaluation of pitch and loudness of the voice. But such qualities as harshness, intelligibility, regularity, and so on, are difficult to rate since they are based on the listener's subjective preferences and expectations. Finally, a judgment upon vocal appropriateness or adequacy requires the listener to be trained to evaluate far more than the sounds of the voice. He must consider the speaker's background, personality, intelligence and the tasks for which the voice is employed.

Without such special training the listener may turn to his knowledge of poetry, literature, and drama for descriptions of voices. Poetry describes the sounds of the voice by means of onomatopoeias. "The Orator", by W. S. Gilbert, for example, imitates the sound and appearance of a confused and pompous speaker.

Rumble, blunder, stumble, thunder,
Wrangle, tangle, jingle-jangle,
Fluttery, stuttery, bog, fog,
 Missing his tack,
 Changing his track,
 Losing his threads,
 Mixing his "heads",
Flash! Dash! Splash! Crash!
Slowly, fastly, grimly, ghastly,
Firstly, secondly, thirdly, lastly.

Voices of some patients who visit our clinics can be described onomato-
poeically as:

The hollow rumble of a humble bumbler
The insistent hiss of a lisping miss
A low crow no woe wont slow
A tumbling booming hullabaloo
A rickety-rackety buzz-whip clatter-clip
A banal slack nasal quack
The appeal to thee to feel free glee
The sleepy peep of a cheap creep

Literature also contains many descriptions of sounds that can be used
as analogies for human voices. The voices of humans are compared to
the sounds of machines or animals:

THE FOGHORN

Loud, long, and dismal bellows it made. The first one seemed especially long.
It couldn't have lasted more than a few seconds, yet it seemed it would never
cease. Loud and disturbing, they came at regular intervals, making the silence
in between seem short and irrelevant.   (A. Vivante)

THE DUCK

[...] the mallard mother quacks unintermittently. If I ceased for even the space
of half a minute from my melodious 'Quahg, gegegegeg, quahg, gegegegeg',
the necks of the ducklings became longer and longer, corresponding exactly
to 'long faces' in human children –   (K. Lorenz)

BOW-AND-ARROW

A sharp crack mingled with a deep thrumming, which one never forgets when
one has heard it only a few times: so strange is it, so thrillingly does it grip
the heart.   (E. Herrigel)

THE SUBWAY

    The jabbering, the silly monologue,
    The endless spilling, spilling of the mind,
    A straining to be free like a chained dog.
    Something that drives like sperm, frantic and blind.
                              (M. Moore)

Dramatists often allude to the after-effects of voices on the listener.
Some voices lull us to sleep, others cause us to take notice. If we pay

attention to our spontaneous responses while listening we may be able to characterize vocal behavior in the following way:

She will sing the savageness out of a bear.
                                                    (Shakespeare)

A man of loose tongue, intemperate, trusting to tumult,
leading the populace to mischief with empty words.
                                                    (Euripides)

The function of human sounds

We use sounds in an effort to fulfill several basic human needs (Greenacre 1952a). The first of these is the need to be aware of ourselves – to establish and maintain a self-image. We need to know where we are in space, to recognize how we are related to other people, and to gauge the results of our own behavior. Such information about our existence is based on the reception and evaluation of stimuli, including those that are a result of our own activity. The sounds we make, for example, stimulate our own ears; this process is one of several feedback circuits that maintain the self-image. We hear our own words, sneezes, whistles, and other noises because they are directly transmitted through the bones of the body, and are also reflected from external obstacles. As experiments with artificial feedback disturbances have amply demonstrated, it may be almost impossible for an individual to remain coordinated and rhythmical unless he can hear himself. Small wonder that the deaf are at such a tremendous disadvantage when it comes to establishing a satisfactory self-image. Very few have the creative gifts of a Beethoven or Smetana with which to compensate for their inner silence. Robbed of the pleasure and safety that comes from listening to themselves, the deaf must rely exclusively on vision, smell, touch, taste, and movement to maintain a sense of their own existence.

No person can live alone in isolation from others. Sound is an all-important medium for breaking through one's personal shell to make contact with people. From birth to death the individual screams, gasps, rattles, and calls in order to let others know where he is and what he is doing. Life experience teaches him that sounds in the range of one thousand to six thousand cycles per second are most easily picked up by the ears of other people. He learns to produce noises that are likely to be heard and recognized, so that others may react to him.

This experience also teaches the individual to use sounds so as to maintain and control human contacts at the most pleasurable and comfortable level. Those sounds that attract people are used to obtain food, love, warmth and protection. Those sounds that annoy are used to keep people at a distance or to drive them away if necessary. Screeching voices, explosive noise, tiresome slogans, insipid music, and many other forms of sound are used for this purpose. These distinctions must be kept in mind when one tries to help people with speech problems. The patient may suffer from serious conflicts about closeness which need to be recognized and treated before improvements in sound-production can result in improved human relationships.

While the use of words is often a primary requirement for successful communication, it is not the only way to transmit information by sounds to other people. Body rumbles, friction noises, and other unintentionally produced sounds may be more effective than words in conveying messages about hunger, fear, anger and other inner states of the sender to a sensitive listener. And words cannot be used for communication unless the inflection, tempo, tone quality, and other nonverbal aspects of speech effectively cue in the listener to how these words should be interpreted (Skinner 1957).

As cues or guides in verbal communication, sounds can be divided into those that introduce, those that accompany, and those that separate the speaker's words. Every speaker must introduce himself and indicate that he intends to start speaking. Introductory sounds and gestures include such things as pounding with a gavel, clearing the throat, blowing one's nose, or having another individual play a fanfare or make a speech of introduction.

Prefatory noises like loud inhalation, grunts, or smacking of the lips may alert the listener for what is to follow. Some persons emit sounds like "ugh", "hmm?" etc. as if to ask the listener, "Are you with me? Shall I go on?" When a listener is slow to respond, or deliberately avoids paying attention, the speaker may be forced to repeat his introductory sounds or to build them up until an effective breakthrough occurs. Some people use accellerando finger taps, others make nonverbal noises like "UUHH-ahh-eh-e" in the manner of a Rossini Overture.

Whenever he emits words, a speaker must accompany himself with sounds to tell listeners what to make of these words. The color of the voice, nasality, tremulousness, breathiness, and other accompanying sounds transmit the emotional tone of the message. For example, the words *I feel fine*, uttered by a disturbed patient, can be entirely misleading unless the listener correctly perceives the depressive quality of the voice. People also emphasize certain of their words and phrases by barks, bangs on the table, swoops from one vocal pitch to another, or a peculiar accent, to bring out the emotional implications.

To separate consecutive verbal statements from each other, a speaker makes punctuation sounds. These are distinctive patterns of rhythm and pitch like the cadences which punctuate music. To indicate '.' the speaker rapidly lowers the pitch of his voice. To indicate '?' he raises the pitch before an expectant silence. Silences give the listener time to digest what he has just heard and to join ideas smoothly. Punctuation sounds and silences also indicate that an interchange is coming to a close. The speaker may signal the approaching end by droning, repetitiousness, or such noisy behavior as rattling papers, pencils, a watch-chain, cigarette lighter, or other handy items.

In the fabric of human relationships that we call society, sounds often serve to prepare a suitable atmosphere. The blend of noise at a cocktail party, for example, creates an atmosphere, one of impersonality. There are tinkling glasses, jumbled voices, and soft music which, like the haze of cigarette smoke, the undulations of the guests, and the gestures of the host establish an atmosphere for informal conversation. The verbal interchange has to be brief, impersonal, and brisk. With the background noise of the cocktail-party statements like "How are you" are taken as greetings, not questions. In another setting the words would have a different implication. In the psychiatrist's consultation room, for instance, atmosphere is provided by a muffled silence. This, plus other cues of privacy, prepare the patient to respond to "How are you?" with a detailed recital of his personal problems. It would seem clear that human sounds are involved in the manipulation and management of social situations, whether these involve conversation, intrigue, seduction, entertainment, education, or other mutual activities.

Summary

This chapter presents information from several fields of inquiry, including musicology, phonetics, and individual and social psychology, to show how human sounds function in communication. From our present state of knowledge, the following conclusions seem warranted:

(1) Human sounds range in complexity all the way from simple physiological noises emitted by the internal organs to highly specialized spoken and instrumental sounds which necessitate extensive social experiences both for the sound-maker and the listener.

(2) Historical facts suggest that human beings usually employ sounds directly to alert, attract, annoy, distract, alarm and otherwise influence each other, and indirectly in the form of words, musical themes, specific noises, and other symbols in order to exchange ideas.

(3) Science and technology in the twentieth century may significantly change the nature of speech, music, and other forms of communication with sounds due to the impact of intense mechanical noise upon hearing and the results of long distance contacts via telephone, radio and other electronic devices between individuals and groups.

(4) The human body may be regarded as the most versatile of sound-making instruments since it is used to produce sounds not only with the vocal tract, but also with the bony structures, joints, internal organs, skin, and surrounding objects.

(5) The effects of sounds come about through stimulation of a listener when his ears, which may be viewed as exquisitely sensitive microphones, respond to vibrations. He can also be burned, agitated, and otherwise directly affected by sounds of high intensity or ultrasonic frequency.

(6) Control over human sounds is provided by inner neurophysiological filter-like devices that regulate the flow of auditory stimuli between the ears and the higher brain centers, and by outer social and environmental conditions which determine when, where, by whom, for what occasion, and for how long human sounds may be produced.

(7) The human voice is a multidimensional phenomenon which includes the personality of the speaker, the acoustic characteristics of the sounds he produces, and the subjective responses of those who listen to these sounds. Descriptions and measurements of the voice which are limited to only one or another of these dimensions introduce distortions into the analysis of vocal behavior.

(8) People use sounds to assist in self-evaluation and to initiate and maintain contact with each other. Those whose speech or hearing is impaired may experience profound difficulties in the establishment of a self-image and in the development of satisfying human relationships.

2

THE SOUNDS OF HUMAN BEHAVIOR:

A Survey of the Literature*

(1960)

The problem

Sounds are pressure changes which, when they impinge on human ears, constitute signals for communication. The purpose of this paper is to bring together information about sounds from sources which may not be generally available to clinicians and other students of behavior. Behind this survey of the literature is the assumption that sounds, while not the only signals for message exchange, nevertheless are the most important ones for patients and their physicians, especially psychiatrists. Indeed, it has been said that psychiatrists are basically listeners (Menninger 1957), and some recent publications about speech show that sound is as important as the meaning of words when it comes to the interpretation of what patients are talking about (Pittenger and Smith 1957; Eldred and Price 1958).

While many gaps still remain in our understanding of principles which govern communication with sounds, it is remarkable how many publications from superficially unrelated fields actually contribute to this problem. Several sciences employ different terminologies and vary in their scope, yet deal essentially with the same phenomenon: viz., people communicate with sounds. Acoustical engineers explain the physical basis for sound and account for its transmission, absorption, and reverberation through space (Beranek 1954). Linguists show that people habitually solve communal problems by making certain sounds called words (Bloomfield 1933). Musicologists demonstrate that sounds universally serve man in the realization of creative and recreative needs (Einstein 1938). Psychologists know that sounds are used to express pleasure, pain, and other

---

* Reprinted from *Logos*, 3. 1: 13-24 (1960).

emotions (Ruesch and Kees 1956). For lack of space some of these contributions, especially those dealing with acoustics, have had to be somewhat neglected. I have chosen rather to highlight the issues about sounds which seem most pertinent for persons who listen, interpret, and cautiously make sounds in the presence of disturbed people.

Animals communicate with sounds

Living organisms utilize sounds to obtain information about the world they live in. Spiders, for example, with accordion-like slits in their legs pick up vibrations that range in frequency from 100 to 50,000 cycles per second (Lear 1959). Thus they are warned by the squeaks of predatory bats or enticed by the buzzing of insects trapped in the spider web. Scientific study of animal sounds began with Darwin, who described and compared the various noises and gestures of emotional expression. He concluded that "the vocal and other sound-producing organs, by which various expressive noises are produced, [...] were first developed for sexual purposes, in order that one sex might call or charm the other" (Darwin 1955). Anatomical studies led Negus to another conclusion: in terms of phylogenetic progression, hearing probably preceded purposive sound-making. Hearing, according to Negus, evolved "as a means of detecting the sounds of nature or the involuntary noises made by animals [...]" and the range of hearing "[...] is likely to be adjusted in accordance with the pitch of the sounds which it is desired to hear [...]" (Negus 1949).

Each animal learns which of the many sounds that occur within its genetically determined range of hearing are the ones desirable and necessary for survival. As Lorenz, Hess, and others have demonstrated with ingenious experiments, the pattern for an animal's response to sound is imprinted shortly after birth. They presented freshly hatched ducklings with a decoy that emitted "gock, gock, gock", and then compared the subsequent responses of these animals to silent versus 'gocking' objects (Hess 1959). Some of the communicative sounds made by animals lie outside the human range of hearing, and this has led to the false idea that these animals are silent. With modern electroacoustical devices it has been possible to record some inaudible animal noises. For example, Griffin showed that certain bats make sounds between 40 and 80 kilocycles per second and navigate through dark space by listening to the echo of these sounds from walls and obstacles (Griffin 1958).

No doubt animals and humans have much in common when it comes to communication with sounds. Porpoises, according to Lilly, seem to make distinctive noises that resemble the sounds we have come to associate with expression of pleasure and pain (Lilly 1958). Some neurophysiological studies even suggest that animals, like people, listen only to what they want to hear. For example, Hubel and coworkers show that in cats the auditory cortex responds to auditory stimuli only when the sound indicates food, a person, or similar objects, or when its source is visible to the animal (Hubel et al. 1959).

Human uses of sounds

Human beings differ from spiders, fish, bats, and other animals in that the number of sounds they use for communication is much greater (Fletcher 1953). For example, the English language has 32 primary speech sounds, called phonemes, like *a*, *f*, or *p* (Bloomfield 1933). In addition, there are eight compound phonemes like *aw* or *ow*. And nine secondary phonemes conveyed by loudness or pitch change in the voice indicate whether words are questions, demands, exclamations, or other kinds of statements. According to Pierce and David, the human ear can discriminate among some 400,000 sounds (Pierce and David 1958). How did we learn to organize these sounds into patterns like speech and music?

The ancient history of human sounds will probably never be written; there was no way to preserve the sounds that people made. Phonetic writing, a far from perfect way to denote verbal sounds, probably did not exist prior to the Egyptian civilization (Gardiner 1950). *Neumes*, a primitive form of musical notation, gave no clue to the actual pitch of the sounds that were used (Fleischer 1895). Fortunately musical instruments, sculptures, and other archeological remnants have provided historians with some clues from which a theory of the origins of human communication with sounds may be constructed (Kinsky 1930). Presumably primal man enjoyed great freedom of vocal expression and noise-making. Schneider states that music originally included "whispering, speaking, humming, singing, and even yelling" (Wellesz 1957). The urge towards contact, according to Revesz, led to the invention of words, about the time that tools came to be used several 100,000 years ago (Revesz 1956).

Fears about death, famine, earthquakes, and other natural phenomena probably drove early people to make sounds, presumably in an effort to imitate and magically control nature. Sachs and other musicologists have traced many modern instruments like drums, flutes, and violins back to the rattles, whistles, and other primitive implements of ancient religious festivals (Sachs 1940). Warfare, economics, family structure, and other social elements gradually affected the use of sounds, as Farnsworth, Wellesz, and others have shown (Farnsworth 1958; Wellesz 1957). For example, the Egyptians cunningly employed trumpets and drums to summon their troops and encite them to battle. Their flutes and pipes stirred the populace to rapture and excited erotic frenzy for the festival of Osiris. Among the Jews, vocal sounds in the form of psalms and chants served to induce religious feeling in the temple, while harps, viols, and trumpets came to be reserved for politics and warfare. The Bible, for example, cites the soothing effects of music on Saul and other important personages, and gives accounts of battles, like that of Jericho, where victory was attributed to the noise of trumpets.

Acoustic study of sounds, and systematic analysis of their effects on human behavior, probably originated in Greece. Mathematicians like Pythagoras analyzed the physical attributes of the auditory stimulus through measurements of vibration frequency (Helmholtz 1885). Symbolism was also studied; in Plato's Cratylos one reads about early linguistic theories (Plato 1937). Knowledge about sounds was applied in many practical ways by the Romans. For example, certain Roman generals stationed musicians in empty camps or lonely outposts for the specific purpose of confusing the watchful enemy. And Nero, who was a trained singer and instrumentalist, boosted his own popularity and discredited his rivals by employing a claque of more than five thousand persons for public meetings. He instructed this mob in the art of applause, distinguishing *bombi*, like the buzzing of bees, *imbrices*, like the sounds of rain or hail on a roof and *testae*, like the crashing of pots (Wellesz 1957).

Traditions regarding human sounds developed somewhat differently in the Western world than in the East. In the Orient, for instance, music remained basically monodic and speech emphasized pitch as the differentiator of meaning. Special attitudes about sound-making prevailed among the Arabs. Noise was banned in the Seraglio, for example, where the dropping of a dish might be punished with death, often at the hands of a mute executioner (Cable 1959). In Europe, the rules of the Roman Catholic Church also restricted certain forms of sound-making, resulting, among other things, in competition between sacred and secular forms of musical expression. Additional impetus to the development of daring and original tonal combinations came from the musical notation devised by Guido d'Arezzo. His visual display of pitch on horizontal lines enabled composers to write down and teach complex patterns of sounds (Einstein 1938).

Sounds of nature attracted great interest during the Renaissance. Jannequin and other musicians portrayed battles, hunts, street scenes, aviaries, and other subjects with a virtuosity equal to that of the great painters of the period (Lowinsky 1954). A rhythm notation invented by the mathematician Johannes de Muris enabled composers to write sounds that were amazingly life-like. Risque texts and onomatopoieas were also popular.

During the 18th century, several authors tried to account for the effects of sounds on human behavior by the analysis of musical form. As Wessel points out in an unpublished study, these aestheticians fell short of their goal because they failed to distinguish between the sound-maker and the listener, and lacked sufficient information about physiological factors in emotion (Wessel 1955). Nevertheless, their generalizations are still pertinent. Marpurg, one of the outstanding scholars, stated, for example: "Sorrow should be expressed with a slow-moving, languid, and drowsy melody, broken with many sighs, and often caressing a single word in which exquisite tonal material should be used, plus a prevailing dissonant harmony [...] Fear, anxiety, anguish, and despair are expressed with tumbling and downward progressions placed mainly in the lower register" (Wessel 1955).

Philosophical speculations which still haunt contemporary research into sounds dominated 19th century thinking. The pervasive romanticism of the time surely distorted people's judgments. Kierkegaard, in an essay entitled "The Immediate Stages of the Erotic or the Musical Erotic", argued that music is peculiarly abstract (Kierkegaard 1959); and the "ranz des vaches", a mountain tune played on the Alpine horn, was so suggestive of depression that men of the Swiss Guard would inevitably desert or commit suicide on hearing it (Barzun 1956). Perhaps this rampant emotionalism accounts in part for the modesty of 19th century scientists. It is worth noting, for instance, that Helmholtz closed his outstanding work on sounds with the following remark. Referring to the psychic motives which determine what people hear, he said: "I prefer leaving to others to carry out such investigations, in which I should feel myself too much of an amateur" (Helmholtz 1885). And Freud, whose ideas about the perception of noises and words attest to his competence in matters of sound, wrote next to nothing about music (Freud 1954).

When people make sounds

Of all the activities of human beings that result in sounds, those leading to words have been investigated in greatest detail. Studies about words are customarily divided into those of SEMANTICS, which deal with the meanings of words, and those of PHONETICS, having to do with speech events without reference to meaning, or, as Fry puts it: "[...] a process which involves a series of transformations from the stage of the linguistic memory to that of air pressure variations [...]" (Fry 1955). Psychiatrists and other clinicians generally make no distinction between the meaning of words and the speech act since the latter itself means something in behavior – for example, to make contact or to express anger (Feldman 1949).

The motor aspects of speech have been thoroughly investigated. How movements of the chest, larynx, mouth, and other body parts produce sounds is lucidly described in a recent book by Pierce and David (1958). Words result from a coordinated motor pattern which, according to Stetson, involves three muscle groups: (1) Intercostal muscles release the sound; (2) mouth and throat muscles shape it; and, (3) chest and abdominal muscles arrest it. He parenthetically suggests that the motor patterns of speech, piano playing, dancing, and other forms of expressive behavior are basically alike (Stetson 1951).

The neurophysiological basis for language is not completely understood. Most of the information stems from observation of people with brain damage (Penfield and Roberts 1959). The function of the cerebral cortex has been carefully investigated, particularly in connection with the aphasias. It seems generally agreed that certain parts of the brain are more actively involved in language and speech than others. Evidence for three cortical speech centers is presented in a recent book by Penfield and Roberts: Wernicke's area in the posterior temporal and posterior-inferior parietal regions; Broca's area in the posterior part of the third frontal convolution; and a supplementary area within the mid-sagittal fissure. Destruction of Wernicke's area produces the gravest aphasias (Penfield and Roberts 1959). The observations of Luria, a Russian neurologist, should also be mentioned here. On the basis of over 800 cases of brain injury, Luria concluded that lesions in the left temporal zone cause a breakdown in auditory perception of phonemes that in turn affects pronunciation, writing, and symbolization (Luria 1958). According to his theory, the brain handles sounds in a hierarchical fashion, with one sound acting as a signal that organizes the rest of the word and differentiates its meaning.

This idea fits well with an assumption underlying much contemporary language research: words have to contain certain sounds in order to be recognized by listeners. Liberman and co-workers, for instance, believe that speakers make specific sound patterns that can be identified in terms of their acoustic properties (Liberman 1957). But Licklider and many other investigators find no single dimension of speech to be critical for communication. Licklider states: "Since speech can be severely distorted without becoming unintelligible, it is reasonable to suppose that the normal stream of speech contains many more discriminative clues than are necessary. If distortion removes or confuses some of these clues, the others carry the message. An important aspect of any message is the extent to which the component elements are interrelated. As long as each element is unrelated to the others, each element can carry a separate parcel of information, but the listener is required to make no mistakes. If some relation exists, the amount of information per element of the message is reduced, but the listener's job is simplified. If the listener hears any of the related elements, he knows something about the others. By sending related elements in the message, the talker is, in effect, repeating himself. From the point of view of efficiency, human speech seems a poor device, but what is lost in efficiency is regained in resistance to distortion" (Stevens 1951).

The inefficiency of speech for communication has often been recognized by psychotherapists. Ruesch, for example, states that "Every good therapist eventually arrives at the inescapable conclusion that verbal accounts cannot adequately represent analogically codified events. Furthermore, verbal denotation cannot adequately represent experiences and skills which are accessible in terms of action only" (Ruesch 1955). Some patients even use speech to hide personal data or to avoid emotion. As Meerloo points out, "All manner of speech habits are employed to escape the danger of self-revelation. Stuttering, stammering, 'sloganizing', boasting, whining, scolding, the using of catch words and truisms are all resorted to" (Meerloo 1959).

The study of human sounds which are not words is still in its infancy. Moses summarizes what is known impressionistically about such non-verbal aspects of speech as rhythm, melody, stress, and register (Moses 1954). Starkweather, Goldman-Eisler, and other investigators are trying to identify the vocal cues with which speakers express certain emotions (Starkweather 1956; Goldman-Eisler 1958). To date, the correlation of vocal patterns like pitch, loudness, and word-rate with differential emotional states has disclosed nothing that would surprise experienced clinicians. For example, high pitch and rapid speech often correlate with anxiety, while low pitch and slow speech may be associated with depression (Eldred and Price 1958). Undoubtedly, with suitable electro-acoustical devices and rigorous experimental designs, expressive voice qualities like whininess, bitterness, or flatness can also be correlated with acoustic patterns.

Noises used for communication have also received some attention. Heartbeats, breathsounds, abdominal rumbles, and other autonomic by-products are described in the literature on physical diagnosis (Douthwaite 1954). Burps, blathers, coughs, finger-nail clicks, flatus, and other noises patients make during therapy are discussed by Scott, Ostwald, Merrill, and others (Scott 1955; Ostwald 1960a; Merrill 1952). I have reported whistling as self-stimulation and as a form of ambiguous communication (Ostwald 1959). Several psychoanalytic studies on screaming, yelling, humming, and other expressive noises are available (Scott 1958). A recent report by Robertson and Shamsie treats the problem of gibberish in a schizophrenic patient (Robertson and Shamsie 1959). Greenspoon's study of the sound *mm-hm* suggests that this noise, by indicating agreement, may be used to control the responses of other people (Greenspoon 1955).

The place of musical performance in human communication has been discussed, with minimal recourse to aesthetics, by several writers. Kohut, using the psychoanalytic model, relates music-making to the three components of the personality: for the id, music serves primarily as emotional catharsis for repressed wishes; for the ego it provides playful mastery over threats of trauma; for the super-ego, music brings about enjoyable submission to rules. Kohut finds that musical activity contributes "[...] to the relief of primitive, preverbal tensions that have found little psychological representation and it may provide for the maintenance of archaic object cathexes [...]" (Kohut 1957). Ehrenzweig writes more specifically about musical form. He considers vibratos, trills, and glissandos analogous to the doodles, shading, and other expressive devices used by painters (Ehrenzweig 1953). These sounds, he feels, free the performer from rigorous demands made by the composer and provide the listener with unexpected stimuli.

When people listen

Customarily listening is divided into two components, one having to do with the ears, the other involving the central nervous system. This artificial distinction between peripheral and central aspects of auditory perception gradually disappears in the face of mounting evidence that central mechanisms actually control what the sense organs perceive and are in turn regulated by feedback from these organs (Galambos 1954). Yet for descriptive purposes, some arbitrary dividing up of the listening process is inevitable.

The mechanical properties of the ear are succinctly described by Békésy (Stevens 1951). There seems to be good agreement that incident sound waves agitate the tympanic membrane and are transferred to the cochlea by oscillation of bones in the middle ear. But what happens thereafter is still largely a mystery. Several new theories which are well summarized in a recent article by Licklider now supersede the Helmholtz resonance-place theory of hearing (Licklider 1959). The SIGNAL DETECTION THEORY does away with the concept of auditory threshold and puts in its place a statistical-decision process. It

is formulated in such a way as to be applicable to detection trials in each of which (1) a signal, of specifications known more or less completely by the listener, is either presented or not presented, and (2) a listener makes a response signifying whether or not, according to his judgment, the signal was presented.

The THEORY OF SPEECH INTELLIGIBILITY partly preserves the concept of auditory threshold but

postulates a 'neural noise' which acts in precisely the same way as random-process noise of external origin and, in fact, adds to the external noise, just as in the theory of signal detection.

The PITCH PERCEPTION THEORY

assumes that the acoustic patterns delivered to the two ears are subjected to mechanical frequency analysis in the cochleas and that the products of that analysis are then subjected to a twofold coincidence or correlation analysis in unspecified centers of the nervous system. The first coincidence analysis in a sense correlates the signals from the two ears and mediates sound localization in phenomenal space. The second coincidence analysis, through a process called autocorrelation, exposes periodicities that may have appeared only in the envelope, and not necessarily in the wave-form per se, of the acoustic stimuli (Licklider 1959).

The neural mechanisms of hearing were comprehensively reviewed by Galambos and new information constantly accumulates, making this phase of sound-reception increasingly complex. According to Galambos, "In addition to the classical afferent pathway shown in most textbooks [...] auditory connections involving the cerebellum and the reticular formation have recently been defined. Furthermore, a system of neurons descends from cortex to medulla, possibly having as its final link the olivo-cochlear pathway that is known to end in the region of the internal hair cells" (Galambos 1954). His experimental work with cats, reported in 1956, suggests that via this pathway auditory inflow may be suppressed peripherally by central stimulation in the medulla (Galambos 1956).

Physiological limits of hearing can best be determined with standard audiology tests involving pure tones, spondee words, and other neutral stimuli (Newby 1958). Nonverbal responses of the listener, such as a change of skin resistance measurable electrically, are useful for testing immature, hysterical, or unreliable subjects (Newby 1958). It is generally accepted that the human ear is sensitive to sounds between 16 and 20,000 cycles per second, age accounting for some variation in this range (Fletcher 1953). This entire spectrum is not necessary for communication, however. Human speech, for instance, occupies the 60 to 8000 cycle per second band with a predominant center from 500 to 2000 cps; musical instruments make sounds between 50 and 10,000 cycles per second; and signalling devices like whistles concentrate sound in the 1,000 to 4,000 cycle per second band. Thus the listener must tune in, like a radio, on one or another segment of the sound spectrum.

How to tell whether people are 'tuned in' or listening to certain sounds is one of the most exasperating problems in clinical medicine. In the first place, listening can occur in the absence of external stimuli, as everyone knows who is familiar with hallucinations, auditory reveries, musical inspiration, and similar phenomena. Secondly, to find out what a person hears, we must ask him to say or do something, which immediately puts us on the receiving end. Finally, the subject of listening is tinged with many taboos and misconceptions, due partly to the fact that prior to the phonograph a sound once made, was gone forever, causing observers to have all sorts of mystical, omnipotent, and frightening theories about what had happened.

Many of these imaginary and fanciful notions about listening have been tapped by psychoanalytic investigators. Jones, for instance, wrote about the delusion that impregnation occurs through the ear (Jones 1951a). Knapp, in a review of the subject, concluded that "the ear, often an unobtrusive part of our body scheme, plays a definite role in psychic life. As an orifice and appendage, it may readily substitute for anatomically similar areas – the vagina, anus, or mouth, on the one hand, the phallus on the other" (Knapp 1953). An embryological basis for such substitutions is also suggested by findings like those of Hilson, who demonstrated that congenital anomalies of the ear and the genitourinary tract often go together (Hilson 1957).

Social values control listening insofar as some sounds, churchbells for instance, are supposed to be heard while others, say dirty words, are not. Isakower first pointed to the auditory sphere as the "nucleus of the super-ego". He called the auditory mechanism "one of the most important apparatuses for the regulation of relations with the environment and with the introjected representation of interests in that environment [...]" (Isakower 1939). Further contributions to the social psychology of listening can be found in Barbara's recent book (Barbara 1958). He finds listening to require discipline, concentration, patience, skill, comprehension, and participation on the part of the listener.

More widespread effects of sounds on human behavior are discussed by Davis, Broadbent, and other contributors in the *Handbook of Noise Control*, a book devoted exclusively to individual and social aspects of noise (C. Harris 1957). There is general agreement that some noises can cause bodily injury. Damage to hearing results only from repeated exposure to loud noises and usually begins at 4,000 cycles per second. Burns can occur when a source of ultrasonic waves is close to the body. Unpleasant sensations result from vibration of the eyes, labyrinth, and other organs in the head when an individual is exposed to high-intensity noise. Sudden sounds cause startle reactions manifested by all the physiological signs of stress. If the subject cannot adapt to this stress, noises may interfere with his efficiency and well-being.

Broadbent discusses the subject of annoyance in some detail (C. Harris 1957). He postulates an "internal blink", which may last as long as one second, in response to a sudden noise. As with the eye blink, all sensory input is momentarily shut out. Noises are generally recognized to interfere with verbal communication, since they may obscure the sounds of words. But this does not necessarily impair word recognition, since speech involves additional cues from which the listener can glean what is said. A listener who is familiar with the speaker, his language, the subject under discussion, and the situation recognizes more words than the one who is not (Stevens 1951).

Sounds in human relationships

Verbal behavior is mediated by sounds which people make and by visual depiction with phonetic symbols of the things they make sounds about. Skinner introduces his brilliant study of this most characteristically human activity with the following remarks:

We need separate but interlocking accounts of the behaviors of both speaker and listener if our explanation of verbal behavior is to be complete. In explaining the behavior of the speaker we assume a listener who will reinforce his behavior in certain ways. In accounting for the behavior of the listener, we assume a speaker whose behavior bears a certain relation to environmental conditions (Skinner 1957).

This interaction between speakers and listeners differs depending on their age, sex, and biological needs for each other. An unborn infant, for example, relates to its mother primarily as a listener, and she – as far as sounds are concerned – is mainly a noise-maker. Little is as yet known about such prenatal communication patterns. The ear is already fully developed before birth, and it has been suggested that noises transmitted through the amniotic fluid and the bones of the head can affect the growing fetus. Indeed there is some evidence that intra-uterine babies respond to sounds. Sontag and Wallace reported increased fetal movements following noises made close to the mother, especially a doorbell buzzer placed over the fetal head (Sontag and Wallace 1935). They reported responsiveness to sounds in the thirty-first week of intra-uterine life. Partly from these observations and similar studies of premature and newborn infants, Greenacre postulated a prenatal predisposition to anxiety which "favors an inadequate development of the sense of reality and furnishes additional predisposition to the development of severe neuroses or borderline states" (Greenacre 1952b). Vascular pulsations, breathing, walking, singing, and speech may also affect the unborn child. Greene suggests that the mother's rhythmic noises might serve the fetus as a protective barrier against erratic external stimuli (Greene 1958).

Once the baby is born, the situation partly reverses itself: the mother now becomes a listener and the child sounds off. (Rarely an infant may vocalize while still in the uterus, a phenomenon reported in myths, repudiated by Leonardo da Vinci, but recently confirmed by obstetricians) (Panconcelli-Calzia 1954). Infant screams are remarkably efficient sound signals. No amount of electro-acoustical filtration seems to make them unrecognizable. Unlike open mouths, wet diapers, and other visible signs of baby needs, screams cannot be ignored by averting the eyes or closing a door. Thus most mothers learn to differentiate sounds which indicate that the baby is hungry, cold, lonely, or in distress (Brody 1956).

Subsequent steps in the development of communication with sounds have been investigated by Lewis, Spitz and others (Lewis 1936; Spitz 1957). Lewis, on the basis of painstaking observations, concluded that within a few hours after birth infants produce vowels and nasal consonants indicative of discomfort. Shortly thereafter, back consonants indicating comfort can be heard. Subsequent babbling and imitative noises are seen as precursors to syllables, words, and phrases. Spitz observed that negation and affirmation as linguistic concepts develop as the baby moves its head, largely in search for milk from the mother's breast. This finding could explain the universality of certain speech patterns. According to Greenberg, "there is a slight tendency for certain sounds or sound combinations to be connected more frequently with certain meanings that might be expected on a purely chance basis. Conspicuous instances are the nursery words for 'mother' and 'father' and onomatopoeias for certain species of the animals" (Greenberg 1953).

Various speech disturbances may result from frustrating experience in interaction of the child with its parents. Stuttering, for example, is an abnormality in the flow of spoken words. According to Glauber, who has written extensively about this subject, the mother's anxieties initiate stuttering, and the father's ambivalence maintains the neurosis (Eisenson 1958). Glauber states that stuttering is "generally accepted as a pre-genital conversion or a narcissistic neurosis, that is, one in which primarily the executant part of the personality, the ego, is defective or in-sufficiently developed." There is some evidence for a constitutional pre-disposition to stuttering. While long-term therapeutic results are not too good, temporary relief of the speech symptom can be produced with psychotherapy, feed-back delay, masking noise, and other measures (Diehl 1958).

Lesser forms of speech pathology occur in all of us. Blocking, hesitation, slips of the tongue, and other phonetic symptoms can be explained on the basis of unconscious conflicts (Freud 1935). Mispronunciations and the sort of phonemic 'twists' that one usually labels affectation can be studied psychoanalytically. The recurring sound-sensation *MM*... for example, was traced, by Greenson, to "the memory or fantasy of the pleasurable experiences of being at the mother's breast" (Greenson 1954). Voice quality also has psychological meaning. A falsetto voice, for instance, was shown by Ferenczi to occur whenever the patient wished to "coquette with me or please me, so that he was more concerned with the effect of than with the content of his talk" (Ferenczi 1950a). Some physiological correlates for voice pathology have been demonstrated. Holmes and co-workers, for example, showed that stress precipitates vascular and mucosal reactions in the nasal turbinates (Moses 1954).

Mutism, or the absence of speech, is a more serious problem. Formerly ascribed to deafness, this disorder is now recognized more and more as an expression of childhood schizophrenia (Kanner 1957). The patients, as Sherwin has observed, can respond to sounds, and can sing, scream, or make noises (Sherwin 1953). But they rarely learn to use words as symbols for communication, and treatment is discouraging. Jackson, in a seven-year follow-up study of non-speaking children, proposes "an inherent susceptibility, or a genetic flaw of varying gravity, which may balk the most thorough and prolonged efforts at rehabilitation" (L. Jackson 1958).

It seems appropriate to close a paper about sounds with a few words about silence, or the absence of sound. In human affairs, silence has an important place since it has come to be associated with mourning, religious experience, creativity, intellectual effort, and other forms of behavior (Witzleben 1958). Most investigators feel that silence symbolizes death. Patients in psychotherapy use silence defensively and as a hostile maneuver, and few symptoms are as disturbing as protracted silence (Levy 1958). Some people tolerate silence so poorly that they must 'fill it in' with sounds at all cost, a technique which Sheehan has quite aptly labeled filibustering (Eisenson 1958). The French writer Maurois expressed a related idea when he stated: "Men fear silence as they fear solitude, because both give them a glimpse of the terror of life's nothingness" (Maurois 1958).

Summary

Books and articles from various fields including linguistics, acoustics, psychiatry, and musicology are surveyed in order to bring together some pertinent information about the sounds of human behavior. Recent animal studies have shown that many organisms heretofore thought to be 'silent' communicate with sounds; some animals even use sounds as signs leading to specific behavioral responses. Human beings, it seems, not only use a greater number of sounds for communication than do animals; they are able to use sounds symbolically. This means that social customs and personal attitudes which determine the interpretation of symbols have a very significant role in the usage of human sounds.

Until recently there was no way to record sounds directly, so that the history of human sound is extremely sketchy. Philosophical and scientific problems in the study of human sounds are briefly discussed. It seems that currently more reliable information is available about sound-making than about sound-perception. This is unfortunate since perception of sounds is one of the factors which controls the making of sounds. There is much room for further investigation of human sounds, and several fruitful areas, including the development of speech in children and the disturbances of speech in interpersonal relationships, are briefly mentioned.

3

WHEN PEOPLE WHISTLE*

(1959)

The shrill, high-pitched musical sound produced when air is forced
through a small opening or against a thin edge is called whistling. This
paper treats whistling as a special form of human communication. A
simpler form of communication than speech, it requires less training in
the production and perception of sounds. Yet whistling is more difficult
than noise-making, whose sounds are by-products of unskilled movements
like eating or breathing and are universally understood. In terms of its
history and in connection with the experiences of the whistler and the
listener, whistling provides interesting information about the psychology
of sound. A study of whistling therefore belongs in the analysis of human
behavior.

The history of whistling

Though the exact function of whistling in the animal world is not known,
there are many examples which may shed light on human whistling. The
wild 'whistling swan' of North America, for example, emits a soft,
distinctive, musical tone. The large mountain marmots of the northwest
also whistle, and are nicknamed 'whistlers'. There is a whistle pig (wood-
chuck), whistle fish, and whistle moth. Possibly whistling sounds serve
these animals to recognize each other, to stay in groups, to frighten
predators, and to time their reactions for feeding, mating, and other
self-preservative acts (Lorenz 1952).

Humans whistle by directing a stream of air through the mouth or
nose. While there is almost no written information about whistling, one
can assume that ancient tribes whistled (Wellesz 1957). Instruments used

* Reprinted from *Language and Speech* 2. 3: 137-145 (1959).

to whistle, as well as visual depiction of musicians using pipes and whistles have been recovered from archeological diggings. Savages generally used whistles made of cane that were often blown with the nose. In Mesopotamia, mouth whistles capable of making one to three distinct tones were used. The Chinese employed clay whistles in the form of frogs, birds, and other animals. Tubes of bamboo with reeds inserted into the walls were used for whistling during funeral processions, and Pekin puppet plays still use the *koouchyntzyy*, a free-reed whistle, to imitate chickens and infants. The 'whistle pots' of the South American Indians consisted of two communicating earthenware vessels, half filled with water.

Occasionally whistling was used as a form of language; and such languages may have characterized many early hunting cultures. The only whistle language in existence today goes back to the 15th century. The 30,000 inhabitants of La Gomera, one of the Canary Islands, communicate by whistling, often to the exclusion of speech (Classe 1957). Their language, called 'Silbo', is audible for several miles and is ideally suited to the mountainous terrain for greeting calls, message exchange, and joke telling. Only the pitch of the whistle is varied to indicate different 'words'.

With the growth of instrumental music in Europe, whistles came to be used in the form of Pandean pipes, and later on as the 'piccolo', or little flute. Whistles also figured in the mechanical orchestras of the 18th century. They were blown by steam or air, like high-pitched organ pipes. Instructions for the use of the bird-whistle were also published at that time. It would appear that whistling gradually came to be associated with the activities of socially underprivileged or poorly educated persons. In any event, throughout Europe and even in the United States upper class persons may tend to frown on whistling and may outlaw it in formal restaurants, art museums, and other public places.

Today whistles are also used by children as toys and by steam-kettles and policemen as warning devices. Several contemporary examples of whistling deserve mention. In the movie, *The Bridge on the River Kwai*, British prisoners whistled "Colonel Bogey" while marching as a means of keeping up their morale in the face of oppression during captivity. Engineers concerned with the mechanical production of artificial speech by machines like the 'Voder' make use of hissing and whistling sounds (Pierce and David 1958).

Numerous colloquial expressions hint at the usage of whistles in social discourse. One might *whistle for* ('demand') *a handout, go whistle* ('tell secretly') *a story, whistle down the wind* ('argue to no purpose'), or *whistle off* ('dismiss') *an employee.*

How humans whistle

It is possible to whistle without using an instrument. One simply exhales through the mouth and controls the amount of air with the speech organs. The vocal cords are abducted as in breathing, the tongue stays on the floor of the mouth, and air is expelled more or less forcefully through a small opening provided by puckered lips or spaces between the teeth. Some whistlers make a narrow opening by placing two fingers in the mouth. The pitch of a whistle can be varied by altering the shape of the mouth cavity, usually with the tongue.

The whistler uses more energy than in speech because he needs considerable muscular control and co-ordination. Those who cannot close the lips firmly or shut off air flow through the nose may have great difficulty. Children can rarely whistle adequately before the age of five or six. Uncontrolled human whistling usually occurs only when there is accidental leakage of air from the respiratory tract. Persons with articulation defects or badly fitting dentures may whistle while they speak. Artificial openings of the windpipe (tracheotomies) occasionally whistle, as do lung adhesions or cavities due to tuberculosis.

The whistler

What the whistler experiences as he whistles is difficult to define since it involves a medley of subjective sensations and personalized values. Yet whistling, as a discrete and nicely defined bit of behavior, has its concomitant emotions which I shall try to spell out.

To begin with, when a person whistles he experiences tension in the muscles of the mouth and face that is accompanied by buzzing and tingling feelings in the skin of the lips and the mucous membranes of the buccal cavity. Such tensions and sensations are similar to those experienced during any process that involves oral gratification – viz., biting, tasting, chewing, salivating, kissing, talking, smoking, etc. And since oral gratification, at least in those people who were mothered during infancy, involved the simultaneous satisfaction of other needs besides hunger – closeness, warmth, protection, etc. – whistling may call forth a more general hedonic state than usual in the whistler (Greenacre 1952a).

In addition to the mouth and face, whistling involves the respiratory structures. These structures – chest, abdomen, lungs, windpipes, and throat – move of their own accord, regulated by neuronal and chemical processes beyond voluntary control. But the whistler in effect willfully imposes his own rhythm, amplitude, and organization pattern on these automatic movements. Psychological studies show that if the individual is rewarded by attention or praise when he first gains control over such automatic processes, he may continue to expect satisfaction from this display of skill (Greenacre 1952a). As will be shown later, whistling arouses the attention of listeners, so that the whistler's bodily mastery is almost universally rewarded in some way.

Studies of children suggest that products of the body, like matter from digestion, warm air from breathing, or sounds from the vocal tract, may become invested with great interest, pride, and pleasure once the individual masters the movements that result in such products (Greenacre 1952a). Occasionally children will play with their products, and create fantasies in which these inanimate things begin to have a life and existence of their own. Whistling results in a sound, and this like other products of his willful effort, may be cherished and idealized by the whistler. On the other hand, whistles, like other body products, may come to be regarded as dirty and undesirable. For instance, a child may be taught to believe that his air 'smells bad' or is 'too noisy', with the result that he experiences guilt while whistling or stops this pleasurable activity altogether.

Some of the emotions that accompany the act of whistling would appear to result from wishful thoughts and magical fantasies in the mind of the whistler. Whistling, because it involves the production of wordless sounds, may bring back memories of that very early period during which the child could not distinguish between those sounds which came from the outside world and those sounds which came from his own body. During this phase of personality development, one is unsure of the significance of sounds. One cannot tell whether a certain noise, say one's footsteps, has personal meaning referable only to his own body or has a public meaning with some reference to the world of other people. In this confused state, the individual may come to believe that the sounds he produces have some causal relationship to what he experiences. Whistling, like other noises he makes, may thus be associated with fantasies of omnipotence which, unless corrected by reality, can lead to delusions of grandeur. Occasionally parents or other adults inadvertently encourage magical behavior in their children and thus reinforce fanciful thoughts about whistling and other sounds. For example, nurses have been known to employ whistles to 'make the child urinate', and kindly grandparents not infrequently 'whistle away' the aches and bruises of a youngster.

Certain magical ideas associated with whistling are reinforced by beliefs and superstitions prevalent in the culture at large (Diserens 1926). For example, there is an old myth among mariners to the effect that to 'whistle for a wind' will bring a fresh and vigorous breeze to fill the sails. Tales about whistles are numerous in the folklore of various cultures. Suffice it to say that magic whistles which attract birds are described in Celtic tales, and flutes which have power over serpents, demons, and beasts appear in the legends of almost all cultures. Pan, the god of shepherds and flocks, invented the syrinx, a pipe that produced whistling sounds. With it he startled wanderers in the dark forest. He also used his whistle to enchant King Midas, and one day challenged Apollo, the god of the lyre, to a musical contest.

Another way to explain what the whistler experiences is to look upon whistling as a form of nonverbal signalling (Ruesch and Kees 1956). Wordless signals usually have a vague and imprecise meaning. They do not usually communicate ideas but serve rather to attract attention. One requirement of this kind of signal is that it must be easily perceived by others. Whistles are sounds much easier to hear than words. They tend to be pure tones which concentrate sound energy into a narrow segment of the frequency spectrum instead of spreading it – as in speech – over a wide band. Furthermore, they occur most often in the frequency range of 1,000 to 4,000 cycles per second to which the human ear is most sensitive. Thus the whistler can be sure to be heard by random listeners even at a considerable distance. Alone in the woods or on a prairie, for example, he can signal to birds and other animals. Most people seek companionship and may be rewarded with the pleasant company of a pet or a child if they whistle. In addition to making contact with another being by whistling, the whistler can expect whistling to evoke a sympathetic reaction. Nonverbal signals like yawns, laughs or cries, lead to immediate emotional rapport; whereas words, which have to be translated and interpreted by the receiver, result in delayed or symbolic behavior.

Last but not least, whistlers, since they produce melodies, rhythms, and other sound patterns identifiable as music, experience pleasures akin to those of the performing musician (Kohut 1957). When he 'plays on his musical instrument', the whistler conforms to some of the traditions, rules and formulas, which, over the course of time, have come to be associated with beauty. He also identifies himself with publicly adored figures such as famous composers and artists.

The listener

Some of the effects of whistles upon a listener have been mentioned in connection with the whistler, who, whenever he is alone, is simultaneously the listener. Listening to one's own whistle may have yet another function – that of echo-location. Griffin and others have found that many animals determine their position and direction in space by listening to the reflection of their own noises (Griffin, 1958). Bats, for example, can fly in total darkness thanks to their ability to navigate by reflected sound. Some blind persons judge distances in the same way, by a form of echo-location known as 'facial vision'. Whistles, as clear penetrating sounds, may serve such a purpose, and a person who 'whistles in the dark' is not necessarily afraid but may merely be exercising his unconscious sense of echo-location.

As to the listener who is not also the whistler, his behavior in response to the sound of whistling is a complex pattern. Part of his behavior is due to the fact that sounds can produce an arousal reaction. That the human organism has a deep-seated native capacity to be aroused by sounds is known from observing the startle patterns of intra-uterine infants and newborns (Greenacre 1952). This capacity appears to be enhanced whenever the listener expects to hear a sound, as when an alarm clock wakes him from sleep, or an air-raid siren alerts him in time of danger. When a person is engaged in repetitive or monotonous work, sounds tend to alleviate fatigue and to increase his efficiency. This is one reason why music is used for improving the morale and work output in factories and for reducing depressions in mental hospital patients.

Whistles not only arouse the listener, they may bother or annoy him. The high-pitched whistle of sufficient sound energy will cause discomfort and pain in the listener's ears. After continuous exposure, the listener may become temporarily deafened to the tones of the whistle; and even permanent damage to the structure of the ear has been reported. It is reported that certain annoying sounds can precipitate convulsions in susceptible individuals (Bevan 1955).

As the result of its arousing and annoying potential, whistling has come to be used for the purpose of controlling people – particularly people in groups (Ruesch and Kees 1956). Thus a whistle blast may initiate a marine assault during combat. Whistles signal the start of runners, boxers, or other athletes towards their goal. In the case of human groups that are unorganized and unprepared, whistling, together with other signals, calls attention to a group leader. Such is the case of the students who file into the classroom in an orderly fashion when the whistle blows, or the police whistle which breaks up a riot. The story of the Pied Piper of Hamelin tells about an exodus from the village of children led by the sound of a whistle. Whistles can also be used to halt movements. This fact is known to hunters who kill rabbits by causing them to stop in their tracks at the sound of a whistle. The traffic cop and the referee also 'call a halt' by whistling.

Whistles convey specific meanings to the listener only when they are associated with significant ideas or images. This may happen in the case of whistles that have a specific acoustic character, such as those of whizzing bullets or speeding trains. Some people learn to identify each other on the basis of distinctive whistles; and in some families, members have whistles which they use to call to each other over the hullabaloo of a crowd or at a distance. Occasionally, whistles have a stereotyped meaning for a large segment of the community. The wolf whistle, for instance, has come to signify sexiness. Similar patterns of sound are also used to indicate amazement, surprise, astonishment, and other emotions. Rhythmical whistles that resemble the sounds of walking, the heartbeat, machinery, or other familiar phenomena are relatively easy to associate with specific thoughts or images. But much of the time whistles lack a definite rhythmic form and, like many radio sound effects, have a general sound that suggests vague ideas and moods (Turnbull 1951). For instance, whistling that rises in pitch suggests something approaching and leads to a feeling of alarm and suspense. Whistles that fall in pitch suggest something receding and create the impression of weakness, cowardice, or failure.

If a whistle first alerts the listener and then causes him to have vague thoughts and ambiguous feelings, we say that the whistle has put him into a state of suspiciousness. He begins to wonder what is really going on, and tries to find out. He strains his ears and eyes, and searches restlessly for the origin and significance of the sound, much like a hard-of-hearing person who receives only a fragment of the information contained in speech. He remains dissatisfied until he locates and understands the noise. Suspiciousness can lead to panic; it also seems to be a useful, self-protective form of behavior in the face of danger. For example, during World War I the British Army trained a unit of specialized 'Sound Rangers' whose responsibility it was to listen for the whistles and explosions of enemy artillery bombardments (Innes 1935). In the face of enemy submarines, sea-captains learned to listen suspiciously for telltale underwater sounds. For the purpose of testing machinery and motors, listeners and listening devices are employed in order to discover any whistles, rattles, and other vague noises.

Sounds are also among the most important clues for the evaluation of health and disease in clinical medicine (Douthwaite 1954). Pathological whistling, although it does not occur as frequently as abnormal lung or heart sounds, occasionally indicates serious physical malfunction. For example, in veterinary medicine, the whistling horse requires immediate attention; the whistle is symptomatic of obstruction of the respiratory tract because of laryngeal paralysis. Pathological human whistles include those resulting from asthma, diptheria, and other conditions that interfere with breathing. An inability to whistle may also be of pathological significance, and has been reported as one of the diagnostic signs of myopathy or paralysis.

Psychiatrists occasionally observe exaggerated responses to whistles in patients with emotional disturbances. These hypersensitivities are diagnostic clues that can point up severe underlying psychopathology. For example, a woman seen in our clinic gradually became tense, confused, and distractible following the birth of a child. One day her husband came home and found her in a disorganized state; she talked continually of the whistle of the teakettle, and insisted that the whistle had stopped because "God turned it off". A psychiatrist made the diagnosis of a post-partum schizophrenic reaction and admitted the patient for treatment. After her recovery, analysis of the patient's abnormal response to whistling revealed that her mother had been in the habit of using a tin whistle to summon her children to meals. Following the birth of her child, the patient had felt a great need for help from her mother but was unwilling to ask for it directly. Instead she made great demands on her husband. When he was unable to fulfill her wishes, she began to pray to God for assistance. The patient began to imagine that she was the Virgin Mary, and in this setting she interpreted the whistle of the teakettle, which resembled that of her mother's whistle, as a sign from God.

Another patient with hypersensitivity to whistles was a man who requested treatment because of jealousy, suspiciousness, and homosexual tendencies. One day he met a girl who he became convinced was a Lesbian because he had heard her whistle. He stated that whistles were used as a secret code among homosexuals, particularly when they wanted to attract each other. Analysis of this notion led to the information that the patient's father, a clergyman, had regularly requested his son to listen to rehearsals of his Sunday sermons. The little boy, unable to comprehend the words, was spell-bound by his father's oratory and would sit in a trance throughout the sermon, seemingly hypnotized by the sound of his father's voice. The undulating and pure-tone quality of whistling always reminded him of his father's voice, and anyone who whistled exerted an irresistible fascination upon him.

The function of whistling in human relations

Since whistling exists in many human and animal groups, it evidently plays a significant role in relations between individuals within these groups. In human society, whistles, like other sounds, help a person to orient himself in the world and permit him to maintain comfortable contacts with other persons at crucial moments. It is not only that the echo of his whistle provides the whistler with a sense of his whereabouts and assists him to avoid obstacles in his path. When he whistles, he hears his own sound directly, and this, like speaking, singing, humming, or any other form of sound-making, gives him knowledge that he exists. It is like looking into a mirror or touching one's body. Such self-evaluative activities prove to the individual that he is alive, intact, and awake. It is the most immediate and reliable way to reassure oneself (Ruesch and Kees 1956).

Whistling also helps the individual to maintain his equilibrium during times of danger, boredom, fear, and loneliness when he cannot share his feelings with others or when such sharing would lead to trouble. During these times of stress or excitement, unpleasant emotions are contagious. The individual must control them, lest these emotions begin to reverberate between him and others and, like an echo, produce confusion. Whistling may strengthen his self-control. The whistler does not talk, yet he communicates. He keeps busy during the time of waiting, yet he is not overactive. This is probably why whistling, like foot-tapping, smoking, chewing, and similar activities, occurs so often when people wait for a departure, prepare for a performance, and endure many other tense and potentially disagreeable moments. Whistling 'while we wait' is simultaneously energy-conserving and energy-expending. Rather than fidget about and stir up others, the person quietly whistles. Yet the activity of whistling produces some fatigue, thereby soothing and calming the whistler.

The whistler communicates too in a very specific way with his fellow man. With a whistle he implies all sorts of inner moods, motives, and thoughts which keep the listener guessing. Like other nonverbal indicators of emotions, the meaning of the whistle cannot be definitely pinned down, so that the whistler is safe from criticism, discovery, and punishment.

He can get away with expressing a whole range of feelings – hate, disdain, coolness, nonchalance, pity, and tenderness – by whistling, and who will be the wiser? He can safely express many of the things for which he has not yet learned words, or for which no words exist, or whose verbalization is out of the question at the time (Ruesch and Kees 1956).

Thus in effect whistling can bring people closer together. It is a form of communicative behavior which requires no training on the listener's part to be perceived and understood (see Table I). While it does take practice, co-ordination, and effort to produce a whistle, whistling demands less training and skill than is necessary for speech, which requires facility with word symbols.

TABLE I

Type of sound	Training required for:		
	Production of sound	Perception of sound	Interpretation of sound
Spoken words	+	+	+
Tunes	+	+	
Whistling	+		
Noisy activity			

Comparison of training required for utilization of sounds.

Whistling is even a simpler form of communication than is music because the listener must be receptive and tolerant in order to appreciate a musical message (Diserens 1926). But whistling is not simply noise that results from random movement. Acoustically, whistling resembles a pure tone, has melodic form, and may even be rhythmical. Noises, on the other hand, are rough, irregular, and disorganized acoustic patterns. No planning or effort is needed to produce a noise, since one makes noise simply by walking, swallowing, or breathing.

Conclusion

From this information about whistling in human and animal behavior, whistling appears to be a special form of communication which lacks the complexity of speech and music, yet is more complex than simple noise-making. The experiences of the whistler concern mouth and body movements that may be pleasurable, as well as thoughts and emotions that range from excitement to depression. An analysis of the effects of whistling upon listeners shows that whistles arouse, annoy, alarm, and control others. Finally, whistling has its function in human relations. Whistling seems to help calm a person who is in danger and distress. It reinforces the whistler's belief that he is alive and aids in self-orientation. By whistling, an individual can establish contact with others. People whistle to communicate feelings which cannot be readily expressed in words.

4

HUMMING, SOUND AND SYMBOL*

(1961)

Sounds that have no dictionary meaning may nevertheless be informative under certain circumstances. For instance whistles, body slapping, clicking with the fingernails, and other human noises are used to transmit fairly complicated messages when the rules about the usage of such signals are known to both sender and receiver (Ostwald 1960b). The purpose of this brief report is to discuss the possible significance of humming and to present a number of clinical observations about this interesting form of human sound-making.

Some facts about the hum

The hum is a pleasant, soft, musical sound produced by singing with the mouth closed. A hum has a mellow tonal quality; it is composed of a laryngeal fundamental with few overtones, and resembles the sound made by a bass flute. As a form of pleasurable self-stimulation, humming excites the throat, mouth, and nose, setting the surrounding skin and mucous membranes into vibration. This leads to a warm, tingling feeling over the lower part of the face. Intense humming may also involve acoustic resonance of the facial sinuses and other head structures like the teeth, lips, and nose; it has a rich, cello-like quality. The loud hum which causes the teeth and bones of the jaw and throat to resonate adds a light tickle to the pleasant sensation.

The humming of animals provides us with some clues as to the function of this sound in human behavior. Purring, for example, is a hum commonly associated with cats. It is restricted almost exclusively to domestic cats and other Felidae. According to Bell, cats purr "because

* Reprinted from *The Journal of Auditory Research* 3: 224-32 (1961).

they have entered a certain emotional state: they are relaxed, and are without any form of apprehension, being at peace with the world around them." (Bell 1960). During the cat's relaxed state, the muscles which control the vocal cords apparently slaken, and the cords move in the stream of respiratory air, producing the purr.

Some animals hum when they try to elicit attention from each other, as for example the Panama Howling Monkey; the baby makes a humming sound when it seeks coddling from its mother (Bouliere 1954). Apparently animal hums can also become meaningful for human listeners: it has been noted that certain creatures turn to humans for mothering and affection, particularly when a human being offers himself as a substitute source of love to the animal shortly after it has lost its parents (Lorenz 1952). In such cases the human pseudo-parent, particularly if he or she is also lonely, may use the animal as a focus for private fantasies. Children develop fanciful ideas about the sounds of animals this way; and it is not surprising that in a child's mind the buzzing of insects, the fluttering of hummingbirds, the chirping of grasshoppers, and other nonhuman noises may come to have elaborate imaginary meanings (Searles 1960).

The exact evolution of humming in the history of mankind is not known. One theory is that primitive man, like the higher apes, may have used a relatively small number of speech sounds for communication (Revesz 1956). According to this point of view, cries, grunts, screams, and other noises of primitive man probably sufficed for communication about shelter, food, and sex. In line with this idea, one might suppose that humming, which is a relatively easy sound to produce, also played a role in aboriginal communication. Perhaps as groups began to organize for hunting, agriculture, and other communal enterprises, man standardized his primitive noises and came to use the hum as a more specific linguistic sign. A short humming sound, the phoneme /m/ occurs in all European languages, and according to Voelker makes up about $4\frac{1}{2}$ per cent of the consonants occurring in formal English speech (Irwin 1947).

But what about nonverbal humming? Some additional clues come from the field of musical composition: humming adds a quasi-instrumental quality to vocal music, one which many listeners find ethereal, unreal, and mysterious (Grove's Dictionary 1954). For example in the opera *Rigoletto* by Verdi, wordless singing is used as a sound-effect to suggest the howling of the wind. Contemporary composers (Boulez, Nono, and others) also make extensive use of humming as a means of bringing varieties of vocal color into their instrumental works.

Another useful fact is that humming is a diagnostic sign in medicine:

a hum indicates the site of certain disease processes to the alert physician. For instance, engorged blood vessels have characteristic hums due to eddies of slowed-down blood. Hyperthyroidism, splenic peritonitis, arterio-venous fistulas, and pregnancy can also be diagnosed on the basis of distinctive humming sounds (Douthwaite 1954).

Emotional meanings of humming

In the analysis of any bit of human behavior, it is well to consider independently what this behavior means in emotional terms, how it is used in action, and for what it comes to stand symbolically. Let us first consider the emotional meaning of humming since this is more difficult to put into words than are its actional or symbolic meanings. During early infancy when the human being is unable to express himself in words, humming seems to become a part of the total emotional experience of being with mother. Many steps are involved in this process: following birth, the infant and the mother are in a symbiotic relationship that resembles their physiological interdependency in the uterus. The infant instinctively tries to nurse on the mother in order to be nourished. He makes mouth movements in anxious anticipation of the feeding, vigorously sucks during food-intake, and smacks the lips afterwards while pleasantly satiated (Spitz 1957). Unless the mother resists this instinctive behavior, she usually enjoys feeding the infant and the associated physical intimacy. In this setting of mutual contentment humming may be heard for the first time. The mother herself may initiate the hum, as many do while feeding their children, singing lullabies, and rocking them to sleep.

It is difficult, if not impossible, for a person to remember this infantile phase of life. But occasionally during dreams, intoxication, or revery states some memories of very early childhood may come to consciousness and from these one can reconstruct the emotional meaning of humming. For example, in a study by Greenson, a patient in psychoanalysis began to experience a humming sensation in her mouth (Greenson 1954). Later she dreamt about a velvet cloth, and this brought to mind thoughts about delicious tactile, temperature and taste sensations localized predominantly in the mouth and hand. Following this she experienced the memory or fantasy of pleasure at the mother's breast.

Many mental traces are later superimposed on these early memories of nursery experiences: nursing is not uniformly satisfying, and particularly with clumsy, hasty or angry mothers the infant may experience oral frustrations which can be remembered in later years. Especially when the

teeth erupt, the physical and psychological relationship between mother
and child undergoes a change. The baby feels pain in the mouth and feeding becomes associated with new kinds of mouth movements (Kucera
1959). The jaws become more active, the lips are closed, and along with
an increase in bodily motility, more vigorous biting and chewing occurs.
The child is now capable of acting destructively; psychoanalytic studies
indicate that he may develop fears of aggressive impulses, in particular
a dread of biting and hurting the mother (Abraham 1942). The significance
of humming in such negative affect states is not yet known. But we do
have some information about the way people use humming in action as a
way of dealing with the outside world, which will now be considered.

Humming used as a masking noise

In addition to its use as a stimulus for self-induced affects, which has
already been mentioned, humming has an important behavioral function
in communication between people. It is used as a self-regulated 'masking
noise' to screen out sound stimuli from the external world. An acoustic
explanation for this phenomenon will immediately become apparent if we
remember how valuable pure tones (such as humming) are in the production of masking effects (Beranek 1954). When a person hums he can blot
out most of the sounds of speech, as well as other noises of the environment occurring in the masked portion of the sound spectrum. For
instance, a sufficiently intense hum at 500 cycles per second would mask
sounds in the 1000 to 2500 cps range, which is where some of the essential
cues for intelligibility of speech – for example the second formant – are
found.

This may explain in part why people hum when they do not want to be
disturbed by external sounds and noises. Many hum to themselves while
concentrating on tasks, particularly if these involve abstract thinking or
fine motor skills. Patients in psychotherapy occasionally hum in an effort
to ignore what the psychiatrist has to say. Self-distraction may also be
one of the mechanisms involved in the anesthetic effects of masking
sound, for instance as applied in dentistry (Gardner and Licklider 1960).

Among schizophrenic persons humming is associated with a more
general withdrawal from the realities of the outside world. For example,
a patient observed in the psychiatric clinic used humming to remove himself from uncomfortable environmental situations. This man had never
learned to speak in articulated words. When one tried to talk with him, he
made a variety of grunts and hisses, and periodically started to hum. While

humming he would slip into a revery, smile inappropriately and remain out of contact with the real situation that confronted him. He picked his nose, ate the contents, engaged in small jiggling movements with arms and legs, and emitted flatus. For this very disturbed person humming was clearly part of a deeply regressive act.

Psychoneurotic patients may use humming as part of an attempt to keep troublesome fantasies out of awareness. This is particularly true if the hum is in the form of an obsessive musical theme. Sherwin reports a patient obsessed with a tune from *Lady in the Dark*. The tune was used to cover up some feelings about his mother which the patient could not consciously recognize and accept (Sherwin 1958). In a similar case, a patient in psychoanalysis found himself obsessed with the music from an aria of Bach's *St. Matthew Passion*. The words of the aria, which he could not remember, had to do with murder, a subject particularly difficult for him to think about in an openly conscious manner.

Humming can also be the result of inhibition of aggressive activity directed towards the outside world. In our culture there is less objection to humming than to the sudden expulsion of air by belching or flatulence. In contrast to air expelled through the mouth, as in coughing, burping, the expiratory phase of yawning, and speech, humming produces a softer sound. Hence a youngster is less likely to be scolded for humming than for louder noises; if the humming is musical, he may even be praised. The humming child runs into little or no danger of interference with his activity from others. Yet his form of self-expression contains a particularly autistic element, for the very reason that it is not interfered with. Not subject to correction by other persons, emotions and fantasies associated with humming may remain unchecked, permitting the child to enjoy an unreal sense of power and superiority in his private world. We shall next consider some of these fantasied symbolic meanings of the human hum.

The symbolic meanings of humming

Since we have already learned about the infantile association between the hum and blissful feelings in the mother-child setting, it is not too surprising to discover that for many persons humming and similar forms of musical behavior are symbolic substitutes for love. This was well demonstrated by the case of a depressed painter who requested psychiatric treatment at a time in his life when he had few, if any, truly affectionate relationships. He had previously sought love in casual affairs, but seldom attached himself longer than a few days to another person. This attitude resulted in considerable conflict about whether to let himself feel attached to his physician during a course of psychotherapy that might take months if not years. After a few interviews he began to experience profound anxiety when faced with the prospect of revealing his private thoughts and feelings to the psychiatrist. He dealt with this problem at first by adopting a highly intellectual approach to therapy. Being an artist, he was able to engage in pseudo-aesthetic dissections of everything he saw. He commented critically on the color patterns of paintings and furnishings in the room, disconnecting and anatomizing everything in sight. This intellectualization worked as far as aggressive and destructive impulses were concerned. But when it came to passive and erotic strivings, these were expressed musically. The patient found himself thinking about and actually humming certain fragments of music, invariably tunes from songs or other compositions with unmistakable meaning. For instance, instead of talking of a wish for closeness and affection, he might hum Grieg's "I Love You".

Like any sound which has no generally agreed-upon definition, humming can have multiple and contradictory symbolic meanings. The dictionary mentions that humming may convey disapproval, embarrassment, and dissent. Why do so many persons consider humming sounds annoying? A possible explanation is that the unconscious connection between humming and the loss of maternal love may be recognized. Since every human being has to undergo the pain of separation from the mother, and humming may represent an attempt to recover from this, one can see that the hum could symbolize a counterfeit or dehydrated version of mother-love. Like many gestures, the hum seduces but does not satisfy; humming is like thumb-sucking without the thumb.

Seidenberg has made interesting observations on the way a child may attribute unpleasant symbolic meaning to a humming sound: a mother kept an electric egg beater running outside her child's bedroom supposedly to help him overcome his fear of noises. When the child later came to psychiatric treatment, because of extreme passivity, it was found that in his fantasies the child had managed to conceptualize his mother's vagina as a dangerous instrument with internal whirling blades (Seidenberg 1958).

Another example of the sexual symbolism of humming – in this case a mental image of musical tone – comes from Strawinsky's autobiographical accounts: One night before going to bed the composer was troubled by a certain tonal interval which kept coming to his mind. He dreamt about this: The interval "[...] had become an elastic substance stretching exactly between the two notes I had composed, but underneath these notes at either end was an egg, a large testicular egg. The eggs were gelatinous to the touch (I touched them) and warm, and they were protected by nests. I woke up knowing that my interval was right" (Strawinsky and Craft 1959).

Since in humming air must pass through the nose, it is not surprising that the hum so often has a symbolic meaning connected with the erotic. In fantasy, the nose frequently represents a bisexual organ (Saul 1948). In analogy to the penis it protrudes from the body, emits substances, and is covered with skin; and like the vagina the nose is hollow, permits insertion, and is lined with mucosa. Like nose-picking, humming is a displaced form of masturbation among certain emotionally disturbed persons.

The verbal meanings of humming

There are two forms of humming in verbal discourse: the word *hm* and the phoneme /m/. The word *hm*, according to Jaffe, constitutes a significant portion of the verbal responses of psychiatrists (Jaffe 1958). Since its meaning is not defined in the dictionary, this word is open to a number of possible interpretations.

Hm tends to be understood as a question when it has an upward inflection that resembles the sounds associated with doubt or pleading (Sapir 1949). Two staccato *hm*'s uttered in rapid succession with a rising inflection generally suggests affirmation (Greenspoon 1955). An up and then downwards inflection of *hm-hm* suggests a number of feeling states such as surprise, amazement or interest. Undulating *hm*'s suggest unrest, anguish, uncertainty, or alarm, probably because of the resemblance to the sound of a whine or siren.

For the phoneme /m/ we must again turn to studies of language development. The earliest communicative signals emitted by humans are mainly cries composed of sounds resembling the vowel [a], [ɑ], [e], [ɛ], and the consonants [h], and glottal stops. According to Irwin [m] constitutes less than 1 per cent of all the consonant sounds produced by the child during the first month of life (Irwin 1947). This low incidence easily leads one to underestimate the importance of the hum-like sound during infancy.

Lewis linked /m/ specifically with the sucking mouth movements of newborn infants waiting to be fed (Lewis 1936). He observed that "if the child phonates while making these anticipatory sucking movements, the sounds produced will approximate to the labial and dental consonants.

If, further, he is in a state of discomfort, such as hunger, and phonates nasally – as we have seen he does – then the consonants produced will inevitably be *m* or *n*." By the age of six months, when teeth have started to appear, [m] makes up 3 per cent of the baby's consonants, rises to 9 per cent shortly after the first birthday, and stays close to 8 per cent for the next year and a half.

To become linguistically meaningful, the child's spontaneous utterance of /m/ must be reinforced by parents or other speaking adults. Such reinforcement can occur in a variety of ways. What usually happens is that the baby's random mouth noises are mistaken for formed speech elements. Parents may be delighted to find that their baby can already make recognizable sounds. In their eagerness to communicate, babies may repeat the mouth sounds which please their parents. But as a phoneme, /m/ can only function in conjunction with other speech sound; in isolation it has no verbal meaning. To what extent its early association with oral factors causes the /m/ to impart a maternal feeling to words which contain this phoneme is not yet known. But note the high incidence of /m/ in words signifying mother (mom, mummy, mutti, mere, madre, etc.), and at the beginning of female names (Mary, Martha, Margaret, etc.). This may be one way in which the emotional hum of children survives as a depersonalized linguistic sign in adult communication (Greenberg 1953).

Summary

Humming is a sound produced by singing with the mouth closed. It may be used to express pleasurable emotions related to mother-love and satiation. Humming can also be involved in aggressive and masturbatory behavior. As a masking noise, humming helps certain people to withdraw from external stimuli during states of revery, intellectual work, and obsessional preoccupation. In verbal discourse, humming occurs as the word *hm*, which may signify assent, negation and other possible meanings. The phoneme /m/ may provide words in which it appears with an emotional flavor that recalls the primal mother-child relationship from which humming sounds originate.

5

LINGUISTIC CONTRIBUTIONS
TO THE STUDY OF HUMAN SOUNDS*

(1971)

People make various sounds, especially with their mouths. Many of these
sounds, when uttered according to specifiable rules of phonology and
syntax, are used to convey meanings by referring symbolically to things
and events not present in immediate reality. The study of these sonic
behavioral phenomena – i.e., the making of meaningful oral sound
sequences – falls into the domain of linguistics, a branch of science
dealing with language. No observer or student of sonic behavior can
ignore this field of knowledge, and my purpose in the following paper is
to indicate some of the major contributions which linguistics has made
to the understanding of human sonic communication.

Like so many scientific fields today, linguistics is in the throes of an
'information explosion'. Books and journals range all the way from the
broadest consideration of semiotic systems to the narrowest focussing on
artificial codes or computer 'languages'. Also, like many other sciences,
there is no fixed or permanent boundary between linguistics and its
neighboring fields concerned with human behavior – psychology,
psychiatry, and the social sciences. Some experts in language have had
their major educational experiences in one of these neighboring fields.
Indeed, the label 'linguist' is sometimes applied not to a trained language-
scientist at all, but refers to a person who is fluent in several languages.
Practical knowledge in communicating sonically with many different
kinds of people, in many different kinds of social settings, and within
many different language and dialect regions would seem to be a useful
prerequisite for work in linguistics, whether this be done in academic
settings or in clinical situations.

---

* This paper is based on a series of lectures given in 1969 and 1970 at the Langley
Porter Neuropsychiatric Institute in San Francisco.

Historical and comparative linguistics

Questions about the origin of languages have excited curiosity since ancient times. One finds a number of theories about human soundmaking described in the Book of Genesis, by Greek philosophers (Plato and Aristotle especially), and by Indian scholars as early as 800 B.C. Of course since we only have access to the thoughts of these early linguists by way of what they left behind in writing, this information is very incomplete. Writing transforms speech into a radically different symbolic medium in which sounds are no longer audible and the evanescent quality of spoken utterances disappears. More and more emphasis is placed on the permanency of meanings that can be stabilized across groups and between generations. The temporary and affective constitutents of soundmaking tend to disappear when written down or put into print. Thus we see a surge of interest in the practical matter of translating one language into another, which became necessary with the spread of Christianity. For scholars, a knowledge of Latin grammar was universally required. Printing in the sixteenth century led to the proliferation of textbooks and dictionaries, and the amount of information available about language steadily accumulated (Waterman 1970).

Language study in the modern sense began in the nineteenth century with the work of Rasmus Rask (1787-1832) and Jakob Grimm (1785-1863), who compared the different Germanic languages and postulated that shifts in the pronunciation of speech sounds were largely responsible for differences between these languages. Their discoveries initiated an era of HISTORICO-COMPARATIVE LINGUISTICS which led to the systematic description of all Indo-European languages. Studies of Sanskrit broadened the empirical basis for making linguistic comparisons. The German scholar August Schleicher (1821-1868) likened languages to quasi-organismic entities with properties like growth, maturation, and decay, and linguists began comparing the degrees of logical complexity of languages spoken by different ethnic groups. Strongly influenced by the theories of Charles Darwin and Friederich Hegel, a number of linguists in the nineteenth century tried to discover proto-languages *(Ursprachen)* from which the so-called 'primitive' languages of pre-Christian cultures were thought to derive. These theories were drastically undermined by archeological discoveries at the turn of the century which disclosed how truly 'advanced' many of the ancient cultures had been.

Today the comparative study of languages is of historical interest because it sheds some light on how people may have lived and thought about themselves and the places they inhabited. Statistical methods are now used to 'date' the changes that take place in the way words are pronounced and grammatically organized into meaningful sentences. In addition, the search is on for deep-seated or 'universal' features of linguistic symbolization which must underly the constantly changing speech-patterns of the world (Greenberg 1963). Comparative linguistics focusses on collective rather than individual behavior, and its time scale is in terms of historical epochs rather than momentary events.

Structural linguistics

Ferdinand de Saussure (1857-1913), a Swiss linguist, tried to separate the collective and more time-enduring aspects of linguistic CODIFICATION from the individualistic and more transitory phenomena of SPEAKING. This distinction made it possible to conceive of temporary and really quite arbitrary 'bonds' between patterns of spoken sounds and what these sounds are meant to signify.

To communicate linguistically, people must have (1) certain internal ideational schematizations or conceptualizations, and (2) sets of names to label these inner concepts with. Language provides the conventionalized labels for a person's inner concepts. Unless he talks about his ideas, they are not communicated in a verbal format. But by doing so, the individual is obliged to cast his thoughts into the depersonalized or 'abstracted' forms of public phonology and the rules of syntax and semantics required by language. If he exceeds the acceptable limits of these linguistic rules and formats, his vocal utterances will become incomprehensible to others. For those creative people who cannot or do not want to transform their inner mental schemas and ideas into understandable verbal patterns, other symbolization systems may be more satisfactory. Art for instance – painting, sculpture, photography, cinema – allows for a more spatially-depicted, dimensionally-articulated, and visually-based form of communication of our inner concepts. Music, another 'nonverbal' medium, allows for communication of the more continuous emotional moods, rhythms, and tensions of inner experience without making it necessary to impose the very rapid discontinuities or the arbitrary vocabulary rules of linguistic speech (Rosen 1971).

Even prior to the time that structural linguistics was appointed to the task of depicting and explaining patterns of relationships between the sounds and meanings of speech, a German philosopher and linguist, Wilhelm von Humboldt (1767-1835), had emphasized that language compels people to structure their experiences in accordance with certain conventionalized rules. De Saussure tried to make it clear that this structuring has two dimensions: one is a linear or SYNTAGMATIC organization of sequences; the other is an associative or SEMANTIC organization of simultaneities. These two dimensions interact whenever an identified speech pattern signals a semantic distinction, or vice-versa, whenever a semantic distinction is depictable in speech.

It remained for the Slavic linguist Nikolas Trubetskoy (1890-1938) to devise a PHONOLOGICAL METHOD for demonstrating these semantic-syntagmatic interactions in speech. This method has focussed mainly on those physical properties of speech sounds which have perceptual consequences. Whenever the phonetic contrasts between two sounds are capable of transmitting a semantic difference, then this feature of speech is considered PHONEMIC. A linguist can thus characterize certain aspects of any speech sound by denoting the meaningful contrasts in terms of a code. The naive assumption of one-to-one relationships between sounds and meanings is no longer permissible. The phonological method (Jakobson, Fant and Halle 1952) gave a very powerful impetus to the development of modern language science.

Within the last two decades, important reformulations of linguistic theory have been made, reflecting contemporary developments in zoology, information sciences and other fields to be discussed shortly. For example, Charles Hockett (1960) has proposed that all bio-acoustic communication systems be analyzed in terms of certain design-features such as directionality, rapid fading, feedback, and semanticity. While animals communicate very efficiently with signal-systems that display only some of these design characteristics, human languages require them all, and perhaps even some additional features that have not yet been scientifically studied. In a courageous endeavor, the linguist Kenneth Pike (1967) has revised the conceptual framework of language study with the hope that speech behavior and all other aspects of the totality of human functioning can be brought into a comprehensive unified theory.

Psycholinguistics and the theory of generative syntax

Very rapid technological developments especially in physics during the first half of the twentieth century forced scientists to reconsider their theories of man's relationship to his environment. Interdisciplinary groups which began meeting during and after the second world war recognized the artificiality of some traditional academic boundaries between fields of inquiry. In this context, a Committee on Linguistics and Psychology began meeting in 1952, the result of which was the new field of Psycholinguistics (Osgood and Sebeok 1954). Psychologists had traditionally explored memory, perception, cognition, intellect, affect, and other so-called MENTAL PROCESSES. In doing this it was necessary either to objectify behavior in experimental situations, or to delve into the introspections of psychologically sensitive subjects. Both of these approaches to the mind require language – in spoken or written form – as a means of giving instructions and obtaining certain observations. The psychologist Karl Buehler (1934) had pointed out that language has a tripartite function in human communication: (1) TO EXPRESS the speaker's intentions and ideas; (2) TO APPEAL to the listener for a response; and (3) TO REPRESENT aspects of past, present, and future reality in an abstracted, timeless fashion. A recently translated volume about psycholinguistics by H. Hoermann (1971) interconnects the older European traditions of linguistic research, including Buehler's theory, with the newer, mainly American (U.S.A.) contributions to the psychology of language.

The earliest psycholinguistic models were based largely on concepts of electrical communication, especially those used by the telephone industry to help design better cables and equipment in facilitating the rapid flow of information between places at great distance from each other. Basic to these early models was the notion of fixed CHANNELS, with definable band-width and impedence properties, through which patterned signals have to move. Signals go from a SENDER to a RECEIVER. Efficiency in the communications network is increased when there can also be backflow of signals to the sender, i.e., a FEEDBACK indicating how correctly his information is being received. Translated into psychological terms, these formulations call for the notion of DECISIONS that have to be made about encoding, transmission, and decoding of this patterned information.

The simplest way to represent a decision-making process is to think of it in terms of 'yes-or-no', a binary decision easily mimicked by an electronic circuit switch ('on or off'). A series of binary decisions can then be indicated, and precisely quantified in terms of BITS OF INFORMATION. To deal with any chunk of sound, the human speaker-listener is expected to make several crucial decisions, (at least "seven, plus or minus two"), described by G. A. Miller (1967) approximately as follows:

A language-user must

- AUDIT the sound as a representative sample of human speech.
- MATCH this percept with his internal criteria of a phonemic code.
- ACCEPT this utterance as part of a syntactic structure.
- INTERPRET this sentence as being semantically meaningful.
- UNDERSTAND how this message functions within a general context of information.
- BELIEVE that such knowledge has validity and relevance for personal conduct.

Little is known as yet about the exact ordering of such decisions inside the human brain. Does the central nervous system in fact perform its decision-making functions in the hierarchical and systematic fashion suggested above? Modern technology has made it possible to program electronic computers to carry out certain of these logical sequences, with tremendous speed. Indeed, some intriguing ideas about possible ways that logic-circuits can be combined into so-called TOTE UNITS have been put forward, in the hope that these models could help explain how language-users plan sequences of words and sentences for speech (Miller, Galanter, and Pribram 1960). But the fact that in spite of many serious attempts, no electronic device has yet been built that listens or talks in a way even remotely reminiscent of human dialogue indicates that the more global and intuitive forms of communicative intelligence which go along with language behavior have yet to be scientifically explained.

The linguist Noam Chomsky has made what are widely considered to be some of the most daring and powerful contributions to this field of inquiry. He took for granted that the decisions underlying our use of sounds for speaking have to be made very quickly and in carefully pre-organized sequences. During natural speech, a syllable takes at most only one-quarter of a second, and such a 'unit' already contains many items of information about phonemic and morphemic contrasts of which one is unaware unless speech is artifically slowed down. Only at certain strategic moments are there ordinarily interruptions, which can be used more-or-less consciously to deliberate, and to plan what one says and how one says it. Chomsky (1965) reasoned that a fundamental distinction has to be made between (1) the overt PERFORMANCE that a language-user manifests at the time of speaking and listening, and (2) the covert COMPETENCE that a language-user has for generating any number of speech sequences and for interpreting speech correctly. He set about to construct a system of rules or ALGORHITHMS which could be helpful to explain how the surface structure of a person's actual speech performance is related to the deeper structure of his underlying linguistic competence.

Chomsky's theories about the generation and transformation of syntactic structures are concerned with idealized speaker-listeners who presumably know the language of a homogeneous speech community perfectly, have no limitations in memory, and never make any mistakes. Obviously such people don't exist. But this important aspect of the almost mathematically-abstract theory of generative-transformational grammar was not always appreciated.

The goal of generative linguistics is to define the complete grammar of a given language, i.e., to specify the full set of OPERATIONAL PROCEDURES required to generate all acceptable sentences in that language. Assuming this goal could be achieved, then by comparing and contrasting the grammars of several languages, it ought to be possible to develop an understanding of what it is about all human beings, independent of national backgrounds and cultural-origins, which allows them to engage in the sort of semiotic behavior that is called verbal-linguistic (Fodor and Katz 1964). For the reader who does not wish to wade through the complexities, subtleties, and controversies of generative-transformational theory, I would recommend an excellent popular article that appeared recently in the *New Yorker Magazine* (Mehta 1971).

Developmental linguistics

A delightful testing ground for ideas about linguistic soundmaking is the nursery, where one can observe the miracle of language-acquisition in infancy. Naturalists of the nineteenth century, including C. Darwin himself, had recorded the unfolding vocabulary of their growing youngsters. As children master the use of language, they can more precisely express their wishes. In addition, adherence to the rules of linguistic soundmaking fosters a social collaboration between the child and his parents for the fulfillment of these wishes. The studies published prior to the mid-1920's usually focussed on a single child growing up in one particular family, and scientists were therefore reluctant to make broad generalizations which could apply to language acquisition universally.

Under the influence of embryological and psychoanalytic theories, observers began organizing their data about infant speech according to DEVELOPMENTAL STAGES. McCarthy (1946) was thus able to classify 126 items of linguistic development between birth and age 3, and quantitative methodologies encouraged this cataloguing approach to development. Various aspects of motor and mental functioning were measured at regular intervals to establish where a child's communicative behavior fits into statistically normalized growth curves. It soon became clear that two growth processes are simultaneously at work in the child's development of language. One process manifests itself in an orderly sequence of MOTOR-PATTERN ACQUISITIONS (Winitz 1969). Babies first mostly vocalize cries, coos, and gurgles, then go on to articulate babbles, syllables, and finally recognizable word utterances at around one year of age.

The other process in language acquisition is a specialized part of the progressive maturation of PERCEPTUAL-COGNITIVE SKILLS (Gibson 1967). Infants have an ability to 'tune-in' on the behavior of older human beings, which is manifest by their preference for the human breast as a food-source, the human face as a visual target, and the human voice as an auditory stimulus. Particular sensitivity for language seems to be present from a very early age. Already when only a few weeks old, the normal infant appears able to discriminate certain phonological contrasts of speech (Eimas, et al. 1971). My hunch is that just as the visual system is biogenetically prepared for IMPRINTING with the mother's face, so is the auditory system pretuned for organizing itself in terms of the mother's vocal-speech behavior, with the consequence that the infant 'follows' the adult model.

During the earliest phases of ego-development ($1\frac{1}{2}$ to 3 months) an infant's vocal output gives few if any hints as to how his internal sensory-motor maturations are progressing. Indeed, the baby's EXPRESSIVE VOCAL BEHAVIOR is so undifferentiated at this time that even the deaf infant behaves as if he were communicating with sounds. COOING (around six weeks) and reflexive BABBLING (around six months) are observed whether or not the infant is exposed to speech, suggesting that these early components of the soundmaking repertoire are acquired due to activation of an innate brain-mechanism (Lenneberg, et al. 1965). After six months of age, however, a child's vocal behavior shows increasingly definite evidence of speech imprinting. His babbling begins to have a PROSODY that is more and more speechlike (Crystal 1969). By the age of nine months a kind of segmental structure is noticeable which resembles speech closely enough to suggest to many parents that their babies are uttering SYLLABLES.

Thus it seems clear that by the time a truly semantic content is apparent in the baby's soundmaking – i.e., his FIRST WORD produced approximately at one year of age – some of the critical phonetic contrasts of the linguistic code used by his family have already had to be assimilated. This does not imply however that the baby, when communicating (i.e., 'speaking') with other members of his household uses sounds semantically in the sense of making meaningful verbal statements. What the child might be saying when he utters a 'word' or two can only be deciphered by observing and knowing him in the context of his interpersonal relationships with caretaking family members. For at least another six months, until age 1 ½ years, the speech output is holophrastic, condensed, and primarily emotive. Viewed from the standpoint of the child's intellectual organization at this stage, one can say that there is as yet insufficient dissociation between reflexive motor displays and internal mental reconstruction of learned experience. Thus the baby cannot make unambiguous semiotic references.

Nevertheless, a remarkable comprehension of the grammatical orderliness of language seems to underly emerging speech productivity of toddlers as they approach their second birthday. Behavioral repertoires – both verbal and nonverbal – blossom in extraordinary ways during this time, and even the most sophisticated psychologists have expressed considerable uncertainty about how to measure and interpret a two-year-old child's intellectual accomplishments (Bayley 1966). By visiting the youngster once or twice a month at home and taping all his speech during interviews, several psycholinguists have collected enough data to allow the construction of a few hypotheses about possible steps in the child's acquisition of syntax and grammar (Bellugi and Brown 1964). Generative grammars have been written as a way of characterizing the linguistic competence of small children at different ages.

The first simple SENTENCES are usually just two-word utterances, thought to represent combinations of items from two functionally distinct classes or categories of words (McNeill 1970). The OPEN CLASS contains nominalizing words like *Daddy* or *shoe*, while the PIVOT CLASS contains modifiers like *my* or *here*. Word combinations are assumed to be a manifestation of the child's first efforts to express grammatical relations. Only by combining two words, e.g., *my daddy*, *Daddy shoe*, is he able to discover that it is possible to indicate contrasts in semantic meaning. Later yet the child begins to use connecting predicates for making his meaning more precise – *Daddy take my shoe*.

Augmentation of the vocabulary, and increasing complexity of sentences are two of the specifically linguistic aspects of memory, attention, and sensory-motor coordination which go closely together in the child's maturation. There is no easy answer to the question of what precisely

are the brain structures that predetermine the sequences of this psychobiological process, which involves much more than simply the organization
of the deeper structures of grammar (Lenneberg 1967). Environmentalists
emphasize that no matter how perfectly a child's 'language acquisition
device' may be working, his exposure to the speech spoken by the community is always a critical factor which limits the repertoire for one child
and enhances it for another. Such factors as social-class dialects, the
influence of the school-system, and the varying opportunities for acquiring
a second language must be taken into account (Fishman 1971). Personality
before mid-adolescence is plastic and impressionable. Language along
with other semiotic functions is fashioned in an as yet quite mysterious
interaction between brain and behavior.

Neurolinguistics and patholinguistics

One of the most fruitful approaches to the problem of how the human
brain organizes sounds for linguistic communication has been to study
the anomalies and peculiarities of speech. Language pathology readily
draws attention to itself because of blocked or disrupted patterns of
interpersonal communication which ensue when previously well-integrated
soundmaking breaks down (Brain 1961). Another topic of great practical
importance is the inability of some children to learn how to speak
properly, or in a few tragic cases the failure to acquire language altogether
(Vetter 1969). Until recent years, research in this field was done mostly
by physicians who have access to patients with various forms of neurological disease. Therefore in this part of our discussion we must go
somewhat beyond the purely linguistic contributions.

Two French clinicians – Marc Dax (1771-1837) and Paul Broca (1824-
1880) – independently discovered that damage to the left side of the brain
can produce aphasia, a nonspecific term referring to the loss or profound
disruption of verbal skills. Subsequent neuropathological studies led
to the conclusion that the upper portion of the left temporal lobe, called
'Wernicke's area', is concerned with the process of SPEECH DECODING,
while the lower part of the left pre-central motor strip, called Broca's
area, is responsible for the LINGUISTIC ENCODING of information. The
British neurologist Hughlings Jackson (1834-1911) emphasized that
integrated processes of VERBALIZING could best be understood in terms
of 'internal aspects' – thinking, abstracting, and symbol formation – plus
the 'outer' manifestations – speaking and listening. Jackson's formulations
required a dynamic concept of brain-functioning, and he objected to

static notions of so-called speech-centers.

A historically-significant breakthrough came about as the result of contributions made by Sigmund Freud (1856–1939), a Viennese neuropathologist, to the study of brain-thought-language interrelationships. Freud (1891) proposed that the semiotic functions which result in speech reflect a functional arrangement of neural networks between auditory, visual, and motor areas of the left cerebral cortex. Disturbances could result not only from localized destruction of these areas, but equally from interferences in the flow of messages between them. At that time there was insufficient technical knowledge about the electrochemical transmission systems of the brain to explain how 'functional' disruptions of neural networks might be accounted for.

To analyze the verbal processing of information, Freud urged his patients to recline, relax, and allow their conscious attention to wander. Any sensations, images, or memories which could be observed were to be transformed into speech. It soon became apparent that this process of FREE-ASSOCIATION came into conflict with a process of CENSORSHIP. To explain this conflict and its effects on a patient's semiotic behavior, Freud and his followers devised a complicated METAPSYCHOLOGY (Rapaport 1960). Instinctual drives were postulated as the internal motivators of all human behavior. Repeated collisions with socio-environmental reality cause children to inhibit their biologically-determined primary emotional expressions. The resulting pent-up energy must be released via indirect or symbolic modes for communication. Language was said to be one of these so-called SECONDARY PROCESSES which allow the 'ego' (a theoretical construct) to accomplish socially-acceptable discharges of drive energy. Knowledge about how to use the language code was considered to belong to the 'super-ego', a part of the ego that incorporates cultural rules.

Psychoanalytic approaches have remained useful for the clinical assessment of those disturbances in language functions that can be related to conflicts between personal-motivation and socially-sanctioned opportunity (Laffal 1965). But neurophysiological explanation of the linguistic brain mechanisms has continued to be of much greater interest to organicists, especially the aphasia experts. After World War I, they tended to abandon the strict localization theories of the nineteenth century, referring instead to a broader and more abstract SCHEMATIZING function of the cerebral cortex. Pick (1931) characterized this cortical language function as (1) the activity of an anatomically definable *Sprachfeld* which takes care of segmentation, codification, and other discontinuity processes, plus (2) the closely related 'musical functions' which manage continuities and deal with more abstract auditory-symbolic integrations.

Technological advances account for many of the recent breakthroughs in neurolinguistic science. For example, the use of quick-acting anesthetics injected directly into the carotid arteries has made it possible to study the two cortical hemispheres independently. When the artery supplying the dominant hemisphere – usually on the left – is injected, a patient briefly loses the ability to comprehend and produce speech (Milner et al. 1964). Disconnection of the two hemispheres due to congenital absence of the corpus callosum, or its destruction by disease or surgery, also shows that linguistic functions are for the most part managed on one side while nonverbal intelligence resides in the contralateral hemisphere. These experiments on disease-processes usually involve adults.

In childhood, parts of the cerebral cortex are as yet 'uncommitted'. Prior to mid-puberty there is considerable plasticity in the functional integration of language, and even massive brain injury does not necessarily lead to permanent aphasia. The Canadian neurosurgeon Wilder Penfield has studied the different cortical areas at the time that the brain of conscious patients is exposed for surgical treatment. He found that electrostimuli have contradictory effects. In certain areas the electrode would cause the patient to vocalize and speak, often about detailed memories including noises and visual components of the scene being recalled. Other areas of the cortex, when stimulated, had the opposite effect: the patient stopped talking and felt himself unable to procede with further verbalizations (Penfield and Roberts 1959). In the last few years, neurosurgeons have experimented with electrodes inserted through the cortex of the brain into different structures of the white matter and basal ganglia. In cases of Parkinson's Disease, Epilepsy, and other conditions which disturb verbal communication, clinical improvement has been noted when scar-tissue is electrosurgically removed.

These patients with very advanced forms of disease usually have had to make secondary and tertiary social compensations to a primary organic disability, and their collaboration as research subjects in language experiments is often difficult to obtain (Horowitz 1970). On the other hand, healthy subjects cannot afford to have their heads opened for neurosurgical probing. Thus it has become necessary to search for indirect methods to study neurolinguistic functions, for example with ELECTRO-ENCEPHALOGRAPHIC METHODS. Low-voltage electrical activity is recorded by attaching thin wire-electrodes to the scalp. The frequency patterns, wave-forms, and changing intensities of brain-biorhythms can be analyzed under differing conditions of consciousness and arousal. Comparisons are made between the two cerebral hemispheres and frontal, parietal, temporal, and occipital lobes of each side. It is more difficult to study the limbic system which deals with important visceral-emotional processes, and the interhemispheric callosal connections that integrate verbal and nonverbal semiotic processes.

Using computer-averaging techniques, scientists are able to obtain information about the precise electrical brain-wave patterns which occur while a subject engages in some clear-cut mental task, for example two-signal auditory discrimination or visualizing words vs. nonverbal patterns. Because an AVERAGE-EVOKED-RESPONSE depends on multiple repetitions of identical time-locked stimuli, the information to be processed has to be quite simple, of short duration, and with stimulus-onset no longer than 20 milliseconds. Nevertheless, it has been possible to localize some brain activity associated with repetition of short words (McAdam and Whitaker 1971), and to show that different neural events take place in the left cerebral hemisphere during the analysis of linguistic versus non-linguistic parameters of the same acoustical input (Wood et al. 1971). Lengthier and supraphonemic constructions such as sentence-planning, verbal ideation, and semantic interpretation of meaning – both normal and abnormal – are still among the deepest mysteries so far as the neuro-physiology of language is concerned.

Summary

I have discussed five major fields of linguistic inquiry which contribute to the understanding of human sounds.

(1) Historical linguistics traces the evolution of natural languages throughout the world.

(2) Structural linguistics characterizes the phonology, syntax, and semantics of any given language.

(3) Psycholinguistics investigates how language is actually used by a speaker or group.

(4) Developmental linguistics studies the acquisition of verbal skills from infancy through adolescence.

(5) Neurolinguistics relates normal and deviant language performance to the various nervous system functions.

The emphasis here has been on language as heard and spoken for purposes of meaningful communication of ideas. The more emotional and symbolic uses of sound in speech, nonverbal behavior, and music will be treated at greater length in the next sections of this book.

SECTION II

ACOUSTIC DENOTATION OF HUMAN SOUNDS

INTRODUCTORY STATEMENT

Every transformation of sound into non-auditory sensory-motor pat-terning entails a modification of the emotional experience that is so characteristic of time. Sounds help us to appreciate and relate to the temporal aspects of an environment. Rhythms, recurrences, and se-quences define this time-world just as shapes, structures, and outlines define space. Thus in approaching the phenomena of human sound-making for the purpose of scientific study, one is forced to oversimplify the interesting sonic events, or to deal with them abstractly, in verbal or mathematical terms.

The following papers are concerned with the problem of denoting sounds acoustically, according to their physical structure. In contrast to Section I which is a largely verbal-descriptive account of the semiotics of human sound, Section II focuses on certain technical issues involving acoustic analysis, measurement, and spectrography, especially of human vocalizations. The first two articles, 6 and 7, are both directed towards establishing an acoustical MODEL for what is known in psychology as the "personality stereotype" (Kramer 1964). In daily conversation generally and clinical diagnosis particularly, such information about 'the way a person sounds' – whether angry or depressed, happy or involved, officious or lackadaisical, etc. – becomes very much part of the internal imagery that we develop of that person. The work which has been done over the past 15 years with the SEMANTIC DIFFERENTIAL method (Osgood et al. 1957) is applicable to this problem of verbally depicting various evaluative qualities. Experiments with vocal self-confrontation also are pertinent to this research approach, insofar as they show that considerable cognitive-dissonance may be experienced, often unpleasantly, whenever one's stereotyped notion of his own voice is compared with a tape-recording (Holzman et al. 1966).

Paper 6, if written today, would have to spell out with greater precision what is meant by (1) information about the state of the speaker (e.g., rate and rhythm of speech), (2) information about the words spoken (e.g., stress and intonation) and (3) information about paralanguage (voice quality, nonverbal aspects of communication). As it was more than a decade ago, one made crude assumptions, for instance that the voice is a 'musical instrument' or a 'noise source', so as to move from the level of clinical impression to that of objectification. Paper 7, which is more directly applicable to psychiatry, has a better delineation between speech-communication on the linguistic (verbal, intellectual) level as contrasted with the paralinguistic (nonverbal, emotional) level. But some of the statements made about physiological production of certain vocal patterns have turned out to be incorrect. Paper 8 relates acoustical findings to clinical studies.

The detailed results of early research conducted with acoustic methods have been reported elsewhere (Ostwald 1963). Essentially what we found was that half-octave band methods may suffice to distinguish certain very gross variables – e.g., inhaling an ammonia solution in an experimental situation, or using electroconvulsive treatment clinically. But after the publication of *The First Five Minutes* by Pittenger et al. (1960) it became more and more difficult to justify acoustical research that ignores the temporal aspects of soundmaking as much as the cross-sectional methods of acoustics are forced to do. In their book, Pittenger, Hockett, and Danehy took the first five minutes of a recorded interview and converted each sound into a written symbol. Words were denoted with phonemic signs derived from standard linguistics, while paralinguistic cues such as silences, getting-louder, increasing-tempo, register-shifts, and noises are denoted with special signs. The transcription is accompanied by descriptive statements about the sounds on the tape, plus interpretive comments about what was probably happening during the interview. Some deal with covert, physiologically-determined motives; for example, the patient's disinclination to speak and her desire to smoke at one point may represent "a wish for oral intake rather than oral output." Other interpretive comments are about the overt behavior of the psychiatrist in the presence of his patient; for instance, slight breathiness on the part of the therapist may be part of his "machinery for signalling calm kindness or – a failure to conceal completely his own affect" about the patient. Intriguing labels were attached to certain sound-events, for example: "opaque intonation", "fracture", "fade-in", "topic-inertia", and "accuracy-compulsion", which made one eagerly want to see how closely the interpretations correspond with what actually happened during "the first five minutes". Unfortunately, there was never a sequel to this work.

Papers 9, 10, and 11 show the impact of these developments in semiotic theory on our own work. They also demonstrate the effects of an intended audience upon communication, insofar as each was written for a particular kind of professional group. Paper 9, which was our first study with the Kay-Sonagraph, was designed specifically for the annual meeting of the Association for Research in Nervous and Mental Disease. *Disorders of Communication* was the general topic of this conference. My hypothesis was that symptomatic paralinguistic behavior is designed to 'under-cut' verbal behavior. This idea corresponds with neurophysiological theory, e.g. the Pavlovian point of view, about primary signal-systems of emotion. Autonomic cues are mediated by the limbic areas of the brain, which lie closer to the subcortical centers in charge of self-preservative and defensive operations. The secondary signal-systems, to which language belongs, are cortical and serve to regulate behavior according to learned societal demands for conformance and, if necessary, delayed action. The significance of acoustic research to this field can best be understood by reading G. Mahl's discussion of all the papers on the topic of vocal behavior which were presented at the meeting (Mahl 1964).

Paper 10 was written for a conference of workers in neurology, pediatrics, and education. It steps away from the general category of 'emotional disturbances' to deal more specifically with disturbances of speech. Psychiatry classifies these disorders in the category of SPECIAL SYMPTOMS "for the occasional patient whose psychopathology is manifested by a single specific symptom" for example, tic, speech disturbance, or enuresis (Gruenberg et al. 1968). Actually, as I shall attempt to demonstrate in Section IV of this book, there is no clear dividing line between the symptom and the syndrome to which it belongs. Classification of any behavior deviation as a 'special symptom' is simply a way of saying that we cannot as yet clearly recognize a syndrome.

Paper 11 was intended to do just that, i.e. to delineate a syndrome. The patient is a disturbed teen-ager who carries the official diagnosis of schizophrenia but also has had temporal-lobe epilepsy. The clinical study of this patient involves diagnostic interviews, sound spectrography, and X-ray methods. The paper was written for an audience of general physicians, and tries to synthesize ideas about neurodynamics (brain functions), psychodynamics (internal representation of experience), and sociodynamics (environmental control factors) in disease.

6

A METHOD FOR THE OBJECTIVE DENOTATION OF THE SOUND OF THE HUMAN VOICE*

(1960)

The nonverbal characteristics of speech are of importance in the investigation of human communication. Rate and rhythm of word utterance, for example, provide listeners with clues of the alertness and mood of the speaker (Pittenger and Smith 1957). Stress and inflection patterns give information on the way a speaker's words are to be interpreted. The sound of the speaker's voice is another dimension of nonverbal behaviour. The purpose of this report is to describe a method for denoting the sound of the voice in objective visual terms.

The human voice is a complex sound, which, like the sound of a musical instrument, consists of a fundamental tone and numerous harmonics (Helmholtz 1885). While the exact mechanism of voice production is not yet fully understood, there is fairly general agreement among phoneticians that overlapping physiological processes are involved. The central nervous system controls movements of the lungs, larynx, and mouth, which form and shape the voice. Resonating chambers like the chest, throat, and skull modify the voice in terms of its frequency-intensity characteristics. Feedback of information from the speaker's ears and from outside listeners further determines what is said and how it is said, in particular in regard to those vocal utterances which we call words. One expects, therefore, that the sound of the voice will vary from one speaker to the next depending on his body build, the integrity of the various organs involved in voice production, the emotional and physiological fluctuations which affect these organs, and the demands of the external environment.

Correlations between the voice and other components of human behaviour have been attempted with varying degrees of success since

* Reprinted from *Journal of Psychosomatic Research* 4: 301-05 (1960).

ancient times, when off-stage voices were used to portray different personages in plays and pageants (Ostwald 1960a). Several studies have appeared showing how voices may be correlated with body build, sex, age, occupation, and other personal characteristics of speakers (Licklider and Miller 1951). There is also some evidence that changes in the sound of the voice correlate with situational characteristics such as truth-telling, expression of emotion, and social attitudes (Licklider and Miller 1951). Such studies are of great importance for psychotherapists, singing teachers, speech correctionists, and other professionals who evaluate vocal behaviour and train people to use their voices more effectively.

Scientific investigation of the human voice as it is used in speaking must take into account the fact that no clear-cut distinction can be made between voice and speech. When a person speaks he produces a series of sounds which carry acoustic energy in the frequency range between approximately 100 and 6000 c/s.[1] At several points along this spectrum, the sounds of his voice reach levels of concentration, called formants. According to Liberman and his co-workers at the Haskins Laboratory, definable interrelationships over time between several formants account for the appearance of phonemes, which are recognizable speech sounds like vowels and consonants (Liberman 1957). It follows therefore that to denote the sound of the human voice as it actually occurs in speaking, one must include all of its acoustic components. Isolation of one energy level, for example the fundamental pitch, would ignore many of the acoustic cues which provide intelligibility and give a voice its individual and distinctive flavour.

The method described here for denoting the sound of the voice reduces all sounds emitted by the speaker to a meaningless noise, thus eliminating any possible distinctions between his voice and his speech. A tape-recording is made in an echo-free environment. An omnidirectional microphone (Electrovoice Model 655C) placed horizontally in front of the speaker's mouth at a distance of 10 inches has been used. The subject is asked to read a brief standard paragraph, and after a warming up period this is recorded with a magnetic tape-recorder (Ampex Model 601). Immediately after the reading, a 1000 cycle calibrating tone is recorded on the same tape. A 4-foot loop is made from approximately the first two sentences of the tape-recorded speech. This is played backwards through a Sound Analyzer (H. H. Scott Model 420-A), the pre-recorded

---

[1] The term 'hertz' (Hz) is now used, in place of the older term 'cycles per second' (c/s or cps) for the vibratory frequency of sound. [P.O. 1973.]

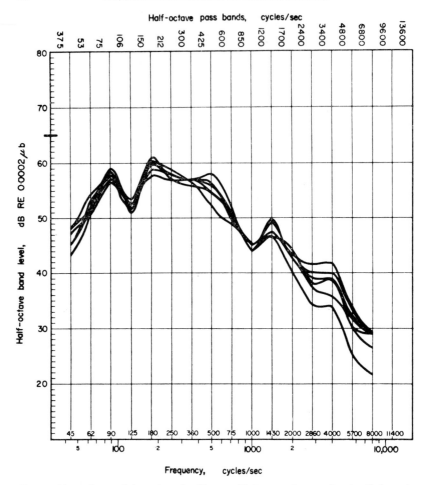

Fig. 1. Six analyses of the voice of a 27-year old depressed man, showing little variation from one week to the next, and poor distinction between the formants, possibly
accounting for the indistinct quality of his speech.

calibrating tone having been used to adjust the analyzer to a base level.
The operator of the sound-analyzer hears only a meaningless jumble of
noise and, undistracted by meaning and other verbal cues, records the
absolute sound level and the distribution of sound energy in half-octave
bands. After relatively little experience with acoustical instruments it is
possible to repeat the readings in this way with a very high degree of
accuracy.

    The result of each sound analysis is plotted on prepared graph paper
with frequency in c/s as the abscissa and half-octave band level in decibels

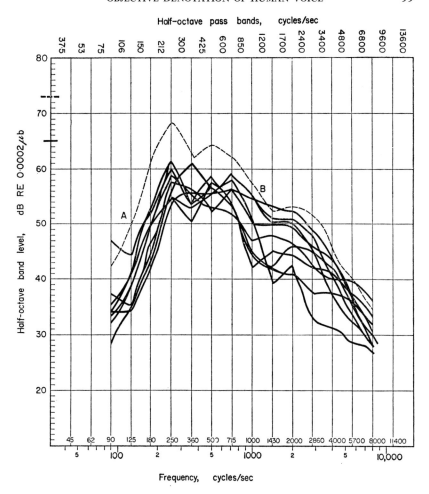

Fig. 2. Weekly analyses of the voice of a 22-year old hysterical woman in psychotherapy, showing a basic pattern resembling that of a 10-year old child (AB) and
irregularities which probably represent her dramatic use of the voice.

re 0·0002 microbar as the ordinate. Each voice is thus denoted in the
form of a graph, and, by equating the absolute sound levels of the various
sound analyses, the graphs can be superimposed for comparison. Figure 1
shows the results of repeated weekly analyses of the voice of a 27-year
old man suffering from a psychoneurosis with depression. His voice
was weak, muffled, and lustreless. The analyses, which vary little from
one week to the next, show the fundamental tone (F_0) concentration at
90 c/s, and relatively little differentiation between the first and second

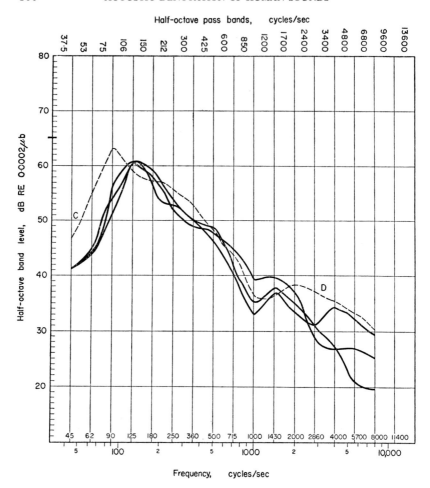

Fig. 3. Analyses of the voices of 4 organically impaired males, showing a drop in acoustic energy above 200 cycles per second. The heavy curves are from 3 senile patients. The dotted curve (CD) is from a young man with bilateral frontal lobe damage.

formants, which may account for the indistinctness of his speech.

Figure 2 shows 9 weekly sound analyses of the voice of a 22-year old woman with hysterical and psychosomatic symptomatology. The graphs, made from recordings taken directly during psychotherapeutic interviews, demonstrate how the personality-bound characteristics of the voice overlap with its situational characteristics. There is a regular pattern, resembling the voice of a 10-year old child, which is reproduced for comparison at a level 8 db above the other curves. This denotes the pinched, childish, immature quality of the patient's voice. The irregular patterns which fluctuate from one week to the next denote her hysterical, screechy, demanding way of speaking, and her use of the voice as a means of attracting attention and evoking sympathy.

Figure 3 presents sound analyses of 4 different patients. The heavy curves represent the voices of 3 senile men. The tell-tale feebleness and quakiness of their voice is apparent: there is a rapid falling off in acoustic power above 200 cycles. It is not yet known whether this characteristic results from a diminished elasticity of the speech organs of old people, or whether it is a function of disturbed cortical control of speech. That the latter may be a factor is suggested by the similarity between the shapes of these curves and the record of a physically robust 20-year old man who sustained bilateral frontal-lobe damage in a motorcycle accident (dotted curve CD).

The method lends itself to the investigation of the voice in the fields of neurology, psychiatry, and phoniatrics. It may also be applicable to comparative linguistics, noise control, and related fields of communication research. The sound of the voice is, however, only one dimension of communicative behaviour; the above method for denoting the sound of the voice is objective, simple, and relatively inexpensive but it cannot be used as a research tool in the absence of other diagnostic methods.

Summary

By playing tape-recorded speech backwards through an acoustic analyzer, graphs are obtained which display frequency vs. sound energy per half octave band. This method makes no distinction between voice and speech. It is used to study psychiatric patients and may be applicable to other problems in behavioural research.

7

VISUAL DENOTATION OF HUMAN SOUNDS*

Preliminary Report of an Acoustic Method

(1960)

The purpose of this report is to present an acoustic method for denoting human sounds. Correct interpretation of the sounds emitted by patients is one requisite of psychiatric diagnosis. Whenever these sounds are words it is relatively easy to record them in writing, to communicate about them with colleagues, and to discuss their meaning with patients. The words of patients are also excellent subjects for research, since they lend themselves to established linguistic and semantic methods of analysis (Osgood 1954). However, patients make many sounds that are not words (Ostwald 1960a). They groan, grunt, burp, bellow, whine, wheeze, and produce noises. As Kris, Milner, and others have shown, these and other nonverbal sounds play a primary role in the communication of affects (Kris 1952b; Milner 1956). Speech itself is used expressively; stress and inflection patterns of the voice often carry more important information about the speaker than do the words he uses in speaking (Starkweather 1956). This is why a psychotherapist ignores the meaning of 'I'm feeling fine' if these words are uttered in a tearful voice.

The human voice is a complex sound made up of many tonal ingredients, and there have been several successful attempts to denote this sound visually. Musical symbols may be used to represent the melody and the rhythm of speech (Sherwin 1953). Phonetic and phonemic symbols can be used to denote sounds that resemble those which make up spoken words (McQuown 1957). Speech spectrography isolates the formants or overtones (Potter et al. 1947). This method is probably the most accurate and detailed way of denoting human sounds. At the present time it is expensive and requires the services of a highly skilled interpreter. A simpler method, the one reported below, makes use of a technique for sound

---

* Reprinted from the *Archives of General Psychiatry* 3: 117-21 (1960).

analysis that has been standardized by acoustical engineers for the measurement and analysis of noise (Peterson and Brüel 1957).

The patient's sounds are recorded in a quiet, echo-free environment. A microphone with tape-recorder which is sensitive and reliable between at least 90 and 5,000 cycles in the frequency spectrum must be used; this will take care of most of the sounds that are used for speech. In the work reported here, an Electrovoice Microphone, Model 655C, was placed horizontally in front of the patient's mouth at a distance of 10 inches. An Ampex Magnetic Tape Recorder, Model 601, was used. Spontaneous utterances during interviews were recorded, and in many cases the patient was asked to read a standard paragraph containing all speech sounds which contribute to loudness. Immediately after the recording was made, a 1,000 cycle calibrating tone from a transistor oscillator was put on the same tape. Only a small segment of the tape was used in the final sound analysis: a loop containing 6 to 10 seconds of speech usually selected from the initial minute of the recording.

The loop containing speech is played backwards by the tape recorder into a sound analyzer previously adjusted to base level with the pre-recorded calibrating tone. An H. H. Scott Sound Analyzer, Model 420-A, was used for the denotations presented below, which are for half-octave bands of sound. The same machine can measure octave or larger bands, which is less time-consuming but has less resolution. When the operator makes his readings he hears a meaningless jumble of noise and, undistracted by meaning, measures the sound level in each band. He must also measure the total sound level for each sample if he wishes to compare different samples with each other. Since speech sounds fluctuate quickly, it is necessary to estimate the average level for each reading from the maxima and minima shown by the decibel meter. After relatively little experience with acoustical instruments I was able to repeat my readings with enough accuracy to rely on direct vision for the sound level readings. For even greater accuracy it is possible to pinpoint the sound levels by photographing the excursion of the needle, or by using a condenser and DC Electrometer.

The result of each sound analysis is plotted on prepared graph paper with frequency (in terms of cycles per second) in the abscissa vs. intensity (in terms of decibels re 0.0002 microbar) in the ordinate. Looking at the graph of each analysis, one can tell at a glance the relative predominance of various tones in the voice of the patient. Except insofar as a rapidly-speaking person may put out more sound energy than one who speaks slowly, these graphs give no information about temporal aspects of soundmaking like rhythm or word rate. In the figures shown below, all graphs were equated for a total sound level of 65 decibels and the peaks of the curves were superimposed whenever possible in order to demonstrate the differently shaped graphs more clearly. In the analyses done so far, four patterns seem to predominate. Statistical study, using the intensity levels in various half-octave bands, is currently being planned so as to determine how closely these patterns correlate with descriptive analyses of the same sounds. Verbal labels which I have attached to the patterns illustrated below are commonly-used sound symbols; the scientific value of such symbols has been emphasized in recent publications by Brown and others (Brown 1958).

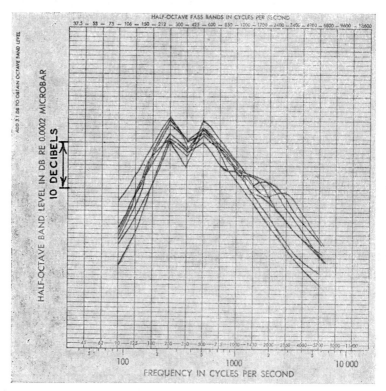

Fig. 1. The 'sharp' voice. Sound energy is concentrated in adjacent octave bands.

Figure 1, the 'sharp' voice, shows what is usually called a nagging, insinuating, querulous tone of voice. Of the seven curves shown here, one came from a 10-year old boy with a behavior disturbance while the rest came from adult female patients with various diagnoses. Acoustic analysis shows how energy is sharply concentrated into two adjacent octave bands. This produces, through reinforcement of overtones, a loud, sharp. and clear sound. Its effect on the listener tends to be generally alerting, alarming, and demanding.

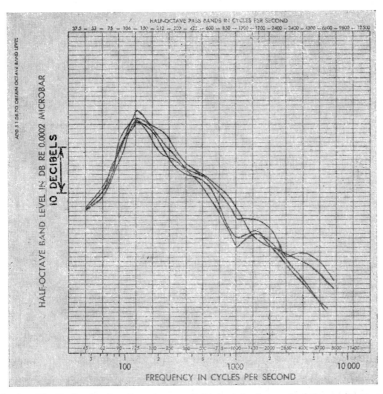

Fig. 2. The 'hollow' voice. Sound energy is high at the low end of the spectrum, and drops rapidly in the higher frequencies.

Figure 2, the 'hollow' voice shows what is often described as a flabby, rattling, quavering quality of voice. Three of the curves shown were taken from senile men, and the fourth came from a young man who sustained bilateral frontal-lobe contusions in a motorcycle collision. Acoustic analysis shows that energy is concentrated at the low end of the spectrum and then falls quickly, without any appreciable overtone reinforcement. This leads to a soft, indistinct, muffled sound and has an effect, on the listener, of inaudibility, paucity, and fuzziness.

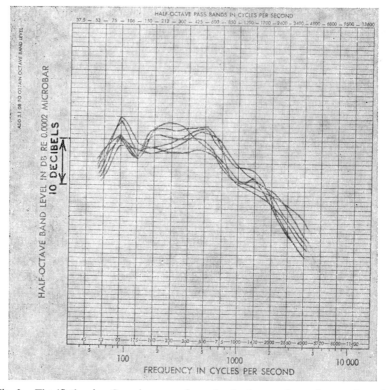

Fig. 3. The 'flat' voice. Sound energy above the fundamental tone is spread out in an irregular, dissonant pattern.

Figure 3, the 'flat' voice demonstrates another pattern. This time we are dealing with what may be called a smudged, lusterless, hesitant way of sounding. All the curves came from males who are neurotically depressed, obsessive, and inhibited in their behavior. An acoustic analysis of this sound reveals that energy output above the fundamental tone is spread out over almost two octaves. This may be indicative of gliding back and forth over many notes which, in the face of a strong fundamental tone, results in dissonance, even harshness. This kind of flat sound spectrum, in its effect on the listener creates ambiguity, unpleasantness, and lack of clarity.

Figure 4, the 'robust' voice demonstrates the graphic appearance of the tone of voice commonly known as extrovert, aggressive, and confident. The samples used here came from professional men and women, some known for their excellence as teachers or lecturers. Acoustic analysis of their voices shows that the sound is distributed over a relatively wide range in the spectrum, coming usually to a peak about midway in this distribution. This indicates that the voice is modulated evenly, rising and falling in a symmetrical way. Such a sound pattern tends to arouse interest, pleasantness, and admiration in a listener.

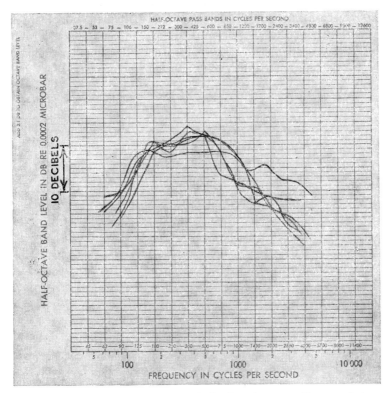

Fig. 4.   The 'robust' voice. Sound energy is distributed over a wide range, but comes to a peak about midway in the spectrum.

This method for visually denoting human sounds has a variety of applications. It may be used to compare the vocal behavior of individual patients from one moment to another, thus indicating any changes associated with psychotherapy, drug treatment, or other measures. As a diagnostic tool it may be used to compare various patients and groups of patients. From the research point of view, it is possible that this method, in combination with other measurements, might be used to gain insight into some of the subtle psychophysiological mechanisms underlying vocal behavior.

Summary

A graphic denotation for human sounds can be obtained by playing loops of tape recordings through an acoustic analyzer. A standardized method for this procedure is described. Preliminary studies indicate that there may be a number of recurring sound patterns produced by the voice during speech. These are labeled 'sharp', 'hollow', 'flat' and 'robust' voices. It may be possible to correlate these and other sound patterns with clinical variables such as personality, psychopathology, stress, and treatment.

8

THE SOUNDS OF EMOTIONAL DISTURBANCE*

(1961)

Sounds communicate emotions. This observation has been made by psychiatrists, musicians, and poets throughout history, and is repeated by every mother who listens to her baby. The purpose of this paper is to define the phenomenon, and to present evidence for the existence of specific acoustic signals that transmit information about emotional disturbance.

The study of human sounds

That sick people produce tell-tale acoustic signals was known to healers in primitive societies and to the earliest scientific investigators. Ancients wove the noises associated with illness into their myths and primitive rites (Frazer 1959); physicians recognized groans, rattles, coughs, wheezing, and other diagnostic signs (Hippocrates 1950). Accurate verbal description of these sounds was difficult, however, and taxed the onomatopoeic vocabulary of even the greatest poets and writers. Since words never did full justice to the actual sounds of disturbed persons, music took over the task of portraying them accurately. (During the Renaissance, musical portraiture of human behavior developed into fine art; conventions like minor intervals to describe sadness and chromaticism to denote anguish still are used in 'popular' music today [Cooke 1959]). The English naturalist William Gardiner depicted a number of emotional expressions with the use of musical notation (Fig. 1), for instance (1) the natural ebullitions of mirth and gaiety, (2) growling of the voice,

* Reprinted from the *Archives of General Psychiatry* 5: 587-92 (1961). Mr. George Wilson assisted in calibration of the acoustical equipment used in these studies, and Mr. Sanford Autumn applied statistical analyses to the data.

Fig. 1.   Emotional states depicted musically by Gardiner (1838): (1) mirth, (2) growling, (3) laughter, (4) crying, (5) sorrow.

(3) laughter, (4) the puling cry of a spoiled child, and (5) a person weighted down with sorrow and pain (Gardiner 1838).

Medical scientists contributed to the study of acoustic symptoms with inventions like the stethoscope and diagnostic techniques of percussion and auscultation (Ackerknecht 1955). During the 19th century methods for objective acoustic measurement were developed: first crude flickering flames, light-beams, or strips of metal, and later more accurate khymographic techniques (Beranek 1954). Helmholtz and his co-workers finally made it possible to identify human sounds in terms of precise intensity-frequency patterns (Helmholtz 1885).

Today increasing use is made of electromagnetic devices for measuring sound: Fletcher (1953), Rudmose (1948), Potter (1947), and others have already greatly advanced our understanding of acoustic communication. In their efforts to improve speech intelligibility via the telephone, these scientists initiated a search for acoustic cues that enable listeners to

distinguish one word sound from another (Licklider and Miller 1951).
A very important by-product of this work was the discovery that spoken
language is highly redundant, i.e., that when a person speaks he produces
many more acoustic signals than are necessary for correct speech perception (Shannon and Weaver 1949). Which of the many acoustic signals
in speech are involved in the communication of emotions? Attempts to
answer this question have led many clinicians to study the human voice
(Trojan 1959). They noted rapid register shifts (Moses 1954), extraneous
vowels (Mahl 1956), and other vocal pathology in the presence of
psychiatric illness; Grünewald showed constitutional factors to be related
to vocal sound intensity levels (Fig. 2). Such findings make one suspect
the existence of dynamic mechanisms whereby the emotionally disturbed
person produces a specific acoustic impact on the listener. Our work is
directed towards the elucidation of such mechanisms. The first step has
been to define the acoustic impact.

Acoustic analysis of human sounds

Preliminary investigations indicated that acoustic patterns are subject
not only to the physiological laws governing respiration and phonation,
but to social rules regarding the acoustic expression of emotion as well

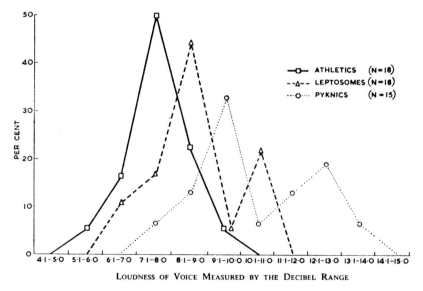

Fig. 2.   Vocal intensity as related to constitution (from Grünewald 1957): Intensity
increases in the order athletics-leptosomes-pyknics.

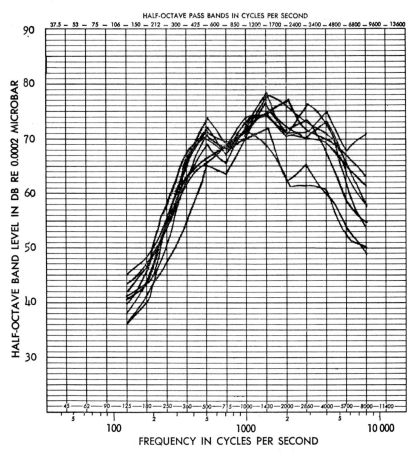

Fig. 3.   Cries of 9 human infants, measured in half-octave band intensity levels at the peak of each cry.

(Ostwald 1960b). Any objective approach therefore had to first find an acoustic unit that is compatible with physiological mechanisms of sound-making and also essential from a social point of view, so that no amount of language change could possibly force it out of the repertory of human sounds.[1] One human sound which fits these qualifications is the cry of infancy, an acoustic signal that is unlearned, transcultural, nonverbal, of brief duration, and easy to tape-record. Experiments with newly born infants in the hospital nursery led to the development of a method for

[1]   Linguists have noted a variable but progressive discarding from the vocabulary of words and word patterns that have lost their social usefulness (Greenberg 1953).

quantifying this sound in acoustic terms, based on half-octave band analyses of sound fragments lasting 1 to 4 sec. (Fig. 3).

The first application of this method to psychiatric patients led to the following results (Ostwald 1960c): (1) An obese, infantile, dependent hysterical female showed a basic intensity-frequency pattern with octave-doubling in the mid-range of the acoustic spectrum which was identical to the acoustic pattern of children's voices. This pattern changed from week to week as she alternately pleaded, attempted to seduce, or otherwise histrionically acted-out unconscious conflicts in the setting of her psychotherapeutic relationship. (2) An obsessional, effeminate, conscience-stricken, depressed male showed a persistent stereotype of vocal expression with the fundamental tone invariably fixed in the 75 to 106 cps band, and the midrange formant pattern smeared out in a flat way across the spectrum. (3) Four organically disturbed patients, 3 in the geriatric category and the fourth, a young man who had sustained bilateral frontal lobe lesions from a motorcycle accident, showed a pattern of acoustic inadequacy characterized by a single concentration of sound energy in the low end of the spectrum. There was steady and persistent dropping off in energy of the mid-spectrum, and unmistakable wasting-away of sound in the upper-frequency region responsible for speech intelligibility. These findings were later expanded into 4 distinct categories of human sound: (1) a 'sharp' voice characteristic of excited and complaining persons who needed to make themselves heard in dramatic ways, (2) a 'flat' voice produced by depressed and obsessional people who presented an irritating but indistinct acoustic facade to the listener, (3) a 'hollow' voice of organically ill or emotionally drained people who could not muster enough energy to sustain and clarify their speech, and (4) a 'robust' voice characteristic of persons who spoke loudly, emphatically, and needed to be heard, to impress, and to influence others (Ostwald 1960e).

So far part of our hypothesis has gained support: Sounds of disturbed persons can be objectively characterized in terms of acoustic impact patterns. But what about the effects of such impact patterns on the auditory system of the listener? Examination of the intake characteristics of the human ear provided an important lead in pursuit of the answer: It revealed that sounds in the mid-portion of the acoustic spectrum produce a much stronger listener reaction than do equally intense stimuli at the upper or lower extremes (Beranek 1954) (Fig. 4). This is why people whistle, scream, or make other sounds to stimulate the auditory *fovea centralis* when they need to get attention quickly (Ostwald 1959). Further support of the hypothesis therefore demanded that some significant

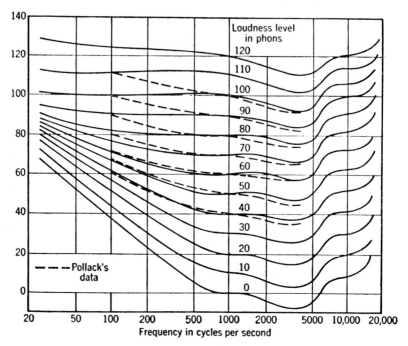

Fig. 4. Sensitivity of the human ear, in terms of equal-loudness contours for pure tones (Fletcher and Munson 1942) and bands of noise 250 mels wide (Pollack 1952). From Beranek (1954).

concentration of acoustic energy in the voices of emotionally disturbed people be located.

Repeated inspection of the acoustic records of psychiatric patients indicated that certain peaks along the intensity-frequency spectrum were more recurrent and prominent than others. To discover whether any of these change significantly with emotional distress, we subjected 20 persons to an olfactory stress. Each subject – these were not patients – took a deep breath from an ammonia solution and uttered a standard sentence in order to minimize linguistic factors. This was tape-recorded and compared to the same sentence spoken without the bad smell. (The sequence was reversed for half the group to control for the effect of order on the results). Changes of intensity level in 15 adjacent half-octave bands of the acoustic spectrum were then compared.[2] Two points along the acoustic

---

[2] The Signed Rank Test for Paired Observations was applied, after changes in sound levels for each of the 15 adjacent bands had been corrected for the absolute change in sound level of the entire acoustic product. The level of significance was fixed at 0.05.

spectrum, 125 cps and 500 cps, showed statistically significant changes. At both of these points the change was in the direction of an increase of acoustic intensity with stress.

What about psychiatric patients – do they emit anything like these artificially induced 'stress sounds'? To find out, we next applied the acoustic method of analysis to 30 acutely disturbed patients, recording their sound immediately on admission to the hospital and repeating the recording after 2 or more weeks of treatment. Intensity measures for the frequency bands centered at 125, 500, 1,430, and 5,700 cps were converted to loudness units in sones (Stevens 1956) and compared. Word rate, variability between spontaneous speech and reading, and total loudness were also compared.

Results – characteristic changes

Three patterns of change associated with treatment are illustrated in Figures 5, 6, and 7. Figure 5 shows the before-and-after-treatment acoustic analyses of a 64-year-old salesman who was admitted to the hospital during the depressed cycle of a manic-depressive psychosis. After 2 weeks of treatment, which included 5 electroconvulsions, his reading voice showed a loudness rise of 4.3 sones, the band of maximum increase (2.2 sones) being that centered at 500 cps. There was also a

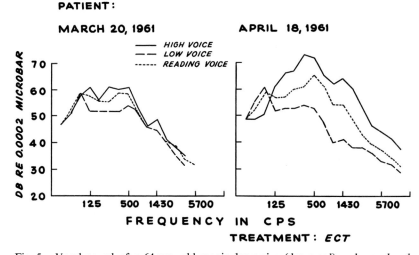

Fig. 5. Vocal sound of a 64-year-old manic-depressive (depressed) male, analyzed before and after electroconvulsive treatment. High and reading samples show a rise of intensity and pitch.

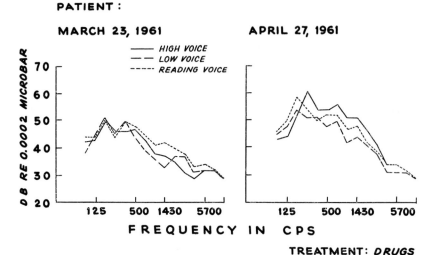

Fig. 6.   Vocal sound of a 16-year-old schizophrenic female, analyzed before and after
drug treatment. All samples show a rise of intensity and pitch.

considerably greater variation between his high and low speaking voices
and his reading voice. In addition, his reading had slowed down an average
of 0.06 seconds per syllable. Figure 6 shows before-and-after-treatment
comparisons for a 16-year-old girl admitted during an acute schizophrenic
state. After 5 weeks of treatment that included phenothiazine-derivative
drugs, her reading voice showed a loudness rise of 1.6 sones, the band of
maximum increase (0.6 sones) centering at 1,430 cps. The voice also
showed less compactness, and her reading had speeded up an average of
0.06 seconds per syllable. Figure 7 compares the sound of a 32-year-old
woman in an acute psychoneurotic hypochondriacal state before and
after treatment, which consisted of supportive psychotherapy and rest.
While there was some increase in over-all loudness (1.3 sones), the most
striking feature of the change was the greater acoustic stability as shown
by the pulling together of the high, low, and reading voices. Change in
reading rate was not significant.

A statistical analysis of these data for 30 psychiatric patients was
carried out[3]; the clinical variables selected for study were: age, sex,
diagnosis, form of treatment, duration of treatment, and improvement
as rated by the ward psychiatrists. Changes in 2 acoustic measures were

[3]   The Mann-Whitney U-Test was applied, with statistical significance set at 0.05
(Siegel 1956).

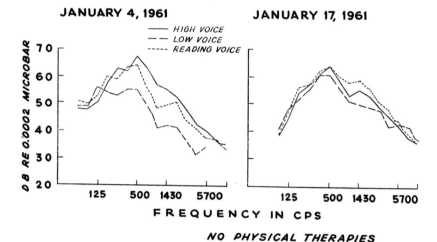

PATIENT:

Fig. 7.   Vocal sound of a 32-year-old hypochondriacal female, analyzed before and after therapy. Low and reading samples show a rise of intensity and pitch.

found to be statistically significant: the measure of total loudness, and the measure of loudness rise in the band centering at 500 cps. These significant changes were revealed only by the treatment variable, and with both measures the change was in the direction of an increase in loudness after electroconvulsive treatment and a decrease after pharmaco-therapy.

That a change at 500 cps (centering the 425-600 cps band) should be significant is of great interest, since it is at this point along the acoustic spectrum that the new-born infant emits its first cry (Ostwald 1960d). Also the fact that sex does NOT differentiate any significant acoustic change in these patients seems to indicate that sounds produced by acutely disturbed psychiatric patients stem from a primitive, pregenital pattern of response. Studies are now in progress which may shed further light on this phenomenon.

Summary

This paper examines the idea that emotional disturbance may be com-municated by specific acoustic signals. Descriptive studies of this problem are reviewed. Acoustic analysis with contiguous band-pass filters offers an objective approach. After treatment, acutely disturbed psychiatric patients show a statistically significant change of loudness in the acoustic spectrum centered at 500 cps. This change is in the direction of a rise in loudness after electroconvulsive treatment and a fall after pharmaco-therapy. The fact that the change occurs at 500 cps (centering the 425-600 cps band) is of additional interest in that this position along the acoustic spectrum corresponds with the fundamental tone of the human baby-cry.

9

ACOUSTIC MANIFESTATIONS OF
EMOTIONAL DISTURBANCE*

(1964)

Aberrations and peculiarities of soundmaking are crucial diagnostic
clues in clinical psychiatry and have evoked considerable research interest
since Freud's initial effort to explain speech disturbances psychopatho-
logically (Feldman 1959). Most subsequent studies have relied on the
clinician's ears or on a secretary's typescript to determine when and what
kind of speech abnormalities occur during interviews (Mahl and Schultze
1964). Recently, microlinguistic methods have been applied to psychiatric
interview material, with the result that we are beginning to get clarification of what patients are doing on the PHONEMIC level to call attention
to their emotional problems (Pittenger et al. 1960), but so far, few investigations have been carried out on the PHONETIC level of sound-
making. Consequently little information is yet available about physiological processes which underlie those pathognomonic twists and disruptions of speech which one hears in the consultation room.

   Acoustic methods offer one striking advantage for research into this
problem; they help disclose the physical structure of sounds produced by
patients. This enables one to make statements about the soundmaking of
emotionally disturbed individuals without having to use a terminology –
for example, that of descriptive linguistics – applicable to verbal communication, that very aspect of behavior which the symptomatic non-verbal
soundmaking of patients is evidently designed to undercut (Ruesch 1955).
My first investigations of acoustic psychopathology were carried out
with an H. H. Scott Half-octave Band Analyzer, and the results have
been reported elsewhere (Ostwald 1963). The purpose of today's paper is

* Reprinted from *Disorders of Communication* XLII: *Research Publications*,
A.R.N.M.D.: 450-465 (1964).

to present some detailed observations about disturbed soundmaking, using the sound spectrograph to study this behavior acoustically.

Spectrographic analysis of sounds

The sound spectrograph (Kay Sonagraph) has been extensively used over the past 15 years to study acoustic characteristics of normal speech, with the result that some fairly precise information is now available about 'distinctive features' of the verbal language code (Jakobson and Halle 1956). Its application to pathological forms of soundmaking is much more recent however (Lehiste et al. 1961), and no systematic studies have yet been published. The spectrograph can analyze 2.4 second segments of sound by filtering it into contiguous frequency bands between 0 and 8000 cps of the acoustic spectrum. Energy contained in each band is converted to heat which burns a sensitized paper placed on a continuously rotating drum. This produces the spectrogram, which is essentially a 'picture' of sound, comparable to a microphotograph of visible tissue studied histologically. Broad-band (300 cps) and narrow-band (45 cps) spectrograms can be made, roughly analogous to low-power and high-power microscopy. Broad-band spectrograms reveal the formant-structure of vowels and other acoustical details important for speech perception. Narrow-band spectrograms – which is what I shall be presenting to you – reveal finer details in the harmonic configuration of the sound. Both kinds of spectrograms can denote pauses, which show up as clear areas, non-tonal noise, which shows up as amorphously distributed mottling, and variability in sound intensity, which shows up as variations in the degree of darkness on the spectrogram.

Figure 1 illustrates the narrow-band spectrographic pattern of normal speech.[1] The first spectrogram is of a male speaker, the second of a female, both uttering an identical test phrase: *Joe took father's shoebench out*. The over-all pattern of energy distribution over time is determined by the linguistic material in these words and by paralinguistic factors such as rate of speaking, clearness of articulation and the frequency and intensity characteristics of the voice. Note that the female voice, which is higher in pitch than the male voice, shows somewhat clearer delineation of tonal harmonics. Both spectrograms show vowel formants and consonantal noise. Let us now compare these spectrograms of normal speech with

---

[1]   All spectrograms shown in this paper were made with high-shaping, compression = 9, and mark level = 9.

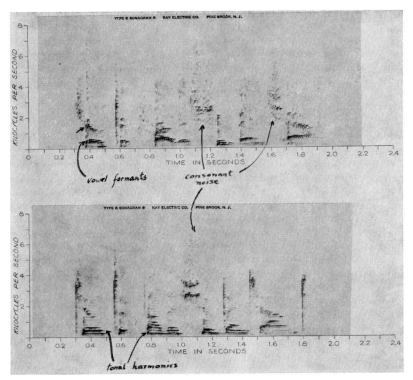

Fig. 1. Narrow band (45 cps) spectrograms of normal speech. The male voice (above) shows the formant structure of vowels. The female voice (below) in addition illustrates the harmonic structure of these tonal sounds. Both samples also show consonantal noises. The words recorded here are *Joe took father's shoebench out*.

eight examples of soundmaking which are taken from severely disturbed psychiatric patients whose psychopathology has come to dominate their use of language and their paralinguistic behavior.

1. Rapidly intermittent sound

To start with one of the most extreme deviations from normal speech, I shall illustrate some characteristic sounds produced by hospitalized psychotic patients. The first spectrogram in figure 2 shows a machine gun-like outburst of intermittent sound. This represents part of a deteriorated and stereotyped pattern of behavior produced by a 40-year-old autistic woman who has spent most of her life in state hospitals. She accompanies this ugly glottalized sound with curious shaking of her head, for which she has been nicknamed 'Billygoat'. Spectrographically we see

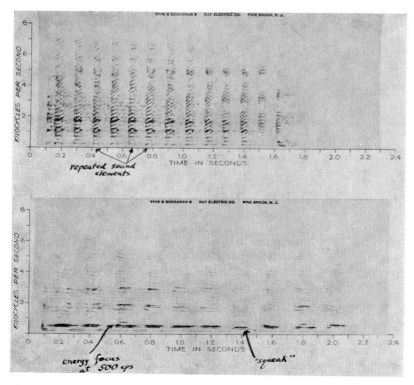

Fig. 2.   Spectrograms of rapidly intermittent non-verbal sounds produced by psychotic patients. Note the stereotyped uniformity of the sounds produced by a chronically autistic woman (above) as compared with the somewhat more variable 'blathering' of an acutely schizophrenic boy (below).

14 individual acoustic fragments – each about 0.05 second in duration – within a space of about 1½ seconds. Each one of these tiny acoustic particles contains a very sharp rise in the frequency of tonal harmonics, something one cannot consciously hear as such but which may account for the extremely tense quality of her sound. Separation of the individual fragments of this mechanical sound is most noticeable above 3200 cps.

The second spectrogram illustrates blathering (Scott 1955), part of the regressive soundmaking indulged in by an adolescent boy during an acute schizophrenic excitement. He made these chains of repetitive sound when one would try to speak with him, and afterwards he called himself a 'blabber-mouth'. The picture shows his blather to consist of 10 almost identical 0.1 second acoustic fragments within an interval of 2 seconds. Except for the seventh fragment, which consists of a noisy squeak, each part of the blather has a harmonic pattern, the main energy component of which is located at 500 cps. It may be worth mention that at 500 cps and around 3000 cps, which also shows some energy concentration in this patient's spectrogram, is located what has been called a 'singer's formant', a focus of sound regularly found in the voices of trained singers (H. Harris 1962). In other words, one could say that this patient's blathering comes closer to singing than to speaking. In previous studies of sound by means of half-octave band analysis, I was unable to locate any significant differences when the outputs of 20 experimental subjects were measured before and after an olfactory stress, EXCEPT FOR THE HALF-OCTAVE BAND CENTERED AT 500 CPS. Similarly, in a clinical study of 30 psychiatric patients before and after treatment, the only significant ($P \geq 0.05$) change in acoustic energy output occurred at 500 cps (Ostwald 1961a).

2. Predominance of noise

Interruption or replacement of normal speech by predominantly noisy sound is illustrated in figure 3. The first spectrogram shows sound emitted by a woman of very low intelligence who became excited during a discussion about going to a dance with her boyfriend. She suddenly stopped speaking and began instead to pant and to make a few tiny squeaking sounds. The spectrogram shows her sound to consist almost entirely of noise which is spread out evenly across the frequency spectrum, except for some increased density around 2000 and 3000 cps. The picture resembles that of 'cavity noise', which results from the turbulence of respiratory air as it rubs against the sides of the oral cavity. Throughout 2.4 seconds there is only one tonal sound, a 0.1-second fragment whose major harmonic focus is at 2800 cps. Another interesting acoustic manifestation is a peculiar short clicking noise which occurs four times, at points of transition between inspiration and expiration, presumably as a result of some soft-tissue friction in the patient's nasopharynx.

The second spectrogram shows similar noises produced by a patient who was being treated for a chronic schizophrenic disorder. He has profound identity problems and feels that when he was a very small boy someone may have got inside him and taken control over his thinking. Whenever he becomes particularly aware of this inside outsider, he tries to expel it by means of vigorous snorting, to the accompaniment of sudden jerking of his pelvis and torso. The sound you see here was recorded during such a paroxysm. It consists of stretches of cavity noise, for example a prolonged burst between 1.6 and 2.4 seconds, as well as short

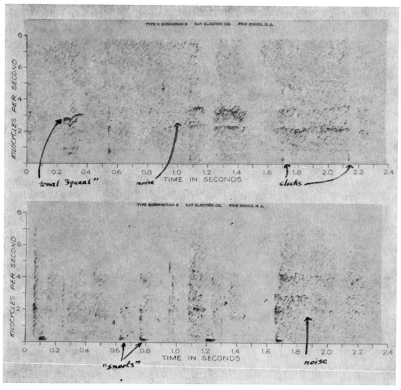

Fig. 3. Spectrograms of predominantly noisy non-verbal sounds. Above: harsh breathing, clicks, and a squeal produced by an erotically excited mentally retarded woman. Below: snorting and paroxysmal breathing of a schizophrenic patient.

recurrent clicks of noise. There are five tiny harmonic foci at around 150 cps, the longest lasting about 0.06 second. These brief tonal hums denote his snorting sounds.

3. Prolonged emission of continuous sounds

At the opposite extreme to the rapidly repetitious soundmaking described earlier stands the prolonged emission of continuous sound. Two examples of this uninterrupted soundmaking are illustrated in figure 4. The first spectrogram shows a roar produced several times each day by a psychosomatic patient who attempts thereby to relieve intolerable hungerlike sensations. Spectrographic analysis shows the sound to contain fragments of tone and noise, both going on continuously for slightly less than 2 seconds. The harmonics are very broken up, but a fairly definite focussing

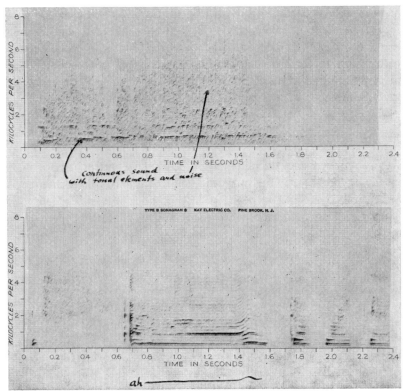

Fig. 4.   Spectrograms of prolonged non-verbal sounds. Above: a roar, containing
noise and tones, produced by a psychosomatic patient. Below: an embolophrasic *ah*
which interrupts speech. Note the frequency 'wobble' at the end of this sound.

of energy seems to occur between 500 to 600 cps. Resonance energy in
higher reaches of the acoustic frequency spectrum also looks choppy and
ragged, as though the patient is never quite sure which resonance cavity
is being used, and to what extent.

The second spectrogram shows a prolonged sound emitted by a patient
whose soundmaking will be used to demonstrate several other forms of
acoustic psychopathology. She is an extremely excitable, immature,
psychoneurotic woman in her twenties who sought therapy for alleviation
of obsessional ideas and a tendency to suddenly contract the muscles of
her face, neck and shoulder girdle. In this instance she interrupts her
speech with a long musical sound, a sort of *ah* that resembles the embolophrasic noises of stutterers. The spectrogram shows this sound to consist
of an unvoiced stop followed by a tonal sound (with formant structure)
that after a momentary frequency-fluctuation settles down to a steady

harmonic level, particularly well delineated around 800 cps. After 0.7 second there is another very sudden frequency-level change, which sounds like a quick rise of pitch but which actually consists of a rise-and-fall pattern lasting close to 0.2 second. This 'wobble' resembles another phenomenon that has been noted in the voices of singers, a vibrato-like 'catch' when they wish to portray emotion (Potter et al. 1947).

4. Ultra-rapid frequency shifts

The wobbly frequency fluctuations produced by the patient just presented is only one example of her more widespread pathology in pitch-control. She appears to suffer from a sort of 'laryngeal tic'. The pitch of her voice jumps nervously between one level and another, almost like an acoustic

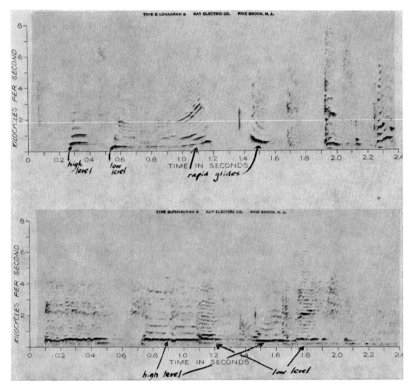

Fig. 5.   Spectrograms showing very rapid non-linguistic frequency shifts. The record at the top shows quick glides between high and low frequency levels in the sound of a female psychoneurotic patient with tics. The lower record, taken from the schizophrenic boy who blathers, shows abrupt, 'yodel-like' shifts in frequency levels.

counterpart to the visible jerking of her body. The pattern is illustrated in the first spectrogram of figure 5, which shows dramatic up-and-down swings in tonal frequencies. This starts with a fundamental of 500 cps which drops to 250 cps within a space of 0.3 second. There shortly follows a very precipitous rise in the frequency level, leading to a brief silence interrupted by a noisy click. Then there is an equally abrupt fall in frequency, denoting a non-verbal 'gasping' sound. At the end of this specimen, the frequency again climbs abruptly but this time ends with the sort of 'wobble' described earlier.

The second spectrogram illustrates very rapid non-phonemic intonation changes in the speech of the schizophrenic patient whose blathering was illustrated earlier. This peculiar 'yodeling' in vocal pitch was a very striking part of his psychotic disorganization. For example, on certain days he would alternately produce the high-pitched sound to mimic his mother, saying such things as *pay attention, be a good boy*, and the like, and the low-pitched sound to portray himself responding to these verbal commands. One night the nurse on the ward even found the boy alternately emitting the high voice out of one side of his mouth and the low voice out of the other. The spectrogram shows these two tonal patterns in rapid alternation. The high-pitched sound, which has its harmonics spaced more widely apart, shows the fundamental tone at 450 cps; the low-pitched sound has its fundamental at 220 cps. The ultra-rapid switch from the high to the low voice is particularly clear at 1.1 second. You will also note a prolonged *eh eh eh* at the beginning of the record between 0.1 and 0.5 second, a sound which resembles the embolophrasia shown in figure 4.

5. *Sustained unvarying frequency levels*

The opposite of rapid frequency fluctuation is no fluctuation at all – a frequency level which is sustained and sounds monotonous. This phenomenon is illustrated in figure 6. The first spectrogram shows the enfeebled, hollow sound produced by a middle-aged man with arteriosclerotic brain disease, who suffers from a reactive depression. Note that only the fundamental frequency of his voice is clearly defined. The frequency remains on one level for a total of 1.2 seconds of sound, and only rises once for 0.2 second, on the word *other*. It is also worth pointing out that this patient's sound is almost completely lacking in formant structure and that the individual words run into one another, which further reduces the intelligibility of his already substandard speech.

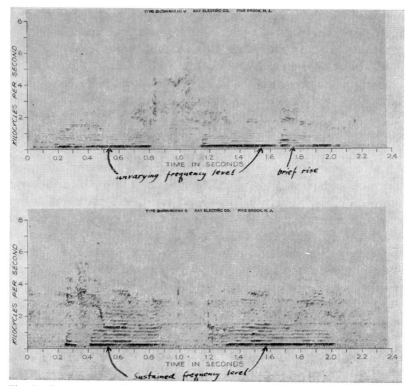

Fig. 6.   Spectrograms of monotonous speech with little variability in the frequency pattern. The top figure illustrates the sound of a depressed, arteriosclerotic man in his fifties and the bottom figure illustrates a withdrawn pseudoneurotic schizophrenic girl in her twenties.

The second spectrogram shows an almost identical phenomenon in the sound of a young woman who became depressed during late adolescence and developed a pseudo-neurotic schizophrenic syndrome in her twenties after her brother entered a state hospital. The lack of frequency variation in her sound coincides with a general flatness and inability to express emotion. Although there is some suggestion of a formant structure in the vocalic portions of her speech, generally it is only the fundamental tone which shows any major concentration of acoustic energy, a pattern which I have called 'hollow voice' and described in greater detail elsewhere (Ostwald 1960e).

6. Abrupt lapses in acoustic output

Another manifestation of emotional disturbance is characterized by a sudden lapse in the patient's production of sound. The first spectrogram of figure 7 illustrates this phenomenon in the case of a 30-year-old man who is being treated for a severe sexual perversion. He is quite assertive and generally speaks in a fully resonant, tenor voice. But from time to time his soundmaking falters. This usually occurs at the beginning of certain words or syllables and is related to an acute sense of embarrassment associated with particular ideas he may at the moment wish to express or to hold back. The sample illustrated here has to do with a discussion of his speaking over the radio, and it is when he begins to say *radio* that the soundmaking suddenly gives way. This shows up in the spectrogram as an acute drop in the intensity of the sound, indicated by a lighter portion on the graph which lasts for 1 second, during which interval the acoustic energy level is very low, and there is no resonance above

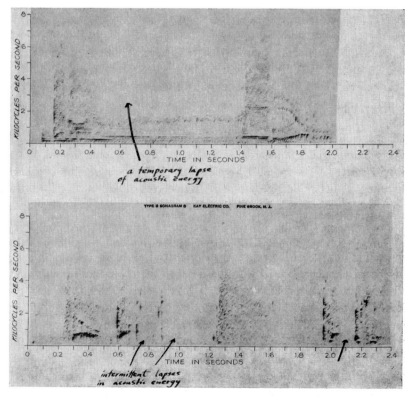

Fig. 7.   Spectrograms illustrating abrupt lapses in sound energy output. Above: one second 'stammer' in the speech of a male patient. Below: lapses in the sound produced by a woman who tried to talk at the end of expiration.

1500 cps. Then he recovers his power on the vowel *a* of *radio* and goes on with a more normal speech pattern.

The second spectrogram illustrates a similar phenomenon in the speech of a middle-aged woman who is receiving treatment for a severe psycho-neurotic tension state. She insists on trying to speak without first taking air into her lungs. Consequently the sounds she makes are unsupported by phonation, appear choppy and spasmodic and are difficult to understand. This sample contains the words *self-conscious talking*. Her acoustic energy output practically disappears after the morpheme *self* of *self-conscious*. All one sees are a few miniscule mouth-smacking noises between 0.7 and 1.0 second where there should be a formant structure. Only the end of the word is clearly visible through a 0.4 second noise, representing the terminal hissing *s* consonant.

7. *Suddenly increased sound levels*

Converse to the phenomenon just described is a sudden momentary rise of acoustic energy. This was quite prominent in the soundmaking of a 16-year-old boy who was in the hospital for treatment of an acute schizo-phrenic excitement during which he felt convinced that his nose was stopped up and that he was going blind. In the first spectrogram of figure 8, he speaks in an excited, whiny, nasalized voice which has practically no resonance energy above 4000 cps. Suddenly the intensity level of his sound starts to go up; at 1.3 second the harmonics become broader, darker and better defined, and the frequencies begin to climb. At 1.6 second there is a break in the tone, and after 0.1 second one sees noise. Throughout this time the resonance level has gone up above 5000 cps. The sound remains more intense for another 0.4 second, while the fre-quencies fluctuate in the rapid way I described earlier.

The psychoneurotic girl with tic-like changes of vocal frequency and the *ah*-like sound prolongations this time demonstrates acute energy-level elevations, which constitute another acoustic manifestation of her emotional illness. She suddenly overemphasizes certain words or parts of words, out of context and not in keeping with linguistically meaningful stress patterns. The sample illustrated spectrographically in figure 8 starts with the words *and so and so had*. The *had* is the focus for a tonal burst of sound at 2000 cps which is accompanied by a sudden jump in upper-frequency resonance from 5000 cps to 7500 cps. This is followed by a peculiar inspiratory wheeze and three brief stutter-like noises.

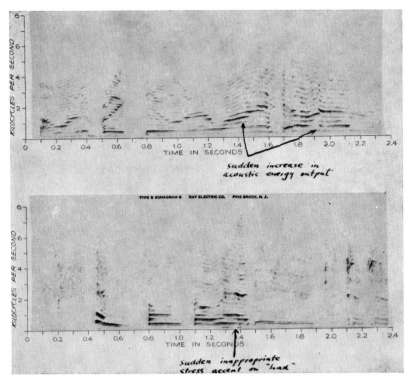

Fig. 8.   Spectrograms of acutely increased acoustic energy outputs. Above: sudden rise in frequency and intensity levels, capped by a noise: this was produced by an acutely schizophrenic male. Below: an inappropriate stress accent produced by the patient with tics whose other acoustic abnormalities were presented earlier.

8. Hyperresonant tonal sound

Finally I wish to describe an acoustic manifestation of emotional disturbance which is characterized by an excess of tonal sound and might thus be contrasted with the predominance of noise described earlier. The first spectrogram of figure 9 shows the sound of a middle-aged woman who suffers from recurrent depressions for which she has received electroconvulsive treatment. She speaks in a whiny, pleading, babyish way. The spectrogram shows an almost entirely tonal pattern, with extremely clear demarcation of harmonics, in particular the fundamental frequency and second harmonic. This phenomenon, which can most readily be seen between 0.8 and 1.0 seconds, has been described elsewhere as a 'sharp voice' which tends to make itself readily heard (Ostwald 1960e). There is practically no noise to be seen in this patient's spectrogram and her

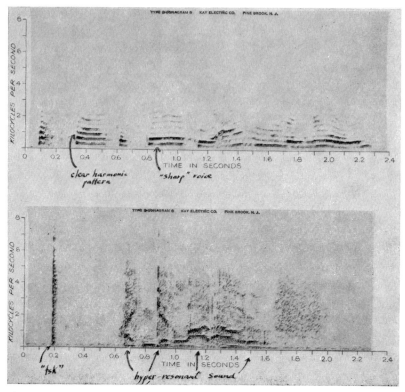

Fig. 9. Spectrograms of hyper-resonant tonal sound. Above: a depressive middle-aged female patient with a 'sharp' baby voice; the harmonic pattern is unusually clear. Below: the sharp voice of a phobic male patient who speaks in a booming, unrealistically confident-appearing manner.

resonance energy hardly ever gets higher than 3000 cps.

The second spectrogram shows the hyperresonant voice of a man who suffers from chronic anxiety and multiple phobias. He cannot work and is unable to live with his family. He has a pompous, exuberant facade which belies his basic timidity, and the sound you see here is part of this front. The formants are unusually clear for a narrow-band spectrogram, and there is a great deal of tonal resonance energy. The spectrogram also shows two noises, one at 0.2 second denoting a brisk self-critical *tsk*, and another between 1.6 and 2.0 seconds denoting a dramatic exaggeration of the final *f* in his utterance.[2]

[2] I wish to acknowledge the assistance of Jesse Sawyer, Ph.D., Associate Professor of Linguistics and Director of the Language Laboratory, University of California, Berkeley, who made the use of a sound spectrograph available for this study and greatly helped me in regard to the interpretation of the spectrograms.

Discussion

The spectrograms presented above illustrate different sounds produced by psychotic and severely psychoneurotic patients during clinical interviews. These examples were selected from a large amount of tape-recorded material currently being analyzed. The advantage of studying non-verbal sounds in this way is that it converts the acoustic information into a visual picture which can be inspected at leisure and scanned for patterns easily missed by the unaided ear. Eight such patterns were analyzed above, and it became apparent that certain of them could be seen as pairs of contrasting opposites, for example: predominance of noise / hyperresonant tonal sound, ultra-rapid frequency shifts / sustained unvarying frequency levels, abrupt lapses in acoustic output / suddenly increased sound levels, and rapidly intermittent sound / prolonged emission of continuous sound.

Other patterns will undoubtedly emerge from this sort of acoustic specification of psychopathology, and I look forward to the day when all pertinent clinical phenomena can be accurately described in terms of their acoustic morphology. This should be of definite benefit for medical research. For instance, acoustic specification of sounds may help clarify certain problems which arise from the disruption of normal speech patterns due to organic pathology of the nervous system (Brain 1961). Furthermore, a structural approach might enable us to deal more objectively with the elusive functional disturbances of speech called stuttering, stammering, dysphonia, dyslalia, and the like.

Finally, better understanding of pathognomonic sounds produced by sick persons should help us to explore the meanings of these sounds, in the sense that they are signs pointing to a specific disturbance in a patient's life-pattern. For example, the structure of hunger-cries must be known before one can scientifically study the preverbal communication of hunger between child and mother (Ostwald 1962). Satiation, tension, arousal, quiescence, pleasure, excitement and other affective states are similarly waiting to be studied in terms of their acoustic manifestations and the role that acoustic signals play in communicating information about these states. Emotionally disturbed individuals undoubtedly use and abuse such acoustic signals in their interactions with others, and detailed knowledge about this interesting aspect of disturbed communication should be helpful for diagnostic and therapeutic work in psychiatry.

Summary

Eight acoustic patterns are presented from application of the sound spectrograph (Kay Sonagraph) to abnormal forms of soundmaking among psychotic and severely disturbed psychoneurotic patients whose speech was tape-recorded during clinical interviews. These patterns are described in terms of unusual temporal organization, the predominance of noisy or of tonal sounds, the abrupt elevation or diminution of acoustic intensity levels and excessive or deficient fluctuations in acoustic frequency levels. Visualization of sounds enables one to study in detail the ACOUSTIC MORPHOLOGY of pathognomonic sounds associated with various diseases. Such structural specification of diagnostic cues may be important in differentiating between organic, functional and emotive patterns of speech disturbance. It should also enhance the scientific analysis of how acoustic signals are used and abused for non-verbal communication about hunger, satiation, pain, pleasure, fear and other affective states.

10

SPECTROGRAPHIC DIAGNOSIS OF SPEECH DISTURBANCES*

(1965)

Introduction

One of the most vexing difficulties in the scientific study of speech disturbances is that objective statements about specific manifestations of speech pathology often cannot be made. This problem arises not only from differences in the LEVEL of the analysis of the pathology – for instance the neurologist deals with the central and peripheral nerve mechanisms controlling speech while the laryngologist is concerned with the voice organ itself – but stems also from limitations in the descriptive terminology developed by various specialties dealing with speech problems. The purpose of the present paper is to suggest that as a first step towards solving this difficulty we must approach the PRODUCTS of speech disturbance, i.e., the sounds made by the patient, in as objective a manner as possible. Acoustical methods are, it is submitted, one way in which this goal can be reached, and some examples of acoustic analysis of abnormal speech will be briefly presented.

The brilliant investigations of NORMAL speech sounds which have been carried out over the last 20 years or so in several phonetic laboratories throughout the world are well known. The book of Potter et al. (1947) for example, gives in an almost dictionary-like way the acoustical parameters of various English phonemes, and this can serve as the baseline against which abnormal sounds may be compared. Since this valuable work appeared there have been many similar studies going into greater detail and clarifying allophonemic variations in speech. Jakobson and Halle (1956) have proposed a way to classify the acoustical properties, or so-called 'distinctive features' of speech sounds. While this scheme is

* Reprinted from *Journal of the Neurological Sciences* 2: 271-77 (1965).

not as complete or universally applicable as was originally hoped, it does give us a scientific way of dealing with the communicative linguistic sounds of human beings. Where information is definitely lacking at the present time is in the field of paralanguage (Sebeok and Hayes 1964) and here we must presently be guided in our methods and theories by the work of zoologists and other investigators of the sound languages of animals, such as bird song systems, underwater sounds of fish, and insect noises (Lanyon and Tavolga 1960).

Method

The sound spectrograph (Kay Sonagraph) which is presently the instrument of choice in studying biologically meaningful sounds, consists essentially of a bank of electro-acoustical filters that convert sound into heat energy. The sound is fed to the machine either from a microphone into which the speaker talks directly or from a tape-recorder which reproduces what the speaker has previously said. The output from the filters goes to a heat-stylus which burns marks of varying degrees of darkness onto paper placed around a revolving drum. The pattern which appears on this paper is called the SPECTROGRAM.

Figure 1 shows a spectrogram of normal speech.[1] The horizontal axis

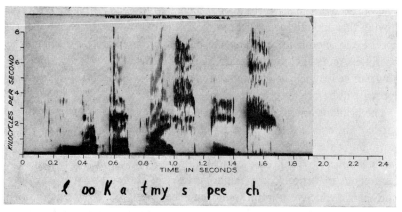

Fig. 1. Normal speech, showing dark bands (formants) of vocalized sound, noises produced by articulation, and the typical temporal distribution of phonemes.

---

[1] For demonstration purposes, the standard English alphabet has been used. Naturally, a phonetic alphabet is desirable for studying in detail the phonemic and acoustic relationships.

denotes elapsed time. On this axis we see a regular recurrence of sound impulses that represent the different phonemes articulated by the speech apparatus. The vertical axis denotes the frequency composition of these sounds. At the low end of the frequency spectrum – between approximately 85 and 3500 c/s – there are heavy, dark, smoothly-outlined bands of sound energy which tend to change in position from one phoneme to the next. These bands are called FORMANTS. They represent the relatively large amounts of vocal sound produced during speech by the larynx and in the major resonating cavities. The upper frequency spectrum – from approximately 3500 to 8000 c/s – shows more widely and unevenly distributed regions of sound. These are the consonantal NOISES produced during speech by the lips, teeth, back of the tongue, and other articulating surfaces. Normal speech shows a well-organized pattern of formants and noises separated by brief moments of silence. These brief silences denote the normal spacing of words as well as interruptions in the flow of sound necessitated by the stop consonants.

Case studies

Now let us look at a spectrogram of disturbed speech. In figure 2 it can be seen that almost the entire picture is made up of noises and silences. Some of the noise is collected into formant-like bands, suggesting that the resonators are already engaged to produce a vowel. But except for a split-second formant burst toward the center of the picture, vocalization is held back until the very end of expiration. At this point the sound

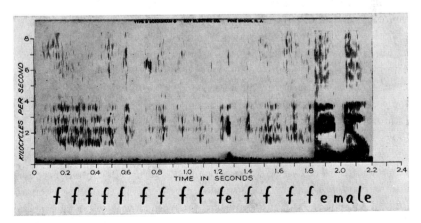

Fig. 2.   Abnormal speech, showing perseveration of the initial fricative noise followed by hasty vocalization at the end of respiration.

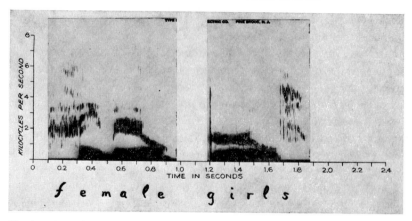

f e m a l e 　　g i r l s

Fig. 3.　Normal spectrographic appearance of the words *female* (contrast with Fig. 2) and *girls* (contrast with Fig. 4).

abruptly emerges, and the entire utterance *female* is expressed with great haste, leaving two jammed-up formant clusters that are almost indistinguishable from one another. Contrast this with the normal spectrographic appearance of the word *female* as shown in figure 3. The initial consonant is quickly released to produce a vowel which leads smoothly into the short bilabial *m* sound. This in turn opens up into the vocalic *ei* followed by its terminal transition to *l*.

The patient whose spectrogram was shown in figure 2 is a 24-year-old man with a communication disturbance since early childhood which has not responded to speech therapy. His twin sister has an abnormal EEG and had a grand mal convulsion in high school. While the patient's neurological examination is negative, his history reveals other signs of pathology, including adolescent impulsivity, fire-setting, and voyeurism, and in adult years a tendency to obsessional thinking and compulsiveness. The spectrogram in figure 4 illustrates a different kind of speech disturbance. Instead of the hyperabundance of noise and silence displayed by the previous patient we now see a preponderance of vocal sound and very little noise. The patient is trying to say *girls*, a sound which normally looks like the second word shown in figure 3. Normally the opening *g* shows up as a clear vertical stripe of noise and leads immediately into a vowel composed of two easily-seen formants. These merge into the *l* sound after which there is a burst of noise denoting the sibilant *s*. Now when we look at the patient's speech on figure 4 we see a weak articulation of *g* followed by a normal vowel but no terminal consonant cluster. Instead there is a 0.3 sec gap of silence after which the patient starts over. But

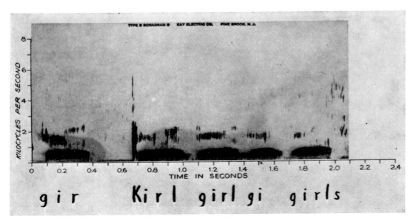

Fig. 4.   Abnormal speech. The patient cannot complete the word *girls*.

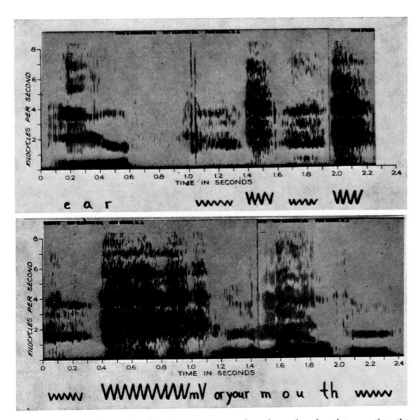

Fig. 5.   Abnormal speech, showing a pattern of prolonged noises interrupting the flow of words.

this time he produces an excessively hard attack that almost resembles the phoneme k. Again he almost completes the word, but not quite, and three more times he starts over. Only on the fifth try does the word come to termination with the pluralizing s. The patient whose spectrogram we see here is a 22-year-old man. His father died when the patient was only 4 years old, and while there are no neurological and electroencephalographic findings, his history points to serious disturbances in other areas of functioning in addition to speech. He has been quite obese, suffers from periodic depressions accompanied by violently sadistic fantasies, and engages in overtly homosexual behavior.

Figure 5 shows a spectrogram of another kind of disturbance. This patient's speech comes to a complete stop in the middle of a sentence. Then after a pause there is a sudden noise lasting for 0.3 sec followed by

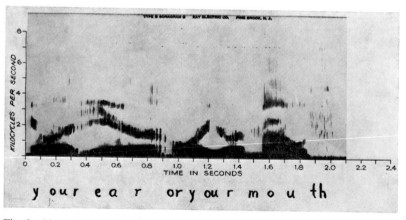

Fig. 6.   Normal speech of the same sentence shown in Fig. 5. Compare the duration and fluency of these two spectrograms.

a much louder noise of about 0.2 sec. This pattern of alternating soft and loud noises is repeated several times. Only after producing a segment of very loud noise lasting almost 0.75 sec does the patient again make word sounds. Normally this sequence of words would look like figure 6, showing that the phrase is completed without interruption in approximately 2 sec. The patient in figure 5 who takes twice as long to say the same thing is a 20-year-old man. He has suffered from paroxysms of muscular twitching, and uncontrollable, tic-like gyrations of the body since age 6 when he was struck by a car. The family history is replete with psychopathology and the patient's father also has a speech disturbance.

In the course of treatment the patient developed a full-blown paranoid illness during which his speech became normal and his bodily paroxysms almost completely subsided.

Finally we may inspect the spectrogram of a very peculiar sound-making disturbance (see Fig. 7). Except for an unusually high frequency

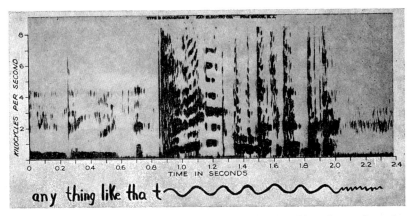

Fig. 7.   Abnormal speech, showing the interruption produced by a burst of pseudo-language.

level of the formants, the speech proceeds normally for 0.8 sec. Then there is a sudden explosion of noise followed by a series of rising formants which display a harmonic pattern going all the way up to 8000 c/s. This denotes a progressive elevation in pitch like one finds in a cry. The musical pattern stops for about 0.1 sec and then rapidly descends in pitch, followed by a series of short sonic bursts. Each of these has both formant and noise structure resembling normal speech, but the bursts do not fit the acoustic pattern of known words. Yet the silent spaces indicate that the patient is articulating these sounds, and at a rate that is much faster than her normal speech. The patient is a 59-year-old widow who started to make these and other strange noises several years ago after recovering from a paralysis of the right arm. Some of the sounds are accompanied by aggressive body thrusts and sexual gestures. She claims to have no control over this behavior and complains that her speech disturbance is very distressing to others. While psychological tests suggest organicity, neurological examination has been negative. Electroencephalograms made during her attacks show no clearcut seizure patterns, but some occasional slowing. We think she suffers from an adult variant of the GILLES DE LA TOURETTE syndrome.

Discussion

One can readily see how the visualization of speech disturbances helps one to understand what the patient is doing and assists in diagnostic work. This information about the phonetics of abnormal speech can be added to the clinical data of the patient's illness. In addition to this practical application, sound spectrography has been useful in research (Ostwald 1963). For example, we have used acoustic methods to study the cries of newborn babies and to compare the cries of identical twins with those of fraternal twins. We have acoustically studied voice changes associated with an experimental stress situation. The effects of electro-convulsive treatment and other therapies on the vocal behavior of acutely disturbed patients have also been investigated. Currently a study of acoustic correlates of mood change is in progress.

In terms of the theory of communication disturbances, it seems that the sound spectrograph helps to bridge the gap between speech physiology on the one hand and language coding on the other. The spectrograph makes a picture of the actual sound produced by the patient. This frees the investigator from having to use alphabetical symbols to refer to speech events. While alphabetical symbols are useful for reading and writing, they cannot possibly portray the speech act in its dynamic complexity. The sound spectrogram on the other hand gives a picture of the interlacing processes involved in speech. Several investigators are presently correlating spectrographic manifestations of soundmaking with X-ray pictures of the speech tract in action. This should provide very important knowledge about the etiology of speech disturbances and may even help to point the way towards more effective therapies.

Summary

This paper briefly presents four cases of speech disturbance and spectro-graphically illustrates the sounds emitted by the patients. It is felt that this way of objectifying the actual sounds produced by patients is a necessary step in the scientific analysis of communication disorders.

11

SPEECH DISTURBANCES IN A
SCHIZOPHRENIC ADOLESCENT*

Case report and spectrographic study

(with Alan Z. Skolnikoff)
(1966)

Speech and language rank among man's most important tools for coping with life's problems. In medical practice we often encounter disturbances of speech and language functions, either as primary communication defects which thwart social adaptation or as secondary symptoms of brain disease. Psychiatrists are concerned particularly with the primary communication defects, of which schizophrenia is one of the most common. The schizophrenic's peculiarly rambling sentences and inappropriate vocal inflections are among the easiest clinical signs to recognize, especially if the first contact with the patient is by telephone, when visual cues do not distract the physician. There may be other and more subtle auditory cues as well, and the purpose of this report is to describe these by means of speech spectrography, a method of acoustic analysis recently introduced into clinical psychiatry (Ostwald 1963).

Case report

A 15 year old male high school student had shown disturbed reactions to people since early childhood. He responded poorly to parental direction, and in school he had to be placed in special classes in spite of good intelligence, especially in mathematics. With the onset of puberty he became quite effeminate, behaved in a foolish and bizarre fashion toward others, and did his work slowly and compulsively. At home he often barricaded himself in his room and at one time became so aggressive toward his parents that they called the police to protect themselves.

The patient's physical development in infancy was normal. Shortly after his birth the mother again became pregnant, and when the boy was

---

* Reprinted from *Postgraduate Medicine* 40. 1: 40-49 (1966).

only 13 months old she left him with an older couple for three months. On entering nursery school he became asthmatic and allergic to flowers. At age nine he had several epileptiform convulsions of the jacksonian type which were easily controlled with anticonvulsants. His electroencephalogram, which had shown a spiking pattern in the left temporal lobe, returned to normal. During puberty a frightening fantasy world of ghosts and goblins began to haunt him. He became so engrossed in reading fiction that he would believe events in the story were happening to him. Subsequently he refused to read novels or short stories for fear of being caught in an unreal world.

When this patient was admitted to the hospital, examination revealed an overgrown, restless, gawky adolescent with unkempt hair and a rich stubble of beard. While walking he made bizarre jerking movements with his hands. To engage the attention of people he liked, he frequently thrust his face immediately in front of theirs instead of talking to them. The patient's speech was strikingly abnormal; his voice sounded nasal and indistinct. Poor breath control often left him gasping for air after he had exhaled before speaking. Articulation was also impaired and, because his mouth closed insufficiently, the consonants sounded mushy and unclear. He also occasionally drooled accumulated saliva.

The results of physical and neurologic examinations were normal. Psychologic tests failed to show any sign of organic brain disease but revealed clear-cut evidence of a severe schizophrenic thought disorder of a chronic nature. The electroencephalogram was normal.

To explore further this patient's speech disturbance, physical actions of his mouth and pharynx during speech and swallowing were studied with X-ray motion pictures made by Dr. Earl Miller of the Radiological Research Laboratory, University of California School of Medicine, San Francisco. The lips and tongue operated normally. At times the soft palate did not completely close off the nasopharynx, resulting in a fuzzy nasal sound. But at other times the patient seemed able to control his speech and, during diagnostic examination by a speech therapist, he performed almost normally. In his daily conversation with other people the patient was generally difficult to understand; we therefore concluded this to be a part of a schizophrenic pattern of communication.

Spectrographic study of speech disturbance

We tape-recorded the patient's speech during six clinical interviews and analyzed the tapes with a sound spectrograph. This instrument converts

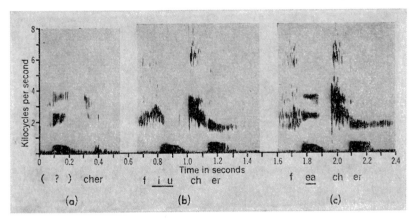

Fig. 1.   Comparison of a word spoken by the patient (a) with similar words spoken by normal persons (b and c) shows a lack of proper acoustic cues for identifying the patient's vowel sounds, particularly in the first syllable.

speech sounds into visible patterns that can be scanned repeatedly and studied in detail. The resulting spectrograms show the tone-frequency patterns vertically and the time pattern horizontally. The loudness intensity of sounds is denoted by degrees of darkness on the 'visible speech' tracings.

Example 1. It was difficult to identify certain of the patient's vowel sounds; consequently the words containing these unidentifiable vowels often could not be understood. Figure 1a shows a word uttered by the patient which sounded like *preacher*, but according to the meaning of the sentence could not possibly have been *preacher*. Actually the patient was trying to say *future*.

When a normal speaker utters the word *future* (Fig. 1b), it has a more distinctive physical acoustic shape. There is a diphthong, a sound that changes from one vowel to another, after the initial consonant *f*. This diphthong is made up of a sound like *i* (as in *pit*) followed by *u* (as in *school*). Because the initial consonant merges with the vowel, one cannot see clearly the beginning sound of the *i*. But one can see clearly the shift from the *i*, which carries energy at 300 and 2000 cycles per second, to the *u*, which carries energy only at 300 cycles per second. These energy-carrying bands are referred to as 'formants'.

A comparison of normally spoken *future* (Fig. 1b) with normally spoken *feature*, the word shown spectrographically in figure 1c, demonstrates that the latter contains the characteristic acoustic structure of *ee* as in *eat*, which is very different from the diphthong *iu*. The *ee* formants

146   ACOUSTIC DENOTATION OF HUMAN SOUNDS

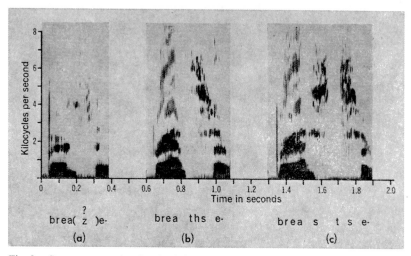

Fig. 2.   Spectrograms showing indistinct consonants uttered by the patient. It was difficult to decide whether the patient's word (a) was intended to be *breaths* (b) or *breasts* (c).

occur at 300, 2500 and 3700 cycles per second. Now we see why the patient's utterance in figure 1a was so unclear. First of all there is an almost total absence of sound above 4000 cycles (4 kilocycles). This means that the frictional noises enabling us to recognize consonants, in this case *f* and *ch*, were missing. Also, the vowel formant at 2000 cycles kept changing position, preventing the listener from knowing whether he was to hear *ee* or *iu*.

Example 2. It also was difficult to identify some of the patient's consonant sounds. Added to the ambiguity of his vowels – as shown in example 1 – this consonant dyslalia led to all kinds of misunderstandings. For example, figure 2a shows an utterance of the patient which sounded like *brea(z)*, taken from the sentence *they have to take brea(z) every little while*. The part in parentheses sounded vaguely like the consonant *z* as in *zebra*. There was insufficient acoustic distinctiveness to make it sound like a normally spoken word such as *breaths* (Fig. 2b) or *breasts* (Fig. 2c). (All three spectrograms include part of the next word, the *e* of *every*.) In the context of the conversation, *brea(z)* made no sense whatever, and even repeated listening to the tape recording did not reveal what the patient was trying to say. However, he later produced a clarifying statement, *We have to breathe every little while*, which dispelled the possibility he had been referring to a delusional idea regarding *breasts*.

Example 3. When a listener lets such a patient know that he cannot be

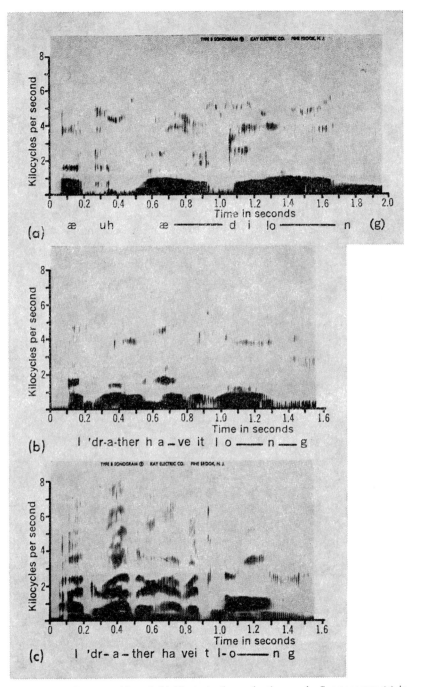

Fig. 3. Spectrograms (a) and (b) illustrate the patient's speech. Spectrogram (c) is that of a normal person saying the same sentence as that shown in (b). Note the absence of distinctive acoustic features in the patient's speech, particularly the poor quality of his vowel formants (resonance-energy bands) and lack of clearly articulated stop consonants.

understood, the patient, instead of clarifying his speech, often modifies the word structure of the sentence, continuing nevertheless to produce sounds that are difficult to decipher. Again the listener must rely on the context of the conversation to derive the intended meaning. In this instance the patient was discussing the problem of getting a haircut. He uttered the almost totally unintelligible phrase illustrated in figure 3a, which sounded something like *I'd rather 'twould be long*. After the listener indicated he could not understand, the patient said, *I'd rather have it long*. Figure 3b shows that this utterance has the same poorly differentiated phonetic pattern as the first, with the exception that the sounds were now produced somewhat more briskly. But a comparison of this with a normal speaker's utterance of *I'd rather have it long* (Fig. 3c) shows that in the normal speech all the sounds can be identified. What helps is that the stop consonants *d* and *t* momentarily interrupt the outflow of sound and that the vowels have their typical formant structures. The patient's

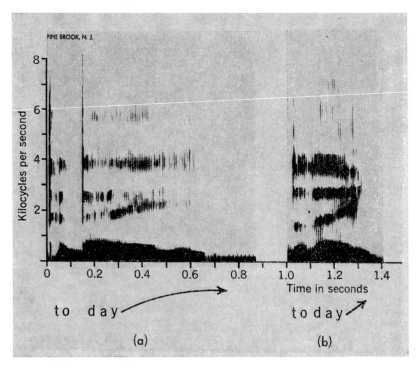

Fig. 4a.   Elongation of patient's terminal vowel sounds produced a baby-like pleading sound at the end of questions. (b) The same question as spoken by a normal person.

spectrogram (Fig. 3b) lacks these distinctive features. The sound flowed out almost entirely without interruption by stop consonants, and the vowels lacked precise formant structure.

Example 4. The patient's speech demonstrated an exaggerated intonation pattern, an inappropriately high and prolonged rise of the voice, especially at the end of questions where normally the rise in voice is brief. Figure 4a shows the final word of a question ending with *today*. By the upward intonation the patient produced a pleading sound which indicated that he wanted something very badly. This intonational pleading was reminiscent of the demand behavior of children between one and two years of age when they pull someone's arm, stomp on the floor, or whine to emphasize the urgency of wishes which cannot yet be expressed in words. Compare this with the same word spoken at the end of a question by a normal speaker, figure 4b.

Example 5. This same dyscontrol could also be seen as a terminal 'dribbling out' of sounds at the end of sentences. Figure 5 shows the words *the end*. Instead of really stopping after *end* the patient continued to make a sound lasting one and a half seconds. This was a predominantly breathy sound, with large amounts of noise between 4 and 7 kilocycles imposed on formants at 500 and 1700 cycles that caused the sound to resemble the vowel *e* as in *yet*. This noise-vowel combination sounded something like *hehehe*, suggesting a mirthless laugh. Neither the content of the patient's speech nor his facial expressions suggested laughter at this point. Clinically one received the impression of 'inappropriate affect'.

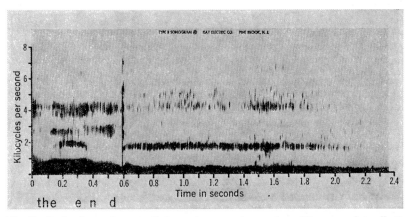

Fig. 5.   Patient's poorly controlled speech gave an impression of 'inappropriate affect'. His mouth did not remain closed after finishing the word *end* and a mirthless laughlike sound persisted for almost two seconds.

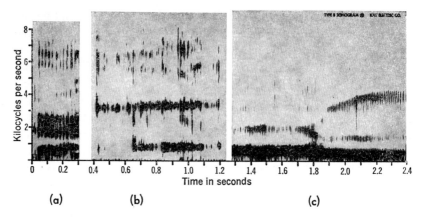

Fig. 6.   Spectrograms of noises produced by the patient at times of great emotional tension or excitement: a rasp (a), a froglike *squeak squawk* (b), and a growl that sounded like *aw-er* (c).

The spectrogram shows how this disturbance in affective display arose from the patient's poorly controlled speech behavior.

Example 6. There were times of emotional expression when the patient abandoned speech altogether and produced a great variety of oral sounds and noises which were not words at all. Figure 6 illustrates a number of these nonverbal sonic manifestations. The spectrogram shows loud screeching rasps (Fig. 6a) emitted during a phase of motor excitement and aggressive grimacing while the patient acted in a foolish manner, refusing to answer a question and poking fun at the interviewer. This screeching rasp resembled sounds birds use to communicate (Lanyon and Tavolga 1960).

Figure 6b shows another animal-like sound. This was a peculiar *squeak squawk* that started on a very high tone and after about 0.2 second turned into a lower-pitched sound with formant components at 1000 and 3500 cycles. This sounded like a frog. The noise occurred during a phase of intense exasperation when the patient adamantly refused to engage in any verbal communication. He had been upset by events in the ward and his behavior generally was more slovenly and negativistic than usual.

Figure 6c shows a growling sound which began with a very intense *aw* vocalization that turned at 1.8 second into the sound *er*. This, too, was an expression of angry resentment and represented a negativistic turning away from speech.

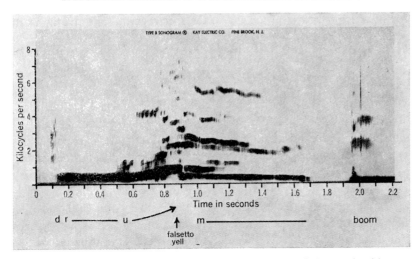

Fig. 7. Illustration of patient's attempt to fuse verbal linguistic speech with non-verbal prelinguistic behavior. The patient first vigorously yelled the word *drum*, then repeatedly said *boom-boom-boom* while striking his body as if he were both drum and drummer. Spectrograms shows only the first *boom*.

Because babies before they learn to speak make sounds and noises that are not dictionary words, the patient's behavior was interpreted as a sign of regression to an infantile pattern of soundmaking. At the same time, his growling, squawking and screeching were a form of imitative behavior, much like that of a young child playfully imitating animals, automobiles and other noisy objects.

Example 7. There was an intermediate phenomenon between speech and nonverbal noisemaking when the patient fused emotive noises with words. These noise-word mixtures were more than just playful episodes of animal sound that interrupted the stream of talk. We now heard a more bizarre, annoying, overloud kind of acoustic behavior in marked contrast to the indistinct, low-intensity, faulty speech which is described in examples 1 and 2.

Figure 7 illustrates the word *drum*. The patient dragged this out over a period of 1.6 second, which is about four times as long as normal. In the middle of it, during the vowel, the patient embarked on a 0.2 second yell, the falsetto configuration of which strikingly resembled the acoustic structure of a baby's cry. It was not possible to interpret the significance of this behavior from acoustic cues alone; visual observation of the patient was also necessary. He struck his body with his fists as if he himself were a drum. Indeed, a series of imitative *boom-boom-boom* utterances, one of which is shown at the end of the spectrogram, followed the word *drum*.

Etiologic and therapeutic implications

Two conditions must be met for a child to learn normal speech. First, his brain has to be capable of correctly receiving, storing and integrating information based on auditory input. Second, he must be exposed to a speaking environment and encouraged to speak during the critical formative years of early childhood. Of particular importance for learning speech is the period from 9 to 18 months of age, during which meaningless babbling begins to change into comprehensible words (Bullowa et al. 1964). At this time the baby starts to recognize and produce what linguists call 'distinctive features', i.e., minimal differences between speech sounds. For example, the baby learns to distinguish *d* from *t* because *t* is accompanied by a slight burst of air while *d* is not. To make the sound *oh* he purses his lips in order to distinguish it from *ah*. If the growing child cannot hear the distinctive features of speech or does not learn to reproduce them, his soundmaking will remain undifferentiated and rudimentary, and listeners will have difficulty in understanding what he says.

The patient described had this problem. His sounds lacked certain distinctive features (examples 1, 2 and 3) and he persisted in producing infantile sound elements which normally are abandoned in kindergarten (examples 4 through 7).

How can this communication defect be explained? One turns first to a neurologic conjecture: Possibly the left-cerebral pathologic condition which in adolescence produced right-sided jacksonian seizures had earlier in life impaired the patient's ability to learn to speak. Slater, Beard and Glithero (1963) have suggested that epilepsy, especially in cases in which the electroencephalogram demonstrates foci in the temporal lobe, may be causally related to schizophrenic disorders. After studying over 800 persons with brain injuries, Luria (1958) concluded that left temporal lesions cause a breakdown in auditory perception of the distinctive features, impairing a patient's ability to recognize and reproduce speech sounds.

Psychologic considerations suggest a second possibility in the case under consideration. Through separation from his mother at 13 months of age, the patient may have lost vital encouragement to communicate. Clinical studies of emotionally deprived children (Spitz 1945) as well as laboratory experiments with monkeys (Harlow and Harlow 1962) have demonstrated clearly the disastrous consequences of depriving babies of maternal love. Also, the presence of a newborn sibling in his environment after the mother returned home may have reduced the patient's incentive to learn. Only 16 months old and yearning for his mother's love, the boy witnessed how effectively cries, screams, burps and other nonlinguistic noises evoked maternal concern. At the very time that he should have been exposed to and practicing linguistically more distinctive sounds, his attention was repeatedly drawn to the infantile sounds of a newborn rival to which his mother in her postpartum state of auditory hyperacusis was particularly responsive. In raising her two children, the mother undoubtedly was compelled to compromise between the patient's requirements for learning to speak and the new baby's need for nonverbal communication (Ruesch 1957).

Treating the behavior of this schizophrenic adolescent required caution to prevent a sudden awareness of his 'deficiencies' in speech and other social skills from flooding him with acute feelings of intense depression or panic. He had already developed a compensatory talent, excellence in mathematics, which enabled him to do fairly well at school as long as the other students and teachers tolerated his behavior. An institutional night-care program provided him with more supervision and greater structuring of the environment than could have been possible in the patient's own home.

This patient also needs group therapy and speech training. When his speech has become more comprehensible and he has achieved greater emotional stability, individual psychotherapy of the 'talking out' kind will help him to tolerate both the pleasures and the frustrations that attend long-term human relationships. Hopefully he will then be able to resume a place in society, to work productively, and perhaps to marry and raise a family.

Summary

This article demonstrates in detail some of the speech abnormalities produced by a schizophrenic adolescent. The patient, a 15 year old male high school student, showed behavioral deviations in very early childhood and had several epileptiform convulsions at age nine. Sound X-ray motion pictures revealed no structural pathologic abnormality of the speech tract. Sound spectrograms showed that his words lacked distinctive phonetic features, with the result that the patient's speech was often unintelligible. Dyscontrol over speech functions was especially evident at the end of sentences. The spectrograms also showed a propensity for noise-making and demonstrated the fusion of linguistic behavior with prelinguistic behavior.

Organic and psychologic elements in causation of this patient's speech disturbance are discussed, with particular emphasis on the possibility of temporal lobe damage plus maternal deprivation. The patient responded well to psychiatric treatment. He continues to live in an institutional setting while attending school during the day and requires further speech therapy as well as psychotherapy.

SECTION III

LISTENING – THE PERCEPTUAL EXPERIENCE OF SOUND

INTRODUCTORY STATEMENT

Auditory behavior encompasses a number of patterns which, while dissectable for scientific purposes, are really interdependent and coordinated parts of a listener's experience. First is his readiness to take-in sounds, what the physiologist calls AUDITION. This requires a physical mechanism for sound reception – i.e. external-ear canals, middle-ear bony structures, and inner-ear cochlear apparatuses for transducing acoustical energy into neuronal signals. Next is the listener's ability to orient himself to sounds, what the psychologist calls ATTENTION. The neural linkages between cochlea and brain have to be given a certain priority in order that external acoustical stimuli achieve conscious recognition as sound. Finally there is the listener's willingness to commit himself as to the meanings of sounds, what the semiotician calls INTER-PRETATION. Auditory information processed by the brain has to be evaluated and categorized according to immediacies of social existence, the varied experiences of the past, and the anticipation of a future which seems relevant to the listener. Naturally the three aspects of listening – audition, attention, and interpretation – do not necessarily occur in this sequence. For example, the interpretative functions of listening may already be strikingly active before any acoustical information is processed. This is the expectation which for example enables a person to 'hear' something before it happens.

The papers in Section III all deal in one way or another with auditory perception. The opening paper, 12, was written for a symposium on Experimental Psychopathology held at the Third World Congress of Psychiatry, in Montreal, Canada, 1961. It reviews the information then available about effects of four types of sound – (1) words, (2) music, (3) noise, (4) body sounds – and of course the emphasis is on psycho-pathology. One of my interests at the time was to explore the specifically

noxious and therapeutic possibilities of acoustical stimulation. Originally
this paper had a second section dealing with some clinical experiments in
which patients could select different kinds of sounds, or were asked to
describe what they felt after exposure to certain kinds of sounds.

Two of these experiments are described in papers 13 and 15. They deal
with noise and music respectively. Paper 13 was designed to comment
on the problem of noise from a psychopathological point of view, i.e.
the abnormal aversive reactions to sounds that some individuals complain
of while by and large the same sounds are tolerated by the rest of society.
The observations and conclusions described in this paper should obviously not be used to argue simply that people who object to noise are in
some way deviant or exceptional persons. On the contrary, I am very
much in sympathy with the idea that noise is rapidly becoming a sort of
'environmental pollutant', especially in cities and industrial areas where
levels of noise are steadily increasing (Welch and Welch 1970).

Music ought to be easier to tolerate than noise, but paradoxically many
people describe a new musical composition they don't like or understand
as 'noise'. This happened to Beethoven and Wagner just as it's happening
to some of the innovative composers today. The problem is further
complicated by the fact that a number of contemporary composers have
used tape-recorded machine-racket, tire-squeals, cocktail-party conversation and other noises as part of their musical compositions. There is also
the problem of temporary threshold shifts in audition resulting from
exposure to loud rock 'n roll music (Dey 1970). While the musician and
listener might say the experience is pleasurable, a more 'objective'
approach claims that what is listened to is dangerous noise.

Since I am both a practicing musician and a practicing psychiatrist, I
am occasionally consulted about such questions. My first opportunity
to make a public statement about music came in 1960, when the American
Association of Music Therapists had its annual meeting in San Francisco.
Paper 14 is the result of that, and serves as a general introduction to the
subject of music and human emotion which is such a vital topic in the
semiotics of sound. Paper 15 discusses 'background' music, which for
many people is a mixed blessing when piped into elevators, buses, or
hotel lobbies. Paper 16 is a very succinct statement of my views in 1965
about music and emotions, delivered as part of a session on "Arts and
Humanities" during the American Psychiatric Association Conference
in New York City. This session featured a good deal of actual musical
performance and, like all nonverbal matters, is impossible to translate
into exact word equivalents. Because I believe that musical enjoyment

is part of a social experience and that the musician is the carrier of a specific kind of tradition in any culture, I wrote an essay about the music lesson which appears here as paper 17.

Paper 18 which closes Section III moves back into the field of psychopathology. It is the case study of a patient with audio-visual synthesia which can be a perfectly normal phenomenon in childhood. Like the subjective experience of listening, the subjective experience of visualizing is difficult to describe. One is forced to use words which, unless one has the gift of a poet, cannot always approximate the sensory meanings. Manfred Clynes has written about this problem in terms of bio-cybernetics, and I would like to recommend one of his papers (Clynes 1969) to the interested reader.

12

BEHAVIOR CHANGES
PRODUCED BY SELECTED ACOUSTIC STIMULI*

(1961)

Most experimental and therapeutic procedures in psychiatry incidentally serve to organize the acoustic environment of patients. Hypnosis, for example, focusses auditory attention upon significant words and human body sounds (Kubie and Margolin 1944; Trojan 1960); psychoanalysis encourages the production of emotionally meaningful words and noises (Scott 1958); milieu, conditioning, and re-educative therapies all make use of repetitive verbal and nonverbal acoustic stimuli (Cameron 1956; Ostwald 1960b). Can systematic manipulation of the acoustic environment be used as a PRIMARY technique for influencing human behavior? The purpose of this paper is to explore this question through a review of available knowledge.

Within the context of human behavior, four types of acoustic stimuli regularly produce changes in human behavior: These have been called (1) words, (2) music, (3) noise, and (4) body sounds.

Words

Definition: Words are acoustic symbols whose meaning is shared by at least two persons, a speaker and a listener (Skinner 1957).

(a) Isolated Words

In psychiatry isolated words are used primarily within the framework of psychological testing, specifically in the form of word-association tests (Rapaport 1946). The listener is instructed to utter the first word which

* This study was supported (in part) by grant T-59-144 from the Foundation's Fund for Research in Psychiatry. Presented in The Section on Experimental Psychopathology, Third World Congress of Psychiatry, Montreal, Canada, June 6, 1961.

is brought to his mind as the result of the acoustic stimulus. This is a useful way to quickly disclose areas of thinking which are dominated by conflict (Jung 1910), to elicit bizarre ideation, or to evaluate the patient's capacities for reality-testing (Weinstein and Kahn 1955).

A modification of the word-association technique involves presenting stimulus words at sound-intensity levels below the auditory threshold for tone-recognition, or in the presence of wide-band masking noise (which in effect raises the threshold) (Tanner 1958). This makes it possible to show how a stimulus word not only influences output behavior, but also affects input behavior in the sense that the meaning of the word contributes to its audibility. For example, Dixon demonstrated that words with sexual meaning have a tendency to stimulate symbolic associations even when presented "below awareness threshold" (Dixon 1956). Beech reported that "sex" words presented 5 decibels below the 1000 cps threshold to a woman suffering from anorexia nervosa led to significantly more "food" responses than did "neutral" stimuli (Beech 1959). These and similar observations have necessitated reformulation of the auditory threshold concept in more dynamic terms; a recent version of auditory theory postulates a hierarchy of mental criterion levels which determine the making of decisions that account for the threshold process (Green 1960).

'Four-letter' words deserve special mention as verbal stimuli because of their capacity to evoke explosive emotional discharge. Characteristically composed of a short vocalic phoneme sandwiched between two consonantal sounds, these words are often echoic substitutes for physiologic body sounds (Wentworth and Flexner 1960). The sudden release of tension brought about by such words has been compared to similar phenomena in tic-states and epileptic seizures (Hollander 1960).

(b)   Organized Word Patterns

Words strung together into sentence chains influence each other according to rules inherent in the grammar of the language (Halle 1959): Information carried by single words is modified, repeated and reinforced so that listener resistance and channel noise may be overcome (Shannon and Weaver 1949). In addition, the effects of organized word patterns depend on assumptions about language shared by speaker and listener. Thus words can be used both to inform and confuse, to satisfy and frustrate, to please and annoy (Ruesch 1957).

One way to neutralize this ambivalent function of words is through incessant repetition, as employed in certain forms of indoctrination, advertising, and psychotherapy. Repetition wipes out subtleties of meaning, reduces words to a sequence of noises, and elicits crude emotional reactions. This technique has been used to 'drive' unwanted information into the ears of patients. According to Cameron, chronic neurotic attitudes are thereby brought to awareness, anxiety is stirred up, and a realignment of defenses including ruminative preoccupation with the acoustic 'implant' may take place. In resistant cases repetition produces unbearable tension, attempts to escape from the situation, or a kind of projection whereby the patient hears only what he wants to hear (Cameron 1956).

(c) Paralinguistic Speech Sounds

Paradoxical changes in behavior produced by verbal stimuli have led to the recognition of two sets of acoustic signal systems in speech: One serves to identify the words, the other provides instructions as to interpretation. The latter set of acoustic stimuli is called paralinguistic; it comprises tempo-changes, register shifts, and alterations in tone-color of the voice (Pittenger et al. 1960). The effects of para-linguistic sounds have been of interest to poets and orators for centuries (Ostwald 1960a). Increased tempo, intensity, and pitch arouse attention, while decrease accomplishes the opposite; regular rhythms and low, pure tones are soothing, whereas choppy rhythm and harsh vocalization stimulates excitement (Trojan 1960). Vocal cues also provide speech with punctuation analogous to signs like commas, question-marks, and quotation-marks in written discourse. When these acoustic punctuation signs are incorrectly used, as by schizophrenic children (Goldfarb et al. 1956) the listener cannot place subjects, verbs, objects and other parts of a sentence in proper relation to each other. Quantitative changes in the use of paralinguistic sounds have also been reported: depressed patients omit some of the crucial dynamic accents, and hysterics clutter their speech with nonverbal gasps (Moses 1954). These symptoms make it difficult for the listener to tell whether the patient's words are meant to be denotative, expressive, or appealing (Buehler 1934).

Music

Definition: Music is nonverbal sound that has been patterned into units of relatively long duration by composers or entertainers.

(a)   The Ingredients of Music

Musical patterns are produced when the basic dimensions of sound (time, frequency, and intensity) are systematically manipulated. These manipulations result in subjective experiences called rhythmic, tonal, and dynamic (Ostwald 1960d).

RHYTHM experience results from contrast between accented and unaccented sound, between sound and silence, and between repetitive tonal patterns (Sachs 1953). In some manner that is not yet understood, musical rhythm gives the listener an external frame of reference with which he may consciously or unconsciously couple various rhythmical activities of his body, such as foot-tapping, walking, head-nodding, arm-waving, or dancing (Farnsworth 1958). Autonomic effects of music have also been reported (Stovkis 1958); Shatin showed that chronic schizophrenic patients have a significantly higher pulse rate in the presence of rhythmic sounds than without this stimulus (Shatin 1957).

TONE experience results from relatively discrete localization of energy along the audible acoustic spectrum, which is generally held to be between 20 and 20,000 cycles per second. Among babies the range of audibility goes much higher, and with age it is considerably reduced; females have a larger auditory range at all ages than do males (Corso 1959). Persons with so-called absolute pitch can identify tones from their vibration frequency. More commonly, tones are remembered in terms of melodic, less frequently harmonic, context (Revesz 1954). Tonal memories are apparently stored in discrete areas of the cerebral cortex where they are linked to recoverable somesthetic, visual, verbal, and situational engrams (Penfield and Roberts 1959). Not infrequently an isolated tonal pattern comes into consciousness having lost its direct memory associations, similar to the way dissociated verbal fragments may appear in obsessions, dreams, and fantasies (Sterba 1946). Tonal patterns may also undergo condensation, reversal, rotation, and other structural changes before they reach consciousness (Friedman 1960).

A significant part of the tone experience has to do with tone-quality, which is a function of the harmonic wave-form character of the acoustic stimulus. As far back as Pythagorean science it was recognized that certain harmonic patterns are inherently pleasing while others tend to be innately ugly. But clear neurophysiological correlates for these judgments have not yet been established (Galambos 1954).

DYNAMIC experience stems from fluctuations in the intensity of the acoustic stimulus pattern; vibration frequency is also a factor since the auditory threshold is lower for vibrations between 1000 and 5000 cycles per second than for other frequencies (Beranek 1954). The effects of acoustic intensity on the human listener will be discussed in connection with the subject of noise.

(b)   The Social Function of Music

Since music is used primarily for entertainment its effects are difficult to investigate scientifically. By and large the single most demonstrable result of music is enjoyment. From time immemorial music has been associated with festivities, dancing, and ceremony (Ostwald 1960b); even today's 'age of anxiety' sees people attending jazz and opera, buying phonograph records, and operating juke-boxes with an enthusiasm equaled only by Old's self-stimulating rats (Olds 1956). Among contemporary studies of this phenomenon only those by Langer, Kohut, and Ehrenzweig can be mentioned here. Langer (1942) attributes the enjoyment of music to man's innate desire to symbolize; she thinks of musical activity as the most suitable way to communicate ABOUT the emotions. Kohut (1957) finds that music facilitates regression, thereby allowing preverbal tensions to be released without disturbing more archaic object cathexes. Ehrenzweig (1953) sees music as communication between the unconscious of the musician and that of the listener; for this to succeed, both participants must understand the form elements of music, which, like a code, disguises the unconscious message it transmits.

Without doubt music is also an important factor in stimulating what is called the spiritual side of the human psyche. It is often used in conjunction with prayer, mourning, and solitude. Many persons consider music to be uniquely soothing in times of anguish or confusion. Music has also been introduced into factories, offices, stores, and lobbies as a booster of morale. Several studies show music to increase the work output of individuals and groups, but this effect may actually be the result of general improvement in work conditions such as higher wages, cleaner lavatories, or friendlier supervision (Diserens 1926). Some studies indicate that music stimulates motor activity (Shatin 1957), but failure to rule out paramusical factors make these investigations scientifically suspect.

The therapeutic use of music is similarly difficult to evaluate; for many years the emphasis was on developing a musical pharmacopoeia, but little more was accomplished than to vaguely divide musical compositions into soothing and exciting ones (Schullian and Schoen 1948). Lately more attention has been paid to the variable effects of different musical instruments, such as the cello (Alvin 1960), hand bells (Brunner-Orne 1958) or piano (Sherwin 1953). As with most therapies, success with music seems largely to be a function of the therapist's personal magnetism and devotion. The best results are reported by those who not only perform very well on their instruments but also have a clear under-standing of the patient's emotional problems (Sherwin 1958; Tilly 1948).

Reports have recently appeared about the anesthetic effects of acoustic stimulation; a device for delivering mixtures of music and noise to patients via earphones is available for dentists (Gardner and Licklider 1960). According to investigations recently conducted by Borland, these effects are due primarily to suggestion, auditory stimulation being a factor which promotes the necessary hypnoidal state (Borland n.d.).

Noise

Definition: Acoustically speaking, noise is unwanted sound (C. M. Harris 1957); within the wider context of information-theory, noise refers to interference with communication (Shannon and Weaver 1949).

(a)   Stressful Noise

Whether noise can produce physical stress in the form of pain and organic damage depends among other things on the intensity-level at which it reaches the listener (Davis 1951). According to Parrack's recent review, acoustic stimuli whose sound pressure level exceeds 120 decibels re 0.0002 microbar lead to unpleasant auditory sensations like pressure, pain, and tickling. Prolonged exposure results in varying degrees of temporary deafness and may lead to irreversible elevations of the hearing threshold if the cochlea and other inner-ear structures are damaged. Noise above 110 decibels may also affect the vibratory receptors of the skin, giving the false sensation that one stands on something which vibrates. Noise above 135 decibels affects the vestibular apparatus leading to a loss of space orientation. At 140 decibels, particularly when composed of low-frequency elements, noise affects the abdominal and thoracic walls, with the result that the subject feels nauseated and may vomit. Noise of 145 decibels and higher affects the stretch receptors of muscles, joints and tendons, interfering with proprioception and precision movements of the limbs. Skin heat receptors are activated by noise at levels above 150 decibels producing "heat pain" (Parrack 1961). At ultrasonic levels, 50,000 cycles per second and up, noise heats up tissue, can produce skin burns, and may damage deeper tissues by depolymerizing long protein chains. Few studies are yet available about the effects of stressful noises on human adaptation over long periods of time. Poor morale, fatigue, psychosomatic symptoms, and absenteeism are mentioned by persons who are exposed to high-intensity noise around jet airplanes and power-machines, but psychological factors in these reactions have not yet been fully investigated (Broadbent 1957).

(b)   Annoying Noise

In addition to being stressful, noise is annoying. A number of investigators attribute this primarily to the fact that noise can interfere with verbal communication. For example, Kryter showed conversational speech to involve a dynamic intensity range of 30 decibels. To speak intelligibly in the presence of continuous noise, a speaker is forced to work harder; to be heard, he must emit sound that is at least 18 decibels more intense than the noise. The listener also has to work harder in noise, since his masked auditory threshold goes up linearly as the intensity level of the noise rises (Kryter 1950).

A second explanation for annoyance comes from the fact that noise reduces auditory self-perception. Feedback mechanisms are interfered with when one cannot hear one's own sounds, and this leads to various forms of decompensation (Chase et al. 1959). Speech becomes retarded, blocked, slurred, and repetitious, and the subject feels frustrated and grimaces when he does not immediately hear what he says (Black 1951). Mahl, using a 93 decibel white noise to block self-corrective feedback, noted changes in both form and content of speech: the normal rhythm and intonation patterns were lost, and speakers produced unusual noises. They also laughed aggressively and erotically, and revealed information which ordinarily would not be divulged (Mahl 1960). Goldfarb produced aggressive behavior, panic reactions, and acute paranoid states in schizo-phrenic children by interfering with their auditory feedback (Goldfarb and Braunstein 1958).

Finally, annoyance can be traced to unacceptable meanings which one consciously or unconsciously attributes to noise (Ostwald 1961b). Being a relatively formless acoustic stimulus, noise frustrates the listener's demand for precise informative cues from the external environment. Like a person whose hearing is impaired, the listener to noise projects various imaginary and autistic interpretations which may disturb him (Davis and Silverman 1960). Attempts were made during World War II to use this principle in order to produce casualties among combat troops. Noises like the whining of bombs, shooting of guns, and screams of the wounded were found to produce anxiety and collapse. This only occurred among inexperienced and immature personnel however, and no methods were successfully devised for delivering such noises to an enemy at sufficiently high sound levels (Burris-Meyer and Mallory 1960).

Body sounds

Definition: Body sounds convey information directly, without recourse to symbols. Only within recent years has objective study through tape-recording of body sounds become possible (Tembrock 1959); hence many of these sounds are not yet labelled.

(a) Animal Sounds

The sounds of insects, fishes, frogs, bats, birds, and some mammals have been studied, and it is possible to show that specific body sounds are related to food, enemies, sexual behavior, parent-young relationships, and group movements (Lanyon and Tavolga 1961). Animals make sounds to inform each other of danger, to signal the availability of food and shelter, as a means of releasing species-appropriate behavior in partner or group, and for unknown reasons. For human behavior, animal sounds play a significant role in folklore, myths, and fairy tales. Individuals deprived of meaningful human contacts may also turn to animals, whose sounds then become an expressive and possibly a denotative language. Searles has described the animal sounds of certain regressed schizophrenic patients who bark, cackle, squeal, and yelp (Searles 1960).

(b) Human Body Sounds

A hypothesis for the transmissibility of emotions with body sounds is that these are informative cues which occupy a mid-point between words and noises. Without losing his foothold in the realm of verbal discourse which makes use of discrete, sequential signals, the listener to body sounds circumvents many of the decision-making steps involved in digital decoding (Ruesch 1955). Yet he also avoids the ambiguity that results from the reception of a continuous stream of nonverbal signals like hand gestures, facial grimaces, or uninterrupted noise. Body sounds tend to convey sufficient information to enable the listener to establish a rough idea about the sender's age, sex, habitus, physical condition, and emotional state, but they do not clarify details of the sender's past history or his present trends of thought.

Among the first human body sounds to be investigated were those used for medical diagnosis, like breathing and the heart-beat. A study of respiratory sounds by Kubie and Margolin showed them to have a hypnotic effect when amplified and returned to the ears of the breather and other listeners (Kubie and Margolin 1944). Clinicians also observed that panting produces anxiety (Moses 1954) and that breathiness tends to convey a sense of intimacy (Pittenger et al. 1960). Wheezing seems to stimulate protective parental activity; it is often used by asthmatics as a distorted means of expressing oral aggressive needs (Knapp and Nemetz 1957). The heart-beat is thought by some to contribute to the sense of rhythm (Hodgson 1951). Greene suggests that when the human fetus becomes responsive to the vibratory if not the auditory aspects of acoustic stimuli, regularly recurring sounds of the mother's body including the heart-beat might serve as a kind of protective barrier against erratic external noises (Greene 1958). Salk claims that the behavior and development of newborn babies can be influenced by exposing them to tape-recorded heart-beats in the nursery; he found that in comparison to a control group the infants in the sound-exposed group showed a significant increase in body weight, greater regularity and depth of respiration, less restlessness, fewer respiratory and gastro-intestinal upsets, and a significant reduction of crying (Salk 1960).

Gastro-intestinal sounds attract listener attention to specific parts of the sound-maker's anatomy and physiology; this has been held to be of importance in the direct or vicarious gratification of biologic needs (Scott 1958). Infants instinctively make smacking sounds with the mouth and lips when they want to be fed (Lewis 1936). Many of these sounds later drop out of the child's repertory under pressure of linguistic demands, but may return during states of emotional or organic illness (Ostwald 1961a). Burping is a post-prandial sound which Western adults inhibit except in certain group settings where it produces laughter, surprise, pleasure, and other positive discharge emotions. This may be due in part to its ambiguous resemblance to flatus. Anal noises, also originally produced in the nursery, call attention to defecation and are associated with the disemboguement of odors. Mixed pleasure, disgust, and other affective states are aroused in the listener, whose reactions vary accordingly (Merrill 1952). The sense of discomfort and anger which stutterers produce in themselves and listeners by expelling sphincter-like speech sounds may also be due, at least in part, to the resemblance that these acoustic stimuli bear to infantile anal and oral noises (Glauber 1958). An intimate relationship between the sounds of urination and human auditory responsivity has often been noted (Van der Heide 1941), but no comprehensive study of this phenomenon is yet available. An anatomical investigation by Hilson suggests that the development of the ear and the urogenital tract may in some way be inter-related (Hilson 1957). Conditioning factors due to the coincidence of water sounds with toilet training seem more plausible, however.

A number of body sounds are derived from or represent exaggerations of the vocal and articulatory processes of speech. Whistling serves to attract attention to the sound-maker and expresses a 'keep calm' attitude (Ostwald 1959). Humming produces oral pleasure and also screens out external stimuli (Ostwald 1961c). *Ah, er, uh,* and other hesitation sounds indicate that the speaker experiences anxiety or conflict (Mahl 1956).

Summary

This paper is concerned with information about the effects of four kinds of sound: (1) WORDS, which codify specific mental data, (2) MUSIC, which is pleasurable sound patterned into relatively long time units, (3) NOISE, defined as unwanted, stressful, or annoying sound, and (4) BODY SOUNDS, which directly convey information about biologic needs without recourse to verbal symbols.

13

PSYCHOPATHOLOGIC MECHANISMS IN
AVERSIVE RESPONSES TO NOISE*

(1961)

Recent years have witnessed a striking increase in the amount of noise produced in our society. Aviation and rocketry have brought noise into hitherto quiet suburbs (Von Gierke 1957), composers of classical music are using noise in the concert hall (Hodeir 1961), and dentists employ noise in an effort to reduce pain (Gardner and Licklider 1959). A certain number of persons react negatively to these developments; they claim that noise is injurious, detrimental to health, or undesirable from an aesthetic point of view (Broadbent 1957). It is the task of the psychiatrist to investigate the possible psychopathologic basis for such complaints. He becomes suspicious whenever people vehemently denounce unwanted sounds; this is too reminiscent of myths and delusions about bright light, cold air, hot spices, and other allegedly noxious external stimuli which so often are blamed when our suffering really stems from some internal conflict or frustration (Jones 1951).

To understand the psychopathology of noise-aversion we must explore the hidden unconscious meanings that obtain for noise in the listener's mind; an excellent approach to this effort is discussed in a recent paper by D. M. Green which shows how the auditory threshold may be affected by the listener's criteria for perception (Green 1960). Using these and similar concepts as a theoretical framework, I have been studying noise reactions in the setting of clinical psychotherapeutic work with patients. To convince myself of the dynamic meaningfulness of noise I exposed 12 mentally-ill persons and 7 normal volunteers to various forms of nontraumatic noise. Time does not permit the detailed presentation of all

* Presented in Session T, *Physiological and Psychological Acoustics*, 66th Meeting of Acoustical Society of America, May 13, 1961, Philadelphia, Pennsylvania. Abstract published in *J. Acoust. Soc. Am.* 33: 858 (1961).

NOISE   RESPONSES

VERBAL BEHAVIOR

- *COMPLAINS*
- *DEMANDS*
  CESSATION OF TEST
- *IMITATES NOISES*
- *STOPS TALKING*
- *RAMBLES*
  INCOHERENTY

PERCEPTUAL BEHAVIOR

- *LOOKS ABOUT*
- *STARTLES*
- *LISTENS*
  ATTENTIVELY
- *CLAIMS*
  NOT TO HEAR
- *FAILS TO REACT*

EMOTIONAL BEHAVIOR

- *BECOMES TENSE*
- *RESTLESSNESS*
  OR TICS
- *EMBARRASSMENT*
- *ANGER*
- *PLEASURE*

SYMBOLIC BEHAVIOR

- *MISINTERPRETS*
  NOISE
- *CONFUSES MEANINGS*
- *PRIVATE*
  ASSOCIATIONS
- *IGNORES*
  EVERYDAY MEANING
- *PHOBIC FEARS*

noise-reactions that were observed. For the sake of clarity I have divided these into 4 categories of behavior: (1) verbal, (2) perceptual, (3) emotional, and (4) symbolic, which are schematized in figure 1. In actual clinical work these categories of behavior always overlap; therefore, the conventional case presentation method will be used in presenting my data.

First is an example of what can happen when, in the mind of the patient, a noise becomes symbolically equated with an actual threat. This may be observed among confused listeners who cannot distinguish between appearances and reality, or among fearful listeners who are generally hyper-sensitive to external stimuli. Often confusion and fear go hand-in-hand, as demonstrated by the following case:

A 72-year-old spinster who had supported herself for years in the Army as a file-clerk, gained admission to the mental hospital after months of increasing suspiciousness and hostility towards her neighbors. She threatened to assault anyone who dared to come near her. During her stay at the hospital I had a chance to study her responses to the Wilmer Test. This is a sound-association technique, resembling the Rorschach inkblot test, that consists of 21 recorded sound-stimuli, each 20 to 50 seconds in duration and made up of various mechanical noises, human and animal sounds, speech, and music (Wilmer 1951). Many of her responses indicated that she experienced noise as a threat of assault. She apparently lacked the ability to discriminate between signs of external activity and the real possibility that this activity might overwhelm and engulf her in some way. For instance, stimulus #1, which consists of the noise of a train leaving a station and includes the sound of passengers together with various depot noises, led her to the remark "something terrible coming on – some sort of attack – a woman screaming – something immediate, but it was too noisy to determine the reason." While talking about her reactions to these noises, the patient appeared fearful, close to panic. A similar response occurred when she listened to stimulus #4, the noises of a crowd yelling "ya, ya" and a clock striking: "a definite warning calling for some immediate attention. I've heard many an air-raid and recognized what it all meant. I've heard many of them, but I'm telling you, in God's name, honestly I do not recognize a thing that calls it to my attention." After she listened to stimulus #6, the sound of an organ playing and a poem being read in a muffled voice, her reaction of fearful panic changed gradually to one of fatigue and apathy and she said: "I'm growing weary of things I cannot identify." The next day, when the test was continued, she still complained "it's wearing me out again." It is of interest that with this patient her aversion for noise was the first symptom of an increasingly delusional attitude towards auditory signals in general. During her second week of hospitalization she showed a decided unwillingness or inability to interpret the meaning of sounds. For instance, when I said to her "I'm sorry you're having such a rough time", she replied "not cooperative?? I'm trying to be docile, it's the lady-like thing to do." During the night she misinterpreted the sounds of nurses making rounds, patients coughing, and other ward noises as "a weird, whiny-toned voice of death calling out my name, saying 'Mary's dead'."

Next I would like to illustrate the influence of very strong dependency needs on the perception of noise; this can be observed in certain immature personality types. These patients occasionally make spontaneous comments about noises during their psychotherapy hours which are helpful clues to the way they perceive acoustic stimuli (Ostwald 1960a).

A 27-year-old salesman, who was profoundly anxious whenever he found himself alone on a job and unable to depend upon a person of authority, complained to me about the noises of the San Francisco foghorns. These reminded him of the sounds his father used to make when expelling gas from the rectum. The patient's idiosyncratic noise-aversion was a symptom of his pattern of unconscious seeking for a dependent contact with men. During another session this patient angrily complained of the noise of running water which he noticed coming from the bathroom. He had the notion that someone was taking a shower, and was reminded of a wish to be bathed and taken care of like a baby, a desire which he frequently indulged in fantasy and which interfered with his ability to function independently.

With patients who have organic disturbances of the brain one can more clearly observe the operation of primitive, regressive modes of thinking in connection with the perception of noise (Goldstein 1948). An example of confusion between the 'aural' and the 'oral' significance of noise is illustrated by the next case:

This 20-year-old man of Philippine background came to the psychiatric clinic as the result of repeated efforts made on his behalf by social agencies towards vocational rehabilitation. He had had a serious motorcycle accident three years previously which left him with some neurological deficit due to frontal lobe brain damage. This resulted in a tendency to express himself in a literal, overly concretized manner. His manner of listening resembled the behavior of a hungry puppy, in that he attended with great eagerness, listened closely to each tape-recorded sound, turned towards the loudspeaker, and tried his best to describe meticulously the effects that each sound had made on him. Listening to stimulus #4, the noises of a crowd, with a clock striking in the background, he told me "it is lunchtime, and everybody is getting ready to get chow and eat it." Stimulus #11, the noises of splashing water, led to this patient's comment "can I get a glass of water? My throat is dry." Stimulus #16, sucking noises, were interpreted as "a baby suckin' on his nipple", which is an extremely unusual interpretation of this noise. And stimulus #18, the noises of wood being broken and cloth being torn, led this man to comment "this could be the sound of someone eating French bread, the crust, hard crust." In going over the protocol, one gets the impression that this patient had the tendency to make of listening for noise a symbolic substitute for the obtaining of food, with the result that, metaphorically speaking, he took noises in not through the ears but through the mouth.

Another interesting pattern of noise response can be observed in patients who, for psychological or organic reasons, favor the auditory system as a channel for taking in information from the external environment (Knapp 1953). This kind of reaction is characterized by an indiscriminate seeking for acoustic stimulation as a means for making direct, nonsymbolic contact with the outside world. The following patient was also tested with the Wilmer noises.

He was a 42-year-old married cashier who came for psychiatric treatment after a heart operation had precipitated in him various physical symptoms that included partial blindness, thus providing some realistic cause for his helplessness. Unable to use vision as a way of perceiving the outer world, this patient seized upon any acoustic signal as a potential sign of assistance and friendly contact, ignoring in the process any of the more obvious meanings of the sound. For instance, his associations to stimulus #1, the noises of a TRAIN LEAVING a crowded railway depot, were "there were people waiting around the railroad station on the platform, and THE TRAIN WAS PULLING IN, and they were waving at friends and relatives." He interpreted stimulus #3, the noises of a baby crying amid the din of seagulls as "there are birds flying back and forth, and hunters are blowing on a whistle trying to coax the birds closer to them." Stimulus #14, another baby cry sound, this one mingled with the soft singing of a woman's voice, was heard as "she's trying to rock the baby to sleep. I get the sense of complete happiness and relaxed contentment. I can almost feel the mother, the child, the crib in the room." Not only did this man indicate a positive seeking for contact through his responses to noises, he also gave evidence of a most profound denial of the possibility that such contact might not be obtainable. This was most apparent in his reactions to stimulus #20, which include the words *shut-up* uttered in an angry, definitely rejecting fashion. To the patient this sound indicated "a man in a gay mood just good-naturedly saying 'shut-up'."

Finally I would like to briefly mention a psychopathologic response to noise which consists of the patient's inability to recognize that a noise which is distressing originates in the outside world. The patient seems to experience noise as though it comes from some internal acoustic source. In a sense this is the reverse of auditory hallucinosis, whereby the listener perceives as though coming from the outer world some kind of stimulus or message that originates in his own mind. This confusion between the inner and the outer world can be seen for example when certain acutely ill schizophrenic patients show aversive reactions to noise (Searles 1960). Naturally one does not want to subject these patients to any unnecessary stress, but I did observe this response in the case of a 14-month-old baby studied with the Wilmer Test.

This child was brought to the clinic because of emotional and mental retardation attributable to a congenital defect. In response to a number of acoustic stimuli from the Wilmer Test he grimaced, became restless, or began to cry. Several times at the height of his aversion reaction he would hit his face or head with both hands. This would stop at the end of the stimulus. Towards the conclusion of the test he seemed to have become accustomed to the noises, and even expressed a positive interest in some of them. An interesting response occurred in connection with stimulus #19, consisting of the noise of a drill press. He just sat quietly and listened to the noise, but the moment it was turned off he was acutely startled, as though the sudden quiet had surprised him.

What conclusion can be drawn from the clinical observation of noise reactions? One feature which seems to emerge from the psychopathology of noise is that mentally and emotionally disturbed persons tend in general to overlook the actual stimulus properties of noises. These patients seem to mask the sounds they hear in such a way that the appearance of external reality which is suggested by acoustic stimuli becomes more compatible with the fulfilment of basic biological drives towards nourishment, protection, contact, and pleasure. To the extent that noise is an amorphous, nonspecific, acoustic stimulus, it is particularly subject to the sort of perceptual distortion just described. In normal behavior we either ignore noises or scan them for any meanings that potentially increase our chance for biological health and survival (Ostwald 1961d).

The disturbed person not only seems unable to ignore certain noises; in his urgency to restore an equilibrium with the world he attributes to a given noise certain stimulus properties that it does not possess. This increases the possibility for misinterpretation of reality, reduces effective contact with the external environment, and furthers withdrawal.

While on the surface this looks as though noise is potentially harmful, actually one must consider that noise-aversions may be adaptive: the individual distances himself temporarily from a threat with which he cannot cope. His problem is not solved when one removes the disagreeable acoustic stimulus through more efficient techniques of noise-control. In fact the reduction of external stimuli may have dire consequences for individuals who are unprepared to cope with the onslaught of internal stimulation which is thereby released (Levy et al. 1959). It would seem that any practical solution of the noise problem involves not only acoustical noise-control measures but an intensive campaign aimed towards making listeners more realistically interested in and tolerant towards the noise of the environment.

14

SOUND, MUSIC, AND HUMAN BEHAVIOR*

(1960)

Sound is the basic medium for music, and music is an avenue for contact between the music therapist and his patients. The purpose of this presentation is to delineate those elements in communication with sounds which form a groundwork for more specialized and uniquely human forms of behavior called music.

Music has been approached from the acoustical, psychological, social, and historical points of view (Ostwald 1960b). In the following discussion music is treated as one form of human sounds. This makes possible a formulation of the musical process in terms of two major theories about behavior: It enables us to utilize the theory of psychoacoustics, based on findings of Helmholtz, for an explanation of nonsymbolic aspects of sound (Olson 1957), and the framework of psychoanalysis, derived from Freud, for an understanding of the symbolic functions of music (Friedman 1960). As we shall see, sound involves a cycle of events – movements by the source, dispersal of signals in space, and responses on the part of a listener. Music also uses this cycle, but adds to it the expressive needs of composers and performers, the aesthetic standards of the culture, and the social needs of an audience. The following remarks are aimed at highlighting certain aspects of each element in order to relate elements to each other; no complete or exhaustive analysis of individual elements in the musical process is intended.

Sound

What we call sound is a cycle of events that arbitrarily may be thought to begin when movements produce acoustic vibrations.

* Reprinted from *Music Therapy*, E. H. Schneider (ed.): 107-25 (1960).

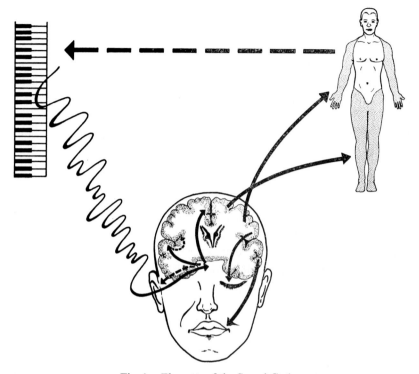

Fig. 1. Elements of the Sound Cycle.

The full cycle, as illustrated in figure 1, consists of the following
elements: (1) movement produces acoustic vibrations which are transmitted through space; (2) a listener picks up some sounds and converts
them into signals for interpretation by the nervous system; (3) decoded,
classified, and integrated into larger perceptual entities, sounds become
part of the pattern of symbolic and manifest behavior; and (4) the listener
regulates the source of sound (dotted feedback arrow). Let us now
examine each of these elements.

The human body as sound-maker

Because of the fact that movement sets up acoustic vibrations, each and
every one of us is a sound-producer much of the time. Whether we want
to make sound or not is a secondary consideration; in reality we cannot
help it. We are born into this world with a small but substantial body
mass and one of the first things we do is to make noise. The instrument

we use for this has been some time evolving: the larynx. It has its origins in a valve whereby the first land-dwelling fish could separate food, water, and air (Negus 1949). The human larynx is activated during the first moments of life, once breathing sets in. It is of interest that the cry of infancy is one of the loudest sounds human beings ever make. Acoustic studies show that the baby cry has an average sound level of approximately 84 decibels re 0.0002 microbar. This is a sound level equivalent to the noise of an unmuffled truck. The loudness of baby cries is usually about 35 sones – which is 4-6 times as loud as the sound made by a speaking adult. The pitch of the baby's cry has also been studied. Its fundamental frequency is usually at 500 cycles per second, or close to the open A string of a violin. This tone is heavily reinforced at 1,000 cycles and 2,000 cycles per second, which is the midrange of an extremely high-pitched musical instrument, such as the piccolo.

From acoustic analyses of baby cries it becomes apparent that this sound has certain musical characteristics. But it is not music because it is not produced in conformance with certain social patterns which will be discussed later.

I have already touched on intensity (loudness), frequency (pitch), and waveform (timbre) of sound in connection with the baby cry. These are three of the six physical properties of sounds that are significant in human behavior. Table 1, taken from Olson's textbook (Olson 1957)

TABLE 1

Acoustic Characteristics of Sound

Property	Sensation
Intensity	Loudness
Frequency	Pitch
Waveform	Timbre
Envelope	Attack-Duration-Decay
Portamento	Sliding
Vibrato	Wavering

shows these properties as related to the sensations they bring about. A study of these acoustic characteristics of sounds has already been extremely productive for the scientific investigation of speech (Fletcher 1953) and holds promise for research in music perception (Babbit 1960).

Portamento is well demonstrated by the cries of animals or children. It is caused by sliding from one pitch to another without a break in time, like a trombone or violin glide. The portamento has a very provocative effect on the emotions since it takes the listener's ear quickly from one point of reference to another and yet another without giving it a chance to stay put. Portamento may be compared with stroking the skin; its arousal and irritant value is a useful property of danger sirens, howling winds, baby cries, and other sounds that must be urgently attended to.

Vibrato is well demonstrated by the wailing sounds of an Iranian singer. Its rapid changes, referred to by the engineer as "frequency and amplitude modulation" have a puzzling and often irritating effect on the listener. For this reason the vibrato sound is not too popular in music and has to be used in moderation, as every string player and singer knows.

Sounds span space

The speed of sound differs with the medium through which it travels: 344 meters per second through air, 5,000 meters per second through steel, 70 meters per second through soft rubber, and 1,540 meters per second through salt water. These figures from Table 2, also taken from Olson

TABLE 2

Speed of Sound

Medium		Meters per second
Gases	Carbon Dioxide	258
	Air at 20 °C	344
	Steam	405
	Hydrogen	1,270
Liquids	Alcohol (methyl)	1,240
	Gasoline	1,390
	Water (13 °C)	1,441
	Salt Water	1,540
Solids	Soft Rubber	70
	Cork	500
	Pine Wood	3,600
	Steel	5,000
	Hard Glass	6,000

(1957) give some indication of the extent to which listeners are at the mercy of their physical environment.

The fact that sound vibrations must traverse space and are slowed down or speeded up by the substances they pass through may have some bearing on human behavior. For example, the heart beat of the pregnant woman passes through multiple layers of blood, lymph, fat, connective tissue, epithelium, and muscle before it reaches the ears of the fetus in utero. The sound is secondarily affected by reflection from bony and cartilagenous surfaces, and mingles with other body noises such as those of digestion, breathing, walking, and speech. It is not yet known whether the sounds of an expectant mother have any direct effects on the development and growth of the embryo. It has been suggested by Greene and others that sounds transmitted to the fetus through the mother's body are involved in the very earliest process whereby the organism learns to distinguish between itself and the outside world (Greene 1958). Dr. Lee Salk of New York has gone one step further. He observed that newborn infants gain weight more rapidly, cry less frequently, are less restless, and have fewer respiratory and gastro-intestinal upsets when they are raised in a nursery in which a tape recording of the rhythmic thump of the adult heart is played continuously (Salk 1960). Apparently the sound has a way of reminding the infant of certain conditions of life inside the mother, thus helping it to adjust to the new and different conditions of the nursery.

The human body as sound receiver

One of the commonest and also one of the most misleading ideas is that we hear with our ears. Actually the ear is a specialized part of the body surface which allows sound waves from the outside to enter and be converted into nervous impulses (Von Békésy 1960). One might compare the ears to the tuner component of a hi-fi set. Like the eyes, the nose, the fingers, the skin, and other surface structures of the body, the ears serve to make contact with the external environment and to convert signals from this environment into information for the use of the organism. Not only do the ears allow sound waves to enter the body and be converted into neural signals, they also make sure that certain sounds are kept out. The ears tune in only those stations that broadcast on channels between 20 and 20,000 cycles per second. The lower frequencies cannot be heard, but they may be experienced as vibrations or atmospheric pressure changes, while the ultrasonic frequencies are felt as tingling, burning, and painful sensations in the skin (United States Army 1950).

Like the tuner in our hi-fi set, the ear is controlled by human thinking systems which make changes whenever a station brings in programs that are noisy, repetitive, uninteresting, or frightening. We do not yet know how the brain manages to switch channels so as to bring in a new station, although important research studies on this process are currently under way (Licklider 1959).

Two explanations have been proposed to account for the way the brain makes the ears cut down the amount of sound which is let into the body. Galambos (1956) suggested that a series of shutter-like devices in the central nervous system can reduce the input of auditory signals at various levels between the cochlea and the cerebral cortex. Another explanation, forwarded by Hugelin and colleagues (1960), is that the sensitivity of the ear is diminished due to contraction of the small muscles inside the ear. This occurs as part of a generalized arousal response during which muscles throughout the body become more tense.

The human uses of sound

In this phase of our discussion we hover over the intellectual abyss created by the body-mind problem. So far we have stayed in the realm of the physical; we dealt with tangible things like vibrations, sounds, ears, and nerves. Now we approach the psychological world, and will have to use abstract terms like thoughts, feelings, and actions.

Let us start with the most uniquely human use of sound: verbal communication. Whereas prehuman organisms had already reached the point at which sound was useful for communication about things, it was man's destiny to use sounds linguistically to form ideas (Brown 1958). Mammals make sounds, primates have danger calls, but only man produces phonemes, morphemes, syllables, and words, stringing these together into a logical and efficient symbol system. Only man can describe, abstract, and create with sounds (Hockett 1960).

But man's ability to abstract meaning from sounds and to systematize the noises made with the mouth resulted in more than verbal language. The importance of the achievement, as Levine has explained, is that it "marks not only the beginning of verbal language but also the end of man's days as a lone wanderer upon the face of the earth. For with the development of verbal language, the advance was begun from coexistence among man-creatures to communion among mankind." (Levine 1960).

It is precisely the use of sound for communion which we find so often to be altered among mentally and emotionally disturbed persons. For example, a patient who has recovered from a psychotic depression may describe certain sounds heard during the illness. He may talk of the 'voices' of God, parents, lovers, or unidentified enemies. In retrospect, ideas about these sounds are recognized to have stemmed from internal stimuli in form of memories, wishes, and thoughts about the figures in question. But at the time of the hallucination when such insight was lacking, the patient 'peopled' his environment with nonexistent person-ages, and, like an omnipotent stage-director, controlled what they said and how they said it.

Similar phenomena have been observed during sleep when we dream, and when individuals are isolated in prisons, jungles, or experimental laboratories (Levy et al. 1959). Here the unsocialized individual, centering more interest on himself than on the outside world, interprets what he hears in an illusory way. Instead of the rustle of leaves he hears giggling girls; rather than the thump-thump of his own heart he hears the foot-steps of a giant, and so forth. To put it another way: the dreamer, the prisoner, and the psychotic put the wrong labels on the sounds they hear.

How does the human organism normally label and classify the sounds it uses? In trying to answer this question let us first look at the way an electronic brain, like the R.C.A. Synthesizer, does this. As I already pointed out, six physical properties of sounds have been isolated: intensity, frequency, wave-form, envelope, portamento, and vibrato. Numerical values can be assigned to each sound on the basis of these isolates, for instance 261.63 cycles per second for the frequency of middle C. An electronic machine labels every sound according to these numerical values, using a system of binary decimal code numbers (Babbit 1960). It must be assumed that the labelling of sounds by a human being is far more complex than that by an electronic machine, since the latter has no emotions, moral sense, personal relationships, or life cycle. The tabular comparison of sounds in Table 3 shows some of the factors that we take into consideration when it comes to the labelling and classification of sounds (Ostwald 1960a). At one end of the scale are sounds whose social meaning is nonexistent or minimal. These are primarily body sounds, too weak to be heard except under unusual circumstances. The sounds of the heart have already been mentioned. For the physician, who listens to these sounds by putting his ear directly to the chest or with a stetho-scope, such sounds are classified on the basis of their diagnostic signifi-cance. Intestinal rumbles, lung sounds, and crepitation point to certain diseases.

TABLE 3

Tabular Comparison of Sounds

Type of sound	Smooth muscle activity	Striated muscle activity	Volitional control of behavior	Experience with people	Language skills	Group audience
Public Speaking	+	+	+	+	+	+
Conversation	+	+	+	+	+	
Songs and Instrumental Music	+	+	+	+	(+)	
Oral Noises	+	+	+	(+)		
Tool and Machine Noises	+	+	+			
Noisy Behavior	+	+	(+)			
Body Organ Noises	+	(+)				

When a body noise can get out through one of the body openings there is a somewhat better chance for its being heard by the casual listener, and so it may be used as part of a more complex pattern of social interaction (Darwin 1955). Wheezing, as in asthma, is useful for communicating about internal distress. Snoring, burping, coughs, and flatulence, are other examples of body noises that have a social value; the usage of such sounds is governed by social attitudes and prejudices. For instance flatulence is acceptable at a men's smoker but not at a ladies' tea party, while belching is expected in a nursery or Oriental restaurant, but not during a sermon or song recital.

Two criteria for the classification of sounds have so far been touched on: their diagnostic function and their social meaning. Another important consideration is biological significance, the weighting of sounds in terms of an orderly cycle of physical growth, maturation, and decline which is man's destiny. The meaning of sounds we make and perceive is intimately linked to this cycle. The newborn infant is unable to make distinctions between incoming stimuli; his whole body jerks in a convulsive-like pattern at the sound of a loud noise. At the age of six months he is first able to localize sounds in space (Chun et al. 1960). Throughout life we continue to show certain traces reminiscent of the infant's startle-response to sound. We jump at a loud noise, smile at a pleasing tone, wince at the sound of a fingernail scraped against a blackboard, and become restless when a baby screams. Like Pavlov's dogs who salivated at the sound of a bell, we show certain automatic, irresistible physiological and mental responses to sounds because of their primary association with infantile life experiences.

By the end of the first year, the child's body has matured sufficiently to exert some control over itself. The child also ripens mentally, and can begin to make some patterned associations between sounds and ideas. The little one is exposed at this time to the spoken words of parents urging him towards cleanliness, speech, and coordinated motor acts. At the same time he hears his own babblings and is also aware of the various noises that accompany his behavior. Flatus, splashes, grunts, laughs, and other sounds associated with bathroom accomplishments assume increasing importance.

Development of speech in childhood involves two simultaneous and overlapping processes: (1) giving up of the childish noises that have no general meaning to adult society, and (2) learning to produce the linguistic signals which make up words. For a while children struggle against the rigidity of verbal language and try to hang on to noisy behavior. They play games with words, blatantly defying adult speech by making up perverse clangy rhymes.

For a while school forces the youngster to curtail his noises and teaches him how to communicate with words. But adolescence finds the verbal facade cracking once more; the rebellious youngster defiles his acoustic space with slang, profane four-letter words, razzberries, yells, and other noises (Wentworth and Flexner 1960). As a young adult he again tones down his sound output, this time in conformance with the requirements of his occupation, profession, social status, and income (Ostwald 1960a).

For communication throughout adulthood verbal sounds tend to predominate. The task of using words becomes progressively easier since they are defined in the dictionary or through custom and habit. Only under special circumstances does the adult revert to nonverbal sound-making. This occurs for instance if he visits a foreign country, becomes psychotic, attends football games, or goes to concerts.

As old age overtakes our soundmaker the balance between words and noises again tips in favor of the latter. Articulation becomes more mushy when the teeth are gone. Brain lesions make for garbled incoherence. Wheezing and snorting reappear. In certain cases the larynx gives out or has to be removed. The heart loses its rhythm, the lungs begin to bubble, bones snap and joints creak. Finally there is a rattle, silence, and death.

Music

The foregoing ideas about sound and human behavior provide landmarks for a subsequent discussion of music. We must now expand our basic framework, which was cast primarily in acoustical and psychological terms, into a broader one that can encompass historical and social dimensions.

Figure 2 schematizes my concept of music, obviously more complex than that for sound. The steps involved in what we call music are: (1) Human impulses seek expression; (2) Specific musical instruments are activated; (3) Aesthetic principles are applied; and (4) Listeners indicate their reactions.

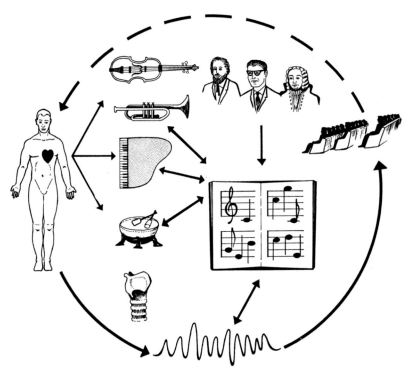

Fig. 2.   Elements of the Music Cycle.

Musical expression

The initial urge towards expression is basically a motoric one resembling that towards running, jumping, throwing, or any one of numerous activities that result from our desire to move and make an impression on the environment outside ourselves (Kohut 1957). In the course of growing up all of us learn how to control body movements to the point where efficient manipulation of the environment becomes possible. MUSICAL EXPRESSION REPRESENTS A REFINEMENT OF ONE ASPECT OF MOTOR CONTROL – THAT HAVING TO DO WITH SOUND-MAKING. The musician, through years of training and patient practice, learns how to extract predictable sounds from an instrument. The composer goes even a step further: instead of acting upon the urge for movement and actually making sounds, he imagines the sounds and translates this fantasy into notational symbols.

Musical symbols are arranged in time, in contrast to painting, sculpture, and dancing, all of which make use of visual space. Furthermore the musical grammar facilitates regulation of time through repetition, condensation, and augmentation of its form elements (Friedman 1960). Whereas speech and poetry also arrange symbols in time, these symbols have definite meanings. Verbal discourse brings to the mind a rapid succession of ideas and images, whereas musical expression sustains and reinforces one mood at a time. This might help to explain why music so effectively harnasses the human emotions: an emotion tends to linger. Like the figured bass in Baroque music which provides a blueprint for harmonic elaboration, an emotion gives the background against which thoughts and actions are played out. A fugue, which repeats the same melody, is a good example of the way music sets up a series of symbols to establish a mood and then proceeds to control this mood in time.

Musical instruments

For a musician the musical instrument is more than a tool of the trade. It resembles a ventriloquist's puppet, being simultaneously a player's right arm and his love object. He works with the instrument many hours each day, keeps it in a special place in his home, and holds on to it during the all-important transactions with an audience. Therefore in music the values of a piano, violin, or clarinet cannot be adequately defined in acoustical terms.

When a youngster is given music lessons, the shape, size, sound, and psychic meanings of the instrument may deeply affect the nature of his thinking about himself and the world at large. The piano, for instance, is a large, stationary object resembling a piece of furniture which a child tends to associate with his house, his parents, and other relatively permanent fixtures in the environment. Unlike a baby or a pet, the piano will not kick, bite, or scream when it is poked. A piano cannot be dropped or pushed over and it is sturdy enough to withstand even more violent assaults. With the piano one can perform complete musical works without assistance of other instruments; the piano permits solitude.

A young violinist has other advantages. His instrument is small, and he can embrace it like a doll, learning to overcome some of the real and imagined threats of being a small and helpless child. The violin is fragile, and while the youngster cannot play with it, he can clean his fiddle and put it to bed each day, or take it along for walks to school or the homes of friends. Sounds can only be coaxed out of a violin, and in order to make music the violinist needs others to play with. His instrument drives him into orchestras, quartets, and various ensembles, making him more of a social creature compared to the solitary pianist or organist.

It is easy to see the psychological effects of playing different musical instruments: trumpet players spit and keep their hands glued to one place, whereas harpists gracefully fondle their instrument. Tubas and cellos are impossible for little people, whereas piccolos and violins are out of the question for bearish individuals with large hands.

Musical ideas

Music is organized sound, and human creators are invariably responsible for the ideas which govern this organization. Machines cannot compose, they can only imitate (Hiller 1959). It is easier to show the connection between a musical idea and its creator when the identity of the composer is known. Take for example Carlo Gesualdo, the ruling Prince of Venosa. He was a passionate man, who murdered his wife and child in a fit of jealousy (Grove's Dictionary 1954). Obsessions with death are evident throughout his work. He emphasized pathos in 16th century counterpoint by translating mournful sighs into music. Exclamations, chromaticism, repeated suspensions, and pauses are combined to give the intended effect of acute anguish. He used texts as the following

Wearily I die in my pains,
And she who would give me life,
Alas, she gives me death and will not give me help,
Oh dolorous fate,
She who can give me life, alas, gives me death.

New instrumental effects are also invented by composers in an effort to externalize certain ideas. While some composers today claim to use mathematical, chance, or random processes in composition, a closer look at their systems usually reveals an organizing principle that stems from their personal imagination. In subtle ways the composer's ideas are also affected by his cultural and even political identifications.

Instrumentalists themselves have an influence on the progress of musical ideas. If they can demonstrate the successful execution of novel sound effects, their inventions are picked up and used by composers. For example, Casals has not only influenced contemporary cello technique; he indirectly stimulated the composition of a number of contemporary cello concertos.

New musical ideas do not always come easily into common practice. Reactions like disgust, puzzlement, anger, and rejection follow upon every first attempt at novelty, not only in music but in art and science as well. Even composers, since they are nurtured on traditional and conventional music, show a tendency to misunderstand and resist new musical ideas (Einstein 1941).

Attempts are often made to define musical ideas in verbal or pictorial terms rather than affective ones. Since pictures and words are limited in time and space, they are easier to cope with intellectually than sounds, which lack visible boundaries. But any attempt to concretely define musical ideas through words or pictures is doomed to fail; the musical language is, by its very nature, a nonverbal one. This is perhaps one explanation for the effectiveness of music as a therapeutic agent: music frees us from 'civilized' requirements for logical, verbal, and pragmatic thinking. Yet music does not permit us to withdraw, for in order to enjoy it we must listen. Kohut (1957) formulated this idea in psychoanalytic terms:

The significance of musical activity for earlier psychological organizations is derived from its capacity to allow subtle regression via extraverbal modes of psychic function. It appears to contribute to the relief of primitive, preverbal tensions that have found little psychological representation and it may provide for the maintenance of archaic object cathexes by virtue of its relationship to an archaic, emotional form of communication.

Leonard Meyer and Deryck Cooke also recently made significant contributions to the problem of meaning in music. Meyer (1957) based his analysis of music on the principles of Gestalt Psychology. He translated certain ideas about visual perception into auditory terms, thus making it possible to relate musical forms more directly to higher psychic functions like memory, learning, and enjoyment. Cooke (1959) undertook a more traditional analysis of music, achieving in his book a contemporary realization of 18th century musical aesthetics. Through painstaking harmonic and melodic analyses he draws attention to conventional ways for expressing certain moods and impulses through music.

Finally the illuminating comments by Igor Strawinsky should be mentioned. His earlier *Poetics of Music* (1947) and his more recent *Conversations* with Robert Craft (1959) provide much food for thought on the subject of musical ideas.

The audience

An audience is made up of various individuals who bring vastly different expectations to the musical event. On the one hand there are auditors who listen; they are interested in sounds, trained to recognize form elements, and sophisticated in terms of discriminating styles of composition and excellence of performance. On the other hand there are auditors who do not listen; they participate in musical events on the basis of what is fashionable and go primarily for the satisfaction of social needs.

Since music is a social art, both listeners and nonlisteners are accepted into the audience. But to hold all members of an audience at an optimum level of attention and evoke in each person the maximum enjoyment poses special technical problems. The size, shape, and appearance of the hall, the price of admission, and the advance publicity are all designed to capture the audience. From then on it is the musician's responsibility to captivate it.

In most instances musicians have no way of knowing the relative proportion of listeners and non-listeners in an audience, nor can this distinction be made on the basis of nonverbal cues like silence, applause, coughing, or program-rattling. Such signs are ambiguous; they can indicate either boredom or excitement; they can reflect both enthusiasm and hostility. The musician accomplishes his task by presenting to the unidentified auditors a mixed stimulus pattern made up of expected, popular, regular sounds and of surprising, novel, and irregular ones. Too much of one kind of sound leads to monotony which satisfies only extremists and is rejected by the majority of the audience.

Psychiatric patients in a mental hospital bring to a musical event personal attitudes, preferences, and expectations that differ greatly from those which motivate an audience outside the hospital. It therefore seems unwarranted to apply to music therapy conclusions about audience responses which are based on studies of public opinion, music appreciation courses, or role-playing situations. The exact meaning of music in psychiatric illness is not yet known, and the problem of audience reaction to music is one of the most challenging ones for research in this field (Teirich 1958).

Summary

Sound-making is part of the instinctive behavior pattern of every human being. This presentation focuses on some of the physical factors which govern the uses of sounds and discusses the processes whereby primitive sound-making is transformed into socially desirable forms of communication like speech and music. Music is explained in greater detail, making use of a cyclic model that takes into account the expressive needs of musicians, the aesthetic values of the culture, and differing potentials for response from an audience. Music cannot be defined in terms of specific meanings since it uses nonverbal symbols. Notions as to its general influence on emotions include: the temporal control of mood and the ability to produce healthy regression. Rarely can musical ideas be traced directly to a single source – the personal life of the composer, the skills of instrumentalists, and artistic values of the community are equally involved. The needs of an audience are never uniform, and those of psychiatric patients in mental hospitals present special problems.

15

BACKGROUND MUSIC IN A PSYCHIATRIC CLINIC

(1961)

Music is one of the oldest therapeutic agents known in the healing arts. It was used by witch doctors in early times and is still popular among primitive peoples. Music as a treatment for mental disease was already mentioned in the Bible where we are told that David cured Saul's madness by playing the harp. Music therapy had a prominent place in the Greek temples of healing, where many of the most important scientists and philosophers of that time studied its effects on human behavior. Today music therapy is used for both individual and group treatment of psychiatric patients. Music reduces apathy, encourages movement, and facilitates social contact. Thus it is particularly helpful in the management of severely regressed psychotic patients and in the rehabilitation of geriatric and neurological cases.

There is another use for music which has achieved considerable popularity: This is background music, referred to variously as mood music, musak, or atmosphere sound. It is already widely applied in stores, factories, offices, and other places where people congregate. Background music is intended to foster a pleasant, friendly, and relaxed environment. The availability today of high-fidelity tape recordings that contain virtually any kind of music, and of sound systems that are durable and easy to operate, puts the use of background music within easy reach of every hospital. Indeed within recent years it has found its way into hospital lobbies, wards, and waiting rooms.

Little is as yet known about the indications and contraindications for background music in hospitals. In view of the fact that music in general has a profound influence on human behavior, one can only assume that background music should not be played indiscriminately in the vicinity of sick persons. It would also seem that for mentally and emotionally ill patients certain forms of background music might be disturbing rather than pleasing. The introduction of background music to a psychiatric environment undoubtedly requires as much care as that customarily exercised in selection of furniture, drapes, rugs, and other environmental agents. Perhaps even greater care is necessary, since, under certain conditions background music interferes with verbal communication.

Music, like speech, is composed of sounds that are above the physiological threshold for hearing and below the threshold for pain. Our responses to music are the result of training and past experience in listening. Personal preferences for certain musical instruments, composers, and forms are involved, as well as cultural attitudes which determine whether music should be considered beautiful or ugly, popular or classical, desirable or undesirable. Under no circumstances are the effects of music ever uniform or fully predictable. These factors must be considered before one undertakes to introduce background music into a psychiatric institution. Here, in addition to the needs of various patients, the individual auditory requirements of doctors, nurses, secretaries, and other members of the medical team have to be satisfied.

To explore the possibility of using background atmosphere sound in a psychiatric setting, music was played for one week in the lobby of the Outpatient Clinic, Langley Porter Neuropsychiatric Institute. The lobby is used as a waiting room; a nurse or receptionist is always stationed at the desk to receive patients. She may also answer phone calls and assist the doctors with making appointments. The total number of people in the waiting room varies considerably, as does the amount of conversation, moving-around, and other sources of noise. Before a diagnostic survey or group therapy program begins, there may be as many as 20 patients in the waiting room. At other times only one or two patients are waiting. Children also use the waiting room; they congregate either at the nurses' station or sit at desks where they may draw and paint. These conditions are associated with varying amounts of sound in the waiting room, a factor which becomes important when one considers what will happen when background music is added.

To provide music, a Conley Moodmaster System was used. The Control system was placed on a table next to the receptionist's desk, and two 8-inch loudspeakers in baffle enclosures were attached to the walls of the room. Music was provided by continuous-loop tape-recordings. The recordings were not labelled and instructions were given to play any tape that gave the type of music most desirable and effective for the atmosphere of the lobby. The tape was changed and another type of music played whenever variety seemed indicated. A record was kept of the length of time that each recording was on the machine.

Since there is as yet no standardized background music for psychiatric clinics, three types of music were used that have been standardized in other settings. One type of music was a kind which is customarily used for fashion shows: soft, lilting, gently flowing melodies, predominantly produced by strings. A second type of music used was the kind often heard in restaurants: rhythmic, lively, dance-type music, featuring drums, trumpets, and other band instruments. A third standardized background music was the kind used in offices and factories: a mixture of fast and slow music, including at times popular show tunes. As it turned out, in the waiting room of the out-patient clinic, the preference was overwhelmingly for the type of music used in fashion shows: gentle, soft soothing, with string-tone predominating. For 30 hours and 10 minutes of total playing time, fashion show music was used 19 hours and 25 minutes while restaurant and office-factory music was played 5 hours and 15 minutes and 5 hours and 30 minutes respectively.

More general reactions to the introduction of background music were studied by means of interviews and questionnaires. While the use of music for only one week cannot provide any conclusive results, it was of interest that before the Moodmaster System was actually installed in the clinic, eager interest was expressed in having background music. To the clinic personnel, music seemed like an excellent way to provide increased stimulation for patients and to improve the morale in the waiting room. But this initial enthusiasm quickly gave way to disappointment. Within the first two days the novelty effect of background music wore off and thereafter the music produced a variety of different reactions, reflecting largely the preferences and opinions of individuals who were interviewed. Surprisingly few patients mentioned the background music; they seemed to handle it in a routine manner, much like any other change in the atmosphere of the hospital. Some of the psychiatric residents and consultants found that background music added something, a friendly or cheerful element to the atmosphere. One resident stated, for example, "The addition of background music to the waiting room would greatly improve and relax the formal, strained appearance of the patients, make their presence and conversations less evident, and remove the slightly 'clinical atmosphere'." Others felt that the music detracted from the restful and sober environment and stated that it was inappropriate for a clinic setting. A typical response was "Although initially I had thought the music might be a good thing, I found myself uncomfortable with it and felt too that the patients were entitled to silence if they so desired."

Another significant consideration for the use of background music within a clinical setting was revealed: Most of the questionnaires indicated that background music should be interrupted from time to time by periods of silence. Music, no matter how pleasant, seemed disagreeable if continued indefinitely for long periods of time. While few individuals complained that music interfered with their thinking, some did express the idea that background music creates a problem in talking, answering the telephone, writing notes, and performing other necessary duties. One of the secretaries remarked that especially when children were in the waiting room, the music was not relaxing because it added to the noise level in the room. This suggests that, in addition to periods of silence, the successful use of background music requires that there must be a quiet area where secretaries and nurses may concentrate on keeping their notes and records, and where the telephone can be answered without difficulty.

While the questionnaires did not concern themselves with psychological factors in the response to background music, some of these are sufficiently well-understood to warrant discussion here. There are two ways to listen to music: one requires attention to the music and seeks out familiar, well-liked tunes, timbres, and rhythms; the other involves disinterest in the music and treats the sound as an incidental feature of the environment. Only when the latter way of listening predominates can background music accomplish what it sets out to do, viz. to provide an atmosphere conducive to the performance of tasks. Whenever background music becomes loud or sufficiently interesting to attract the attention of the listener it defeats its own purpose.

It is important to keep in mind that the loudness and interest of background music cannot be controlled by the person who designs the tape-recordings and operates the music system. Loudness and interest are subjective phenomena, determined as much by the attitudes of the listener as they are by the shape and character of the music. As a matter of fact, in every psychiatric hospital there are hallucinating patients who project into their environment loud and interesting sounds that do not exist in acoustic reality.

This points to the need for sound clinical judgement in the use of background music and other forms of music therapy. A psychiatrist must decide whether it is desirable for patients to listen to music when they find themselves with little to do, or whether music constitutes an antitherapeutic escape from reality. Since music has no specific meanings as do words or pictures, patients respond to its generally stimulating character, especially rhythmicity and intensity. Their responses may be a feature of their psychopathology. Therefore, agitated, exciting, and noisy music is undesirable on a ward or in a waiting room where patients show hypomanic states, tendencies toward destructiveness, delirious reactions, or irritability. On the other hand, hypnotic, softly soothing, and similar types of music may tend to further regression among patients who are stuporous, depressed, or lethargic, and must therefore be avoided in certain clinical settings.

In addition to an accurate evaluation of the psychopathology of patients, some knowledge of acoustics is necessary for successful use of background music in the psychiatric clinic or hospital. Loudspeakers should be installed in corners or on walls where a good reflecting surface distributes the sound evenly throughout the room. Drapes, furniture, carpets and other absorbing material must be placed in such a way throughout the room that there is even scattering of sound, and that no disturbing echo effects or dead areas are produced. Of equal importance is that the operator of a background music system should have a sufficiently great number of tape recordings available, so that the musical atmosphere may be quickly changed to suit the needs and desires of the listeners. The play-equipment should be simple to operate, and a sound engineer or other qualified person should be on call at a moment's notice, especially during the first three or four days, to make whatever technical adjustments are necessary. This will partly insure against the development of frustration and annoyance among listeners, especially when the novelty effect has worn off and they begin to realize that music in the psychiatric hospital is not a definitive form of treatment.

A word should be said about the cultural preferences for certain types of music. As was already pointed out, music has certain general effects on behavior by virtue of its rhythmicity, melodic flow, and intensity fluctuations; its more specific influence is due to the familiarity of listeners with certain types of music. For example, the operatic singing of the Chinese is considered very beautiful by certain groups, but to the Western ear generally sounds like noise. Similar cultural preferences exist for the music labelled jazz, rock 'n roll, classical, modern, and so forth. Listeners who are partial to one or another type of music will show unfavorable responses if they are subjected continuously to a type of music that is outside their range of experience. This makes it mandatory that patients and personnel in the mental hospital have an opportunity to personally select the kind of music which is put into their environment.

Background music is a powerful weapon available to combat undesirable mood states, social tensions, and other disturbing conditions in the mental hospital. But this weapon can also be used destructively by adding to the noise level and fostering confusion and irritation. Experienced clinical and acoustical judgement is necessary to determine what kind of background music is to be played, the kind of equipment that can be used, and the proper placement and adjustment of the music to fit in with the total therapeutic program of the hospital.

16

MUSIC AND HUMAN EMOTIONS – DISCUSSION*

(1966)

Any serious discussion of music and human emotions must start by acknowledging that neither the term MUSIC nor the term EMOTION can be defined in any rigorous fashion. One person thinks of music in the traditional sense of tone and rhythm organized according to definite rules of form and style. Another equally valid definition focuses on the practical role of a performer producing vocal or instrumental sounds for the purpose of entertainment. Today's avant-garde defines music as any form of acoustic behavior that listeners will tolerate – including beating the piano with a hammer, sneezing, or random noise.

Definitions of human emotion have the same chameleon-like quality. Some view emotion as basically physiological and neurohumoral patterns. Others prefer the psychological view of subjectively experienced internal states like rage, fear, hate, hope, and elation. Or, a communicational approach which emphasizes the overt exchange of messages across direct channels is found useful.

Scientifically, the only way out of this quicksand of shifting levels and overlapping views is to measure – and because music involves a measurable energy-process, namely sound, acoustic theories of one sort or another have always come into musical aesthetics. Pythagoras probably started it all with a ruler! He measured the length of vibrating strings and found that different string lengths produce different reactions in people. What especially impressed him was that reaction which we call pitch – namely, the judgment of one tone being higher or lower in relation to a second tone. This was a tremendously important discovery. In a shadowy way it predicted what later became known as the Weber–Fechner Prin-

* Reprinted from *Journal of Music Therapy:* 93-94 (September, 1966).

ciple and is today called Stevens' Law – namely, that the magnitude of stimulation is related in a regularly scaled fashion to the magnitude of sensation. This insight prepared the ground for another great leap: recognition by von Hornbostel, Heinz Werner, and other Gestalt psychologists that there is a basic Unity of All Senses – that hearing, vision, touch, taste, and smell are synesthetically interrelated. In the background of all formal aesthetic experience stands this informal synesthetic which has no discontinuities brought about through words. It has only a kind of polarity where heat, bright, light, loud, fast, tense, rough, and high occupy one sensory realm, in contrast to cool, soft, low, dark, slow, slack, and dull at the other extreme. And one would seem to be on pretty safe ground, both in terms of real experience and in terms of experimental data, to claim the high sensory pole for emotional excitement and the low one for depression. This, in fact, has been the substance of Western musical tradition for over 200 years. Friederich Marpurg and his contemporaries in the 18th century documented it with great detail, and the subsequent years have given it a scientific backbone: relaxed and happy feelings go with fast rhythm, consonance, and rising melody; while the sad and pensive moods correlate with dissonance, descending patterns, and drawn-out notes.

But there is much more to music than sensation and feeling. Music is a form of social behavior. It involves a subculture of composers, publishers, managers, instrument-makers, auditorium architects, broadcast and recording engineers, performers, critics, and (last, but not least) auditors – each bringing to the musical activity some particular skill and taking from it some personal reward. As psychiatrists, we may occasionally hear something about the personalities and the illnesses of people involved in the musical life. We also have access to diaries, letters, conversations, and other more intimate documents about the lives of important musical figures, such as Mozart, Chopin, Wagner, or Stravinsky. These people learned the musical language in childhood, and like anything learned that early, music became part of them. Music became their body language and allowed them as adults to preserve something of the rhythmic, syncretic, nonverbal orientation of the child. I think that every successful musician – including so-called popular musicians like Spike Jones or the Beatles – projects some of the vitality and enthusiasm of childhood, not to mention also the fears, the frustrations, and the uncertainties of the child. Have you all seen Pablo Casals' cello classes on television? One cannot escape the feeling that this artist, in his eighties, can still be like a kid enjoying himself with a huge toy. I am sure that much of the infectiousness and the therapeutiveness of music stems from the musician's childlike glee in playing with sounds.

There is, of course, a more intellectual side to it, especially in classical music where a tremendous amount of self-discipline is involved. Pure music is an abstraction about emotion. It has no story to tell – like an opera; it serves no purpose – like an overture; it promotes no behavior – like a march or a lullaby. Pure music, as Suzanne Langer points out in her book *Philosophy in a New Key*, can have no literal, lexical meaning. Music is a symbolic emotional experience. Whatever understanding may secondarily accrue from music represents a kind of social-sharing of the experience – a being-in-harmony with others who sense its beauty.

This, I suspect, may in part account for the success of music as therapy. The essential ingredient perhaps is the therapist's ability to tune in on his patient and to help him when he feels distressed. This may happen with music, or with painting, or dancing, or conversation, or even with silence. And without this clinical sensitivity, no matter how often you play the *Moonlight Sonata* or beat out a rock 'n roll, it will only strike the psychiatric patient as so much noise.

Of course, to be an effective music therapist, one first has to learn to be an effective musician. The recently published "Rockefeller Report on the Performing Arts" reveals an alarming fact – that public support for music (along with other cultural institutions in this country) is on the decline. Gifted people leave the field for economic reasons, and the crop of young instrumentalists to fill our symphony orchestras steadily diminishes. Who nowadays wants to practice the piano when the electronic guitar is so much easier to play? This decline in music as a cultural force is particularly regrettable at a time when more opportunity for leisure is becoming available. What can psychiatrists do about it? First, encourage the musical activities of children and adolescents. Second, help parents to accept their youngsters' at-times-cacophonic musical behavior as something potentially very healthy. Third, do everything in our power to support the teachers of music – the underpaid workhorses who rarely get into the spotlight and whose successful students walk away with all the honors. Finally, toward the musician as patient, show a particular respect for the healing potentialities of time and of nonverbal forces. One of the most poignant events in Bruno Walter's *Autobiography* shows Freud carefully examining the conductor's right arm – the baton hand – which had become hysterically paralyzed after the birth of a child. Avoiding any interpretation of this symptom, Freud told Walter to travel and to open his eyes to scenes of great visual beauty. After returning to

Vienna, Walter was told not merely to conduct his orchestra, but rather to allow the music to conduct him, to move him, and thus to heal him.

17

THE MUSIC LESSON*

(1968)

The music lesson exemplifies one of mankind's oldest and most honorable traditions: to influence constructively the sound-making behavior of the young. Yet, if the history of music teaching is traced back to its origins in antiquity, it will be evident how often this form of education is applied rather selectively only to certain social groups (Oberborbeck 1961). In ancient Egypt (2500 B.C.), for example, music lessons were reserved for ladies of the court. Spartan Greece trained only free youths in music. During the early Christian era musical training was split up to provide the *musicus*, who had an all-around liberal arts training, and the *cantor*, or practical musician. Modern musical training also may show a certain dichotomy, with some teachers focusing on performance, others on the appreciation of music. Music therapy is a form of education that combines both approaches in an effort to provide for the musical needs of a special group of persons. Students of the music therapist, often a music teacher, belong to that in many ways disadvantaged group known as the mentally and emotionally ill. The following ideas about music lessons and music teaching are intended to focus on some psychological principles that make the lesson a unique tool for influencing members of this group. The four brief episodes that follow illustrate successful and unsuccessful applications of music teaching.

FROM MUSIC TO MASTERY. A powerful, 6-foot, 200-pound teen-ager has worn out a succession of schools and private tutors with his rebellious and aggressive behavior. He is the despair of his parents, who are highly educated people and expect at least adequate school performance from their only son. But Martin's single interest is to play the drums. He refuses to open his school books until

* Reprinted from *Music in Therapy*, E. Thayer Gaston (ed.): 317-25 (New York: Macmillan).

a music teacher is found who recognizes and develops the boy's latent intellectual talents. Sensitive to the schizoid pattern of Martin's fantasy life, the music teacher builds a bridge between the rhythmicity of drumming and the orderliness of nature. Martin now finds that mathematics is nothing to be afraid of – there are numbers in music and in science, too. The teacher leads him to appreciate extra-musical knowledge, and the resulting pleasure pulverizes the patient's school phobia.

MUSIC IS NOT ENOUGH. Pampered, coddled, spoiled, and inadequately prepared for life, P at twenty-five decides to make music his career. To the teacher he brings a hypertrophied speaking knowledge of music but a performance capacity only sufficient to justify applause for an eight-year-old. The music teacher tries scales and basic theory. The student does poorly. The teacher tries to encourage performance, with the result that the student seeks night club jobs. Failure follows failure. Only after P enters psychotherapy does he realize that his submission to the teacher is based on a longing for affection and a secret craving for recognition. In hidden fantasies and dreams he sees the music teacher as parent, rival, and boxing partner. As soon as real gratification comes about through work, love, and lasting interpersonal relationships, the patient abandons music and the music teacher.

THE TIDE IS TURNED. L has two major interests in life – eating and practicing the piano. Except for her parents, whose punitive attitudes control her behavior, there are no significant people in her life. A new music teacher is at first only accepted as an inanimate object – part of the piano – a solid, indestructible creature who cannot hit back. But he very gently detaches himself from the instrument and talks with L about her life away from the keyboard. This produces a panic of such proportions that hospitalization has to be considered. A psychiatrist is consulted. After a few discussions, teacher and student can continue their work. It takes years for L to develop comfort in her relationship with the music teacher who, in turn, learns to limit his attention to the patient's keyboard exercises.

WHO WON? On a fellowship for students from a nation once at war with the United States, Kay finds life here a strange but wonderful experience. She runs into trouble when a certain pushiness of personality antagonizes her roommates. Kay's music teacher wisely channels her aggression into a competition, in the hope that she may win a performing contract. Every ounce of energy is spent preparing works of a dazzling-virtuoso nature. Yet Kay only gets to the semi-finals. Another foreign student wins the contest. Seething with rage, Kay makes a nuisance of herself, and the teacher quickly modifies his approach to her talents. Competence in performing and joy in playing will be enough. He convinces the student that she should accept music for music's sake and persuades her to abandon the fantasy of using it as a vehicle for conquering the world.

What elements of personality does the teacher bring to bear on the music lesson? How does he apply the psychological leverage needed to help emotionally turbulent students master this most abstract of all arts? Let us look at the music teacher as listener, as guide, as coach, and as healer.

The teacher as listener

> In music we sense most directly the inner flow which sustains the psyche or the soul. – Michael Tippett

How the teacher listens – with what degree of undivided attention and empathy – often spells the difference between success and failure in the music lesson. In his relationship with the student, the music teacher performs a function that in certain ways resembles a mother quietly contemplating her child. He observes the breathing, the emotional expressions, and the waxings and wanings of inner tension. He focuses his sensory organs – especially his ears – on the student and clears his mind of all thoughts except those pertaining to the music. He places the student on a mental stage elevated above commonplace problems, listening exclusively to him.

Being listened to is one of the most rewarding experiences a human being can have. Communication with sounds, which starts in the earliest relationship between the newborn and its mother, is basic for emotional empathy. Before words ever come into play, each personality experiences the give and take of communication with tones, rhythms, and melody fragments. This is how our needs for comfort, food, warmth, protection, and security are first expressed. The mother who correctly perceives these signals rewards the child with pleasurable, joyful feelings. Frustrated, the child becomes angry, sad, or frightened (Spitz 1965).

Many of these positive and negative emotions may be reexperienced in the context of the music lesson, which is a kind of immunizing experience for a student preparing himself to go out into the world and perform there. The students and patients of the music therapist-teacher have often been cruelly hurt and disappointed in their life performance. One is reminded of the anxious child who cannot overcome his fear of strangers and starts to frown or cry when a person who has not been identified as safe and loving approaches him; he reserves genuine smiles of friendly joy for only the most intimate relationships. Unhappy, lethargic, withdrawn babies, who have not been favored by the growth-impelling powers of maternal love, continue to show an anxious, unsmiling approach to people for years, sometimes all their lives, hardly ever breaking through their shells of social isolation with genuinely warm smiles and laughter. Notice the mechanical rhythms, the harsh humming, and other pseudomusical activities of psychotic children. There is no communication of pleasure. The child is rocking himself, trying to obtain what his mother should have provided. The patient's stiff movements are attempts to find out where legs or arms are located in space – not expressive activities that invite other children to play. His 'singing' is rote imitation, the same fragment of melody repeated over and over again like a frantic search for time stability. These vocalizations cannot induce others to join in games or choruses.

The teacher as guide

> The most beautiful melodies will always indifferently affect the ear which is not accustomed to them. Here is a language that requires no dictionary. – Jean Jacques Rousseau

The music teacher must be concerned with what to listen for. Music organizes time and space by way of acoustic structures. Musical experience based on closely organized rhythm, tone, and volume gradation has been marvelously conceptualized in traditional Western counterpoint and harmony. Eastern music, serial composition, and *musique concrète* call on a more expanded model for the analysis of auditory experience. The following may give a schematic image of what music is able to synthesize.

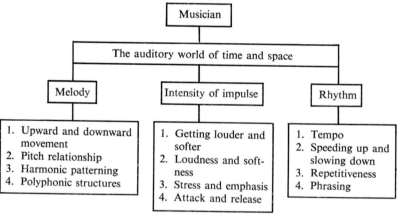

Guides use maps. The music teacher's map was invented by Guido of Arezzo, the genius of the Middle Ages who devised musical notation. Before this time, all music had to be memorized; then a visual aid became available. Notes of the scale were placed on lines and spaces. The *Guidonic*

hand represented the tone system on the fingers of the left hand, a four-lined staff. The right index finger pointed to the notes. This established a visual-motor image in the mind much like an alphabet and its representation in writing movements. Multipart singing in choruses became possible, permitting the symbolic differentiation of age and sex through the different voices – soprano, alto, tenor, and bass.

In guiding a student's understanding, music teachers face the dilemma of too global versus too particular an approach to sounds, movements, and expressive behavior. Globalism reduces intellectual control and may delete from conscious perception the architectural elements that make musical listening such a uniquely satisfying experience. Excess particularization can anesthetize the student's sensuous perception of musical forms. For instance, one of the most exhilarating moments in listening to classical music is the feeling of recognizing themes that, having been exhaustively varied and modulated through the development section, return in their original version. Too particular an analysis of this can deaden the student's esthetic appreciation. If he already senses the closure of a pattern, it should not be necessary to explain every detail of the composer's craftsmanship, the stylistic habits of the period from which the music is derived, or the interpretive capacities of the performer. Beware of turning musical analysis into a dissection. The guiding teacher trusts his students' innate sensibilities for rejecting what is ugly and false in art. Criticism coming out of the analysis of music should be constructive, showing respect for the enormous self-discipline that musicianship requires.

The teacher as coach

> I have no use for a school teacher who cannot sing. – Martin Luther

A music teacher communicates the technical skills of his art. Some do this nonrationally – for example, the famous performers who can convey this information simply through demonstration. Others may know a great deal about how to play an instrument – and this can be communicated – without being master players themselves. A teacher lacking skill or knowledge of technique, however, runs a serious risk. Nothing is so tragic as a student whose interest in music has been squelched by inadequate or incorrect coaching. Technical skill starts with a reverence for equipment. Music is a sport as well as an art, and the entire body enters into musical behavior. The teacher must know how the body breathes, how the bones and joints articulate, and where the important nerves and muscles are

located. For singers and wind players, knowledge of breath control, phonetics, and facial expression is essential. Pianists and violinists have to
learn the pulley system of finger-wrist-elbow and the fascinating many-
levered shoulder joint. A good teacher shows the student how to tense and
relax his body. As coach, he should teach principles that students can
readily apply, but should avoid imposing a set of patterns on the young
musician. Each student develops a personal style of expression, integrating the particular strengths and weaknesses of his own body and tempera-
ment, the necessities of his musical instrument, and the traditional practices learned from his music teacher. Whether to hold the violin at an
angle, whether to sit with elbows above or below the keyboard, how to
balance head with chest register – these are technical matters with which
the coach concerns himself and for which he encourages each student to
find his own solutions.

How to keep musical equipment shipshape should also be taught by
the teacher. Our instruments have taken a long time to evolve their present shape, and each has an interesting history. The flutist should know
the physics of his flute and its forerunners in earlier pipe instruments.
Violinists can be especially proud of their instrument's carpentry tradition,
which includes craftsmen whose products are older than the Declaration
of Independence and just as durable. Organists are privileged to operate
musical machines intimately related to the march of religious history.
And the electronic composer of today is part of a technological achievement that goes back to Pythagoras and ancient Greece.

Even the anatomy and physiology of the ear have a place in music
teaching. This tiny, delicate mechanism has enormous efficiency. It
should be treated with care and respect because of its vulnerability to fluid
collections, inflammations, and injury. What an incredible sensing device;
the ear is capable of responding to air vibrations smaller than the diameter
of a hydrogen atom.

The teacher as healer

Music exalts each joy, allays each grief,
Expels diseases, softens every pain,
Subdues the rage of passion and the plague.
                                                John Armstrong

Healing is not synonymous with therapy. Therapy demands an active
approach, a willingness for the strong to help the weak. To do his job
effectively, a therapist may have to inflict temporary discomfort when

cleansing away the debris of a wound that fails to heal spontaneously. Only after this is done can healing processes take place. Healing relies on the organism's innate capacity to repair itself, and the healer has to wait patiently for this to occur. He maintains optimism while trusting health to overcome disease. Relying on nature and the patient, a healer modestly and humbly mutes his own role in the conquest of a malady. The posture of fighting disease has little place in healing.

Music heals the breach between the direct and the symbolic expressions of emotional impulses. Direct expression of emotion leads to movements and actions – running away in fear, lashing out in rage, submitting to hedonism, or giving up in despair. Man's ability for symbolization makes abstract substitutes for direct action possible – words replace deeds, pictures symbolize fantasies, icons indicate actions. Often we are trapped between conflicting goals in direct versus symbolic expression. Music may provide a bridge to cross this conflict because it is both action AND symbol. The musical experience allows us simultaneously to have very strong emotions and to safely contain these emotions in nondisruptive ways. Music's dual capacity for stimulating and soothing the emotions enables the music teacher to play such a vital healing function in civilization.

Music consists of sounds and silences – both have healing properties. One can even think of music in terms of its ability to organize silence. One important responsibility of the teacher and music therapist may be to prevent choking the patient's environment with music to the point that it becomes intolerable noise. There may be times when he must know how to restrain making music. A closely related healing function is correctly advising the overzealous parents of children who are deficient in talent. Although overtly wishing to foster their child's musical development, the parents' covert purposes may be to exploit the youngster for prestige or financial profit. Exploitation does not necessarily produce bad effects musically speaking, as witness such exploited prodigies as Wolfgang Mozart or Ruth Slencinska. It is the injurious effect on personality we want to avoid. Exploitation gives the child a distorted sense of his own worth; he feels that he exists basically to gratify the needs of others and sees himself as an appendage to their lives rather than an integral entity. Sensing fierce exploitative or competitive motives behind a parent's request for his child's music lessons, teachers should discuss realistically with all concerned the disadvantages as well as the benefits of a musical career.

A cautious, healing attitude also helps in the management of sick children and their families. The wise teacher refers the emotionally disturbed to professional psychiatrists, physicians, and psychologists trained to treat the sick. A knowledge of past experiences with music in the home and family tells the teacher when to encourage further training and when to use other resources for help. He may ask the parents about their own personal experiences with music lessons; whether records are played at home, concerts attended, singing and dancing encouraged. The nursery school or kindergarten child has already been exposed to teaching influences outside the home that may provide useful clues as to whether more or less individual instruction is needed. One should beware of forcing music on a student who does not want to learn; encouragement can turn into discouragement and a fragile glimmer of the potential enjoyment of music may be extinguished forever. "I would have learned to like music had my piano teacher not insisted on scales" is the kind of complaint one hears from some of those whose teachers could not let them go.

To increase our tolerance for new and unexpected sounds may be another of the healing functions of music. All people tend to develop certain acoustical preferences, and some may become conditioned to avoid sounds they do not like. Our basic attitudes toward acoustical patterns probably develop early in life when any sudden and intense stimulus is likely to produce a major reflex response, often a startle reaction. Loud noises can also make an infant uncomfortable and cause him to cry. This cry perhaps adds an unconscious memory trace to the baby's backlog of behavioral experiences with sounds, hearkening back to the ambiguous communication when nobody was quite sure whether the signal was for food, warmth, diaper change, or holding. When vocalizing becomes speech, another layer of values is superimposed on the basic attitude to sounds. Positively, speech is associated with intelligence – "My, isn't Johnny a smart boy to learn so many words." Negatively, speech may be equated with unwanted aggression – "I wish that damn brat would keep his mouth shut." Not only vocal sounds are ambivalently valued in these ways. Rhythmic banging of toys, the cacophony of feet and elbows on the floor or furniture, the crashing of dishes and implements – these and other acoustical elements in a child's behavior elicit both positive and negative reactions from grown-ups. Because a child will identify with his grown-up models, part of his mind can embrace or incorporate such valuations. Inner conflicts may develop between impulses that promote noisy release and those that carry social disapproval. The healer's difficult task is to enter into the child's subjective world of sound valuations in order to reduce, whenever possible, the pressure of such conflicts. If the student can learn to appreciate beautiful (that is, musical) sounds, this may help build up his tolerance for noise (that is, unwanted sounds).

Finale

I have tried, in this brief essay, to compare the work of the music teacher with that of the listener, the guide, the coach, and the healer. Each of these functions may be involved in music therapy, which is the teaching of music to the emotionally and mentally disadvantaged. The music lesson is an ancient and honorable human institution, a mark of civilization. It carries forward the tradition of musical expression, which mediates between the direct expression of emotion and the symbolic sublimation of emotion (Ostwald 1963).

18

COLOR HEARING*

A missing link between normal perception and the hallucination

(1964)

Introduction

Patients rarely complain HOW they perceive the outer world. More often it is WHAT one hears, sees, or smells that causes distress. This may explain why such a frequent and interesting mode of auditory perception – color hearing – does not attract more attention in psychiatry. Individuals who hear in color usually accept this as 'normal' and may even find it pleasurable. The color-hearer usually ignores his condition unless questioned or challenged by persons without this capacity for double-sensation. Bleuler, whose monograph on the subject (Bleuler and Lehmann 1881) preceded his work in schizophrenia, was alerted to his own sound-color synesthesia only after a classmate's casual expression of curious surprise. Some cases of color-hearing are discovered accidentally during psychotherapy (Coriat 1913b).

An investigation of subliminal auditory activity alerted me to this problem of intersensory perception (Ostwald 1963). I found it extraordinarily difficult to fathom what experimental subjects were perceiving in the course of an experiment that required them to listen to some tape-recorded sounds containing sub-threshold baby-cries. Contrary to the reports of subliminal visual perceptions by Fischer and others (1960), my subjects only rarely visualized their remembered images. While one subject did describe a radiator-grille and another (an amateur artist) drew a waterfall, most reports of auditory experiences were verbal, descriptive, and relatively abstract (Ostwald 1961d). That some individuals habitually visualize sounds was a fact only dimly known to me through the literature on music appreciation and musicology (Ostwald 1960d).

---

*   Reprinted from the *Archives of General Psychiatry* 11: 40-47 (1964).

It therefore came as a pleasant surprise when a patient with color-hearing called and asked for attention. When I met her and realized that she was Negro (i.e., 'colored') the question of psychosocial factors in the origin of color-hearing naturally came to mind. But as I studied her case in greater detail, the similarity with other reported cases of color-hearing became more evident (see following Comment and Review of Literature). With today's renewed efforts toward investigating hallucinations (West 1962), it seems appropriate to spend some time also with this complex psychophysiological phenomenon of color-hearing.

Report of case

A 31-year-old, unmarried, Negro college graduate saw me several years ago to talk about her unusual way of perceiving sounds. As far back as she can remember, acoustical stimuli appeared to her not only in the form of auditory sensations, but were also perceived as simultaneous visual patterns in vivid color. All sounds, whether spoken words, musical tones, or mechanical noises produce these colorful visual sensations. In grade school she asked her girl friends whether they too 'hear in color', but was startled to find out that this is not the usual way of perceiving sounds. When she was about 14 years old, she confided in her sister, who it turned out had exactly the same problem. In college she learned that color-hearing is a form of synesthesia, and since then she has read several books on the subject. In fact when I first saw this patient her interest in the problem had assumed obsessional proportions. It was in part her aggressive, overtalkative preoccupation with color-hearing that suggested the need for a psychiatric consultation. Over the next three years I saw the patient approximately twice a week, and our discussions developed a good many insights into what synesthesia meant to her and how color-hearing pertained to her overall life adjustment.

The patient was a thin, stylishly dressed, attractive woman who usually walked rapidly into my office with an alert, watchful expression on her face. She would propel herself into a chair, and after a few flirtatious glances and restless gestures which invited attention, she excitedly launched into a monologue. Her speech was incredibly fast, almost hypomanic, yet quite comprehensible, well organized and appropriately intoned. "Every sound I hear registers as a color", she said, "and where words are concerned the colors I see are very clear. Each vowel, whether spoken by me or by someone else, brings a distinct color sensation into awareness." At my request she described her synesthesia for vowels as follows:

Long vowels: a (ah)   = always pink
               e (ee)   = rust, sometimes orange
               i (eye) = white
               o (oh)   = a strong vivid blue
               u (you) = dark-green bordering on black

Short vowels: a (cat)   = cream
              e (get)   = beige
              i (hit)   = natural straw
              o (got)   = gray
              u (uh)   = dusty green; the u sounds are subject to change
              u (put)   = putty color – muddy, a nasty sound, a brownish-
                          grayish mixture

These colors have various shapes and consistencies, depending partly on the consonants that precede the vowels. Thus, for example:

n   → transparency
l   → liquidity
c and s   → glossiness
r   → vapory, floury quality

The colors are not simply imagined, they are actually experienced visually, projected into external space like one 'sees' visual dreams. "I really see the color when I hear a word", she said, "and if I have time to analyze the spelling of the word, the colors will appear as though written out on a blackboard. With more rapid speech, each word has basic colors depending on the most prominent vowels heard." The range and variety of colors stimulated by different sounds is very complex, and often defies exact description. Even the Munsell Color Charts which describe colors in terms of three attributes – hue, value, and chroma – do not contain all the shades the patient is capable of differentiating, and when put on the spot she points to two very similar shades and says "it's between this and this color". Yet her sound-color responses are extremely consistent. Elmer Owens, PhD, the audiologist who tested the patient's hearing, found no major discrepancies in her color responses to a list of 200 words administered over 12 months apart. But when the sound and the spelling of a word conflict, certain difficulties may arise which she settles in favor of the spelling. For instance, *aisle* was a white word until she discovered it is not spelled *isle*, and since then it has been pink.

Musical sounds also produce visual sensations, single colors in the case of single tones and complex mixtures and patterns when the tones are combined into chords.

             C   = orange
             B   = no color
             A   = peach
             G   = red
             F   = yellow; F # = bright yellow
             E   = brown or maroon
             D   = blue or green
(middle)   C   = gray

Noises are also colored, but there is less variety:

Handclaps   = cream
Baby cries   = cream

Bells   = orange-red
Chimes   = orange-red
Squeaking shoes = orange-red

In addition to the automatic appearance of color sensations when she hears sounds, the patient has noticed that certain words evoke specific visual reactions. For example, her name and the names of persons well known to her tend to have colors not entirely predictable by the scheme for vowels and consonants. Numbers between 1 and 14 evoke the following colors:

1 = silver-gray		8 = brown	
2 = dark-green		9 = charcoal black	
3 = cherry-red		10 = flaming red	
4 = yellow		11 = dark rose-gray	
5 = lavender		12 = red	
6 = natural-straw		13 = lighter than bright-red	
7 = light-blue		14 = yellow	
		(teens add transparent orange)	

Only in the case of seven can she rationally explain these associations. "Seven is always blue because I associate it with heaven which is blue and with God." Numbers, colors, and months are further combined into complex three-dimensional spatial patterns which look something like Figure 1. The patient

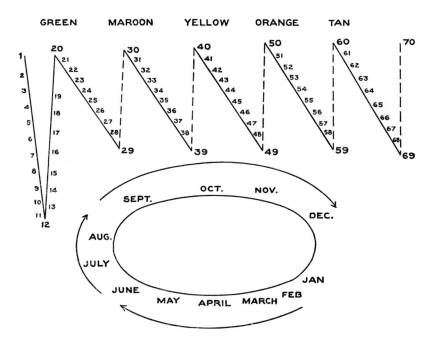

Fig. 1. Reproduction of a drawing made by the patient, of three-dimensional imagery that synthesizes her concepts of colors, numbers, elapsed personal time, and months.

claims that this visual color-space pattern also represents various elements from her life, philosophy, and emotional orientation. For example, the straight line 12-20 symbolizes adolescence, "when mother criticized me for trying to be too perfect." The first element in the zigzag line is a penis, "which I often wonder about – is it brown or colorless. The rest of the zigzag is a vagina, while the circle of months is a uterus." To understand this symbolism, let me briefly review the patient's history and enumerate some characteristics of her personality.

The patient was born and raised on the fringes of the Negro ghetto in a large eastern metropolis. Her father is a pastry cook who came from the Southwest. He had little formal education, is artistically inclined, passive, sensitive, and given to outbursts of brutality and range. Her mother stems from the South. She is better educated than the father, and the patient describes her as more aggressive, controlling, and demanding. The parents separated when the patient was seven years old. While she occasionally sees her father, the mother has really been the central figure in the family and had most to do with the children's upbringing. One sister, a year older than the patient, is a schoolteacher, married, and has a daughter. Except for the usual childhood diseases and a mild chronic acne, the patient has been in good physical health. There is no family background of psychiatric or neurological disease. She supports herself by working as a teacher, or as a secretary-clerk in libraries and administrative offices. Her interests include music, theater, hiking, literature, and art. She attends church occasionally but is not strongly religious. She lives alone but enjoys talking and being with people and goes to concerts and other cultural events with girl friends. She fears and resents men, but will occasionally go on a date with someone she regards as her inferior in education or social background. Her only 'steady' male companion has been a Negro homosexual. She has never had sexual intercourse. Contacts with non-Negroes are limited to work situations, and even here she prefers to socialize with girls or with men of Latin or Oriental extraction.

The patient's early childhood memories reveal a basic concern with colors, textures, and emotions. "I recall mother feeding me mush – she was not as good a cook as my father. Her mush was disgusting and lumpy – I'd object to it but she would insist, giving us mush of different colors and saying 'here's some brown mush' or 'here's some white mush'." Fads based on the color and texture of foods still play an important role in her life. For example, only white rice is palatable; brown rice is "too mushy and not stiff enough." She abhors banana pudding, which is "too lumpy." Bread must be hard and brown, preferably Russian rye or pumpernickel. One of her objections to religious services is that the communion wafer is white. "Jesus might have been a Negro, and brown bread ought to be served". Childhood memories concerning her father are also in color. She vividly recalls an episode in which her father, an amateur sculptor, made a pale-whitish plaster-of-Paris head which he called "Mr. Know-it-all." This head was placed on a table in the living room and was supposed to magically gather information so as to tattle to the parents all misdeeds and sins the little girls might commit.

While she was outwardly aggressive, athletic, self-confident, and a dare-devil type, inwardly the patient has always felt extremely insecure and fearful. Since early childhood she has been particularly concerned with and about her own body. Masturbation is practiced with great frequency, and she dates its onset to age three. Both nocturnally and in the daytime she produces clitoral pleasure by squeezing her thighs. In addition to this "dry process", she recognizes, since puberty, diffuse pelvic sensations accompanied by mucous secretion which are very satisfying but "maybe not a full orgasm." Much of her masturbation occurs "automatically through habit" and is not accompanied by fantasies. But at times she consciously thinks about "intercourse with a partner", particularly when she masturbates to induce sleep. This partner is often a large, heavy woman, like her mother whose bed she regularly shared after her father left home when she was seven years old. But a nipple-like penis is often included in the fantasies, either attached to the partner, or to herself in front near the umbilicus or in back extending from a vertebra. Vaginal insertion is absolutely taboo, and except for one tense speculum examination when she was 22, no fingers, douche-nozzles, or any other objects have ever been permitted entry. Except for a single episode of cunnilingus during adolescence in which she was the active partner, there have been no homosexual experiences. She fears however that her abhorrence for men and friendliness toward women may be interpreted as homosexuality, and sometimes complains "people whisper about perversion behind my back."

Hypersensitivity to cold and pain are important features of her personality make-up. She particularly abhors cold weather, and usually wears heavier clothing than other women, sometimes two sweaters plus an overcoat even on balmy San Francisco days. Pain is felt physically throughout her entire body when she is reprimanded, criticized, or harshly spoken to – another form of synesthesia. Displeasing remarks addressed to her by others "go right through me, cut me, tear me to pieces, destroy me." This exquisite sensitivity to pain stems, she believes, from whippings which her father regularly meted out to discipline his daughters. Whippings on the thighs and legs are recalled with really enormous distress, and while it appears that often the patient provoked such punishment by deliberately misbehaving, especially in adolescence when she was an aggressive, mischievous tomboy, she is filled with rage and revengeful thoughts towards her father. "I often felt like smashing my father's skull – and if I were a boy I'd have killed him long ago." Her mother is never seen as a target for hate, and the patient considers all punishment from the mother – even painful whippings – as justified.

The onset of menstruation at age 16 ushered in fears of forcible abduction, rape, and murder which haunt her to this day and almost entirely forbid her to go out at night or to walk alone. Her one and only romance – in college – miscarried due to terrifying thoughts about possible sexual intercourse, which she believes is "tremendously painful, flesh-tearing, dirty, evil, and immoral." At 22 the surgical removal of a small benign breast tumor precipitated dreadful nightmares of mutilation and dismemberment by her father. Her dreams are often in color. There are recurring themes of violence, destruction, deaths, holocausts, sacrificial festivals, and depopulating catastrophes of various types. At other times her dreams are full of childish and pleasurable images. These dreams are often in bright colors. They show little girls gorgeously attired in luminous gowns; lusciously tinted lollipops; bright circus scenes with delicate animals; porcelain intricately decorated in vivid hues. Depressed dreams are dark in color and show putrifying corpses, or sick and disgusting persons vomiting, with their bowels hanging out and exuding purulent feces. Cloacal and bisexual symbols frequently overlap. For example, in one dream she saw "two telephone booth-like urinals with a male sign on one and a female sign on the other. I entered the booth called 'female' but found 'male' printed on the reverse side of the door. Then I urinated standing up." In fact she urinates very frequently, often only a few drops; she seeks jobs and social situations which permit ready access to a bathroom where she can masturbate and look at other women sitting on the toilet. Confused about the appearance and color of the penis, she tries to peek at babies and little boys in public lavatories. In her dreams the penis often appears as a paper, cloth, or plastic object, from three to six inches long. This imaginary penis has no color.

Comment and review of the literature

John Thomas Woolhouse, an English ophthalmologist living between 1650 and 1735, described a blind patient who perceived colors while listening to musical sounds (Welleck 1931). John Locke in his *Essay Concerning Human Understanding* published in 1690 mentioned a similar case, and in 1735 the first book about simultaneous optical and acoustical experiences appeared in France, written by a Jesuit mathematician – Louis Bertrand Castel. In his treatise on the origins of language (1770), Herder mentioned color-hearing in connection with the idea that emotion provides the basis for all sensation. During the 19th century the concept of fusion between different senses attracted enormous interest among philosophers, psychologists, and artists (Argelander 1927). Rimbaud wrote poetry about the color of vowels (Rimbaud 1948), Scriabin composed music for a color-organ (Scriabin 1913), and Huysmans wrote an incredible novel about a wealthy psychopath who enjoyed every conceivable intercombination between sounds, tastes, smells, and colors (Huysmans 1885).

In medical circles there was by now considerable debate about the pathologic implications of color-hearing, and in 1881 two Swiss medical students produced what must still be considered the definitive monograph on this subject (Bleuler and Lehmann 1881). The senior author, himself subject to very intense intersensory experiences, was Eugen Bleuler. Bleuler and Lehmann interviewed close to 600 persons, of whom 12.5% turned out to have "double-sensations." This condition, for which the general term "synesthesia" was proposed by Millet (1892) is characterized by the simultaneous appearance of several sensations referred to different modalities when in fact only a single sensory system is externally stimulated.

No consistent agreement about the incidence of this condition emerges from what has by now become a voluminous literature (Mahling 1926). Suarez de Mendoza thought 3.5% of the population to have synesthesia, while Lombroso estimated 50%. A recent report (1957) places the incidence at 14% among males and 31% among females (Uhlich 1957).

Color hearing is by far the most frequent form of synesthesia, and all cases share certain common features: The condition appears early in childhood, usually around three to four years. There is a scale-like relation between the sensations, dark colors evoked by low-pitched sounds becoming progressively brighter as the pitch goes up. Vowels and musical tones stimulate clearer and more definite colors than do consonants and noises. The colors are projected into outer space, often directionally towards the source of the sound. They are experienced as mobile three-dimensional patterns which vary in size, shape, texture, hue, and consistency according to the pitch, intensity, and quality of the stimulating sounds. The visual sensation begins and ends with the sound itself, and cannot be altered volitionally, by closing ones eyes, or by looking at real colors. In some subjects imagining a sound produces the same color sensation as actually hearing it. Intellectual knowledge of spelling and phonetics gained in school may modify synesthetic responses somewhat but never changes the unique subjective sensory quality which most subjects have great difficulty describing to others.

Bleuler reexamined his case material 15 years later and observed essentially no changes in the colors evoked by sounds, except that there was some reduction in the intensity and clarity of these "photisms." (Bleuler 1913). He felt synesthesia to be a physiological condition, present in everyone but available for conscious experience in only the minority of adults. Synesthesia is considered a symptom of mental disease when the secondary sensations overshadow or obliterate awareness of the actual stimulus. This happens in certain schizophrenic illnesses (Jaspers 1963), after mescaline intoxication (Delay et al. 1951), and very rarely with D-lysergic acid diethylamide (LSD) ingestion (Rinkel 1966). Bleuler argued vehemently against the notion that synesthetic phenomena result from early childhood experiences whose memory associations are later repressed. This theory had been proposed by Hug-Hellmuth (1912), a psychoanalyst who studied her own color-hearing in great detail. While agreeing with Bleuler's notion about constitutional factors, Hug-Hellmuth strongly emphasized the importance of infantile sexual experiences which, by virtue of stirring up pleasurable and painful emotions, can heighten synesthesias and cause them to become fixed in memories and fantasies.

Pfister, another early psychoanalyst, pointed to similarities between synesthesias and hallucinations, both of which he felt were indirect manifestations of scoptophilia. He described a 17-year-old girl with color hearing who was libidinally inhibited. Her a→ blue synesthesia symbolized repression of heterosexual interest, while e→ yellow stood for repressed homosexuality (Pfister 1912). Coriat (1913a, b) described two unusual cases, both women in their early forties who had come for psychoanalysis. One of these patients visualized numbers in a geometrical arrangement,[1] a zigzag line going up to 10, dropping to 20, and then gradually ascending once more (Coriat 1913b). He postulated a specific physiological abnormality of cortical irradiation whereby sensory stimuli are "derailed" to the wrong projection areas. Wells also argued against the importance of infantile experience. He felt color-hearing to be a primitive form of autistic thinking restricted to elementary sensory patterns and suggested that synesthesias be contrasted with more advanced forms of prelogical thought underlying symbol formation in dreams, hallucinations, and myths (Wells 1919).

After 1921 synesthesia almost completely disappeared from the medical literature. Psychologists and linguists however continued to be concerned with this problem. Von Hornbostel postulated an abstract sense of awareness that unites all forms of sensation, and Heinz Werner confirmed this by a series of experiments in which susceptible individuals were asked to describe changes in threshold sensations produced by "subjectively framed" stimuli (Werner 1948). Werner thought that midbrain and thalamic regions are probably responsible for what he called the "vital" intersensory activity of the nervous system. He concluded that "The basis for synesthesia is an undifferentiated perceptual experience which permits the linking together of the separate realms of sense that is lacking or in abeyance in the highly differentiated and objectified forms of experience." Others have commented on the more frequent occurrence of synesthesias among children and consider this to be of importance in memory function and the learning of language (Reichard et al. 1949). Goldstone feels that both synesthesias and hallucinations reflect a basic process of conceptual confusion in which the subject interprets a sensory message from one mode in terms of another mode. He states "the conceptual distinction

---

[1] Dr. W. C. M. Scott, of Montreal, has called my attention to similar zigzag imagery reported by Francis Galton (1883).

between light and sound is no more automatic than the conceptual distinction between maleness and femaleness. The neural mechanism for making intersensory distinctions may be 'built in' but the experience or perception of these distinctions are more probably of a learned, conceptual nature" (Goldstone 1962). In a similar vein, Mahler and Elkish (1953) have written about the "undifferentiated affective-perceptive engram conglomerates" to explain the fusion and interchangeability of concepts in a severely disturbed 6-year-old boy.

In the patient I described earlier, color hearing was clearly part of a severe personality disturbance. In addition to synesthesia she showed:

1. A generalized hypersensitivity to sensory stimulation
2. Morbid interest in peeking and looking
3. Inhibited sexuality
4. Rejection of femininity
5. Social withdrawal
6. A paranoid attitude
7. Emotional instability
8. Uncertainty as to her personal identity in terms of race, status, and occupation

She came from a turbulent family, was abandoned by her father, and overprotected by her mother. Fluctuating social attitudes toward colored persons in the United States undoubtedly have contributed to this patient's withdrawal and served to intensify her interest in color hearing. Her synesthetic sensory responses to words kept this patient mentally enmeshed in nonverbal fantasy systems and interfered with her utilizing verbal thought, reasoning, and constructive ideation. This was a real impediment to therapeutic progress, and I often felt that this patient preferred to live in an inner world of synesthetic and masturbatory fantasies rather than face an outer world filled with harsh and bitter realities. In her fantasies she could be male or female and white or all shades of brown. It was extraordinarily difficult for me to get her frankly to acknowledge her problems in living, her loneliness, her frustrations, her minority status. She wanted to treat all aspects of her environment – including myself – as some kind of foreign element which could be denied, obscured, even manipulated by magically thinking it to be otherwise. In this respect her color hearing came very close to hallucination.

In the face of these difficulties one can only express amazement at some of the little bits of progress she did make during the years I observed her. For the first time in her life she acknowledged that there is in fact a color problem in her environment and that her inner preoccupation with color hearing is likely to interfere with sensible solution of this problem. She noticed – painfully and hesitantly – that folks do in fact discriminate and that it is not as easy for her as for a white woman to obtain employment, to live where she pleases, and to mingle socially. Bit by bit she overcame some of her fears of going out and started to conquer her shyness in public. She joined a Little Theater group and participated in activities of a hiking club, a group where because of her interest in physical activity and walking she felt particularly at home. She reduced her absenteeism at work, changed jobs less frequently, and exposed herself more courageously to criticism. She traveled more, went on a visit to her family, and developed a warmer relationship with her sister. She even started to entertain friends, learned to cook, and occasionally ventured on a date with a man. When I last saw her she was planning to move to a city where the climate and social environment were more to her taste. While still very much opposed to the idea of sexual love and marriage, she did express the hope one day of having a child. The color hearing did not change, except insofar that it stopped being a major topic in her conversation, and my clinical impression was that the hypertrophied preoccupation with inner synesthetic experiences may have kept this patient from developing more disabling symptoms and helped protect her from a more devastating mental illness.

Summary and conclusions

While synesthesias (perceptions referred to multiple sense-organ-systems upon stimulation of a single sense-organ) seldom cause patients to complain or seek treatment, these phenomena are of considerable psychiatric interest because of their kinship to normal imagery, dreams, and hallucinations. This report is about a Negro woman in her early thirties who has noted color-hearing, an audiovisual synesthesia, since age three. She also manifested generalized hyperreactivity to sensory stimulation, sexual problems, and a chronic disturbance of personality with considerable social withdrawal, autism, and paranoid hypersensitivity. A review of her life development showed how color-hearing – originally a sensory process – became part of her intellectualized obsessional concern with personal problems about sex and race. This confirms Hug-Hellmuth's observations (1912) about the way personal life experiences, by stirring up pleasurable and painful emotions, can heighten synesthetic responses (of probably physiologic origin) and fix these in memories and fantasies. Contrasting and complementary views about intersensory phenomena by Bleuler,

Coriat, Werner, Goldstone, and others are discussed. During the course of normal language learning, children probably link their auditory memories with other internally felt sensations, for example movements of the larynx, tongue, lips, and face (Ostwald 1963). Whether or not color-hearing normally accompanies language development in childhood, or represents a variant with possibly psychopathological implications in later life, is not presently known and merits further investigation.

SECTION IV

EMPATHIC COMMUNICATION
WITH SOUNDS THAT HAVE MEANING

INTRODUCTORY STATEMENT

There is a quality of human communication which heightens the semiotic skills of listening and speaking. We call it EMPATHY (Cooper 1970). The empathic person feels his way into the psychological space of his communicative partners. Whatever he says is spoken with the awareness that several levels of interpretation and misinterpretation are possible. Also in listening, the empathic person recognizes that he is asked to do much more than interpret words. The speech act may be one way of confiding, and the empathic listener is inevitably obliged to react to the concreteness of the speaker's physical existence along with the abstractness of his linguistic formulations. That empathic behavior may be largely 'internal' – i.e. invisible and inaudible to outside observers – does not allow scientists to conclude that this behavior is nonexistent. One can only say that the inner dialogues of empathic conversation have to be studied by methods which are as yet crude and inefficient in terms of the sort of accuracy and reliability necessary for scientific research (Semmes 1966).

Section IV includes papers which were written in attempting to define certain elements of clinical communication, and to portray especially the dyadic clinical situation of patient-with-doctor which requires empathy. Paper 19 is an introduction to one of the clinical arts, usually called AUSCULTATION. This is the semiotic skill of listening for tell-tale sounds of disease. Some of the important contributors to this field are mentioned – Hippocrates, Morgagni, Auenbrugger, Laennec, among others. I then venture upon a model for sonic communication which combines certain elements of psychoanalytic theory and psycholinguistics. Because there is no distinction in my discussion between conscious and unconscious aspects of diagnostic listening, the critical reader may wish to turn to detailed discussions of this problem, e.g., the paper about sign phenomena and unconscious meaning by Rosen (1969).

The next paper, 20, represents my contribution to the interdisciplinary conference on PARALANGUAGE AND KINESICS which Thomas Sebeok organized in 1962, resulting in *Approaches to Semiotics* (Sebeok, Hayes, and Bateson 1964). The instructions for the principal contributors were to prepare a 'state of the art' paper, and mine was to be clinical medicine. Well – that means the state of the art of medicine – an impossible assignment. Thus I limited myself to a discussion of how the patient communicates about disease with the doctor. My bias towards the medical model was immediately challenged at the conference by Ray Birdwhistell, Margaret Mead and others who have to adopt a much broader and more global view of human culture than is required for the practicing physician. The conference was lively and stimulating and truly productive too because of the integrative possibilities in the semiotic approach which colleagues like Shands (1970) have described at much greater length than I.

In applying to actual clinical work what I had learned at the conference, several opportunities presented themselves during the subsequent years. Paper 21 is an example. Written for a book about therapeutic work in prisons – i.e. the 'correctional' community – it describes the interview as a diagnostic and therapeutic instrument. The concept of INNER SPEECH becomes more important in my thinking at this time, due not only to a greater degree of intellectual awareness of Vygotsky, Luria, Piaget, and other writers but because of the personal influence of Harry Wilmer, M.D., Ph.D., a brilliant clinician, writer, and artist who at that time was on the faculty of the University of California School of Medicine where I work. Together we worked on the experiment which is described in paper 22. Wilmer had a great many interesting ideas about the INNER DIALOGUES which I have described as part of dialectic inner speech. We also wrote an article about inner speech and clinical sensitivity – Wilmer providing the drawings and I the text (Ostwald 1969a).

Paper 23 shows that I am not reluctant to move away from the medical model whenever this seems desirable, as for instance in an emergency or during psychotherapy when the doctor has to function as educator as well as physician. Diagnosis always has two sides. One is clarification of what the disease process has been, so it can be stopped, reversed, or adjusted to. This may be largely a professional matter requiring technical knowledge, social support from a 'health-care' system, and a certain amount of in-group jargon. The other side has to do with communication within a larger field – the patient's 'healthiness' as well as his illness, plus the 'illnessness' of the so-called 'normal' surroundings, i.e. the patient's relatives, friend, fellow-workers, and other social co-participants.

To try healing the hiatus between general and professional semiotics of disease, I include in this section a paper prepared for a conference about deafness, a subject I shall return to in Section V. Deafness translators have to be BIMODAL, one avenue ('channel') of communication being audio-aural, the other kinesic-visual. Very fascinating problems of translation are produced, and the meeting in Tucson, Arizona was organized to discuss them. Paper 24 is about the Diagnostic and Statistical Manual of Mental Disorders used in the United States. This is the official language of psychiatric diagnosis and I would like to call attention here to a very interesting alternative to this approach, viz. the description of DISEASE STATES, as explained in a recent European monograph (Silbermann 1971).

You might think of paper 25 as a remedy for the diagnostic struggles described in the preceding papers. It is about psychotherapeutic experience, as exemplified in the work of R. R. Greenson, M.D. I wish that a videotape of Dr. Greenson could be included in every text about semiotics because he is a great performer. His way of talking – expressively, urgently, to the point, with sensitivity and courage – is a model of behavior in the clinical-therapeutic relationship. The article is a book-review, summarizing the essential points made by Greenson about the real vs. the imaginary aspects of a human dyad.

19

SONIC COMMUNICATION IN MEDICAL
PRACTICE AND RESEARCH*

(1963)

Most living creatures make sound. Insects hum, birds warble, whales whistle and human beings speak by manipulating certain sound-producing body parts. In most scientific studies of communication today, there is a distinct emphasis on the linguistic aspects of human soundmaking – the use of speech sounds which are symbols in a language code. But equally important in communication is the use of nonlinguistic sounds – sounds that either convey meaning directly and nonsymbolically, or are part of a code which differs functionally and structurally from formal speech. Some of these nonlinguistic sounds stem from automatic processes over which we have little willful control: heartbeats, breathing and rumbling of the bowels. Others result from the release of internal tensions through expressive behavior: crying, laughter, sighing and certain forms of coughing. Still others are products of societal, occupational or entertainment situations and therefore closely reflect the practices of a particular time and culture: singing, mechanical noise and instrumental music. It would take much more space than we have available here to deal thoroughly with these various aspects of acoustic communication, and I shall therefore focus on one particular subject – sonic diagnosis – which is pertinent from a mental health point of view.

The history of sonic diagnosis

Body sounds have interested healers and diagnosticians since the dawn of recorded history. Even in very primitive civilizations or where medical practice was in the hands of priests and witch doctors, it was observed that life depends on breathing and that silence connotes death (Neuburger

---

* Reprinted from *The Journal of Communication* 13. 3: 156-65 (1963).

1910). Babylonian inscriptions comment on the audible expressions of sick persons, and the Ebers Papyrus (Egypt, circa 1550 B.C.) alludes to DIAGNOSTIC LISTENING. Hindu and Chinese medical writings clearly refer to vocal manifestations of disease, breath sounds, the crepitant noises emitted by broken bones and gurgling of the intestines. Hippocrates (460-370 B.C.), considered by many to be the father of Western medicine, urged every physician to pay special attention to the voice, gnashing of the teeth, yawning, hiccups, crepitation and flatulence. He devised a technique for SUCCUSSION, whereby phthistic patients were vigorously shaken so that splashing noises in the chest might reveal the location and liquefaction of pus collections. Hence, knowledge came very early into medicine that one can glean information about vital body processes by listening to a patient's sonic emissions.

Also the therapeutic effects of acoustic stimulation were well known before Hippocrates (Schullian and Schoen 1948). Certain patients were noted to respond favorably to loud noises made in their presence, ostensibly for the purpose of frightening any evil spirits thought to inhabit the sick body, or to scare away devils responsible for the state of ill health. Other sufferers manifested improvement whenever their illness was dramatically reenacted through song and dance. Later in the Greek temples of healing, music therapy was a crucial phase of every patient's care. Sound as well as silence came to be used in specific medical ways throughout the hospitals of Rome and the Arab world.

Very little new in the way of observation, methods or insights pertaining to sonic diagnosis can be found in the medical history of early Christianity, and the Middle Ages were marked by loss or suppression of much of the earlier knowledge. But during the Renaissance there was curiosity and eager research into naturalistic phenomena, including the sounds of the body. Leonardo Da Vinci observed that certain pelvic noises of pregnant women, previously thought to be intrauterine crying of the fetus, actually represented flatulence. He also wrote a treatise about the voice, which has unfortunately been lost, and studied the acoustics of musical instruments. Other important contributors to sonic diagnosis were the physicians William Harvey, who related thoracic noise to the heartbeat; Robert Hooke, who described wheezing sounds, and Giovanni Morgagni, who commented on various inflammatory noises in the chest (Bishop 1956).

But it was not until the eighteenth century, the time when Bach, Haydn and Mozart created such novel musical experiences, that physicians really started to listen and to find new ways for studying the acoustic manifestations of disease. One of the most remarkable contributors to this field was Leopold Auenbrugger (1722-1809), a doctor whose musical interests were so profound that among other things he wrote the libretto for an opera by Salieri, teacher of Beethoven and Schubert. During visits to his father's inn in Vienna, Auenbrugger noted that the waiters would tap briskly on the sides of wine barrels in order to estimate the amount of liquid. Applying this method of echo sounding – called PERCUSSION – to his patients, Auenbrugger found that he could readily detect inflammatory changes in pneumonia, discover fluid exudations and tell when a heart was enlarged and failing (Jarcho 1961). Auenbrugger wrote two books about mental disease in which his keen auditory sensibility combined with great clinical skill led to important new observations. He described the constant complaining and screams of depressed patients during attacks of maniacal rage, contrasting these patterns with symptoms of equally sick and often suicidal melancholics who hide inner feelings behind a cloak of silence (Menninger-Lerchenthal 1953).

Up to this time, doctors had always listened to diagnostic sounds by IMMEDIATE auscultation, even putting their ears directly against the patient's body. R. T. H. Laennec (1781-1826), a fastidious, flute-playing, French bachelor, considered this form of physical diagnosis to be "uncomfortable, disgusting, and impractical" (Kevram 1960). Rolling some paper notebooks into a hard, hollow tube, he placed one end against the patient and listened at the other. This was the first instrument ever used to study diagnostic body sounds. Later built of wood (see Figure 1) and adaptable for studying heartbeats, murmurs, breathing, voice production and all kinds of friction noises, Laennec's stethoscope had a profoundly stimulating effect on other scientists. For example, Felix Savart (1791-1841), a physician already famous for his invention of the musical pitch wheel, devoted the last ten years of his life exclusively to the acoustic study of heart murmurs (McKusick and Wiskind 1959).

The instrumental approach to human sound reached its apogee in Helmholtz's famous consolidation of acoustics with physiology. Hermann von Helmholtz (1821-1894) was an organically minded German physician with a passion for music but little inclination to do psychological research. He always regretted not having investigated "psychical motives" or studied "utterances and actions of the various affections of the mind" (Helmholtz 1885). Had he done so, an important but obscure piece of research from America – by none other than the son of Benjamin Rush – would perhaps have attracted much wider attention in scientific circles than it did at the time. James Rush (1786-1869) asked: How are feelings

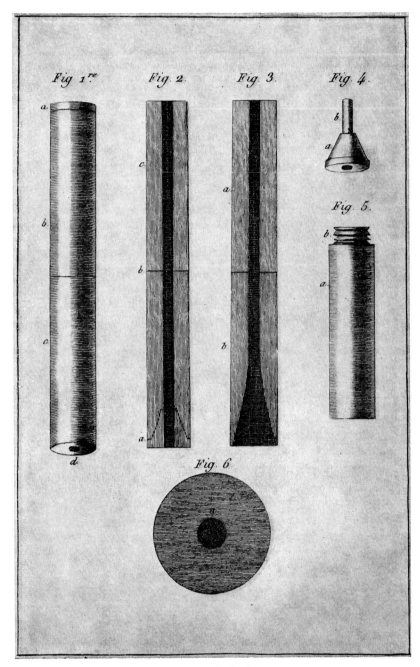

Fig. 1. Laennec's Stethoscope.

communicated acoustically? Carefully observing the various speech patterns used in medical consultations, at social events, in classrooms, at church and in the theatre, he concluded that specific VOCAL SIGNS communicate "conditions or states of mind". Using a modified form of musical notation, Rush showed these signs to consist of definable patterns of "vocality, force, time, abruptness, and pitch" (Rush 1867).

Some aspects of sonic communication in psychiatry

Current understanding of acoustic communication has been broadened through two scientific developments in the twentieth century, both of which also influence medical thought in other fields: (1) recognition that human consciousness is limited in its capacity to comprehend nature; (2) creation of a technology to explore natural phenomena within these limits. That sound-making as well as many other aspects of an individual's personal behavior is unconsciously controlled was demonstrated by Sigmund Freud (1856-1939). More recent psychoanalytic work shows that much of the ego apparatus responsible for interpersonal communication is also unconscious (Meerloo 1959). To speak, an individual must utter sounds most capable of coding his thoughts. He selects these sounds from an array of acoustic symbols whose meaning and temporal organization is limited through social convention. Schematically, the preconscious and conscious decision-making processes which lead up to speech look something like this:

> the speaker adopts an active role
> ↓
> he searches for a potential recipient of messages
> ↓
> he selects an appropriate code for communication
> ↓
> he engages a body system capable of signal emission
> ↓
> he makes sounds.

But this proceeds in the face of inexorable unconscious id demands for direct gratification of libidinal and aggressive urges, leading to conflict with the speaker's superego desire for delayed, socially appropriate communication.

As a result, what was intended to come out of the mouth in the form of informative SIGNALS may emerge instead as NOISE – mispronunciation, jargon, embolophrasic "ahs" and "ums", elisions or reduplications. Speech may even cease entirely, as in hesitancy, blocking and pathologic silence. Or what the speaker cannot convey by means of linguistic signs may instead be broadcast through gesture, grimaces, emotive sound-making or psychosomatic symptoms (Feldman 1959). For example, Freud's infantile neurosis patient emitted noises as a child whenever "he saw people that he felt sorry for, such as beggars, cripples, or very old men. He had to breathe out noisely, so as not to become like them; and under certain other conditions he had to draw in his breath vigorously" (Freud 1925a).

Research problems

There has been an impressive efflorescence of acoustics and speech science in recent years. But few objective methods have so far been applied to the kinds of clinical problems cited above. No standard psychiatric text as yet contains recordings or measurements of any human sound, and many clinicians still rely on a vague descriptive terminology which is miles behind even Rush's primitive effort. To do acoustical research, an investigator will have to get a high-fidelity micro-phone and a properly calibrated tape recorder. He then must arrange his diagnostic and treatment situation in such a way that all pertinent sound events can be collected (Ostwald 1963). Listening to what he has recorded, the investigator may be surprised to find out how much more goes on during an encounter with a patient than was realized at the time. Repeated listening reveals that much of what at first seemed puzzling or trivial contains a wealth of phenomenological data – tonal patterns, stresses, pauses, rhythms, intensity fluctuations and curious noises that are extremely hard to describe. Often these sounds provide clues as to the affective components of the patient's behavior. Reviewing an inter-view's sequential events, the clinician may be able to discover, for example, how a discussion drifted subtly into social palaver and away from more disturbing psychobiological problems like hunger, pain, frustration, greed or ambition.

Linguists have only recently coined a term – PARALANGUAGE – for that portion of human acoustic behavior which deals with emotion, and they are now seriously engaged in trying to find out how this aspect of soundmaking is related to silent communication with the body, called kinesics (Sebeok et al. 1964). It is also important, both clinically and theoretically, to know how paralanguage is learned, what its rules of organization and patterning may be and in which way these differ from principles governing linguistic interaction between persons. In other words, contemporary research attempts to clarify the significant relationships between the code (language) and the activity (speech) involved in sonic communication.

For this task it has become necessary to take acoustical events out of the realm of sound proper and to translate them into forms which can be denoted and analyzed with the aid of other skills than hearing alone. PHONETIC TRANSCRIPTION reduces oral sounds to sets of alphabetical symbols. This is useful if one wishes to study a person's individualized soundmaking in microscopic detail. PHONEMIC NOTATION describes the extent to which two persons are communicating with each other by virtue of sharing a common, socially instigated acoustic code. Clinicians, who must be able to think in terms of individual as well as social processes, should be familiar with both of these approaches to the denotation of sound (Pittenger et al. 1960).

Music deals with larger time segments than phonetic or phonemic transcriptions can handle. Denotation schemes based on musical principles are therefore particularly appropriate for the study of emotive soundmaking. These have been applied in the analysis of singing, humming, paralinguistic phenomena and schizophrenic speech. Musicians, whose role as participants in clinical research and treatment has never been very clearly defined, might be able to contribute in a very telling way to the study of sonic communication (Gutheil 1951). Already trained to perceive and to describe in nonlinguistic terms the sounds human beings produce, a good instrumental musician has personal knowledge about many of the significant relationships between soundmaking, bodily expression, thinking and mood.

Finally, the clinical worker may choose to utilize LABORATORY METHODS for studying sounds. His nonmedical colleagues in noise control, who measure the sounds of jet planes, machinery and other nonliving things, should be consulted. Biologists who analyze sonic communication among animals also have valuable experience to contribute. Devices are available that convert the physical energy contained in a given sound into numerical or visual symbols. To measure a sound, one uses a set of acoustic filters – for instance, the H. H. Scott Sound Analyzer – and determines intensity levels (in decibels) for each particular band of the frequency spectrum. This reveals the CROSS-SECTIONAL STRUCTURE of a particular sound component independent of time. For studying moment-to-moment changes in acoustic energy, it is necessary to apply SPECTROGRAPHY. For example, by means of the Kay Sonagraph one can demonstrate characteristic patterns of repetition, hesitation, overemphasis, energy decay, monotony, melodiousness and hypo- or hyper-resonance (Ostwald 1964b). Since laboratory methods produce a tremendous amount of data, automatic processing devices will probably be necessary to achieve correlation between soundmaking and other clinically significant variables.

Summary

Physicians since time immemorial have used sonic emissions of the human body as informative clues in the diagnosis of disease. Subjective and descriptive approaches to body sound sufficed until the nineteenth century, when Laennec's invention of the stethoscope inaugurated the instrumental study of acoustic signs. Largely because of Freud's insistence on the importance of unconscious dynamic processes in symptom formation, physicians today are aware of the psychopathologic significance of various nonlinguistic sounds. Noises, malpronunciation, errors and other sonic phenomena detectable by ear indicate shifts in the affective undercurrents that influence speech. Modern methods which can assist the clinical worker to study these sonic phenomena more objectively include cross-sectional acoustic analysis and sound spectrography.

20

HOW THE PATIENT COMMUNICATES
ABOUT DISEASE WITH THE DOCTOR*

(1964)

A medical doctor is concerned with total human functioning – the way the body works, how patients think, what they feel, and their activities in family and social situations. He must always emphasize the detection and correction of malfunction, and part of this primary task is to interpret a patient's sign-making behavior correctly, be it linguistic, paralinguistic, or kinesic. The doctor listens to the patient's words in terms of SYMPTOMS that point to disease; he looks for PHYSICAL SIGNS in order to recognize underlying bodily malfunction; he postulates DIAGNOSES as a guide for subsequent management of the problem presented by the patient; and he administers the appropriate TREATMENT to reverse tangible pathology and prevent further disability.

Medical history-taking, examination, diagnosis, and treatment all involve communication between two persons whose individual roles are usually quite clear and whose tasks are also well-defined. This is why clinical problems offer such interesting possibilities for investigation in terms of current theories about processes of information exchange. The purpose of this paper is to highlight but one aspect of the sign-making behavior of sick persons as perceived by physicians: communication without words.

The patient-doctor relationship

An old physician has said:

For him who has eyes to see and ears to hear no mortal can hide his secret; he whose lips are silent chatters with his fingertips and betrays himself through all his pores (Lasswell 1930).

* Reprinted from *Approaches to Semiotics*, T. A. Sebeok, A. S. Hayes, and M. C. Bateson (eds.): 11-34 (The Hague: Mouton, 1964).

Physicians traditionally function in two-person relationships with their patients, and the assumptions of this clinical dyad must be understood if one uses it as a model for research in communication (Frank 1961). From the beginning of his interaction with a patient, the physician alerts himself to visible, audible, palpable, and smellable signs that non-symbolically transmit information about pathology. He is allowed to behave in such a way as to facilitate direct body contact with the patient, touching naked skin, listening to inner noises, and inspecting private openings so as to learn things which may be unknown to the sender. During the course of their interaction the patient (sender) also speaks to the doctor (receiver), using conventional verbal symbols for communication, yet NEITHER SENDER NOR RECEIVER KNOWS IN ADVANCE WHAT CODE IS GOING TO CARRY THE SIGNIFICANT INFORMATION ABOUT DISEASE. In one instance an immobile lump of the breast discloses cancer; another time this information cannot be obtained without surgical exploration and microscopic analysis of suspicious tissue.

A highly charged emotional relationship may arise within this ambiguous communicational setting: the patient tends to relate anaclitically; he bares himself, trusts, and confides. The doctor on the other hand is expected to understand, to heal, and to protect the patient. Outsiders looking through a screen at what goes on, or listening to tape-recordings of what has happened, are likely to miss the very basic ingredient of clinical communication – the sense of intimacy, fear, hope, and other strong emotions shared by the two participants (Roose 1960). Nor can this essential element in patient-doctor communication be artificially produced for experimental investigation (Erikson 1959). Hence *post hoc* description and anecdotal case presentation are generally used for teaching and research in this field. Lately linguistic transcription of verbal material (Pittenger et al. 1960), acoustic measurement of sounds (Ostwald 1960c), analysis of gestures and postures (Deutsch 1952), and physiologic studies (Lacey 1959), have been applied in order to make more rigorously scientific investigation possible.

The language of the body

The autopsy table was medicine's greatest lesson to Man, a lesson in honesty and humility. It is medicine's great spiritual contribution to human culture. (Lawrence Kubie 1961).

The term 'language' is used very loosely in medicine, and not within the specialized framework familiar to linguists. It can refer to any informative, expressive, or communicative activity of the patient – conscious or un-conscious – and may even apply to something happening within part of the patient's body, such as his skin, heart, or gastro-intestinal tract. Much of this has been documented, and for any student of body language there are three invaluable dictionaries: French's *Index of differential diagnosis* (1954), Dunbar's *Emotions and bodily changes* (1954), and Grinstein's *Index of psychoanalytic writings* (1956). From this vast material I shall review only what seems directly pertinent to the work of investigators outside the field of clinical medicine.

The body as a whole

Sizing-up a person is done in a split-second, but often these first impressions outlast later ones. Of particular interest to physicians are striking abnormalities of body size or shape. These usually have physical causes: dwarfism, for example, results from lack of pituitary or thyroid hormone, achondroplasia, vitamin deficiencies, and other metabolic diseases (Hurxthal 1953). Gigantism is usually due to a tumor of the pituitary gland. But total appearance is also influenced by the patient's feeding-behavior and exercise patterns, both of which can be upset through emotional conflicts. For example, obesity is often a sign that oral demands for love and attention are unfulfilled or unfulfillable; and cachexia can result from self-imposed starvation routines designed to achieve delusional goals (Bruch 1961).

Relationships between physique and personality have been described in the work by Kretschmer (1925) and Sheldon (1940). Less well-known to the nonmedical world are studies of internalized concepts of the body and the effects of these 'body images' on appearance and behavior (Fisher and Cleveland 1958; Schilder 1950). Reactions to another person depend in important ways upon how one perceives, evaluates, and uses his own body and its component parts (Diethelm 1955).

The surface of the body

The enveloping skin is a kind of advertising bill-board that broadcasts to the world what goes on under its surface. Fevers, infections, neoplasms, allergies, ageing, and circulatory defects are some of the organic processes which become manifest through dermal change (Andrews 1947). By means of pilo-erection, vasomotor change, pigmentation, exudation, and other signs, the skin also transmits information about the bearer's emotions (Obermayer 1955). Fear gives him goosepimples and pallor, anger produces flushing and mottling, itching annoys the victim and also the onlooker.

Scanning the skin, a trained eye picks up significant pimples, scratches, scars, moles, tattoos, birthmarks, and self-induced lesions which stand out from the smooth homogeneous surface. The primary emotional appeal of that surface is probably related to the infant's instinctive search for its mother; in dreams her breast is not infrequently symbolized as a 'blank' screen (Lewin 1946). Various skin shades and colors also are associated with highly individualized ideas that stem from preverbal thoughts (Knapp 1956).

For example, a Negro patient who had a dark-skinned father and a light-skinned mother alternately denigrated and whitewashed her own brown-ness. Depending on which phase of her ambivalence predominated, she would tan herself – to feel sweatier, warm, and more attractive – or despise the darker shades as dirty, masculine, and dangerous.

The hair of the head is an especially important preoccupation for the dermatologist, who finds that it turns white or falls out under stress. Psychopathology includes hair-fetishism, tearing-out-of-hair, and bizarre dyeing and dressing. Emotional reactions to baldness, haircuts, and visits to the beauty parlor tend to be surprisingly profound.

For example, a college-graduate mother-of-three spent 24 hours in near panic after she sent her 9-year-old daughter out for her first permanent wave. This event apparently symbolized many of her own struggles over sexual identity and maturity.

Paucity of body hair has forced the human animal to cover himself with feathers, furs, cloth, plastic, and other clothing. Flügel (1950) has discussed this in psychological terms, pointing out that the body surface is covered not only for protection but also as a sign of modesty and for decorative purposes.

The face

Hippocrates described the "sharp nose, sunken temples, cold ears, hollow, vacant eyes, open mouth, loose, blanched lips, and livid, muddy color" of imminent death (Thorek 1946). For the living also, the expression of the face is of primary importance in communicating what is wrong. Acromegaly, myxedema, hemiplegia, 7th nerve paralysis, psychoses, wasting, alcoholism, and many other diseases produce characteristic "facies". Thorek (1946) has collected these in a book worth perusing, if for no other reason than to see how unsettling it is to view familiar forms in unfamiliar guises. According to Rangell, facial communication of emotion takes place primarily via the snout, a peri-oral "porthole" [which is] the focus of greatest concentration of effector response to emotions, at least in relation to the external world [...] Within these relatively few inches of body surface, the tone, position in space, and direction of the skin and facial musculature denote how a person is at the moment (Rangell 1954).

Eyes declare the presence of jaundice (yellow sclerae), hyperthyroidism (bilateral exophthalmos), and neurological disorders (pupillary and oculomotor imbalances). Psychiatrists also gauge the sense of interpersonal relatedness by means of eye expression; schizophrenics tend to stare in an immobile, vacant fashion; hysterics may use their eyes to meltingly caress the surface of the doctor's body; suspicious paranoid persons try to focus their eyes inside your head, as though this might enable them to read thoughts directly; the psychopath may shift his gaze watchfully, try to seduce, or give you the "evil eye" (Feldman 1959). Various forms of pathologic weeping have been described (Greenacre 1952c).

Expressive automatisms called tics or spasm disorders may affect the facial muscles as well as other parts of the body. Included here are blinks, squints, sudden scanning movements with the eyes, and contortions of one or another part of the face. Their etiology ranges from epileptic foci of brain irritation (Strauss 1959) to psychoneurotic conflicts (Abse 1959). Unless of organic origin, abrupt facial contortions usually indicate fright-reactions; they are signs of overwhelming fear produced by an external shock or by the undigested memory of a traumatic event in the past. Occasionally it is possible to pinpoint specific maladaptive processes which have produced and perpetuated a spasm disorder (Fenichel 1945).

For example, a young man entered the hospital for treatment of paroxysmal jerking movements of his head, neck, shoulders, and pelvis which were accompanied by sudden harsh snorting noises. Psychotherapy disclosed that in early childhood he became convinced another person had 'entered' his body, and the paroxysms now occur whenever he becomes uncomfortably aware of this inside outsider and tries to shake him out.

Spastic torticollis is an expressive automatism characterized by stereotyped turning of the head to one side. Not infrequently precipitated while being shaved or during military inspections, this disorder may be a symbolic expression of the patient's need to look away from threatening hostile-aggressive impulses which have been unduly stimulated or which cannot be controlled in socially-acceptable ways (Mitscherlich 1961).

Posture, gait, and movement of the body

Posture, gait, and body movements are controlled by the integrated activity of at least three nervous systems: the pyramidal system (for volitional control of movement), the extrapyramidal and cerebellar system (for involuntary aspects of muscle tone, balance, and motility), and the reticular-activating system (for attentiveness, alertness, and overall coordination) (Grinker et al. 1960). Inputs from the external environment directly influence at least two of these – the pyramidal and the reticular-activating systems. Thus social stimuli play a major role in the initiation, reinforcement, and prohibition of various body movements. Furthermore, the patterns of posture, gait, and movement are altered by diseases of muscles, bones, and joints.

Since body movement has such a large number of determinants, no one particular pattern can have much semantic specificity (Rioch 1961). The patient's postures and movements communicate at best something generally about tension and tension-release. Without additional information, one could make no clear distinction therefore between, say, stiffness due to brain tumor, military training, rheumatism, hostility, meningitis, etc. The neurologist deals specifically with such diagnostic tasks. Reflex tests, motor-strength studies, electroencephalograms, and other techniques for getting at underlying neuro-muscular relationships must be used (McDowell 1960). It is important for the non-medical reader to keep this in mind while studying texts about the symbolic (Feldman 1959) and the semiotic (Ruesch and Kees 1956) significance of the various posture, gait, and motility abnormalities.

The hands

Free to move in space and richly represented in the cerebral cortex, the human hand can attain extraordinary importance in communication. Some rudimentary gestures may already be seen in infancy: for example, the newborn presents the palm for grasping, clenches the hands together for balance, and protrudes the thumb in touching the mouth. More elaborate analogues of this infantile hand behavior are later found in saluting, prayer, and the hitch-hiking sign. But only under acoustically unfavorable conditions, such as deafness or continuously intense noise, are hand languages ever systematically developed (Moser 1958). Hand and fingers are terminal peninsulas of the human body and as such particularly susceptible to ageing, arthritis, arterio-sclerosis, and other organic disease processes. Thus it seems extremely doubtful that diagnostic procedures based solely on the hand, for example in terms of its morphology (Wolff 1952), would be accurate beyond the point of the manual stereotypes taught by drama teachers (Stanislavski 1949).

Sometimes in psychotherapeutic work it is possible to obtain insight into the personal meaningfulness of tremors, fidgets, thrusts, and other noticeable hand behavior (Ferenczi 1950b).

For example, an obsessive-compulsive writer, blocked in his efforts to produce a novel, folded his hands and propped them against his mouth during long intervals of silence in the therapy hour. Later he explained this as an expression of deep humiliation and suffering. Another patient stroked the carpet in the office at times when she felt an intense need to be affectionately fondled.

Of further diagnostic importance are the PRODUCTS of manual activity. Sounds produced by hand range from simple mechanical noises to complex musical patterns (Ostwald 1960d): finger-snaps may be used to indicate the 'a-hah!' feeling of sudden understanding. Scratching, finger-tapping, and knuckle-cracking also are used to express emotional states.

Among visible products of the hand, writing has been extensively studied from a psychopathologic point of view. Repetitiousness, clumsiness, fragmentation, ornamentation, and other handwriting characteristics tend to match the expression disturbances of speech and gesture (Roman 1959). Sketching and tracing (Bender 1938), smearing and modelling (Meares 1960), and painting (Shaw 1938) are also used for psychodiagnosis and therapy. Contrary to the artist whose ego integrates a variety of elements into new symbolic forms, a mentally ill person tends to elaborate raw id material through crude, stereotyped visual symbols (Kris 1952).

The feet

In ordinary social affairs one keeps his feet on the ground, encased, out of sight, and refrains from kicking. Not so in medicine where the patient's horizontal posture elevates his feet to a position of equality with the head and the heart. The Babinsky reflex (elevation of the big toe and spreading of the little toes) is one of neurology's most important signs. Part of a mass withdrawal response, this primitive reflex suggests the treeclimbing behavior of monkeys (Wartenberg 1947). Newborns have it:

they engage in rough, pseudo-climbing thrusts and pedalling movements of the lower extremities. Once cortical control has taken over, primitive lower-limb reflexes tend to occur only under conditions of strong emotion or when the pyramidal tract is damaged. During arguments, for instance, the feet tense up; rage produces kicking and stomping; inhibition of aggression may result in hysterical paralysis of the legs. The lowly foot is also subject to circulatory drought and stasis. Arteriosclerosis, varicose veins, elephantiasis, diabetes, and other conditions affecting its nutrient supply tend to create most unpleasant pedal symptoms.

Smell

Doctors must be able to differentiate the stink of uremia, diabetes, alcoholism, lung abscess, and other serious illnesses. Even psychiatric diagnosis may be aided by a good nose, since the sweat of chronically schizophrenic patients carries a peculiar odor that rats and perfume experts are able to detect (Smith and Sines 1960).

The human smell brain lies buried beneath structures subserving 'higher' intellectual processes, yet is closely connected to both the cortex and the hypothalamic emotion centers (MacLean 1949). Its exact function in human communication is not known. Some psychosomatic facts about the nose have been presented by Holmes (1950), and a delightful naturalistic book about the sense of smell is available (Bedichek 1960). That social inhibition may be a factor in reducing nasal sensitivity is suggested by the fact that close to one billion dollars is spent in the United States each year on perfumes, cosmetics, deodorizers, and other toiletries (U.S. Bureau of the Census 1959).

Olfactory sensitivity increases during pregnancy, in certain epileptic auras, and with some brain lesions. But cultural interests in synesthetic phenomena can account for heightened olfactory sensibility; take for example Des Esseintes in Huysmans' "A Rebours" who doused himself with various perfumes. Pathologic oral fixations can also lead to nasal hypersensitivity.

An obese, childish, postpartum depressive patient preoccupied herself with the smell of flowers in my office; a lonely young man dreamt that his mother forbade him to eat canapes with a delicious, pungent smell.

HUMAN SOUNDS

Language is a poor thing. You fill your lungs with wind and shake a little slit in your throat, and make mouths, and that shakes the air; and the air shakes a pair of little drums in my head – a very complicated arrangement, with lots of bones behind – and my brain seizes your meaning in the rough. What a round-about way, and what a waste of time.

(West 1957; quotation from Du Maurier, "Peter Ibbetson")

From the welter of primarily nonacoustic signs described in the preceding section, no physician could get more than a fragmented and self-contra-dictory impression of what is wrong with his patient. To learn more he has to listen closely to the sounds the patient makes, and this involves attention on both verbal and nonverbal levels (Ostwald 1960b). First the doctor 'takes a history', hoping thus to illuminate the sequential pattern of pathologic developments. He asks questions, receives answers, and – if he is a psychiatrist – encourages the active verbalization of fanta-sies and wishes. During all of this, the doctor attends closely to para-linguistic acoustic cues, for example variously intoned forms of "oh" and the nuances which support or belie overt meanings of words.

A few noises and musical patterns have already been mentioned in connection with the language of hands and feet; I have discussed these in greater detail elsewhere (Ostwald 1960a). Other body sounds are systematically elicited from the patient during the physical examination. These range all the way from byproducts of the examination, for in-stance "aah" uttered during visualization of the posterior pharynx, to characteristic diagnostic sounds like the systolic murmur of aortic stenosis. While primarily informative about bodily events per se, many of these acoustic cues also have something to say about a patient's mental con-dition, particularly when these sounds are used in place of words (Scott 1958).

A short vocabulary of body sounds

Acoustic study of human sounds began only recently (Ostwald 1963), and the following remarks should be taken as tentative hypotheses rather than as definitive or conclusive statements about the nonverbal sound-making of patients.

Rhythmic beats. – To come to another person's awareness, the rhythmic beating sounds of the heart need amplification; this is done in the clinic by means of the stethoscope. Only in rare cases of syphilitic aortitis may cardiac pulsations become sufficiently visible for communication, through the patient's rhythmic head-nodding (De Musset's sign). Under conditions of physical contiguity – between mother and child, lover and beloved – the pulse can also be directly transmitted. This fosters a feeling of intimacy and is said to be a factor in the organization of rhythmicity during intra-uterine and early nursery development (Meerloo 1961).

Breath sounds. – Acoustic signals transmitted by air generally play a more important role in communication than do those transmitted by contact. It is possible of course to breathe softly, in which case respiratory sounds are barely audible and have, at most, a mildly hypnotic effect. But due to the larynx, the practice one gets in childhood of stirring others to action with cries, and the amplification afforded by numerous resonating chambers, the respiratory tract is probably man's best instrument for acoustic communication.

Vocalization for speech comes off well in the expiratory phase of respiration. So do sighs, whispers, moans, hums, whistles, screams, and exclamations. Inspiratory sounds, in particular wheezing and snoring, tend to produce annoyance and alarm.

Rasping noises. – While any sound can be noise in the sense of being unwanted (Broadbent 1957), some sounds more than others are especially annoying. These include tooth-gnashing, fingernail-scratching, grinding friction between solid objects, and other noises with a nonharmonic pattern. So far as medical diagnosis is concerned, sounds of this type almost invariably indicate pathology. Rough heart sounds, peritoneal friction rubs, and crepitation in the joints generally point to inflammation, decay, breakage, or new growth which impedes the smooth frictionless gliding of one surface over another. Due to defective phonation or articulation, grating and rasping sounds may also get into the voice and communicate varying degrees of annoyance and unpleasantness. To a certain extent the reactions of listeners to nonharmonic acoustic patterns are further conditioned by the acoustic preference of their community (Farnsworth 1958).

Spasms. – Spasmodic contractions in the gastrointestinal, respiratory, and urogenital tracts at times produce characteristic brief sounds: coughs, gasps, sneezes, retching, cramping, gurgling, and flatulence. These are basically sounds of reflex origin and indicate the body's efforts to eject painful or useless irritants. Under certain circumstances spasm sounds come to be used in communication, however. How this may happen can best be seen through the analysis of a single sound, for example, the cough.

The biography of a cough

The cough is part of an unlearned, reflex ejection-spasm triggered when there is irritation in the patient's respiratory passageway. Acoustically it is an intense, sudden, explosive, noise that can be heard at some distance. Should this noise fall on trained ears – any listener is at least partly trained since he too has coughed at some time in his life – it is then intuitively perceived in terms of something irritating. The listener may himself feel some irritation in the throat. More often however, he finds himself merely sympathetically in tune with the cougher, in the sense that a tacit agreement, 'cough means irritation and riddance spasm', leads to some mutuality. Now the listener may respond to his own reflex impulses to clear the throat, to reduce irritation, even to silence the cougher or escape from the unpleasant situation. Or he may inhibit these impulses and turn to the cougher in helpful ways.

If he is a physician, then the listener uses his own sense of irritation to gauge that of the coughing patient. He may further search for the etiology of the cough, treat the patient, and try to prevent recurrence. These responses may all have the desired effects upon the patient and his cough. But something else can happen too: the patient may recognize that his coughing manages to arouse interest and help from the environment. Should he have difficulty in obtaining these reactions in other ways, he may then be tempted to put more and more vigor into his coughing, which thereby loses its instinctive spontaneity and becomes a pathologic symptom, like a tic. He may even learn to imitate a cough at times when it is not actually the respiratory tract but some other body part that feels irritated. If these counterfeit coughs succeed in eliciting the desired help and attention, then the patient obtains more than the usual amount of control over his environment through coughing. One could call such a non-reflex cough a sort of "verbal" operant (Skinner 1957). However, it seems more correct to think of this kind of sound-making as contrary if not inimical to communication with words. Like other pathologic forms of acoustic behavior used to gratify dependent, passive, infantile strivings, provocative coughing often tends to shut off the possibility of more complex linguistic communication (Meerloo 1959).

Laughter and crying

Repetitive, uncontrolled, spasmodic chains of sound that accompany the release of accumulated tensions are man's purest sounds for emotional expression. Laughter tends to be composed of shorter, more staccato, more high-pitched and more rapidly-repeated tonal elements than crying. For example, the tinkly giggle contrasts easily with the mournful moan as extreme examples of laughing vs. crying. But towards the center of the laugh-cry continuum, it is difficult to make the distinction acoustically; at this point visual cues, such as the square mouth of sadness described by Darwin (1955), become helpful.

Psychiatrists pay a good deal of attention to the conditions that precede emotional sound-making, for instance the tension build-ups before laughter and the feelings of loss which precipitate crying. Laughter can also be produced by a sudden sense of incongruity (Grotjahn 1957).

For example, in the joke-telling situation, the joker subdues the laugher by coaxing him into having evermore discrete fantasies. As soon as the laugher reaches a certain pitch of tense expectation, the joker 'punch-lines' him with information that either is entirely unexpected or might only have been tangentially inferred from ambiguous hints contained in the build-up. Of interest here is the necessary inequality between joketeller and listener: to get a joke to work, the joker must emit verbal symbols continuously (words, puns, metaphors, etc.) while the laugher can emit only non-verbal signs (silent attentiveness, eyes lighting-up with anticipation, outburst of noise after the punch-line). Variations on this theme are found in acted-out jokes and comedy.

Crying is usually a symptom of sadness resulting from real or fantasied experiences of loss (Freud 1925b). As in the evaluation of laughter, the psychiatrist must consider not only a patient's background and physical condition, but also social rules to the extent that these selectively prohibit or encourage certain forms of emotional expression. Also, as with other sounds, crying can be used to arouse sympathy, declare one's helplessness, or express anger. Often the best way to distinguish genuine from counterfeit emotional behavior is for the clinican to allow himself to respond instinctively to his patient and then to introspectively evaluate the depth of these intuitive reactions (Rümke 1961).

Acoustic signalling and the origins of communication

The science of bioacoustics is barely 5 years old (Tembrock 1959). Yet with an eye towards the next section of this paper which deals with stunted and abnormal speech, one must venture a formulation about the ontogeny of normal human acoustic-communication:

Meaningful sound-making originates in the nuclear child-mother relationship. It is here that reflexly produced acoustic patterns first jell into a repertory of signs and then symbols for information exchange. First there is the cry, which is life-saving in any culture that allows a mother to leave her child alone. This sound enables the otherwise completely helpless baby simultaneously to summon assistance and to indicate how uncomfortable it is. At first no mother can tell with certainty precisely what physiologic tensions are rising and which of the baby's vital needs demand satisfaction. Only gradually does the acoustic behavior of the infant become morphologically distinctive enough to enable the mother to discern cries of hunger from shrieks of pain, whines of soiled diapers from plaints for attention, delighted yelps from over-excited yells (Lynip 1951). To learn this 'language' of her newborn, the mother proceeds much like any person who tries to communicate in a strange tongue: she touches, inspects, smells, and lives with the foreign visitor to acquaint herself with his behavior and to decipher the relationships between this behavior and the sounds he makes. At the same time she expects the stranger to do likewise.

Babies make numerous sounds beside cries: smacking, cooing, hiccupping, humming, gurgling, whining, burping, coughing, sneezing, flatus, shrieking, spitting, and more (Kurtz 1961). How mothers seize upon these behavioral cues for information about infants depends in large measure upon their native interest in sounds and their enthusiasm for playing the acoustic detective game. This in turn is probably a function of a mother's personal experience as a child with her own parents and may also reflect the acoustic habits of her particular culture.

For example, a mother may decide that there is no hunger-cry simply by listening for and acting upon the infantile lip-smacking noises which precede crying. This actually occurs, and more general inverse relationships between mothering and crying have also been documented (Brody 1956). One occasionally sees this going too far: I recently learned of a mother who so rarely let her baby out of eye-range that the latter reduced its acoustic output to an occasional mewling whimper.

Clearly then, acoustic communication is historically associated in every person with the helplessness, immaturity, and absolute dependency of his own infancy. The transition from this life period into childhood is characterized by the use of 'family-languages' that contain acoustic elements derived from both infantile sound-making and parental speech (McCarthy 1946). The final step into adulthood requires that the growing person wean himself from the pidgin-languages of his family circle and communicate with symbols useful to the community-at-large. Failure to accomplish this leads to all kinds of disturbances in communication (Ruesch 1957), some of which will now be discussed.

Speech and its aberrations

...Does not the eternal sorrow of life consist in the fact that human beings cannot understand one another, that one person cannot enter into the internal state of another? (I. P. Pavlov 1928: 50).

Verbal communication is a relatively late accomplishment, both in the history of the individual and the history of living things (Hockett 1960). It is not surprising therefore that aberrations of the speech functions are so frequently encountered in medical practice. Those due to developmental anomalies, for instance cleft-palate, or organic disease processes like laryngitis will not concern us here (Luchsinger and Arnold 1959). Neither will I be able to cover the field of neurologic disturbance and its effect on memory, language, and speech (Goldstein 1948). Rather the focus is on relationships between personality disorders and those aspects of behavior which lead to meaningful verbalization.

Nonhuman languages

There are patients who 'speak' like dogs, cats, chickens, billy-goats, monkeys, and other animals. Sometimes this is due to a degree of mental deficiency plus social isolation which in effect keeps the sick person from learning any human language. Cases have been reported of children reared by animals (Brown 1958); also in the hospitals for chronic mental disease one finds patients who have no trace of recognizable speech[1].

Table 1 displays this kind of acoustic behavior; it shows the output of a woman who has been in a State Hospital for 40 of her 45 years. She uses bleats and grunts – accompanied by several stereotyped gestures – to communicate with the staff in a rudimentary way about her feelings and needs. Another patient in the same hospital communicates only by humming; she emits simple song-like tunes as well as repetitious monotonal hums (see Table 2).

Other mentally ill patients know how to speak, but produce the sounds of animals at times when they FEEL themselves to be nonhuman. These are usually schizophrenics who, apparently due to deprivation of security

---

[1] Leonti Thompson, M. D., recorded the two patients demonstrated here.

TABLE 1

The "Vocabulary" of a Mentally Defective Patient

and love early in childhood, turned to nonhuman objects for basic affection and contact (Searles 1960).

Omissions, repetitions, and errors

Even patients who use a human tongue without difficulty are likely to make slips. Their omissions, repetitions, and errors tend to occur during moments of anxiety (Mahl 1956) and often stem from the inability to

TABLE 2

A Mentally Defective Patient who Hums

Song-like tunes:

Simple hums:

resolve some intrapsychic conflict under the stress of having to speak (Freud 1935). For example:

A patient spoke of seeing the movie "To Have and Have Not" on TV. She had previously seen this film during her adolescence, and on the basis of a common appellation (Slim) had closely identified with the female lead, Lauren Bacall. In discussing the movie the patient for a while said nothing about the male lead. This was the first symptom of her speech disturbance: omission of an essential part of the topic. The second symptom, a syllable-repetition, soon followed; when she finally ventured to name the male lead, it came out "Hum-Humphrey Bogart".

The patient denied any awareness of the stutter until I mentioned it to her; and then she reconstructed her thinking in such a way that her speech symptoms became plausible: *Hum* called to her mind *humping*, a slang expression for sexual intercourse which she had guiltily and mischievously used as a teenager.

Two other determinants for the development of some hesitancy in pronouncing Humphrey Bogart emerged through our discussion:

(1) For the past few days she periodically had the fantasy that her husband, a swarthy man who resembles Bogart, might be killed in an auto-accident. This fantasy led to an obsessional idea: "You're not supposed to think about having intercourse with a dead man."

(2) The preceding day she had told me about certain of her ideas regarding pregnancy, but only now remembered how proud of her abdomen she was while pregnant. "It resembled the *hump* of an oriental male god."

TABLE 3

Some Examples of Speech Errors

Level of Disturbance	Type of Error	The Intended Sound	The Actual Sound
Single Sounds:	omission	front	→ font
	addition	remnant	→ remenant
	substitution	affect	→ affuct
	transposition	Yale Journal	→ Jail Yournal
Syllables:	omission	salivary	→ salary
	addition	Marietta	→ Marionetta
	substitution	taken	→ taking
	transposition	Beruf suchen	→ Besuch rufen
	condensation	apprenticeship	→ apprentiship
Words:	omission	you bastard	→ you
	addition	stop	→ please stop
	substitution	working	→ mother
	transposition	feet of film	→ film of feet
	condensation	bowel movement	→ boom
	fragmentation	reminder	→ rema...

Table 3 offers further examples of speech errors collected from a number of different patients and speakers. It is likely that linguistic rules for the formation and decay of language symbols are involved in the production of these disturbances (Zipf 1959). Therefore a combined approach by linguistics and psychiatry to these interesting symptoms seems called for.

Stress, intonation, and pause anomalies

In clinical work one usually studies clusters of symptoms called 'syndromes', not single isolated symptoms. Also in the analysis of verbal behavior, disturbance of a single phonetic variable may have little relevance, since several symptomatic disturbances usually occur within the same speech fragment (Lehiste et al. 1961). The unbalanced STRESS pattern demonstrated by the following patient, for example, occurred in the context of sloppy articulation, repetitiousness, and verbosity.

A middle-aged lawyer, whose fortune and professional reputation had crumbled as the result of personal and economic failures, overstressed certain words and word groupings. Most notable were exaggerated or even incorrect stresses in word couples like *párty pólitics, pólice prótection, póssible pártnerships*. From other information obtained about this man, it became apparent that he had failed to develop emotionally much further than the sexually ambivalent orientation of early childhood. For instance, in the face of extremely vengeful feelings towards women he quite generally directed his dependency strivings towards men.

An analysis of the stress anomaly in his speech showed that the explosive overemphasis was a veiled calling out for his father, whose early death had robbed him of the emotional support needed to cope with a crippled mother and two elderly psychotic sisters. The patient had never given up the infantile babbled form of paternal address, *pá-pá*, in favor of more adult versions: *pápa, papá, father*, etc. Now in his unhappy depressed state, energetic mouthing of the aforementioned word couples gave him an illusory way to magically call out for a father. His associations to the overstressed words (e.g. police, partnership) also revealed fantasies in which an omnipotent agent, usually masculine, was to rescue him from distress.

A number of pathognomonic INTONATION patterns have been noted in the speech of psychiatric patients. Excitable and histrionic persons often exaggerate the normal pitch pattern of the language. When matched by an equally theatrical use of gesture, clothing, makeup, and perfume, these hyperinflections usually indicate a hysterical process (Allen and Houston 1959). The patient seems to use dramatization as a kind of noise to impede the verbal communication of troublesome personal matters.

Depressed patients often restrict the range of pitch variation in the voice. This symptom usually parallels a reduction of vocal intensity and speed. Words are uttered in a lusterless, monotonous way that communicates apathy and resignation.

Anomalous use of pitch cues is noted among patients with schizophrenic illnesses, particularly children and adolescents whose autism also manifests itself through grammar confusion, neologisms, and disconnected word fragments (Boatman and Szurek 1960). Verbal interaction with these patients is extremely difficult since one often cannot extract meaning from what the patient says.

Take for example the 14-year old boy, samples of whose speech are shown in Table 4.[2] During an acute excitement he produced what psychiatrists call a 'word salad' – he was incoherent, babbling, constantly switching between a high and squeaky voice and a low droning one. Sample 1 is a characteristic spontaneous production which, if one tries to impose meaning upon it, can be interpreted in 72 different ways as follows:

$$\text{(Don't) don't tell} \left\{ \begin{array}{l} \text{her} \\ \text{him} \end{array} \right\} \left\{ \begin{array}{l} \text{what} \\ \text{why} \\ \text{by} \end{array} \right\} \left\{ \begin{array}{l} \text{you} \\ \text{yours} \\ \text{her} \end{array} \right\} \left\{ \begin{array}{l} \text{knows} \\ \text{nose} \end{array} \right.$$

TABLE 4

Samples of Schizophrenic 'Speech'

Sample 1:

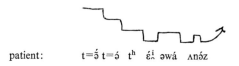

patient: t=ɔ́ t=ɔ́ tʰ ɛ̃́ı̯ əwá ʌnɔ́z

Sample 2:

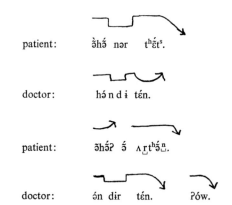

patient: ɔ̀hɔ̃́ nər   tʰɛ̃́tˢ.

doctor: hɔ́ n d ɨ tɛ́n.

patient: ɔ̀hɔ̃́ʔ ɔ́ ʌ ɾ̥tʰɔ̃́ȵ.

doctor: ɔ́n dɨr   tɛ́n.   ʔɔ́w.

Sample 1 shows a verbal utterance that lends itself to 72 ambiguous interpretations. Sample 2 shows a fragment of confused conversation in response to the doctor's question "Do you have any little brothers or sisters?"

Sample 2 of Table 4 shows what happened when one tried to converse with this confused patient. The doctor asks, "Do you have any little brothers or sisters?" Instead of a "yes" or "no" reply, the patient produces an ambiguous sound

---

[2]   This and subsequent linguistic transcriptions were done by William Shipley, Ph.D., Associate Professor of Linguistics, University of California (Berkeley).

(line 1) which the doctor tries to translate into "hundred ten?" (line 2). The patient then makes some more of the same ambiguous sound (line 3) upon which the doctor now imposes the less absurd meaning "under ten" (line 4).

PAUSE anomalies are best observed among stutterers. Fixated at pre-genital levels of psychosexual development, these patients get into a jam when they can neither express their anger through shouts nor inhibit it by keeping still (Glauber 1958). Unlike the overt psychotic who may lose control at this point, the stutterer immobilizes himself and frustrates the listener by emitting a sequence of repetitions, embolophrasias, clichés, or say-nothings.

For example, a 21-year old college student complained of difficulty "tttttalking". He tried to "chchchchchchchchchange" his "ppprogram" for school. He also complained of trouble "pppeeing" and found it "tttttough" going with girls. Table 5 shows consecutive pause anomalies in 5 minutes of a tape-recorded interview with this stutterer.

TABLE 5

48 Abnormal Pause Forms from 5 Minutes of Speech by a Stutterer

áy ə ə ttt...	wə̀z ə ǽkšiliy...
ð̌ɔ́ ʔə ʔə (sigh) ð̌ə ʔə kkk...	tùw ʔə séy...
ð̌ǽ... ʔə...	ð̌êy jist ə lúk...
pppîyíy ə kkk...	álsôw ə túw ə ʔə ʔə...
ænd ə...	àyð̌ík ə ð̌æt ə...
ð̌ə ʔə...	nǎt ə nǎt ə évriy...
hwén ‖ ə sst...	ækšliy ə ʔə...lukiŋ rayt ə ə ə
ð̌ér ə ð̌ér ə ppp...	ǽkšliy ə...
ænd ə ə ə šiy...	wâyày ə lûk ə élshwêr...
ð̌æt ə ə̂p...	ænd ə ð̌êy léft...
kǽnat ə čéynǰ...	mîkst ə grúwp...
áydinôw ʔə ‖ áy...	lûk ə lûkówvir...
(long pause)	hawévir ʔə ow ʔə...
áyð̌íkə méybiy...	hǽdêy ə...
ð̌iy ə θíŋz...	gîv ə ttt...
in ə ‖ ð̌ísiz...	ǽkšliy ə ʔə kə́vird...
ǽkšiliy ə gèt ə́p...	dównt ə dównt ə...
ǽnd ə ‖ sêy àym...	θîŋkày ə ‖ wél...
sêy àym ə ttt...	ǽkšliy ə ppp...
tûwèy ʔə grúwp...	ð̌iyâpizit ə séks...
kin ə ‖ sst	in ə ‖ lâyk ə sspówrts...
sstûwdint ə gə́vəmint...	êniy ə trə́bil...
wél ʔə...	wið̌ ə wə́rdz ǽkšliy...
bə̂t ə ð̌éy...	ǽkšliy ə ə hǽvnt...

Abnormalities in vocal intensity, register, and utterance rate

Illness also takes its toll on the paralinguistic system (Birdwhistell 1961). Like pianists who press different pedals to emphasize important themes, patients selectively vary their vocal intensity, switch register, and change speed while talking.

VOICE INTENSITY can be measured by means of acoustic devices (Steer and Hanley 1957).

For example, Table 6 shows acoustic measurements of the voice of a blind patient. Like many persons without vision, this man compensated for his communication defect by resourceful use of acoustic cues (Schumann 1959). He selected vocal loudnesses over a range of 26 phons in order to convey shades of emotion and to over- or under-score the verbal content of his utterances.

TABLE 6

Loudness Levels of a Blind Patient's Voice during Two Interviews

Patients tries to:	He says:	Vocal Loudness[3]
energetically convey compliance	"Yes, o yes, oh, yes, eh yes sir!"	86 phons
indignantly deny responsibility	"He didn't say who he was"	84 phons
tensely explain	"It's a little bit different; I don't know just how to explain it, but..."	82 phons
criticise	"... an overstaffed office"	80 phons
humbly convey embarrassment	"I guess maybe I don't use it enough, huh, huh"	78 phons
sadly contemplate his condition	"these treatments have done me quite a lot of good because..."	72 phons
painfully discuss his symptoms	"next to a woman I have the strong urge..."	68 phons
sadly acknowledge defeat	"I don't think she cares anymore."	60 phons

[3] Converted from decibels re 0.0002 microbar to phons using the method of S. S. Stevens (1956).

REGISTER SHIFTS have been described clinically (Moses 1954) and can be demonstrated by means of acoustic filters that cut out part of the speech signal (Starkweather 1961) or selectively measure the individual components of an intact signal (Ostwald 1960e). During experimental stress or acute emotional illness, acoustic energy fluctuates particularly in bands centered at 500 cycles per second (Ostwald 1961a).

Table 7 shows half-octave band analyses carried out during the opening (A) and the closing (Z) phases of 11 interviews with a 26-year old salesman who applied for psychiatric treatment following the breakup of his marriage. At that time, he was in a state of acute restlessness, trying to keep a more chronic sense of sadness and unworthiness from undermining his social adjustment. He was the younger of two sons and had usually gotten along pretty well by being a charming, boyish, friendly person and keeping away from intellectual or occupational competition. When on the spot, for example during 'dressing downs' from superiors, he tended to become anxious and behave in an arrogant, provocative manner. This would get him into trouble, which he then tried to escape through passive resignation and submissiveness.

The rapid alternation between provocativeness and submissiveness evident in this patient's social behavior also appeared in his paralinguistic behavior (Table 7). Strident, querulous, effeminate soprano voices (upper curves) would alternate with flabby, resigned baritones (lower curves). These register shifts often took place within sentences, as for example in interview 1 (3-2-60), segment A: His high voice says "putting conversations and things into a negative"; this is cut short by an embolophrasia "b...uh"; the low voice then continues with "course of viewpoint". The end (Z) of the first interview shows this same intra-sentence instability, but now each voice carries more energy than before.

Compare Interview 1 just described with Interview 2 (3-7-60), which shows more acoustic stability both within sentences and within the hour. Now look at Interview 4 (3-9-60), which shows a little fluctuation at the beginning (segment A) but none at the end of the interview which has the voice fixed in a persistent high register (segment Z). A persistently high voice was generally associated in this patient with defensive negative attitudes; for example, after Interview 4 the patient broke two consecutive appointments with his doctor. Later phases of the therapy showed more intrasentence stability than did earlier interviews.

Some most bizarre register shifts can be heard during schizophrenic excitements. For instance, the patient whose productions are given in Table 4 dramatized his preferential use of certain vocal registers by emitting the high squeaky voice from the left side of his mouth and the low one from the right side.

Disturbance in the RATE of speech provides another criterion for the analysis of behavior; utterance rates can be objectively measured and are found to be influenced by personal and social variables (Steer and

TABLE 7

Intrasentence Variations in the Acoustic Behavior of a Patient during Psychotherapy

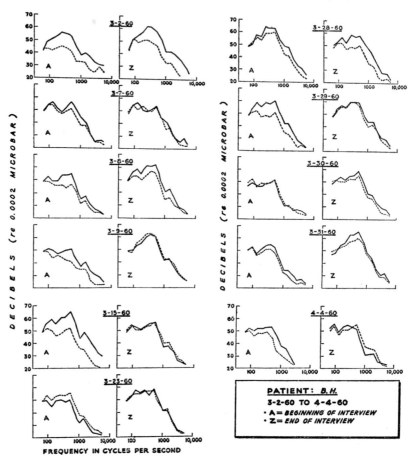

Half-octave band analyses of 11 interviews are shown here. Solid graphs denote the voice at the beginning of sentences, and broken graphs at the end of sentences.

Hanley 1957). Particularly gross disturbances of speech rate accompany the cyclic mental disease called manic-depressive psychosis (Bellak 1952). During the manic phase the patient is under tremendous pressure and his speech speed-up is part of the general psycho-motor excitement. In the depression, speech is remarkably retarded, approaches inaudibility, and may cease altogether.

Defensiveness during psychotherapy is another frequent cause of utterance-rate change. Transient speed-ups or slow-downs may betray the emergence into consciousness of unacceptable ideas and unpleasant feelings.

For example: a self-supporting spinster in her early thirties spoke with extreme rapidity whenever she experienced erotic desires. A rigidly hypermoralistic attitude towards sex made the open recognition of such feelings absolutely unacceptable. Her feverish verbalizations also had the effect of minimizing any questions and explanations the therapist might offer in challenging her repressive attitudes. To be interrupted and talked to was a threat to her fantasy of being an independent asexual person. She recalled that rapid speech used to annoy her mother who complained of inability to understand what was being said. Over the years the patient had thus learned to use loquacity also as a way to keep other people at a distance.

Summary and conclusion

This paper deals with the perceivable manifestations of disease processes which doctors are trained to recognize as symptoms and use as diagnostic cues. Some physical signs point directly to specific bodily malfunctions; others communicate in more general ways about emotional disturbance. Acoustic signals may do this also; but in addition, patients deliberately emit sounds for the purpose of verbal communication. Insofar as illness affects the voice and speech, specific abnormalities of communication with words are discussed, and detailed clinical examples are given.

Both the normal and the aberrant usage of spoken language seem related to man's peculiar cerebral organization, his orality, and the problems posed by his social living. The rift between sound and sense which heralds many human illnesses is a practical consideration for the clinician. But within a wider context one may ask whether these vexing disruptions between acoustic and semantic behavior do not betray a basic flaw in the way man applies soundmaking to the problems he must solve.

How can communication about basic human needs and urgent human dilemmas be improved? An optimistic guess might be that we are on the verge of casting off outmoded ways of discourse in an effort to evolve more universal forms of communication. Perhaps the scientific study of paralinguistic and kinesic phenomena can here make its greatest contribution to the general weal.

21

THE INTERVIEW*

(1967)

The personal interview is an important tool for studying and modifying behavior of inmates in a correctional community. Well-conducted interviews can enhance communication opened up through the group program, while clumsy, inept interviewing can disrupt it. Our heavy reliance on group process sometimes obscures the need for individual relationships, and interviewing partly fulfills this need. Only in the interview relationship can a staff member get a close look at the individual problems of an inmate. Indeed, a staff member must be able to understand and to master the two-person interview before he can deal effectively with the dynamics of an entire group.

Interviews are scheduled meetings between two individuals, usually at a preset place and time. Everything that happens to the participants during this time is part of the interview. Informal chance meetings between inmate and staff member, like a passing greeting or exchange of pleasantries, are not considered interviews, even though such activities may help the two persons to acknowledge and recognize each other, and this may influence the climate of subsequent interviews. On the other hand, so long as the inmate is with the staff member during the scheduled time, this is an interview, even though it can happen that there is little talking because much of the time is spent in silent communication. Interviews may be scheduled by mutual consent when both participants want to meet. In this event both know fairly well what to expect from one another, what questions are likely to come up, and what topics need to be explored. However, it is also possible that interviews are set up on the initiative of one of the participants when he has a problem, for example

* Reprinted from *The Correctional Community*, N. Fenton, E. G. Reimer, and H. A. Wilmer (eds.): 95-106 (Berkeley/Los Angeles: University of California Press, 1967).

an inmate who needs advice or a staff member who has to have particular information. In such instances there may be less mutuality, and the person who takes the initiative has to dispel anticipatory anxiety by indicating the purpose of this scheduled meeting.

How the interview is conducted and what happens during the time spent together will reflect whether the interview is a mutual enterprise or a one-sided operation. It is important to remember that in any large institution – hospital, school, or correctional facility – the clients out-number the staff. Partly for this reason, the scheduling of interviews is controlled by the interviewer, whose time is usually limited by other demands for his service. This gives the interviewer a superior status and carries with it the responsibility for doing whatever he can to get the meeting off to a good start, even though the request for the interview may originally have come from the interviewed person.

Interviews are especially useful at times of transition when inmates and staff personnel are likely to experience the greatest tensions. For example, when a new man first enters the community, interviews can help him adjust to the strange environment and can also help the staff get acquainted with him. Any time when negative forces threaten the continuity of the group work – for instance because of delinquent acting-out by a particularly difficult inmate – personal interviews are needed to forestall and reduce clique formations. Before the inmate is released from the community on parole, when he returns after the first visit with his family, or when he is transferred to another institution, interviews help reduce the emotional turbulence stirred up whenever old inter-personal ties have to be dissolved and new ones established.

Starting the interview

Beginnings of interviews are important because of the jelling effect they create on what is to follow. Many people think that interviews start with talking, when one of the participants asks the first question or makes the first comment. But actually by the time this happens the interview is already under way. The real start of an interview is a visual encounter, a mutual appraisal of feelings and intentions that precede the opening verbal exchanges. Inmate and staff member quickly look at each other for nonverbal signs of tension, angry feelings, friendly attitudes and other subtle emotional nuances. The visual cues most revealing of a person's unspoken expectations and feelings are concentrated in the face, especially the eyes and the region around the nose and lips. Because the face is so richly endowed with expressive muscles, some people develop a 'poker-faced' attitude, or obscure part of the face with a cigarette or pipe, or by holding their chin in such a way that the corners of the mouth are covered up. The hands, the shoulders, posture of the body, and movements and positions of the legs and feet may also reveal information about feelings and attitudes. In this regard it is important to keep socio-cultural differences in mind. For example, an inmate raised in an Italian-American family may use and interpret hand gestures quite differently from an American Negro.

Almost invariably the initial encounter is used to review silently the expectations held before the interview. For instance, an inmate may enter the interview expecting to be punished for a delinquency not known to the staff member. The guilty man may confront a smiling, friendly staff member who is caught off guard. When there is mutual deeper suspiciousness, friendliness may be seen as a mask which hides a punitive attitude. This creates an emotional climate of fear and tension that influences whatever the participants subsequently say and hear.

We usually emphasize the importance of the INMATE's initial visual reactions to the interviewer rather than vice versa. In a professional interview the inmate knows much less about the staff member than the other way around. The staff member has access to legal documents, prison work-ups, medical and psychological reports, and parole and violation records about the inmate, whose only knowledge of the staff member is what has been learned firsthand through previous personal contacts or secondhand through the grapevine. This inequality in terms of background information about each other is another factor that can increase the tension and make the inmate look at the staff member as 'top dog' in the interview.

The conversational pattern

The spoken portion of the interview includes more than an exchange of words which carry semantic meaning. An equally important aspect of speech is the voice used by the speaker to project his thoughts. Words and voice, although inseparable, carry different kinds of information. It may be necessary to attend selectively to one or the other component of the conversation.

Voice belongs to a speaker's personality. It expresses his feelings and is geared to the physiological processes of breathing and phonation (vocal cord vibration) over which he has relatively little conscious control. The sound of the voice also depends on the shape and structure of the chest, head, throat, and mouth. It is therefore possible to identify a person on the basis of his voice, a physical property which can be objectified by sound spectrograms, or 'voice prints'. Words in speech have much more to do with one's learning and education. What a person says reflects where he has lived, who his parents were, what languages he learned, the influence of his teachers, and various occupational and professional roles held throughout life.

An interviewer should listen carefully to both the voice and word content of speech when he conducts an interview. Who starts the talking and what exactly is said may matter less than the quality of attention and selection used in listening. If the staff member is the first to speak, he should listen not only to his own words, sentences, and meanings, but give equal attention to the sound of his voice – its loudness, pitch, rhythm, and tone quality. His voice will have a reinforcing effect on the inmate's emotional reactions, affirming or negating some of the initial impressions based on visual and gestural cues. The inmate's willingness to confide in and trust the staff member, or his eagerness to clam up and remain on guard will throughout the interview be influenced by what he sees in the interviewer's face and hears in his voice.

Similarly, if the inmate starts the conversation, selective attentiveness to both his voice and his words, will often pay off. Pauses, gasping for air, flat uninflected pitch, a harsh or raspy voice quality, the absence or abundance of rhythmic stress accents are all valuable acoustic cues for sizing up how uncomfortable a person is feeling. The better the staff member gets to know an inmate the easier it will be to find out by listening to his voice whether he is sick or well, full of energy or depressed, friendly or angry. Opening remarks of an interview are especially important for this kind of diagnostic listening because the inmate has not as yet had a chance to get adjusted to the personal attitudes of the staff member. Initial statements are apt to reflect more closely what was felt and anticipated before the interview began. Some language experts feel that just about everything which is of any real importance gets communicated during "the first five minutes" of an interview and that whatever happens thereafter has to do with clarification, organization, and utilization of this information.

The interview contract

One of the most important elements to be clarified is the purpose of the interview, the goals toward which inmate and staff member are consciously trying to work. In this respect interviews should not confer on either participant the right to limit his communicative behavior, as may be the case with interrogations where the staff member is obliged to ask the questions whereas the inmate is expected to answer. Interviews also differ from psychotherapy, where the patient is expected to carry the conversational ball much of the time while the doctor may remain largely silent. Interview conversations are true dialogues which allow the participants to share their correctional interests on an equal footing. This equality of interests is the initial contract – the agreement to be candid and honest about the problem at hand.

While it may look simple enough, such a contract is often hard for the inmate to understand and for the staff member to enforce.

Strict adherence to the interview contract may be difficult. For example, an angry, truculent, self-punitive inmate may only be able to go so far as to agree to sit sullenly through the allotted interview time. If he cannot agree to talk, as you expect him to, it is foolish to pretend otherwise by engaging in chit-chat. After a while, he may agree to say certain things about himself, but nothing about the other inmates. Or he may agree to talk about his mother but not his father. Sometimes it is necessary for the inmate to be repeatedly reminded of the contractual nature of the interview, so that when the contract is lived up to the interviewer can give him credit for this accomplishment and when the contract is broken can criticise him for it. Only in this way may a severely antisocial person gradually be able to develop a degree of trust and confidence in his interviewer, a quality of good feeling that hopefully will spread to his relationships with other staff members as well.

Especially when things look bleak – which happens often in the life of the seriously disturbed or recidivistic inmate – a helpful approach is to look for possible agreements and to spell out contractual possibilities. For example, there are men whose negativism and suspiciousness makes them want to argue and disagree all the time. In interviews with such inmates, you may be able to clear the air by saying things like "OK, let's agree to disagree" or "well, we can at least agree on one thing, which is that you don't want to talk to me." This is not only a way of acknowledging reality. It also shows the inmate that the interviewer is not afraid of facing what is going on in this interview and that he can withstand feelings and inner tensions without getting 'mad', going 'crazy' or acting-out in a delinquent way. By watching his interviewer go through this process without becoming upset, an inmate can begin to build up his own resistances against disruptive behavior. This may be one of the first steps in the inmate's identifying with the staff member, a step which has to be taken over and over again if the interview is to become a corrective experience.

The interpersonal relationship

Interviews that proceed satisfactorily allow the participants gradually to establish a personal relationship. The feeling of personal relatedness grows more intense when there is a sequence of successful interviews at weekly or biweekly intervals. Interpersonal relationships kindle strong emotions which can be related to the realities of the interview itself. For instance, an inmate whose parole has just been denied may turn his pent-up anger on the staff member who interviews him, unleashing a barrage of hostile accusations that had to be held back at the official parole board meeting. Unless the staff member is prepared for this and has information about what happened to trigger the inmate's attack, he runs the risk of himself bristling with reactive distress or even reciprocating in a revenge-ful way.

In addition to the more obvious frustrations likely to inflame personal relationships formed in correctional communities, feelings and attitudes that actually have little to do with immediate reality may also have to be tackled. Pent-up emotions derive from memories of past life difficulties which are now recalled in the setting of confinement. For example, the inmate's frustration at being denied parole may awaken reminiscences of very painful disappointments in early childhood. These memories often are incomplete and fragmentary, and the traumatic experiences them-selves may have been repressed, so that the associated feelings do not become too unbearable. Personal histories of many inmates include extremely disagreeable childhood experiences like loss of parents and disintegration of the family. Overwhelming emotional reactions of grief, despair, rage, and attack that were part of these earlier calamities can occur again in an attenuated fashion in all subsequent human relation-ships of any importance, especially when the inmate is reminded in word or deed of the nature of the earlier deprivations.

The correctional interview should not try to deal too directly with the emotional wear and tear of past tragedies that cannot be undone. Instead, the focus usually has to be on more recent avoidable events which precipi-tate troubles that may be reversed. Interviews must try first of all to look candidly at the present life of the inmate, with its daily headaches, frustrations, and dilemmas. Repetitious elaboration of past memories or utopian fantasies may even interfere with the interview's important goal of reality-testing. An inmate may want to display his battle scars in order to distract the interviewer from some current problem in his behavior which he is afraid to discuss. The interviewer should certainly not ignore such evasive tactics. The best way to handle them is to acknowledge that he knows about the many injustices which the inmate already endured. But instead of dwelling on the inmate's past misfortunes, he should be told about the job of discussing the present-day reality which comes first. This directness helps dissolve interpersonal ambiguity and confusion, which are qualities of distorted human interactions from which many inmates have had to suffer.

Definition of the staff member's role helps the interpersonal relationship evolve along realistic lines. There may be times when wishful and magical thinking causes inmates to expect far more from interviews than can be accomplished. For example, some may want the interviews to straighten out their marital problems, others to hear predictions of employment opportunities, all of which relate to intangibles outside the prison over which the staff personnel may have no control. Such requests or intimations of power can sometimes be flattering. It is well to be on guard against this and to avoid promises which cannot be kept. This holds true for matters inside the correctional community as well. The group meetings will help clarify the functional responsibilities of the staff members but such definitions may be temporarily forgotten in the heat of a personal interview. If some misunderstanding about the staff member's role is allowed to persist – in regard to privileges, transfers, job assignments, or progress reports – he risks disappointing, even infuriating, the inmate, whose tolerance for frustration is usually low from the start. On the other hand, the staff member should not belittle himself merely for the reason that he is unable to grant the inmate everything he wants. If pride and integrity about work in the correctional community is not stead-fastly maintained, the inmate whose own sense of self-esteem is low may become pessimistic and embittered toward the interview relationship.

Inner dialogues

When the inmate is talking and the staff member listens reflectively, it may happen that spontaneous inner thoughts reach the staff member's awareness, for example: "Hey, that's a really amazing story – I'd like to hear more – go on" or "Oh no! not that old crap again – I've heard it a million times already – shut up." These are inner dialogues, a kind of abbreviated conversational process taking place between a person and himself. Every child growing up goes through a phase of talking audibly to himself, but later this self-dialogue is gradually internalized and goes on mostly in silence. Occasionally, while one privately rehearses a talk before giving it in public, inner dialogues again are spoken out, for instance in comments like "Gee, that sounded good" or "Hell, it didn't make sense – try it again."

Inner dialogues can help the interview by guiding such crucial decisions as when to continue listening and when to interrupt. There are no cookbook rules for the conduct of interviews; each follows a unique pattern, unpredictable to a certain extent. Outsiders watching the interview through an observation screen notice only the external conversations between inmate and staff member. The inner dialogues, of equal relevance for understanding the dynamics of the interaction, are directly perceived only by the participants themselves. Noticeably, as the inmate becomes an important person, the things he tells the staff member begin to echo inside his listening mind. It is as if the inmate took a place inside the interviewer, who in turn was introjected into the inmate's mind. These 'inside-outsiders' become the partners in inner dialogues, helping the conversation by giving spontaneous cues, ideas, and insights. The inner dialogue can try out different comments, questions, admonitions, or compliments in advance, before these are uttered openly, perhaps inappropriately, thus embarrassing or insulting the inmate and causing him to withdraw. For example, the inner dialogue may ask "Do you know who stole that screwdriver from the machine shop?" Another internal voice may then say, "OK – ask! – he can take it" – which permits the question to be articulated openly. At another time, this kind of question might be squelched by an internal warning of "better not ask it this way – he'll just deny his behavior – the question really sounds like an accusation." In the imaginative inner dialogue the interviewer can take the inmate's point of view and rehearse questions or comments without blurting them out. Each interview is an emotional experience as well as an intellectual one, and the interviewer may be stumped trying to 'figure out' only in logical terms what is happening. There is no coach to tell him what to do next, nor will another inmate, as in group therapy, join the conversation. Reliance on the inner dialogue can sometimes help get an interviewer over a deadlock, and by attending to any concomitant visual fantasies he may be able to recall things of importance that happened during a previous interview with the inmate. Such memories can help provide continuity with the current interview. Also this kind of listening with the inner ear may help bring up novel, meaningful, and spontaneous formulations toward the end of an interview, when separation becomes a problem.

The inmate too has inner dialogues, but the interviewer will not be able to hear these unless he can get this preconscious material to be translated into outer conversational speech. It is not easy to do this in a correctional setting where many inmates may be men of action rather than of words. Their inner dialogues may be full of curses, oaths, and other expressions of hostility which can only be brought out in the presence of the other inmates or when the man is alone. Secrets, fears, magical or 'crazy' ideas which the inmate is afraid to reveal may be deliberately held back. Sometimes there are prayerful, childlike, sexual or loving themes which embarrass the inmate too much to allow for externalization in speech. If this happens he may start to talk compulsively, producing a repetitious and monotonous outer speech to hide painful or embarrassing inner dialogues from himself and the interviewer. The group meeting is an important safety valve for unexpressible preoccupations because here it may be possible for one inmate to say what is on another man's mind, shielding the other and himself from the pain of self-revelation.

Closing the interview

The end of an interview can be difficult because of its symbolic resemblance to past painful separations. Since separation involves two people the staff member must be sensitive to his own role in all types of separations. This issue comes up in group meetings too – whenever someone is transferred, goes on vacation, or leaves the institution – but closing of individual interviews stimulates separation anxiety much more intensely and provides a good training ground for understanding this problem.

Usually closing takes place when the allotted interview time is used up. This matter of time is of utmost importance, especially to the inmate. His 'time' in the correctional institution has been set by others, and he may resent being reminded that he is not in control of time and therefore not of himself. The closing of each interview and the end of the interview relationship can be an unconscious reminder of this kind of personal insignificance.

Sometimes the only way to deal with the problem is by being very matter-of-fact and simply saying "Well, our time is up, we'll meet again next week." This not only reminds the inmate of the reality of impersonal time but also gives him something to look forward to. The other dimension, the personal sense of readiness to quit, is more difficult to assess. When the question comes up, it is well for the staff member to check both the inmate's and his own introspective time sense, the inner clocks of mood and feeling. Every living creature has these internal clocking devices which control and coordinate his behavior. There is evidence to suggest that the inmates of prisons and the patients of mental hospitals cannot successfully correlate their internal time systems to those of so-called healthy, or normal, people. However this may be, it always is beneficial if the staff member asks the inmate and himself whether it FEELS right to quit. This strategy will help keep the interview focussed on its mutuality. Just as each interview must close with some reference to the future, as "see you next week", the end of the interview relationship, terminated by departure from the institution, should also bridge the uncertainty of the future. This is done by the use during the last hours together in discussion of plans for parole, return to work, re-establishment of family life, and other goals of life outside the institution.

When an interview relationship has been particularly useful and friendly, the inmate may on occasion wish to prolong it by writing letters, calling up, or sending messages back to the staff member. There is no need to act stand-offish if this happens, although it is always important to remind the released inmate that any new problems have to be discussed with his parole officer. Once the formal interview relationship has come to an end, a certain amount of informal friendly contact is certainly permissible. Usually however, the reality of pressures of new responsibilities make this impractical for the staff member, and the released man himself prefers to start a new life outside, which does not remind him too often of experiences 'behind the walls'.

22

THE INNER SPEECH OF PSYCHOTHERAPY*

(1967)

Studies of psychotherapy often bog down in the difficult translation from internal psychologic reality into external, social reality. Man's inner life encompasses personal experiences in auditory, visual, olfactory, tactile, vibratory, and thermal terms. By contrast, his social functioning depends on the use of impersonal code systems limited to predominantly auditory and visual modalities. What enables transformations to be made between private experience and public communication? One obvious answer is language, since this can be held internally in the form of verbal thoughts and can also be externalized in the form of speech. Yet even in the realm of language we are faced with a dichotomy between thought and speech that becomes troublesome when patients are requested to free associate (for example, "put all your feelings, fantasies, impulses INTO WORDS"), or therapists try to describe interviews ("TELL ME what happened"). In bridging the gap between thought and speech one may notice a process called INNER SPEECH (Berlyne 1965). This consists of words and sentence fragments which enter awareness in a quasi-auditory form and are not yet sufficiently well organized for comprehensible articulation or have to be held back for reasons of social propriety (for instance, 'censorship'). The purpose of this paper is to review some important contributions to the concept of inner speech and describe an experiment in which this component of thinking was tapped to gain insight into the psychotherapeutic process.

* Reprinted from *American Journal of Psychotherapy* 21. 4: 757-66 (1967).

The concept of inner speech

That one can internally speak to himself by thinking in silent verbal patterns is an observation repeatedly made throughout recorded human history. The very act of writing down one's thoughts is often preceded by a stage of internal preparation which involves self-talk (McKellar 1957). Children playing alone or on the verge of falling asleep may engage in autistic imaginary conversations (Weir 1966). Kubie (1965) described inner speech as part of the stream of preconscious associations, and noted its especially vivid character when the psychotherapist involves himself simultaneously with more than one patient, that is, in group therapy (Kubie 1958).

Within the twentieth century, the concept of inner speech has been reviewed in the French (Egger 1904) and German (Schilling 1929) psychologic literature. Hughlings Jackson discussed it for Anglo-American readers in his famous studies of aphasia. "Verbalizing", said Jackson, has a duality of which "speech is only the end or second half" (J. H. Jackson 1958). Before this external "half" of speech takes place, there is often an internal "sequent conscious and voluntary production of words." He noticed that certain aphasics had lost this ability – they "cannot speak internally". Freud, who was influenced by Jackson's formulations, described the inner "speeches and conversations" occurring in dreams (Freud 1954), namely, at a time when social demands for communication are minimal. In his therapeutic work, he traced these auditory dream fragments BACK to recent memories of actual speech events which presumably had undergone selective repression and unconscious reorganization as part of the dream work. Sullivan, in his introspections, noted that inner speech refers not only back to the past ("a complex function of information I have picked up over the years"), but also FORWARDS, to the future in terms of an intended audience (Sullivan 1954).

The Russian psychologist Vygotsky (1962) made important observations about inner speech (endophasy) when he observed how children incorporate the words of parental speech into their own complex thoughts. He found inner speech to be "condensed, abbreviated speech – almost entirely predicative – speech for oneself – turns speech into inward thought – an autonomous speech function – a distinct plane of thought." Vygotsky cautioned against regarding the transition from inner to outer speech as a simple translation: "It cannot be achieved by merely vocalizing silent speech. It is a complex, dynamic process involving the transformation of the predicative, idiomatic structure of inner speech into syntactically articulated speech intelligible to others." Luria (1961) has since pointed out that inner speech not only transforms thought into verbal expression but is also responsible for "crystallization of the whole expression into its shortened, conceptual scheme." Werner and Kaplan (1963) reviewed the experimental studies of inner speech.

It is important not to confuse those forms of inner speech which the individual directs exclusively to and for himself with the various social aspects of inner speech that are preparatory to external communication. This confusion can be observed in certain hallucinating patients who use one part of their inner speech to cancel out another part (for example, "One voice tells me to say something but then there is another voice that says 'no, don't talk'"). The conflict may also express itself in stuttering. In Freund's (1966) formulation the inner speech interposes itself between "latent speech intent and overt speaking". While scanning his inner speech, the patient discovers words "charged with feeling-tones of displeasure, shame, humiliation and helplessness", and this forces him to decide whether or not to risk using the dangerous words in outer speech. The resulting hesitancy can become an intolerable delay for the listener who expects a certain rate of verbal input to satisfy his own auditory requirements.

While clinicians may be content to regard inner speech in terms of its psychologic reality, scientists must test the reality of this phenomenon through objective, consensual verification. To do so requires an analysis of any external manifestations which might reflect the inner speech processes. A valuable article by Mahl and Schultze (1964) reviews studies of the 'extralinguistic' aspects of verbal communication. Especially revealing are PAUSES in speaking which, to Goldman-Eisler (1964), indicate uncertainty and are taken to be evidence of an active planning process going on in the silent speaker's mind. Similar assumptions can be made about DISTURBANCES in the flow of speech, which in some speakers herald an increased productivity of new and unexpected ideas (Feldstein et al. 1966). Other observable events that have been taken to indicate a significant shift in the speaker's internal milieu include voice changes (Moses 1954), speech mannerisms (Feldman 1959), switching to a foreign language (Krapf 1955), neophasias (Spoerri 1964), and glossolalia (Osser et al. 1973). What about inaudible manifestations of inner speech which are traceable only through concomitant motor patterns? Gould (1948) considered "subvocal" laryngeal movements to be associated with certain autistic activities interpreted as auditory hallucinations, and Lindsley

(1963) has gone so far as to equate OVERT speech with hallucinations. LeBaron (1962) asked hypnotized subjects to indicate their emerging verbal thoughts with "ideomotor" finger signals. Experiments with delayed auditory feedback (Chase et al.) and the motor theory of speech perception (Liberman et al. 1962) both pose interesting new challenges to the concept of inner speech in regulation of overt speech behavior.

A clinical experiment[1]

In the absence of reliable laboratory tools to measure inner speech, we decided to modify a clinical psychotherapy situation in such a way as to facilitate on-the-spot 'capture' of fleeting inner speech phenomena. Video-taping was employed to record nonverbal gestures, posture changes, and facial expressions for immediate replay and analysis (Wilmer 1967). A patient requesting therapy, who himself had observed (disapprovingly!) certain of his inner speech processes, was invited to collaborate in the experiment.

He was an unmarried law clerk in his mid-twenties who requested psychiatric consultation after becoming panicky over the fear of military service. The patient was aware of lifelong problems in social adjustment, having grown up as the youngest child in a home dominated by an aggressive, controlling mother. His father, a quiet, unassuming man, had become moderately successful through hard work and obedient submissiveness. The patient only just managed to break away from home for the first time, and until the letter from his draft board arrived he felt a new and uncomfortably exciting pride over recently having lost his virginity. His overt reason for wanting to avoid military service was that communal army life might expose certain peculiarities, among which were an introverted personality, a strong dislike for physical activity, and a habit of "talking to myself." This almost inaudible self-talk had been part of his behavior since age four, was done strictly in private, and could be inhibited in the presence of others.

The goal of therapy with this patient was to help him tolerate the content of his private reveries which dealt largely with anger, fear, violence, and sexual material. Three technical procedures were employed. First, he was encouraged to articulate his inner speech during interviews. Second, he was invited to use a tape-recorder between visits, record his monologues, and review this material during interviews. Third, he was told that the therapist also would make efforts to attend to his own inner speech

[1] The author is greatly indebted to Harry Wilmer, M.D. for advice and help with this experiment.

processes during and after interviews. To facilitate this, interviews were tape-recorded, and verbal fragments entering the therapist's awareness immediately jotted down. Afterwards these notes were transcribed to give a 'running commentary' of inner speech along with the recorded outer dialogue. Several times a dictating machine was used to directly record inner speech fragments at the moment of occurrence during interviews. Due to the difficulty of talking and listening at the same time, it was usually possible to dictate only telegraphic fragments which, like jotted notes, had to be transcribed afterwards. Once a telewriter was used for making notes during videotaping so that the therapist's written comments could be photographed and fused with the picture of the interview.

The patient was in therapy for approximately six months, the first three of which were used for the experiment. Several distinct patterns in the inner speech were noted, and after the completion of treatment we assigned these to five categories. The present report is limited to a description of these apparently distinct phases of inner speech process.

Echoic inner speech

This is direct reverbalization of some word or sentence fragment which has just been uttered. It appears especially prominent in initial interviews and when the regularity of visits is interrupted. Echoic inner speech seems to make the interview 'stand still', allowing a moment of contemplation. There is a sense of 'taking a closer look' at what had just been said in order to establish a mutuality and understanding of immediate problems.

Example: The patient began a visit by apologizing for coming to the interview with a "cold". This word was echoed internally as a stimulus to several associations regarding fear of contamination, avoidance of closeness, and secondary-gain implications of the patient's behavior.

Improvisatory inner speech

This is a sudden, often quite impromptu hunch that may be evoked by something just mentioned or by a fantasy or memory from past interviews. The response is more complex than simply reverbalizing. It seems to help establish notions of behavior that have predictive qualities. One has more the sense of an inspiration – "Aha – now I'm beginning to understand" – and there is a greater feeling of rapport in the interview.

Example: While the patient articulated a fear of appearing "ridiculous", an inner speech asked: "Why are you afraid to feel ridiculous?" and answered,

"Is it related to what you told me about embarrassment and nudity?" An important element of conflict regarding military service became apparent. The symbolic attainment of masculine identity is linked to the danger of regression through anonymity, overt violence, and exclusion of heterosexual relationships. This seemed applicable to the patient's dilemma.

Schematizing inner speech

Here the inner speech turns to plan-making through a process of symbolic thinking and fantasy. A particular aspect of clinical experience is identified and selected for further analysis. This can result in a program which the therapist may wish to spell out with a certain degree of precision. One senses a logical order, a certain calming down, and is less emotively involved with the immediate interview situation than during echoic or improvisatory inner speech.

Example: While describing sexual fantasies, the patient indicated his interest in a fairly "deep" analysis of oedipal material. The therapist's inner speech cautioned that "what you say is certainly rich with possibilities for exploration of fantasies about your parents. This might keep us busy for a long time." A plan emerged for acknowledging that the patient is indeed afraid of men. This would have to be analyzed in terms not only of the fear of military service but also the passive clinging to his mother.

Dialectic inner speech

These are debate-like dialogues in which verbal exchanges take place. "I say this – he says that – then I say this – and so on." Comments or interventions are 'tried out' in fantasy to gauge whether responses evoked from the patient are likely to be helpful or detrimental to the therapy. These inner dialogues often have a dramatic, highly emotional quality. Again there is much more of an intrapsychic involvement as portions of the patient's introjected behavior engage one's imagination. Arguments, disputations, agreements, and disagreements take place in imagination and one mentally searches for the most 'therapeutic' approach to the problem at hand.

Example: While the patient was talking about his symptoms, the following inner dialogue ensued:
Patient: "I don't know where I'm going..."
Therapist: "But last time you said you were ambitious and knew exactly what you wanted."
Patient: "This time I'm telling you my real thoughts and feelings about that."
Therapist: "Oh – well you're presenting yourself as a cooperative patient, aren't you, trying to make my job easier!"

Meditative inner speech

Precise connections to immediate events are given up as the inner speech turns to commentaries, slogans, or conversational fragments from seemingly unrelated thoughts. There may be a sense of searching for generalizations, interpretations, or 'answers' to basic human problems. On occasion a teacher, friend, or other person engages the meditation through multiparty inner dialogues. The affect may range from pleasant tranquility to uncomfortable yearning.

Example: Mention of the movie *He Who Must Die* evoked fantasies and ideas about pacifism and self-sacrifice. The patient's initial motivations for therapy and questions about his long-range goals came up for review. Comments from personal experience mingled with those derived from authority figures, textbooks and other sources of wisdom. Fragments from Dostoyevsky's *The Brothers Karamazov* came to mind along with psychoanalytic interpretation of historical figures and cultural problems.

Discussion

From the above highly-condensed descriptions of interviews which took place over a period of months, the reader has hopefully concluded that inner speech is not to be viewed as a simple transformation from private thoughts into public utterances. One of the important contributions of contemporary linguistics is to make explicit distinctions between a person's language COMPETENCE and his language PERFORMANCE (Lenneberg 1967). In the sense of linking what we are capable of saying with what we would like to say, inner speech may be one of the mediating mechanisms between language competence and performance. Lashley (1951) expressed this more technically when he wrote:

Internal speech may be carried out wholly by processes within the nervous system, with some unessential discharge upon the final common path for vocal movements. Facilitation of the motor path, either by increased emotional tension or by voluntary reinforcement, increases its excitability until the same central circuits whose activity constitutes internal speech are able to excite the overt movements.

If inner speech is part of an internal psychic process on the level of language encoding-decoding, what is the advantage of calling it SPEECH, in view of the way the term speech usually refers to external social processes?

My answer is that speech signals are used not only for transmitting information between speaker and listener, but can also be used by the speaker to transmit information to himself. This is analogous to the feedback, or servo-mechanism whereby a machine modulates and corrects its own behavior (Foerster 1952). In psychotherapy, the inner speech processing is obviously geared to social requirements of a treatment dyad – where the patient's job is to transform simultaneously occurring emotional, sensory, and cognitive events into sequential structures (that is, language) capable of being made comprehensible to the therapist. The therapist's complementary role is to listen, which requires first of all an auditory scanning of the patient's verbal output. This process is guided by ECHOIC aspects of the therapist's inner speech in which content and style of what the patient says is replayed inside the therapist's short-term auditory memory.

Echoic elements of inner speech may in certain instances be immediately transformed into outer speech by way of the sorts of literal repetitions inexperienced patients sometimes find funny or annoying.

Patient: "I don't think my mother approves of smoking."
Therapist: "You don't think your mother approves of smoking."

Inner speech transmitted in this pseudo-echolalic fashion indicates that the therapist may be developing an internal representation or model of the patient, since similar neuromotor activations must be employed for accurate speech mimicry.

The next step is as subtle as it is complex. Merely by uttering the repetition with a rising inflection, for example, "you don't think your mother approves of smoking?" the therapist reveals that his response may have proceeded to the level of IMPROVISATORY inner speech. It is precisely this subtlety which can confound a computer (Bar-Hillell 1964); the raising of a question in outer speech implies an anticipatory questioning in inner speech, including a set of hunches about the patient's difficulties. By now the therapist has integrated information gained from the patient's verbal output with clues gained by watching him and from knowledge of the history. A working model of the patient as he appears to other people is now present within the therapist.

In addition, the experienced therapist has hunches about how his anticipated interventions are likely to influence the patient. This is where SCHEMATIZING inner speech comes in. The novice lacking clinical experience and psychotherapeutic know-how tends to rely much more on echoic and improvisatory responses than does the experienced therapist, whose inner speech can avail itself of a memory storage full of previous successes and failures with patients. He takes account of ways people are likely to react when their behavior is observed, questioned, interpreted, or commented upon. DIALECTIC inner speech helps to dramatize these variously fantasied possibilities, especially in inner dialogues which allow the introjected image of the patient to reverberate with a consciously felt aspect of the therapist's self. The therapist has managed to free this part of himself for exclusive concern with the patient. An analogous feeling may develop within the patient once he begins to sense that he is not 'just another patient' but occupies a particular role in the therapist's inner life. When the therapy reaches this stage, an understanding of the transference-countertransference processes may be possible (Shapiro 1966).

MEDITATIVE inner speech allows further communication with persons outside the patient-therapist dyad. It is especially noticeable when clinical work is being supervised, as during training. One reason for the unduly passive appearance of some trainees early in their psychotherapeutic work may be that they meditate upon topics not immediately related to the therapy, such as what such-and-such a consultant said last week, or ideas derived from reading and lectures. Significant figures from personal past experience can also 'come to life' during meditative responses, exerting beneficial or pejorative commentary. The inner speech then deals with information derived not from the interview in progress but from long-forgotten memories instead. As an elaboration of the therapist's schematizing inner speech, meditative processes may also be concerned with imagery and ideation about future possibilities in the life of the patient.

Summary

The concept of inner speech, which had its origin in neurology, psycho-analysis, and psychology is here applied to certain conscious aspects of internal information-processing during psychotherapy. Using audiotapes and videotapes, the author has attempted to capture fleeting inner verbalizations while listening to and planning appropriate responses for a patient in therapy. Five patterns were noted: echoic, improvisatory, schematizing, dialectic, and meditative inner speech. Relating these patterns of inner speech to the outer observable speech of the therapist will require more precise methods for correlating behavioral events temporally. There are moments when the inner speech appears to function as a servo-mechanism, controlling and guiding the therapist's overt speech.[2] In terms of contemporary linguistic theory, it may also be said that the inner speech processes are mediating mechanisms between language competence and performance. Thus significantly different patterns of inner speech are to be expected when the behavior of experienced therapists is contrasted with that of inexperienced therapists.

[2]   A monograph by Mysak (1966) has just come to my attention which focuses specifically on feedback processes, including inner speech, in speech pathology.

23

SYMPTOMS, DIAGNOSIS, AND CONCEPTS OF DISEASE: SOME COMMENTS ON THE SEMIOTICS OF PATIENT-PHYSICIAN COMMUNICATION*

(1968)

Diagnosis is a form of pattern recognition. It starts with symptoms and signs (messages) that are interpreted according to certain rules about syndromes (concepts) of disease. In a previous paper (Ostwald 1964a), I described medical semiotics in the traditional context of patient-physician relationships where interpretation of signs and symptoms is akin to the breaking and deciphering of intricate code systems.

Obviously a great deal of communication about disease also occurs outside the specialized network of a patient-physician interaction. Indeed, it may safely be said that many of the most significant communications about disease take place before a physician arrives on the scene, and these preliminary semiotic maneuvers may even determine when the doctor is to be called and in what manner the information about disease is presented to him. Diagnostic work begins on a subjective level the moment the patient feels sick. Symptoms inform him that "something is wrong", which leads to the speculation: "I wonder what I should do about it". When recognition of a change in one's health is coupled with plans for doing something about it, this amounts to a more definitive diagnosis. The next step is communicating one's symptoms to a relative, spouse, friend, or medically trained person, who then asks questions or does some amount of examination in an effort to form his own objective diagnosis.

Each time someone renders a diagnosis about himself to another person, reference must be made to a concept of disease. This may be a highly sophisticated concept, as when the diagnostician is a disease specialist, or it may be a very simple concept, as when a child tells you what ails him. The logical processes are probably similar to those found

* Reprinted from *Social Science Information* 7. 4: 95-106 (1968).

in all forms of language communication, in that messages cannot be interpreted unless there is a conceptual matrix available, and this matrix may vary somewhat from person to person as well as between cultures. One cannot understand words unless it is known to what these refer. Similarly, one cannot make a diagnosis without having concepts of disease.

I do not mean to imply that disease concepts are necessarily consciously-held intellectual entities. On the contrary, the diagnosis "I am sick" is most often made intuitively, on the basis of sensations and feelings that are extremely difficult to put into words. The ability to recognize disease states is undoubtedly an adaptive mechanism which protects our health and keeps us alive. Decisions about disease and diagnosis have to be made efficiently, and I therefore assume the number of basic disease concepts to be rather small, probably on the order of "seven plus or minus two" (Miller 1967). Menninger (1963) postulates only five levels of "dysorganization", and I believe that life as we know it would have disappeared long ago had we to cope with as great an array of disease concepts as our contemporary medical nosology (Thompson and Hayden 1961) seems to suggest. An excellent recent article by King (1967) points out that while progress in medicine consists largely in increased precision, the existence of highly technical and precise diagnostic categories does not mean that they must all be used.

Disease as interference with bodily function

Perhaps the most commonly held disease concept is that of a specific malfunction affecting a part or parts of the body. This may be structural damage, for example fracture of a bone, in which case one thinks of the disease as being an organic one, even though its effect – *i.e.*, inability to move the afflicted limb with appropriate strength – is a functional impairment. The old pseudo-dichotomy between organic and functional diseases is gradually being phased out of medical education as physicians are taught to think in terms of integrated organ-SYSTEMS instead of isolated single organs. For instance, to learn about the function of the heart one sees it as part of the circulatory or cardio-vascular system rather than simply as a pump detached from other parts of the body.

While structure and function are always intimately related, the organic point of view often has a more immediate appeal because one can more easily inspect, visualize and concretize the body's architecture than its movements. Children point to "where it hurts". Oriental ladies use a sculptured model of the body to locate their complaints. The first thing

282 EMPATHIC COMMUNICATION WITH SOUNDS THAT HAVE MEANING

most medical students do is dissect a corpse. This may have unfortunate consequences if the student doesn't simultaneously see muscles, joints, and other organ-systems in action. He is impressed with the simplicity of structure in the absence of function (in spite of the all-too-frequent complaint that anatomy courses are difficult), and risks the psychological attitude of seeing his first patient as being dead.

But once the organically-minded student approaches the anatomy of the nervous system he is bound to make a great discovery. Many structural displacements take place during growth and development because nervous innervations of body segments are laid down very early in embryonal life. As parts of the body mature, their nerves are pulled along to places distant from the original sites. This accounts for the possibility of pain being referred to spots far removed from the source of the irritation. It also means that anyone not familiar with neural distributions produces ludicrously inaccurate symptoms when for some reason the source of the disease lies outside the body.

For example, a young lady whose not altogether perfect fiancé ran his car into a tree after a long and guilty petting session decided she would rather sue him for damage to her health than proceed with their engagement. Her claim that the accident produced leg paralysis was easily disproved by a neurologist's finding of an anesthesia which went up exactly to the level of her miniskirt. This is a socially understandable but neurophysiologically improbable line of demarcation.

Yet even in such clearly hysterical situations the paralyzing effects of psychological conflict can have structural consequences. As 'sick' limbs are no longer used for walking or weight-bearing, their bones become weak, the muscles grow flabby, and the immobilized joints stiffen. Soon what started out as a 'merely functional' disorder turns out to have very obvious and disabling organic pathology. Any one-sided treatment attempts which overlook the patient's somatopsychic unity are doomed to fail.

Disease concepts which limit themselves to isolated body parts have certain administrative advantages. This was beautifully illustrated by a recent *New Yorker* caricature of a doctor's waiting room, one wall of which features a large illustration of the human body. Signs indicate which doctor the patient is to consult. Head complaints go to Dr. X., neck pains to Dr. Y., chest problems to Dr. Z., and so forth. The joke isn't very funny when you consider that patients and doctors are really victimized by such impersonal diagnostic procedures.

Isolated symptoms – the itch here, the lump there, the tender spot over here – may be among the most difficult and nightmarish problems to interpret. Certain very ominous conditions produce only minimal or quixotic signs; on the other hand, fear and anxiety can interfere to such a degree that the patient is unable to give a comprehensive account of himself. The very IDEA that part of his body is not functioning properly and may have to be removed is intensely frightening. This accounts for some of the paradoxical reactions to treatment seen when, much to everyone's dismay, the patient gets worse instead of better after his disease has been 'successfully' treated.

Mr. J. was admitted to the hospital for surgical removal of a femoral bone spur – *i.e.*, a bit of excess bone tissue slowly growing on the thigh bone. Except for a fear of cancer the patient disclosed no reason for wanting the operation done at this time. The surgeon focused his attention mostly on X-rays of the affected region.

The operation took only 20 minutes and was easily accomplished under spinal anesthesia. The wound began to heal well, and everyone was pleased with the results. But on the second post-operative day the patient complained of a "peculiar odor". He mentioned to the intern that someone on the ward seemed to be engaged in "suspicious experiments" and was probably employed by the FBI. The intern joked about this and prescribed a mild sedative. The next day the patient was quite agitated, demanded to see the hospital director, and shouted angrily that a plot against him was being hatched by "communists". A psychiatric consultation revealed the patient to be responding to hallucinatory accusative voices, and antipsychotic medication was prescribed to bring an incipient paranoid schizophrenic disorganization under control. A careful history subsequently revealed that for years the patient had been an extremely shy and socially withdrawn person. He harbored a bizarre quasi-delusional view of his own body, including the bone spur which the surgeon unwittingly agreed to amputate.

Now that surgeons are able to remove organs from one person and transplant them into the bodies of others, new and heretofore unknown diseases will undoubtedly make their appearance. This will raise important issues for social scientists. For example, what compensation procedures are to be followed when the eye you lose in an accident is not your own? Or how is the language of love to be interpreted when the heart that beats in your chest was removed from an executed murderer?

Disease as disturbance in social communication

Many doctors view the brain as an organ of the body, which is correct on an anatomical basis since this vital structure is enclosed inside the skull and is fed by the body's own blood supply. But from a functional viewpoint one surely must concede that brains interconnect people and their social environments. The idea of brain as mediator between man's outer and inner space has been well formulated by Shands (1967). The cerebral portals of sensory input – vision, hearing, and smell – are well designed to receive long distance signals from the world, and neuronal cable extensions bring internal signals like vibration, movement, touch, and taste to the brain.

For healthy functioning, the human organism is as dependent on information from the external environment as he is on his own internal, self-generated signals. Whether we locate 'trouble' inside or external to the body surface seems to be a matter of early imprinting, childhood experience, training, education, and social conditioning. During the first year of life (Spitz 1965) affectionate interactions between infant and mother critically influence the growth of that mental capacity (called ego) which makes decisions about the locations of disturbance. Take the infant's cry: it is simultaneously a semiotic event for the mother, who is depended upon socially for nurturance, and a physiological event for the infant, who breathes, coughs, swallows, and moves according to innate, geneti-cally-determined programs (Lind 1965). Throughout subsequent growth and development there is this interplay between physiological and social reverberations to the child's signals, of which acoustically-mediated ones are of special interest since these may belong to the realm of language.

This is not the place to branch off into a detailed discussion of normal language development, which I shall simply schematize (Table 1). We must assume that the growing child's auditory system is at a certain optimal level of functional capacity before he can perceive the presence of spoken language in his environment. Furthermore, he must have the

TABLE 1

Schematic representation of critical factors in language acquisition.

ENDOGENOUS	EXOGENOUS
Genetic program for building a cerebral language acquisition device	Uterine environment compatible with fetal development
Intact, normally-growing brain tissues	Non-traumatic, nutritionally correct infant care
Auditory system capable of receiving and processing speech sounds	Exposure to human speech behavior in childhood
Organization and maturation of the ego	Emotional ties to significant persons
Development of intellectual functions	Educational opportunities
Neuro-motor equipment for speech-production	Socialization experiences

neurological capacity, or "language acquisition device" (McNeill 1966), to establish rules about how sounds can be used communicatively. Finally, he needs the ability to control his speech-output apparatus in such a way as to make himself understandable. Each step requires appropriate possibilities for linguistic feed-forward and feed-back in the child's social environment. A deficit in one of these developmental steps can throw subsequent maturations out of order, and in a typical clinical history one often finds several deficits simultaneously derailing the child's progress.

Roberta is 16 years old when her father requests "help for her speech". There obviously is a severe disturbance in communicative behavior. The girl emits words in a garbled, often completely incomprehensible fashion, especially when she becomes excited. Distinctive features of many consonants are either absent or scrambled, and the vowels often have an unnatural, "foreign" sound-quality. Only intonation and stress patterns are well preserved, giving listeners the impression that the patient can produce the suprasegmental features of speech but is unable to fill in the discriminative segmentals. A brain disorder is immediately suspected, and the family is indeed prepared for this diagnosis, since the child was long ago enrolled in a special school where organic causation of mental retardation is taken for granted. Our neurological evaluation reveals no localizable lesion to which the girl's language dysfunctions can be attributed, but her resting electroencephalogram shows a generalized dysrhythmia indicating delayed brain maturation, and electrical responses evoked by sensory stimulation show similarly immature patterns.

Closer evaluation of social aspects of the case brings into focus certain additional features which undoubtedly played a crucial role in bringing about this unfortunate disability. First there is the problem of Roberta's father. He was born in the United States, but speaks the American language imperfectly. This results in part from his loyalty to a family and subculture which is Peruvian. His own parents migrated to California and married here, but continued to speak mostly in their native tongue. Roberta's father does not care much for verbal discourse; he is a man of action, a mechanic who functions more successfully on the level of doing things than talking about them. His marriage to Roberta's mother was chaotic. She neglected the home, and even after having a child spent most of her time in local bars. The baby girl was abandoned in infancy, and by the time public intervention became available the now badly starved, depressed, and sick little patient could only be cared for in a hospital. After the parents were divorced, Roberta's father tried to obtain custody of his child, but the court insisted there be an adequate mother in the home. He therefore went to Peru for the specific purpose of finding a new wife as stepmother for his daughter. Two babies born since then have been well cared for and show normal speech and behavior development. Roberta's mother in the meantime has given birth to some more babies which are said also to be mentally retarded, but we don't know whether this is a genetic problem, or results from the mother's neglectfulness, or both.

Why is Roberta referred for treatment now, after all these problematical years? The precipitating stress is quite obvious, though many hours of interviewing her father and stepmother were needed to elicit the information: Roberta has a boy friend, also a retarded youngster. One day in school the teacher found him and Roberta "playing house" in the bathroom, and his intervention prevented copulation. Suddenly Roberta's parents are threatened by her maturation in addition to her retardation. She can no longer be confined to her room (where social isolation actually fosters her retardation). But can she be trusted in the sexually threatening environment at school? This is the dilemma which drives Roberta's father to seek professional advice, the justification for which has to be rationalized as a request (symptom!) for speech therapy.

Disease as dissatisfaction

People are vulnerable to the diagnostic process itself, since diagnosis is a way of saying something is wrong with you, and raises questions like: "What is going to happen?", "How will this disorder progress?", and, most broadly: "What is my future?" In other words, diagnosis implies prognosis. This can be observed in American schools where certain youngsters are identified as being "slow learners" while others are singled out as "fast learners". This labelling process (diagnosis) has the effect of coaxing the teacher to expect more from the fast and less from the slow students, a self-fulfilling prophecy. The same process is found in homes where a mother's favoritism raises one child's self-esteem above that of the less fortunate siblings. The selected youngsters then reinforce the maternal attitudes by promoting themselves through accomplishments or punishing themselves with failures.

Disease diagnosis has the almost inevitable effect of reducing self-esteem. No matter how carefully formulated or tactfully presented, the doctor's words are heard as judgments, even dire or ominous predictions.

A teenager faints during his high school graduation exercises. His mother takes him to a doctor who says: "This is clearly a case of epilepsy". The diagnosis is felt as a damning personal criticism. Having always seen herself as descended from a noble family, the boy's mother suddenly perceives her heredity to be "tainted" (in spite of negative family history for seizure disorders). She scolds her daughters for teasing the epileptic boy into having fits. She flies to Europe to double-check the family tree. None of her children are able to marry for fear of passing the dreaded condition on to another victim.

This is an extreme example, of course. But to a lesser degree the same process can be observed when a correct interpretation (diagnosis of behavior) is made in psychotherapy. The patient feels he has lost something. He never sees himself as quite the same person again. He is forced to realize and accept a certain 'fault' or 'weakness', and feels unhappy even though the new knowledge protects against self-damaging behavior. For example, a nymphomaniac's sexual promiscuity is lessened after learning that this behavior is a self-defeating compulsion to find an affectionately satisfying relationship. But this insight, as it reduces the search for conquests, may also enhance loneliness and accentuate guilt. In cultures that encourage independence and reward aggressiveness, any tendencies toward dependence and passivity are especially difficult to accept.

Clinicians try to offset the depressive effects of their diagnosis. In some medical offices an air of informality prevails which enables the doctor to tell his patient about favorable outcomes of similar diseases afflicting other patients he has cared for. This is supposed to increase the patient's confidence in his doctor, and it may work. But one should be sparing with such bedside manners, since what doctors say and do is interpreted by patients in terms of their personal past experiences with authority figures. Usually it is better to delay giving unpleasant news until the professional relationship is strong enough for the patient to tolerate the diagnostic stress. Any explicit guarantees as to 'cure' or 'improvement' are risky, since failure to achieve the hoped-for results can disappoint and thus additionally hurt the patient.

On the other hand, patients may be dissatisfied with the doctor's uncertainty. Not knowing the complexity of the diagnostic process, they expect quick and unambiguous answers. But diagnoses change as the doctor learns more about the case. Such is especially true when problems stem from hidden lesions which are only uncovered after extensive surgical probing, or where lengthy psychotherapeutic exploration is required to solve complicated neurotic conflicts. Sometimes a diagnosis is inadequate even at the autopsy table, where the cause of death may elude the most skillful pathologist.

Disease as total collapse

Diagnosis of an imminent danger of total collapse can ordinarily be made by lay people, and the physician's presence tends more to reassure the bystanders than to reverse the patient's pathology. Symptoms are often indicative of a drastic change in or interruption of basic biological rhythms, and this is readily brought into awareness. Again, the interpretation of the symptom depends on the receiver's disease concepts. For instance, there are persons who immediately diagnose any cardiac arrhythmia – sudden slowing, speeding up, or momentary cessation of the heartbeat – as critically dangerous for their health. Others wait a moment and when the heart has resumed its regularity conclude they are not in mortal danger. Experiments with operant conditioning of the heart rate show that this can be learned better when subjects do not figure out what it is they are controlling (Engel and Hansen 1966). I think human beings would be in very serious trouble if they had to consciously monitor their own vital functions.

Yet when automatic self-regulating devices built into the human physiology fail to continue functioning, emergency intervention from the outside is mandatory. Modern resuscitation techniques can take care of many problems, like paralysis of respiration (pressure chambers), fibrillation of the heart (electric pace-makers), or urinary stoppage (kidney dialysis). When no machinery is available, the patient has to be linked up to a normally-functioning human being. For example, when breathing stops, you hook up the afflicted person by mouth-to-mouth contact with a healthy breather whose own rhythmic ventilation now temporarily takes over. Should the heart also stop, it is necessary to stimulate a pumping action through rhythmic pressure on the chest or by directly squeezing the afflicted organ. Sudden gushing forth of rhythmically propelled blood, either externally through a wound or internally through a ruptured artery, is another semiotic phenomenon that indicates great danger. Blanching, speeding up of the pulse, and weakness rapidly going on to a state of shock are semiotic clues that the body is attempting to adjust to the dangerous lowering of its blood supply.

The brain's innate rhythmicity may be interrupted in such ways as to cause collapse, which is reversible when the rhythm quickly returns to normal. In our terminology such a major seizure is called 'grand mal'. The patient may have a premonitory sense of doom or some similarly unpleasant or uncanny 'aura'. He may make a tell-tale noise, lose consciousness, fall down, and have a convulsion. Incontinence and marked respiratory slowing can be observed. This is usually followed by deep sleep and a period of amnesia. The cerebral dysrhythmia can be detected only indirectly, by means of an electroencephalogram. Other detectors of ominous change in internal rhythmicity are also employed in the intensive care units of modern hospitals, for instance electrocardiographic devices. When there are undesirable changes, the device automatically institutes certain physiologically corrective actions. On-line computers enable much of the watchfulness previously exerted by nurses and interns to be delegated to machinery. Patients who crave a more personal approach are sometimes upset by this and complain, or develop compensatory (deliroid) symptoms of social deprivation.

The time of crisis seldom permits clearly-formulated, logical communication about diagnosis between patient and physician. Excruciating pain or intense panic negates any extended complex verbal formulations. Thus doctors usually make only brief diagnostic statements and act quickly, above all to bring the acute problem under control.

A struggling, fighting, confused hippie is brought to the emergency room by friends who observed him trying to gouge out his eyes. Whether this is a paranoid panic, hysterical play-acting, an attempt to make trouble, or a drug-induced delirium cannot immediately be clarified. The doctor loses no words. He immediately states "acute schizophrenic reaction" in full confidence that this diagnosis will galvanize the staff into action and legitimize the hospital's care-taking potentials for this patient. His diagnosis serves as a password enabling the patient to be quickly admitted to a treatment ward.

Even after a total collapse is successfully dealt with, there remain possibilities of certain irreversible changes, especially in the brain. Depending on the patient's age, his general intelligence, and the type of damage sustained, there may be limits to what he understands about the diagnosis. For example, a nominal aphasia may preclude the patient's grasping intellectually what the doctor is trying to say. Some clinical studies presently being conducted also suggest that chronic use of psychedelic drugs like LSD may lead to impairment of linguistic skills.

On the other hand, improvement in the clinical condition can also proceed to a betterment in diagnostic comprehension. Recovery from a nervous breakdown may bring with it a certain positive insight, with increased self-understanding and greater tolerance for discussing the problem with the doctor. Certain drugs simultaneously bring about well-being and increased communicability. Amphetamines, for example, produce an internally felt euphoria and an externally manifest increase in word-production and speech fluency (Rockwell and Ostwald 1968). Surgical repair along cosmetic lines can have similar effects. For instance, a skillfully corrected harelip at once improves a youngster's appearance and makes his phonetic behavior more efficient for speech communication.

Summary

Diagnostic processes bear certain resemblances to language processes in general. 'Symptoms and signs' are the perceived facts, and whoever renders a diagnosis interprets these according to disease concepts. This labelling or pattern recognition called diagnosis is obviously not limited to patient-physician interactions, but reflects a general adaptational capacity that preserves health. Symptoms are most easily attributed to the malfunction of part of the body, and this attitude is reinforced by certain social attitudes toward disease as well as the way physicians start their training with dissection.

The human brain and nervous system handle information originating both within the body and external to it, in the social environment. Therefore hurtful external influences, especially when these interfere with maturation of essential neurophysiological processes, may bring about disease. End-state diagnosis may reflect the cumulative effects of sequences of pathological stresses and distortions.

To the extent that diagnostic thinking leads to the concern that something can be done about the disease, a diagnosis also implies a prognosis. After-effects of diagnosis are especially noticeable when the immediate well-being of the patient, his family, or the community is in danger. Thus in emergency situations a diagnosis has to be brief and easily understood in terms of appropriate actions to be taken to reverse the disease. How explicitly this can ultimately be formulated depends, among other things, on the degree of the patient's recovery. Diagnosis can even worsen the disease by lowering the patient's self-esteem, thus promoting a feeling of dissatisfaction. As improvement or recovery takes place, the diagnosis may have to be reformulated several times in terms that not only accurately reflect the patient's changing condition but also take account of any growth or decrement in his language functions.

24

THE LANGUAGE OF PSYCHIATRY*

(1969)

Language is no static equipment, simply to be picked up and applied, like a shock machine, to relieve symptoms. Rather, we deal here with one of the most sophisticated communication systems ever devised, a system which allows man simultaneously to standardize meaning by reference to conventional definitions, and to expand meaning by constructing debatable items of information (Hockett 1960). Elucidating the principles of language is one of today's foremost scientific tasks, made ever more urgent by technological conditions of our time, especially the computer, which is a machine capable of using language in a very "simple-minded" fashion (Miller 1967).

Three properties of psychiatric language

When we turn to the special field of psychiatry, it may be helpful to articulate some basic assumptions which govern the use of language. First, its semanticity: a distinction has to be made between (1) the language doctors use to converse with each other, and (2) the language doctors use when they talk with patients (Ostwald 1968b). Doctors belong to medical societies, groups with an 'in-language' akin to the argot of any subculture which seeks to maintain its individuality. While this technical in-language of medicine facilitates communication within a professional group, it can slow down or completely disrupt communication when naively transplanted to other settings. For instance the lady who is asked have you had "hyperemesis gravidarum" will be struck dumb unless this is translated into "did you vomit a lot during your pregnancy?"

* This paper was prepared for a Social and Rehabilitation Service Workshop on the subject "Interpreting for Deaf People", sponsored by the New York University Center for Deafness Research, Tucson, Arizona, Jan. 29-31, 1969.

Second, allowance has to be made for the extraordinary arbitrariness of psychiatric language (Redlich and Freedman 1966). We are a multidisciplined, multilingual community. Psychoanalysis came from Vienna; group therapy comes from religion; drug treatment has its roots in biological medicine; institutional care is deeply embedded in the social traditions of a community. While the surgeon can readily shift his concrete operations from one hospital to another, the psychiatrist must first 'tune-in' on the particular nuances and referential features of words before he can successfully communicate in a new environment. This holds for patients too, many of whom have to undergo a training period of weeks to months before they can talk with a psychiatrist about their personal problems.

Finally, before we go to work on the problems of translation, we must pay attention to the semiotics of psychiatry (Sebeok et al. 1964). A great deal of what a sick person says is not communicated with words, but rather with the expressions of the face, the movements and postures of the body, and the tone, or paralinguistic aspects of the voice. So-called illnesses observed by psychiatrists are more often disorders of action, mood, and personality. Words may even obscure the problem. Thus a patient may have to be observed in his daily behavior on the ward and his social interactions with other people before one can meaningfully describe his problem. The psychiatric terminology captures at best some rarified abstractions about aberrant human behavior. It condenses a vast amount of behavioral data into a handful of verbal symbols.

The manual of mental disorders

A new edition of the American Psychiatric Association Manual has recently appeared (1968). It offers a comprehensive scheme for describing the bio-psycho-social disorders of man, and undoubtedly will have wide acceptance, especially in the larger mental hospitals throughout the United States. Moreover, the manual has been constructed with a view to promoting an international classification of diseases. Thus one may hope that it could cross the frontier between the world of the deaf and the world of the hearing with greater ease than many other classification systems previously devised. For a very enlightening discussion of the problem of disease classification, the reader might wish to consult Karl Menninger's interesting book (1963) which reduces mental illness to five categories, instead of the ten subdivisions delineated in the new APA Manual. While it is sometimes necessary to use more than one diagnosis to describe a patient's problem, we customarily pay primary attention to that condition which is most serious and most urgently requires treatment.

Before using the psychiatric nomenclature, the translator should know how to spell out certain crucial qualifying phrases and adjectives which indicate whether a condition is acute (of recent onset), chronic (long-standing), in remission (diminished in intensity), mild, moderate, or severe. The full diagnostic nomenclature may be summarized as follows:

1. Mental retardation

This term refers to 'subnormal general intellectual functioning which originates during the developmental period and is associated with impairment of either learning and social adjustment or maturation, or both.' The level of retardation is based on results of IQ tests, which give only a partial view of mental functioning.

Borderline mental retardation	IQ 68-83
Mild mental retardation	IQ 52-67
Moderate mental retardation	IQ 36-51
Severe mental retardation	IQ 20-35
Profound mental retardation	IQ below 20

The presumed causes of the condition are listed as

Infection or intoxication
Trauma or physical agent
Disorders of metabolism, growth or nutrition
Gross brain disease acquired after birth
Diseases and conditions due to (unknown) prenatal influence
Chromosomal abnormality
Prematurity
Major psychiatric disorder
Psychosocial (environmental) deprivation
Unspecified

2. Organic brain syndromes

These disorders are manifested by impaired orientation, memory, intellectual functions and judgment, plus lability and shallowness of affect. They result from diffuse impairment of brain function due to a variety of causes. The brain syndromes are grouped into psychotic and non-psychotic disorders according to the severity of functional impairment.

PSYCHOSIS refers to an impairment of mental functioning that grossly interferes with meeting the ordinary demands of daily life. Recognition of reality is badly impaired. There are hallucinatory and delusional perceptions. Mood is very inappropriate. Causes include senile degeneration of the brain; poisoning with alcohol and other chemicals; infections and tumors; brain trauma; and other physical conditions.

NONPSYCHOTIC BRAIN SYNDROMES do not show the profound levels of disorganization referred to above. In childhood, mild brain damage shows up as overactivity, short attention span, distractibility, and impulsiveness. Sometimes these patients are withdrawn, listless, and unresponsive. They may be repetitive and stereotyped in their behavior, making interaction between child and parent most difficult.

3. *Psychoses which cannot be attributed to physical conditions* (i.e. those factors outlined above)

This is the most important category for the traditional mental hospital psychiatry, i.e. the 'insanities' which cannot be traced to brain disease. SCHIZOPHRENIA is the largest sub-category. It includes a group of disorders showing characteristic disturbances of thinking. Concept-formation is markedly altered, leading to misinterpretation of reality, and sometimes delusions and hallucinations. Emotional responses are ambivalent, inappropriate, and out of harmony. The patient may behave in a withdrawn, bizarre, or regressive way. Traditionally the schizophrenic disorders are subdivided along the following lines:

Simple type – of insidious onset, with marked impoverishment in interpersonal relations

Hebephrenic type – marked disorganization and silliness

Catatonic type – extremes of motor behavior, either excitement or stuporous

Paranoid type – florid persecutory and grandiose delusions, often coupled with enormous hostility and aggressiveness

Acute schizophrenic episode – a sudden break with reality from which the patient recovers within weeks or which goes on to more differentiated syndromes

AFFECTIVE DISORDERS are another important category of psychosis. These illnesses are characterized by an extreme disorder of mood, depression or elation. This dominates the patient's mental life and disturbs his contact with the environment. Subcategories include:

Involutional melancholia – onset during the aging period of severe worry, with agitation, sleeplessness, and other symptoms.
Manic-depressive disease – a cyclic, recurring form of severe depression and/or mania.

PARANOID STATES feature a predominance of delusions, generally persecutory, which lead to secondary disturbances in mood and behavior.
Paranoia: elaborate delusional systems are developed, but don't interfere with daily activities.
Involutional paranoid state: limited to the involutionary period.

OTHER PSYCHOSES include
Psychotic depressive reaction – a profound depression resulting from a traumatic life experience.

4. Neuroses

These illnesses are chiefly characterized by anxiety, which is either felt openly and expressed or held in check by a variety of psychological 'mechanisms' which can lead to other crippling symptoms. In contrast to the psychoses, the neuroses show no gross distortion of reality or profound disorganization of personality. The patient usually has awareness or 'insight' of being ill.
  The subgroups are

Anxiety neuroses – unrealistic fearfulness, physical distress, and panickiness.
Hysterical neurosis – sudden involuntary loss of some bodily function; seemingly in an attempt to resolve (symbolically) the conflicts which are generating anxiety. 'Conversion' refers to a hysterical disorder of sensory or motor function; 'Dissociation' refers to a hysterical disorder of consciousness.
Phobic neurosis – intense fear of an object or situation which UNCONSCIOUSLY threatens the patient.
Obsessive-compulsive neurosis – persistent and unstoppable intrusion of unwanted thoughts, urges, or actions.

Depressive neurosis – an excessive reaction of depression to an inner conflict or outer stress.

Neurasthenic neurosis – complaints of weakness, fatigability and exhaustion which genuinely distress the patient.

Depersonalization neurosis – feelings of unreality and self-estrangement.

Hypochondriacal neurosis – morbid bodily preoccupation coupled with fears of presumed diseases.

5. *Personality disorders and certain other non-psychotic mental disorders*

PERSONALITY DISORDERS are characterized by lifelong maladaptive behavior patterns, often recognizable by the time of adolescence but not necessarily leading to psychotic or neurotic syndromes.

Paranoid personality – hypersensitive, rigid, suspicious, jealous, conceited, and blaming others

Cyclothymic (affective) personality – recurring and alternating periods of depression and enthusiasm

Schizoid personality – shyness, oversensitivity, avoidance of interpersonal closeness, seclusiveness, and eccentricity

Explosive personality – outbursts of rage and aggressiveness, excitability and over-responsiveness to environmental pressures

Obsessive compulsive personality – excessive concern with conformity, overconscientious, rigid, dutiful, and unrelaxed

Hysterical personality – emotionally unstable, excitable, self-dramatizing, attention-seeking and seductive

Asthenic personality – fatiguable, lacking in energy, enthusiasm, and capacity for enjoyment

Antisocial personality – unsocialized, repeatedly in conflict with others, selfish, callous, and irresponsible. Impulsive, unable to feel guilt and learn from experience.

Passive-aggressive personality – aggression is passively expressed, as through pouting, procrastination, obstructionism, and stubborness. This is covert expression of hostility and resentment towards individuals or institutions upon which the patient is over-dependent.

Inadequate personality – ineffectual responses to social, intellectual, and physical demands.

SEXUAL DEVIATIONS are diagnoses for persons whose sexual interests are directed primarily away from people of the opposite sex or towards sexual acts which either are not coitus or are bizarre accompaniments of coitus. This includes

Homosexuality
Fetishism
Pedophilia
Transvestitism
Exhibitionism
Voyeurism
Sadism
Masochism

ALCOHOLISM is a diagnosis for patients who drink enough to damage their physical health, their personalities, or their social functioning.
Episodic excessive drinking – intoxication as often as 4 times a year to a point where speech is definitely impaired and behavior clearly altered
Habitual excessive drinking – intoxicated more than 12 times a year or recognizably under the influence of alcohol more than once a week
Alcohol addiction – patient is dependent on alcohol and cannot function without it.

Drug dependence is used to describe patients who are addicted to or dependent on drugs other than alcohol, tobacco, ordinary caffein-containing beverages, or medically-prescribed agents.
Opiates
Synthetic analgesic drugs
Barbiturates
Hypnotics, sedatives, or tranquilizers
Cocaine
Cannabis sativa (hashish, marijuana)
Psycho-stimulants (e.g. amphetamines)
Hallucinogens (e.g. LSD)

6. Psychophysiologic disorders

This is a group of illnesses with physical symptoms that result from emotional factors and involve a single organ system. The physiological

(autonomic nervous system controlled) changes are usually EXAGGERA-
TIONS of normal emotional responses, e.g.

Skin disorder – rashes and itches
Musculoskeletal disorder – backache, muscle cramps, tension
    headaches
Respiratory disorder – asthma, overbreathing, hiccoughs
Cardiovascular disorder – rapid heart beat, high blood pressure,
    migraine
Blood and lymph disorder
Gastrointestinal disorder – peptic ulcer, inflamed stomach or colon,
    constipation, heartburn, etc. in which emotional factors pre-
    dominate
Genito-urinary disorder – menstruation and urination problems,
    impotence, painful intercourse etc. due to emotional problems
Endocrine disorder
Sense-organ disorder

7.   Special symptoms

This diagnostic category is reserved for 'patients whose psychopathology
is manifested by a single specific symptom'.

Speech disturbance
Learning disturbance
Tic
Other psychomotor disorder
Sleep disorder
Feeding disturbance
Enuresis
Encopresis
Headache
Other special symptoms

8.   Transient situational disturbances

These diagnoses are reserved for temporary disorders of any severity,
including psychotic reactions, that occur in response to an overwhelming
environmental stress. For example

Infancy – a grief reaction associated with separation from the
    mother – crying spells, loss of appetite, withdrawal

Childhood – jealousy associated with the birth of a sibling – bed-wetting, attention-getting behavior, fears of abandonment

Adolescence – irritability and depression associated with school failure – temper outbursts, brooding, and discouragement

Adulthood – Anger and resentment associated with an unwanted pregnancy; fear of military combat; malingering when threatened with severe punishment

Late life – Feelings of rejection associated with forced retirement

9. Behavior disorders of childhood and adolescence

These are more stable, internalized and intractible illnesses than the situational reactions but less so than the psychoses, neuroses, or personality disorders. Characteristic manifestations include overactivity, inattentiveness, shyness, feelings of rejection, over-aggressiveness, timidity, and delinquency. Subgroups are:

Hyperkinetic reaction
Withdrawing reaction
Overanxious reaction
Runaway reaction
Unsocialized aggressive reaction
Group delinquent reaction

10. Conditions without manifest psychiatric disorder and nonspecific conditions

SOCIAL MALADJUSTMENT is a category for individuals 'who are psychiatrically normal but who nevertheless have severe enough problems to warrant examination by a psychiatrist.' A diagnosable illness may be precipitated or develop later. For example,

Marital maladjustment
Social maladjustment resulting from cultural unfamiliarity or divided loyalties
Occupational maladjustment
Dyssocial behavior associated with criminal careers

Conclusion

I have given the language of psychiatry in terms of the latest effort towards a uniform descriptive and diagnostic system developed by the American Psychiatric Association. No one claims it to be a perfect system, nor will it stand for long as an unchanged document. Yet it seems an appropriate starting point for the training of persons who work in psychiatric hospitals and clinics.

For the problem of deafness, modification in the classification scheme will have to follow along the lines of findings reported by Rainer, Altshuler and other investigators (1966). Special emphasis has to be placed on functional, dynamic descriptive categories, such as the special symptoms (7), the situational disturbances (8), the behavior disorders (9) and the nonspecific conditions (10), since these are more likely to be responsive to rapid intervention, education, and preventive approaches in mental health care.

25

GREENSON'S REMEDY
Review of a new book* and some comments about psychoanalysis**

(1970)

Psychoanalysis has had a profound influence on present-day behavioral theory and semiotics. Its originator Sigmund Freud (1856-1939) developed methods for studying mental operations (free-associations, dream-analysis, conflict-solution, etc.) and he postulated basic theories of mental structure (unconscious/conscious, id-ego-superego, etc.). There followed an incredible number of good books and intriguing essays. Freud received the Goethe prize for his literary accomplishments.

But psychoanalysis cannot be learned from books. It is a way of behaving and thinking about emotion. Theories about psychoanalysis make little sense unless you practice the art as patient and/or as therapist. Psychoanalysis in theory is like readings about music, or religion, or sports. They remain meaningless so long as you don't have the actual experience of participation. This is why many psychoanalytic treatises seem deadly dull.

Ralph Greenson's recently published Volume I (he promises a sequel) probably goes further than any text I know in showing what psycho-analysis is like in practice. Several reasons explain this. Greenson is very thoroughly grounded in psychoanalytic theory such as it is. He does not have to apologize for its shortcomings, or try to fill in gaps with philosophy. His teacher and personal analyst, Otto Fenichel, himself wrote (1945) what was a remarkably comprehensive text prior to the days of tape-recorders, television, and other methods for direct study of behavior.

Dr. Greenson is a vivid, dramatic, person – a connoisseur of the arts

---

* Greenson, Ralph R., *The Technique and Practice of Psychoanalysis*, V. I, New York, International Universities Press, 1967, 452 pp., $ 12.50.
** Reprinted from *Semiotica* II. 2: 185-92 (1970).

– articulate and charming. He practices in Los Angeles, where his patients include important figures in the cinema industry. Thus he knows a great deal about the way words are translated into acts, and vice versa. Finally, he is a devoted clinician and teacher, intent on helping people with problems and communicating what he has learned.

The working alliance

The psychoanalytic relationship is much more than a transference-countertransference system in which long-forgotten memories are discussed and archaic feelings are relived. There is also a real, ongoing interpersonal relationship, a bond of mutual dependency which develops between the patient expecting help, and the doctor offering helpfulness. The American psychiatrist Harry Stack Sullivan (1953) based HIS psycho-analytic theory centrally upon this fact, and much of the infighting between Freudian and neo-Freudian theorists represents a struggle over whether to emphasize the 'intrapsychic' or the 'interpersonal' dimensions of psychotherapy. Greenson deflates this false dichotomy. He uses the term "working alliance" to describe the real day-after-day confrontations between patient and therapist, and he preserves Freud's terms "transference and counter-transference" to depict the unreal or imaginary components of the therapeutic relationship.

A working alliance depends on the ability of two people to agree on fundamental principles of conduct. Facts must be separated from fantasies; beliefs from delusions. Thus the psychoanalytic patient must agree to trust the doctor with his most private thoughts. There can be no secrets. "A patient tells me that there is something he cannot and will not tell me. My response is in effect: Don't tell me WHAT your secret is, but tell me WHY you can't tell me about it. In other words, I am pursuing the motive for the secret, not the content... I would ask the patient what kind of feeling he would have if he were to tell me. If he could imagine that he had told me, how would he be feeling. I would go on to ask him: 'How do you imagine I would react if you had told me?' In other words, I would pursue the painful affects and fantasies that the secret material arouses in the patient, including the painful transference fantasy. Then I would pursue the history of this painful transference situation in his past life, i.e., when did this happen to you before?" (p. 130-31).

Silence and speech

Psychoanalytic patients have to be able to endure analytic probing, which is not geared to the usual social amenities of conversation. Some of the probing consists of silent non-response. An analyst is permitted to say nothing for long stretches of time, leaving the patient guessing as to how his verbalizations are being received. Silent unresponsiveness from a person we turn to for help can be devastating. It reminds us of aloneness, of separation from others, of death itself. Silence is one of the analyst's most powerful tools and it is handled with respect. "Silence is both a passive and an active intervention on the part of the analyst. The patient needs our silence because he may need time for his thoughts, feelings, and fantasies to emerge from within himself. Our silence also exerts a pressure upon him to communicate and to face his utterances and emotions without distraction. He may feel our silence as supportive and warm, or as critical and cold" (p. 374).

On the other hand, the patient must be able to hear what the therapist has to say. It is up to the therapist to make sure the patient is ready to listen. And when an 'interpretation' is made, this has to be done in language the patient can understand. The words have to be both emotionally gripping and intellectually satisfying. "The analyst's vocabulary must be aimed at the patient's reasonable ego. The analyst must ask himself the question: how close to the patient's reasonable ego is this insight that I want to impart. The more inaccessible the material is, the more care I must take with my formulations and my choice of words. Furthermore, the analyst's vocabulary should not be too distant from the patient's because that would lend a quality of unreality to the intervention. It must have impact and yet not be shocking – values which can be determined only by the analyst's emphathic identification with each patient in the particular situation. The force and intonation used are often more important than the choice of words. Tone and intonation convey the preverbal and nonverbal feelings, often the unconscious attitudes of the analyst. Furthermore, tone and intonation sensitivity is derived from the earliest object relations, when separation anxiety is a major factor. The tone leads to or away from contact, and is therefore very important for the trust-mistrust balance in the relationship of patient and analyst" (p. 373).

Many people cannot be psychoanalyzed

Obviously the requirements for a psychoanalytic working alliance cannot be met in every case. The patient may lack verbal skillfulness. Or he may hold religious or political beliefs which antagonize the doctor. Some patients fail to reimburse the analyst. Others don't keep appointments, get themselves arrested or hospitalized. Occasionally a patient commits suicide. All of these facts of life explain why psychoanalysis is a very limited approach to the management of mental illness. It cannot be used for handling psychiatric emergencies, in treating psychoses, or as a panacea for social problems. Doctor Greenson is very explicit about the limitations of his technique. But as a practising physician he indicates that the only way to be sure a treatment won't work is to try it. "A valuable method of approach to the problem of analyzability is to explore the patient's endowment in regard to the specific demands of psychoanalytic therapy. As stated previously, psychoanalytic treatment is a time-consuming, long-range, costly therapy that is by its very nature frequently painful. Therefore, only patients who are strongly motivated will work wholeheartedly in the analytic situation. The patient's symptoms or discordant traits of character must cause him sufficient suffering to enable him to endure the rigors of the treatment. The neurotic misery must interfere with important aspects of the patient's life, and the awareness of his plight must be sustained if the patient is to remain motivated. Trivial problems and the wishes of relatives, lovers or employers do not justify undertaking psychoanalytic treatment. Scientific curiosity or the wish for professional advancement will not motivate an analysand to undergo a deep analytic experience, unless it is also combined with an adequate therapeutic need. Patients who demand quick results or who have a large secondary gain from their illness will also not have the necessary motivation. Masochists who need their neurotic suffering may enter analysis and later become attached to the pain of the treatment. They present a difficult problem for appraisal in terms of motivation to get well. Children are quite differently motivated than adults and also need to be assessed from a different point of view" (pp. 53-54).

Psychoanalysis is not a game

Psychoanalysis shares a biological point of view with other medically-influenced behavioral sciences. In this view, "a living organism must be regarded as a nodal point in an extremely complex network of interactions, relations, transactions, AND REMAINS FULLY ALIVE ONLY INSOFAR AS THIS NETWORK IS RESPECTED. Part of the causal network is internal: the biochemical and physiological processes by which the body keeps

alive and active. Part is external, concerned with the interactions between
the organism and other members of the living world, of its own and other
species, and with the non-living factors of its environment." (Waddington
1969).

I have emphasized the quotation just cited in order to highlight the
enormous responsibility which biologically-oriented scientists and scholars have towards a holistic view of man. Thus for the medical scientist,
a sick person is more than a patient. The psychotherapist knows the limits
of his influence. Direct control can be exerted only while the patient is in
the doctor's presence – in the consulting room, at the bedside, on the
operating table, or on the analytic couch. Greenson makes this extremely
clear with innumerable case illustrations. Patients begin to dramatize
their feelings. They shout and swear, weep, kick, wring their hands,
demand physical contact, even get off the couch to embrace the doctor.
His job is always to demand VERBAL expression of the impulses and feelings. If the patient 'acts out' a conflict by dramatizing it, and especially
if such acting-out interferes with talking-out, the doctor is obliged to put
a stop to this behavior. Greenson tells his patients to go back to work –
i.e., talking and free-associating. Indeed, the terms "work" and "working
alliance" permeate his book. To Greenson – and I share his viewpoint
– psychotherapy is no "game". It is very hard work, and both analyst
and patient must get enough rest and recreation to keep on working
year after year.

How not to do it

To bring his personal technique into sharper focus, Greenson also tells
how NOT to do psychoanalysis. Do not make abstract statements about
psychodynamics which are meaningless to patients. Therapists can use
formulations like "You want to bite your mother's breast", or "You are
afraid your father will castrate you" only when a patient has gradually
shown a true willingness to communicate about his feelings on this
metaphorical level. If you bombard a sick person with verbiage of this
order he withdraws, rebels, or simply pretends to understand. Similarly,
if a naive patient talks this way, referring openly to incest or homicide,
it means either he's too sick to undergo analysis or he's pulling your leg.
Yet well known figures in the field of psychoanalysis (and Greenson names
some) have advocated premature direct interpretations as a form of
verbal shock treatment.

Another pitfall is for an analyst to pretend that he can actually make up the emotional deprivations which a patient has suffered in childhood. This technique is based on faulty theory about human behavior. For example, by being kind to a person you simply demonstrate that it is possible to be kind. You cannot UNDO damage done by someone who earlier in life mistreated the patient. If the patient learns from the "corrective emotional experience" of psychotherapy that kindness is a possibility in human conduct, so much the better. But suppose the analyst's kindness makes the patient more painfully aware of unkindnesses that were his lot long ago. This may increase suffering and turn him against the analysis.

The same holds true for discipline. The undisciplined youngster – now an adult patient plagued with symptoms of uncontrollable impulsivity – is not magically cured when a doctor acts like a stern or demanding disciplinarian. There have to be repeated episodes of 'working through' in which the analyst demonstrates by his self-disciplined behavior that impulses can be controlled and behavior modified.

How to produce more and better psychotherapists

In essence a good therapist is true to himself and he must be healthy. Much depends on his genuineness, warmth, and empathy – features of personality which are now receiving more attention from psychologists doing research in psychotherapy (Truax and Wargo 1966). Are these therapeutic features of personality inborn or acquired? The question is important, because there are many, many sick people; and we need to find and train competent therapists. Careful selection of manpower and womanpower for medical and psychological training is crucial.

This brings us then to the social role of psychoanalysis, a topic Greenson doesn't deal with – wisely, perhaps, because it is fraught with controversy. Medical schools today are re-evaluating their goals and their training procedures. One idea is to introduce the 'pathways' program in which students may choose a specialized direction in their studies almost as soon as they enter training. This differs from the traditional four-year program (capped by the MD degree), after which a year's internship and then three to seven years of further specialty training are required. Today's specialist is often technologically overtrained and scientifically under-responsive. Tomorrow's physician will be younger, and his 'path' will be directed towards a specialized role in the fields of medicine, behavior, surgery, or science.

Experienced clinicians will undoubtedly be called upon to give more time in counselling, advising, and preparing young medical students for later career development. Psychoanalysts like Ralph Greenson are in an excellent position to transmit the essence of clinical responsibility and a comprehensive view of human behavior. Yet they seldom participate in the instruction of the medical student. Usually the best 'training' analysts devote their time to teaching 'candidates' in psychoanalysis who are psychiatrists already in their late twenties or thirties.

Perhaps a man of Greenson's vision can think of ways to bring the rich humanistic tradition of psychoanalysis into better rapport with medical practice. There is still too much of a body-vs.-mind dichotomy. An alarming number of medical students get trapped into the fictitious enterprise of trying to separate 'organic' from 'functional' aspects of disease. Patients with obvious problems in living and emotional illness get picked over by specialists looking for lesions in various organs. While this may be financially rewarding for the doctor, and even temporarily satisfying for the patient, in the long run it is a dishonest approach to human suffering and gives inconsistent results.

I hope that Ralph Greenson will one day allow cameras and videotapes into his private office so that his technique, which is so intimately bound up with his personality, can be shown to every young medical student who is struggling with his own social conscience and professional image. That will at least take care of the externals – the observable semiotics of psychoanalytic dialogue. But will it foster understanding of the internals – the psychological substratum of semiotic behavior? Psychoanalysts do a fairly good job in explaining how people intellectualize. Psychoanalysis focusses attention on the preconscious stream of associations and demands that this be transformed into words. But neurosis is not simply a matter of faulty rationalization. Many symptoms interfere with action. In some instances wanted actions cannot be performed; in other instances unwanted actions cannot be inhibited. Dr. Greenson's remedy is to spend an hour a day for several years with someone like himself. His results are good and he is trying to formulate general principles of psychotherapeutic conduct. Only time will tell whether that can be done within the confines of Freudian theory or whether newer models, such as those originating from computer research (Miller, Pribram, and Galanter 1960), are necessary to account for the hidden connections between words and acts.

SECTION V

FRONTIERS OF RESEARCH

INTRODUCTORY STATEMENT

The final section contains papers about some of the topics in the field of human sounds which are amenable to scientific investigation.

The first three papers (26, 27, and 28) deal with the cries of infants. These are uniquely compelling sounds. The sound of an infant stimulates intense emotions and evokes powerful reactions from most everyone within earshot. This appears to be a universal phenomenon, biologically determined, and related to the life-sustaining functions of respiration and nutrition. In addition, the infant cry is the very first piece of human behavior which has social value. It indicates a shift from total silent dependency upon a single being – the pregnant woman – to the possibility of communicating with groups of people in the environment. Crying is the commencement of broadcast-transmission, and I believe that the sounds of infancy represent the forerunners of music, language, and other sound-mediated human symbolizations.

Another important research topic is deafness, or the inability to process acoustical information. I have participated in several conferences devoted to this problem, and paper 29 was written for a meeting organized by the New York State Psychiatric Institute to acquaint psychiatrists with the special problems of communication and social adjustment among deaf persons. Since so much of the rehabilitative emphasis is on oral education and training with sign-language (Mindel and Vernon 1971), I wanted to see what could be offered in the way of alternative communication systems, especially those which utilize modern electronic devices. Hence the paper.

Speech handicaps resulting from causes other than deafness has been another research interest of mine, as already indicated by some of the papers in Section II about acoustic denotation of speech pathology. Paper 30 selects a special problem – that of stuttering – for more detailed treatment. Stuttering is one of the problems in human behavior which continues to defy all attempts at classification. It bounces around as 'symptom' or 'disease', or 'disorder', depending on who is trying to describe the problem and how he wants to help the afflicted person. No matter how much of an effort is made to see stuttering as one manifestation of a general communication process, it keeps popping back as a 'special' symptom. Even the 1968 *Diagnostic and Statistical Manual of Mental Disorders* of the American Psychiatric Association lists "Speech Disturbance" as a primary diagnosis "for the occasional patient whose psychopathology is manifested by a single specific symptom" (Ostwald 1970). My paper was designed to help clinical workers understand some of the practical and research implications of stuttered speech.

The concluding paper was written especially for the present volume in the *Approaches to Semiotics* series. It's aim is to integrate the known facts about sounds and language by way of a kind of systems approach. I take the goal of semiotic research in my field to be the explication of how people use sounds in order to make sense. Obviously there are great gaps in our knowledge about that, and I intend the paper to serve as a kind of framework upon which the few available items of information can be placed.

26

VOCALIZATION OF INFANT TWINS*

A preliminary report

(with D. G. Freedman and J. H. Kurtz)

(1962)

Cries of babies belong to the mammalian pattern of mother-seeking. It seems reasonable to assume, therefore, that this universal trait has a genetic component. To study this component, the voices of speaking twins have already been analyzed (Luchsinger and Arnold 1959). The purpose of the present investigation is to compare the voices of neonatal twins through an analysis of their cries.

Previous studies of the voices of twins and babies

It has often been noted that the resemblance in personal appearance and manner so characteristic of monozygotic (identical) twins may extend to their sound-making behavior. Mothers not infrequently report this, and even trained musicians have been unable to distinguish the voices of identical twins. For example Johann Sebastian Bach's father was often confused with his twin brother by close members of the family (Spitta 1951). Luchsinger (1940) studied the vocal characteristics of 28 pairs of monozygotic and 11 pairs of dizygotic (fraternal) twins from 6 to 30 years of age. He concluded that monozygotes are remarkably similar in terms of the range and quality of the voice, in pulmonary vital capacity, and in laryngeal size and development, whereas dizygotes differ in their vocal range and tone-color (Luchsinger and Arnold 1959). Gedda et al. (1955) also found greater similarities in the voices of monozygotes as compared to dizygotes. They reported that in only 13% of the monozygotic twin pairs studied were both twins able to differentiate between their own voices and those of their twin partners, whereas 78% of the

---

* Reprinted from *Folia phoniatrica* 14: 37-50 (1962).

dizygotic twin pairs could do this. In a subsequent study which utilized acoustic methods for vocal analysis, considerable similarity was found in the fundamental and resonance frequency-spectra characteristics of monozygotic twin voices compared to dizygotes (Gedda et al. 1960).

It must be noted, however, that all of these studies dealt with twins who could speak.[1] Thus, any genetic influence on sound-making behavior must already have been overlaid by the effects of exposure to the linguistic environment. Only a single report of sound-making among non-speaking twins is known to us, but this concerns abnormal (schizophrenic) children (Sherwin 1953). They were identical boys, only one of whom had learned to say any word-sounds by age $3\frac{1}{2}$. While both similarly sang or hummed simple tunes, they also showed distinct differences in their interest in and ability to communicate vocally.

In order to rule out environmental effects upon the sound-making behavior of twins, one must study their spontaneous pre-verbal acoustic productions. Several investigations of the cries of single babies – to our knowledge the cries of twins have never been studied – are available and offer valuable hints as to methodology. High fidelity tape-recordings are needed to accurately reproduce infant cries (Karelitz). Musical notation, for instance as attempted by Gardiner (1838), is useful for the identification of pitch and melody patterns in crying. Phonetic description, as done by Lewis (1936), Irwin (1948), and others provides information about aspects of baby cries which resemble distinguishable phonemic patterns of adult speech. Cinefluorographic study reveals information about physiologic processes underlying the baby cry (Bosma and Smith 1961).

Acoustic analysis by means of contiguous band-pass filters can show the formants (points of energy concentration along the acoustic spectrum) of the cry sound. Several acoustic methods are available: Lynip (1951) used the sound spectrogram to demonstrate typical intonation, cadence, rhythm, attack, and duration patterns of infant crying.

In previous investigations of human sounds we used a half-octave band analysis (Ostwald 1961a). Applied to the peak of a baby cry, this shows acoustic energy to be concentrated into several bands analogous to the formant peaks described in sound spectrograms. The first energy concentration characteristically occurs in the 425-600 cps band, and a peak of maximal energy concentration is usually located somewhere between 1200 and 4800 cps.

---

[1] Luchsinger's study (1961) of twins during the first three years of life [11] came to our attention only after this article was written.

The present study, subjects and method of tape-recording

We tape-recorded 16 pairs of twins under comparable conditions during the first month of life. These infants were chosen randomly from three hospitals in the San Francisco Bay Area and are being seen as part of a long-range behavioral study of twins. At the present time seven pairs of twins have had zygosity determinations based on blood groups; the remaining nine pairs have had zygosity determined solely on the basis of physical characteristics (Freedman 1961). Until the completion of our study, zygosity determinations were not known to the senior author.

The following was used. Recording equipment (Ampex 601 tape-recorder, $7\frac{1}{2}''$ per second tape speed) was set up while both twins were asleep. As soon as one baby started to wake up, we removed it from the crib, and placed it on its back in an unconfined area, usually on a bed or couch. The microphone (Electrovoice 655 C omnidirectional) was held 10 inches in front of the infant's mouth (see Fig. 1), and recording began once the child started to make sounds.

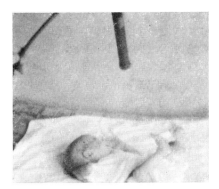

Fig. 1.   The cries of a 17-day-old infant are being recorded on high-fidelity magnetic tape.

As soon as the recording session (usually about 5 minutes duration) for the first member of the twin pair was completed, this baby was taken out of the room, and the second baby was similarly removed from the crib, allowed to waken, and tape-recorded. The first sounds to appear on the tape-recording were usually breath-sounds, lip-smacking sounds, coughs, and other noises incidental to the infant's awakening. Crying began, first in the form of tentative expiratory yelps, as the child became more active and alert. Soon a complete cry, with its sudden attack, rapid rise in pitch, climactic growth of intensity, and final descending glissando could be heard. Cries of this type generally recurred with increasing vigor for about 30-60 seconds, then subsided briefly and started again after some moments of silence. This cyclic pattern of sound followed by silence generally occurred repeatedly until the baby was fed by the mother.

Analysis of the Recordings

After listening to each pair of recordings, we cut the first most complete and characteristically full-blown cry for each baby from the tape. These samples were then made into loops and subjected to half-octave band analysis (H. H. Scott 420-A Sound Analyser) with a technique described in detail elsewhere (Ostwald 1960c). The sound-measurements were read at the peak of each cry, and the results plotted on a curve in terms of intensity in decibels versus frequency centering each half-octave band located between 106 cps and 13,600 cps (see Fig. 2). The same tape-

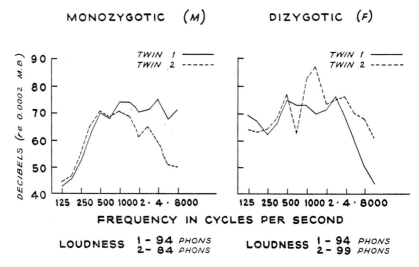

Fig. 2. Acoustic analyses in terms of half-octave band levels of cries recorded 24 hours after birth. Two pairs are shown here, identical twins (left) and fraternal twins (right).

recorded cries which had been analyzed acoustically were next subjected to musical analysis for determination of pitch, rhythm, and melody patterns. In the musical notations (see Fig. 3 – upper part) solid notes indicate the short tones, clear notes the long tones, and glissando lines the slides in each baby cry. Duration was recorded with a stop-watch accurate to 0.2 second, and a guess was made SUBJECTIVELY from listening to the recordings whether they came from identical or fraternal twin pairs. Finally each pair of twin-cries was analyzed by a linguist who compared the phonetic characteristics of onset and termination for each cry, the nature and quality of vocalization, intonation and loudness patterns, and

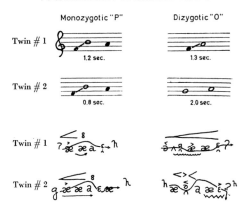

Fig. 3. Musical analyses (top of figure) and phonetic analyses (bottom of figure) of infant cries recorded at 1 month of age. Two twin pairs are shown here, one identical (left) and one fraternal (right).

any intercurrent screams, taps, pharyngealization, bleats, and other sounds (see Fig. 3 – lower part)[2]. Having thus obtained three independent analyses for each pair of tape-recordings, we were now able to rate the degree of similarity for each pair of twin-cries. One point was given for each of the following criteria of similarity that was met.

A. Acoustic Analysis

(1) Less than 5 phons difference in the loudness of the two cries (Stevens' method for converting decibels to phons was used (Stevens 1956)).

(2) An equal number of energy peaks along the acoustic spectra.

(3) Not more than one-half octave difference between locations of the first (lowest-frequency) points of energy concentration along the spectra.

(4) Not more than one-half octave difference between the locations of point(s) of maximal energy concentration along the spectra.

(5) Similar heights of the two acoustic energy curves.

(6) Similar shapes of the two acoustic energy curves.

(7) Similar slopes of the two acoustic energy curves.

(8) Similar degrees of jaggedness of the two acoustic curves.

Table 1 shows the results of the acoustic analyses, how these compared for each set of twins, and the ranking obtained.

---

[2] Lise Deschamps. Concert Pianist, and William Shipley, Assistant Professor of Linguistics, University of California, assisted with the musical and phonetic analyses.

TABLE 1

Acoustic Analysis of Twin Cries

Twin pair	Loudness in Phons	Number of peaks	Location of first peaks (in cps)	Location of Max. peak(s) (in cps)	Appearance of the Curve + = similar; − = not similar				Total number of points (0-8)
					Height	Shape	Slope	Jaggedness	
B 1	93	3	500	1430	+	+	+	+	8
2	95	3	500	2000					
G 1	100	3	500	2000	+	−	+	+	7
2	101.5	3	500	2800					
E 1	93	3	1430	1430	+	−	+	−	5
2	94	3	360	1430					
I 1	99.1	2	1000	1000					
				4000	+	−	+	+	5
2	96.6	3	1430	1430					
N 1	99.2	2	500	1430					
				2000	+	+	+	−	5
2	99.2	3	1430	1430					
O 1	97	3	500	1430	−	−	+	+	4
2	102	2	500	2000					
M 1	94	3	500	4000					
2	84	3	500	500	+	−	−	+	4
				1000					
L 1	97	3	1430	1430	+	−	+	−	4
2	95	2	715	1430					
J 1	98	2	1430	1430	−	−	+	+	4
2	97.5	3	500	1000					
D 1	92	1	1430	1430	+	−	+	−	4
2	93	2	500	2000					
A 1	92	3	500	1430	−	−	−	−	4
2	91	2	500	1430					
K 1	95	2	500	1430	−	−	−	−	2
2	94.5	1	1430	1430					
H 1	93	3	1430	1430	−	−	−	−	2
2	88	2	1430	1430					
P 1	102	4	500	1430	−	−	−	−	1
2	93	2	500	500					
F 1	93.5	2	500	2860	−	−	−	−	1
2	99.2	3	500	1430					
G 1	91	3	500	1430	−	−	−	−	1
2	86	2	500	500					

TABLE 2

Musical Analysis of Twin Cries

Twin pair	Tonal range	Tone(s) of longest duration	Melody: + = Same; − = Different				Duration in seconds	Subjective judgment + = similar − = not similar	Total number of points (0-8)
			Rhythm	Number of tones	Sequence of tones	Number of glides			
P 1	4	B	+	3	+	1	1.2	+	7
2	4	B		3		1	0.8		
I 1	3	A	+	3	+	2	1.4	+	6
2	4	B		3		2	1.3		
D 1	4	A	+	4	+	2	1.2	+	6
2	3	A		4		1	1.0		
C 1	5	A	+	3	+	2	2.9	−	5
2	3	A		3		2	1.1		
F 1	6	B	+	3	+	2	2.8	+	4
2	3	A		3		1	1.9		
H 1	5	A	−	3	+	2	2.6	+	4
	4	A		3		1	1.6		
M 1	3	A	+	3	+	2	2.8	−	4
2	5	B		3		2	1.3		
J 1	3	B	−	4	+	1	1.8	−	4
2	3	B		3		1	1.0		
B 1	5	B	−	4	+	1	0.9	−	4
2	5	A		4		2	0.8		
N 1	3	F	−	2	−	1	0.8	+	4
2	4	F		3		1	0.6		
A 1	5	A	−	4	−	2	1.0	+	3
2	5	A		3		1	1.5		
K 1	5	A	−	4	−	2	2.8	+	3
2	4	A		4		4	1.6		
O 1	3	A	−	2	+	1	1.3	−	2½
2	2	GA		2		0	2.0		
E 1	3	A	−	4	−	3	0.8	−	2
2	3	A		3		2	1.6		
G 1	5	AB	−	5	−	2	1.2	−	1½
2	5	A		4		4	2.4		
L 1	2	A	−	4	−	0	1.8	−	1
2	3	A		3		1	0.9		

B. Musical Analysis

(1) The same tonal range.
(2) Same number of tone(s) of longest duration.
(3) Same rhythm.
(4) Same total number of tones.
(5) Same sequence of tones.
(6) Same number of glides.
(7) Duration difference no greater than 0.2 seconds.
(8) Similar sound as determined SUBJECTIVELY by listening to the cries.

Table 2 shows the results of the musical analyses, how these compared for each set of twins, and the ranking obtained.

C. Phonetic Analysis

Due to the limitations of phonetic methods when applied to non-speech sounds like baby cries, we felt it best simply to compare the number of similarities with the number of dissimilarities for each pair of twin cries. These were scored 0 to 4 points depending on the following criteria.

TABLE 3

Phonetic Analysis of Twin Cries

Twin pair	Similarity/Dissimilarity Score (0-4)
I	4
L	4
A	3
D	3
E	3
F	3
P	3
B	2
G	2
J	2
M	2
N	2
C	1
H	1
O	0
K	0

0 = negligible similarities
1 = dissimilarities outweigh the differences
2 = similarities equal the differences
3 = similarities outweigh the differences
4 = differences are negligible.

Table 3 shows the scores obtained from comparison of the phonetic analysis for each pair of twins, and the ranking.

Results

The degree of similarity (rank) from the acoustic, musical, and phonetic analyses was then compared with zygosity. Also, the scores obtained from the three different methods of analyses were combined into total scores which were ranked and compared with zygosity. The top of each table shows the most similar pairs of twin cries, while the bottom of each table shows the most different cries. The Mann-Whitney U Test (Siegel 1956), with significance set at .05, was applied to these rankings. IT WAS FOUND THAT NONE OF THE 4 RANKINGS DIFFERENTIATED SIGNIFICANTLY THE IDENTICAL TWIN PAIRS FROM THE FRATERNAL TWIN PAIRS.

TABLE 4

The Combined Scores from Acoustic, Musical and Phonetic Analysis of Twin Cries

Twin pair	Total points (0-20)
I	15
B	14
D	13
P	11
N	11
G	10½
A	10
E	10
M	10
J	10
L	9
F	8
H	7
G	7
O	6½
K	5

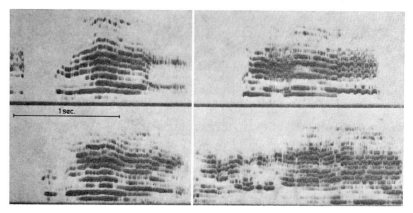

Fig. 4. Spectrographic analysis of cries produced by a pair of identical twins (left) and a pair of fraternal twins (right). The frequencies are from 0 to 8,000 cps reading from bottom to top.

After we had obtained these results we went back to our tape-recorded cries and selected for morphologic study, using the Kay Sona-Graph, a pair of similar-sounding identical twins (A) and a pair of dissimilar-sounding fraternal twins (O). The spectrograms are shown in figure 4. The report of the phonetician (Professor Shipley) reads as follows:

The dramatic thing is the amazing correlation between the spectrograms for pair A. Not only is it possible to match the formants of one with those of the other, but there is an astounding degree of similarity in the temporal sequence of the main cry, even including the final portion. The glottal stricture so clearly marked on the first baby's spectrogram is also represented in the second, but with less of an interval.

What we think about this

Our findings show that certain twin pairs produce cries which are very much alike (for instance pair A which is identical and pair D which is fraternal) while other pairs produce cries that clearly differ (for instance pair K which is identical and pair O which is fraternal). Since these similarities and differences in the cries do not correlate statistically with the zygosity of the twin-babies, it becomes necessary to discuss factors other than zygosity which may account for these findings.

First of all one would expect considerable similarity among the cries emitted by these twins because they were all infants and therefore were relatively undifferentiated in their vocal behavior. Also, infants seem to produce a small number of distinctly different types of cries. For example, we are beginning to differentiate between cries which (at their peaks) maintain a narrow-band concentration of acoustic energy (TONAL) as against cries which develop wide-band spectra (NOISE). The latter cries are more properly called screams. Some babies emit a number of cries followed by a number of screams, while others regularly alternate between crying and screaming. There may be other patterns not as yet recognized. If a single infant is capable of emitting a number of acoustically dissimilar kinds of cries (see Lynip's study (1951) for further discussion of this point), then to sample analogous sounds from twin-pairs for comparison becomes extremely difficult.

Secondly, intrapair variability in weight, physical development and vigor must be taken into account in evaluating the cries of twins. Price (1950) calls attention to one possible bias in twin studies: Monochorionic identicals are in competition for a common placental blood supply, and substantial differences in birthweight and circulatory competence may result. This means that even in monozygotic pairs the first month may witness differences in forcefulness of expiration, muscle tone, and resonance characteristics of the head and chest, not to mention laryngeal maturation which would have a decisive influence on crying behavior. It is to be noted that since one twin is often a vertex and the other a breech delivery, a period of several months may be required for full recovery if there has been a traumatic breech delivery.

Finally it should be mentioned that no matter how accurate the instrument used in the analysis of baby cries, the final decision as to which pair is identical and which is fraternal depends on the judgment of human listeners (or machines programmed to imitate them). And the judgment of a listener in turn depends on memory plus the correct evaluation of non-acoustic information supplied by visual and temporal cues (Pollack 1961). This means that it may be impossible to detect distinguishing characteristics in the sound-making behavior of infants until sufficient time has elapsed for the listener to build up an internal image or model of each infant's behavior.

Summary

Sixteen pairs of infant twins were tape-recorded during the first month of life. Their spontaneous full cries upon awakening were studied by means of an H. H. Scott half-octave-band Sound Analyzer. Analysis of musical patterns and comparison of the phonetic characteristics of the cries were also done. With these methods it was possible to demonstrate similarities in the cries of certain twin pairs and differences in those of others, and this was also confirmed in two pairs analyzed spectrographically. However, the statistical correlation of intra-pair similarity with monozygosity and of intrapair difference with dizygosity was no greater than chance. Consideration must therefore be given to factors other than heredity which determine similarities and differences between the cries of twin-partners during the first month of life. These include variability in the spontaneous crying patterns of the individual babies, and intrapair discrepancies in physical maturation and strength. It is still an open question whether vocal behavior can be directly related to genetic influence, and we plan to continue to study this matter.

27

DIAGNOSTIC USE OF INFANT CRY*

(with R. Phibbs and S. Fox)

(1968)

Diagnostic significance is often attributed to the crying of infants. Mothers complain when their babies 'don't sound right', and pediatricians observe characteristic cries associated with a number of diseases. Within the last 10 years there has been a noticeable increase in published infant-cry studies (Table 1), and one purpose of this article is to review those which are clinically important. In addition we wish to acquaint readers with the results of research conducted in our laboratory which appears to confirm the diagnostic value of cry analysis.

Previous studies of infant cry

The first objective study of infant vocalization using sound recordings appeared some 60 years ago (Flatau and Gutzman 1906) and was remarkable in definitely locating pitch of 20 normal neonates' crying at middle A (440 Hz) of the frequency scale. The only abnormal case demonstrated cry-pitch approximately one octave higher. Twenty years later, psychologists (Sherman 1927; Bayley 1932) described the different conditions that produce crying, and the next acoustical study (Fairbanks 1942) focussed on the cry of the hungry infant. A sonagraphic differentiation between 'hunger' and 'attention-getting' cries was reported seventeen years ago (Lynip 1951). Parmelee (1955) recorded the speech development of an infant, and Truby (1960) categorized several different patterns of crying acoustically. In a half-octave band analysis of normal neonate crying Ostwald (1963) located the fundamental tone between 425 Hz

* Reprinted from *Biologia Neonatorum* 13: 68-82 (1968).

TABLE 1

Milestones in the study of infant cries

1838	Gardiner notated musical patterns of crying
1906	Flatau and Gutzman recorded 30 infants; described pitch and phonetic features of cry
1927	Sherman distinguished hunger, anger or pain, and colic cries
1932	Bayley identified 13 causes of crying in 61 infants
1936	Lewis related crying to language development
1936	Searl related screaming to aggression
1942	Fairbanks traced pitch changes of hunger wails for 9 months (1 infant)
1945	Aldrich, Sung and Knop measured amount of crying in nursery and home environments (50 infants)
1946	Brodbeck and Irwin showed that orphanage environment reduces the types and amount of vocalization (94 infants)
1951	Lynip did the first sonagraphic studies of infant vocalization
1954	Stewart related excessive crying (colic) to parental behavior
1955	McCarthy delineated mass motor activity of crying from specific movements which later differentiate to produce speech
1960	Karelitz, Karelitz and Rosenfeld described cries of cretinism, kernicterus, meningitis and Tay-Sachs Disease
1960	Truby differentiated the acoustics of phonation, dysphonation, and hyperphonation
1961	Bosma and Smith reported cineradiographic studies of crying
1962	Ostwald, Freedman and Kurtz described cries of 32 twin infants
1964	Wasz-Höckert and coworkers described the effects of training on ability to differentiate birth, hunger, pain and pleasure vocalizations
1964	Ringel and Kluppel reported normative cry data
1965	Lind et al. described sonagrams of the brain-damaged cry
1965	Sheppard and Lane developed an automated method for sampling the prosodic features of infant's vocalizing
1966	Eisenson described cry-differences between childhood aphasia and apraxia
1966	Vuorenkoski et al. defined spectrographic features of the 'cat cry'
1966	Bayley found early vocalization to be the only clear predictor of later intelligence scores (among girls)
1967	Chase et al. demonstrated infant cry to be unaffected by auditory feedback delays

This is not intended to show a complete or comprehensive bibliography of contributions in the field of infant vocalization studies, which would require a separate publication. Henry M. Truby, Ph.D., recently presented a detailed chronology of the acoustic research in this decade. (American Speech and Hearing Association, Nov. 1967).

and 600 Hz. Our earlier study of 32 twins (Ostwald, Freedman and Kurtz 1962), pointed to reasons for variability in the results of acoustical measurement of infant cries, including differences in weight, size, physical development and vigor of the children recorded, and sampling of particular cries from the sequence of cries stimulated in each cry-cycle.

No infant emits a uniform series of cries (Sedláčková 1964; Truby and

Lind 1965). Initial outbursts in a cycle, if not apneic, are more irregular than those which appear once the infant is fully aroused and screaming lustily, after which a gradual reduction in intensity of soundmaking may occur, until the baby is again quiescent. Ringel and Kluppel (1964) showed that the "average" expiratory cry of 10 normal pain-stimulated infants was 1.47 sec in duration, with a fundamental tone at 413 Hz and a sound-pressure level of 82 dB, 12 in. from the mouth. P. Wolff (1967) has measured inspiratory as well as expiratory components of cries, revealing duration differences between hungry, "mad", pain-produced, and "teased" crying in 4-day olds.

Many clinical studies use pain-stimulated crying (pinching or snapping the skin). Karelitz and Fisichelli (1962) found that infants with diffuse brain-damage require greater stimulation to produce a standard one-minute crying response than do normal infants, and that the mean latency between pain-stimulation and onset of crying is 1.6 sec for normal and 2.6 sec for abnormal infants (Fisichelli and Karelitz 1963). Lind et al. (1966) found that while latency and duration of the first pain cry is more stable in normal infants than among brain-damaged cases, "one cannot predict when knowing the diagnosis of the child's condition which parameter of the cry recording (latency, first signal or second pause) will give abnormal findings". Karelitz et al. (1960), Illingworth (1955) and other pediatricians have described pathognomonic cries of cretinism, meningitis, Tay-Sachs disease, Down's syndrome, intestinal colic, hunger, and other conditions; some of these clinical observations are now confirmed on an acoustic basis. For example, infants with Down's Syndrome show significantly shorter, less active, and less differentiated cry outbursts than normals (Fisichelli et al. 1966). Another chromosomal anomaly, the Cat-Cry Syndrome, has fundamental tone significantly elevated above 500 Hz (Vuorenkoski et al. 1966), and unusually pronounced formants above 4000 Hz (Luchsinger et al. 1967).

The question arises whether certain features of infant cry may be used to predict a future developmental delay or defect. Karelitz and co-workers (1964) have long suspected and tentatively confirmed a relationship between crying activity in early infancy and pre-school intelligence ratings. The age at which babbling begins is predictive of later intelligence scores among girls (Cameron, Livson and Bayley 1967). But until more is known about cry-transformations, cooing, and other prelinguistic communication patterns during the first year of life (Spitz, 1965), one must procede with great caution in attempting to base any forecasts on the cry-behavior of infants.

TABLE 2

Clinical description of cases

Identifying data			Recording data			Birth data			Follow-up data
Case No.	Sex	Race	Age	Weight	Condition	Weight	Apgar 1′ 5′	Clinical	
Group I									
1	M	Oriental	4 days	2840 g	Normal	2960 g	9 10	Uncomplicated, spontaneous delivery. Physiological jaundice	No evidence of significant clinical abnormalities
2	F	Caucas.	4 days	3800 g	Normal	4080 g	9 10	Uncomplicated, spontaneous delivery	No evidence of significant clinical abnormality
3	F	Caucas.	6 months	—	Normal	No data available			No evidence of significant clinical abnormality
4	M	Caucas.	1 day	2850 g	Normal	2850 g	5 10	Caesarian, mild cyanosis	No evidence of significant clinical abnormality
5	F	Negro	3½ months	3.4 kg	Mild umbilical hernia	1040 g	1 6	Premature, spontaneous delivery. Cyanotic but active at birth	No evidence of significant clinical abnormality
Group II									
6	F	Caucas.	4 months	6 kg	*Neurol.:* generalized irritability *Audiol.:* reduction of auditory responsiveness *Psychol.:* retarded development	3200 g	4 7	Intrauterine transfusions. Caesarian section. Erythroblastotic. Cyanotic. Required intubation	Generalized delay in sensory-motor development and mental development
7	F	Caucas.	2½ months	4.5 kg	*Audiol.:* auditory responses below average for this age Otherwise OK	3000 g	5 8	Intrauterine transfusions. Caesarian section. Edematous, cyanotic, erythroblastotic. Poor respiration, required lengthy hospital care	Normal development except for signs of auditory unresponsiveness

No.	Sex	Race	Age	Weight	Condition	Birth wt.			Delivery	Follow-up
8	M	Caucas.	5, 8, 11, 12 days	~3440 g	Depressed, lethargic infant. Difficult to stimulate to cry. Eating poorly	3700 g	4	5	Difficult mid-forceps delivery. Rt. clavicle fractured. Rt. facial palsy. Multiple contusions. Required resuscitation	Gradual recovery from paresis. Long-term follow-up not available
9	F	Caucas.	15, 22 days	1290 g 1340 g	Receiving intensive care for severe erythroblastosis	1450 g	2		Intrauterine transfusions. Severely depressed infant, born by Caesarian section. Heroic resuscitation methods were required	Post-natal jaundice and diarrhea. Gradual improvement in 3 months of hospitalization
10	M	Caucas.	3 days	3300 g	Good condition except for possible respiratory problems	3730 g	8	9	Uncomplicated, spontaneous delivery	Throughout post-natal care, child was weak, has poor head control. Subsequent development in question

Group III

No.	Sex	Race	Age	Weight	Condition	Birth wt.			Delivery	Follow-up
11	F	Caucas.	2 days	3500 g	Normal	3540 g	9	9	Uncomplicated, spontaneous delivery. Mild jaundice	Child completely failed to develop and died age 3 months because of severe cardio-pulmonary anomalies
12	F	Caucas.	20 days	3160 g	Lethargic, hydrocephalic infant	3100 g	7	9	Normal, uncomplicated delivery	Became unduly irritable and hypothermic. Trans-illumination disclosed absence of cerebrum. Now in a State Hospital
13	M	Negro	7 months	—	Hyperirritable, opisthotonic, exhausted-looking infant. Screams in response to the mildest stimulation	3200 g	—	—	Normal, uncomplicated delivery	No development of normal cooing or babbling. Child developed severe respiratory distress and died 'of unknown causes' age 7½ months. Autopsy findings were non-contributory

The present investigation

Our study was designed to determine whether two acoustical features – duration and pitch – of the expiratory cry sound show any relationship to diagnostic ratings based on clinical evaluation of infants. Both of these features have been implicated in previous studies (see above).

SELECTION OF CASES. Twenty babies were selected from case-material available in a teaching hospital. We went to the nursery looking for presumably normal cases, and asked pediatricians also to call our attention to newborns whose delivery was complicated or whenever future developmental difficulty might be expected. Three cases were the off-spring of mothers hospitalized for mental illness. Each child was tape-recorded in a quiet room after being maximally aroused by exogenous pain-stimulation. In most instances this was accomplished during blood-sample collections, and the same technician was used to administer the skin-puncture. When she was not available, a skin area of the left heel was swiftly and firmly pinched in order to provide comparable results. The recording microphone (Electrovoice 655 C) was held approximately 6 cm directly in front of the baby's mouth and rotated in accordance with any head movements. Each child lay on its back and was unrestricted except for manipulations to the foot. Sound input level of the tape-recorder (Ampex 601, 7.5 ips tapespeed) was adjusted to give no readings in excess of 2 V. In ten cases we were able to record the child on more than one occasion.

DIAGNOSTIC RATING. Each infant was assigned to one of three diagnostic groups on the basis of all clinical data available. We gathered information about the mother's prenatal history; a description of labor and delivery; physical examination of the newborn including Apgar ratings, nursery reports of weight, activity, health status, and laboratory tests; follow-up reports from pediatric examinations, including special neurological, psychological, and audiometric studies in some cases. While no attempt at classification was made before the completion of acoustical studies, we knew about the conditions of these babies through contacts with their doctors, parents, and nurses. However, in seven cases the information was considered too unreliable or limited to permit a clear-cut diagnostic classification of the infant. These cases were therefore eliminated from the study.

Table 2 summarizes the clinical facts, and three diagnostic groups were established as follows:

GROUP I-5 NORMAL INFANTS. While in two cases questions were raised at birth regarding the infant's prognosis (case 4, Caesarian section, case 5, premature birth), no information from subsequent examinations, studies, and follow-up visits pointed to any deviation from normalcy in terms of behavior, growth, sensory-motor maturation, attainment of developmental milestones, or general health status. Case 3 was born out of wedlock in another city and we were unable to obtain reliable data about its birth. But a 3-month observation period disclosed no developmental abnormalities whatsoever, and pediatric examinations were repeatedly negative.

GROUP II-5 QUESTIONABLY IMPAIRED BABIES. In each case very serious questions arose at birth or during the observation period regarding the child's health.

Cases 6, 7 and 9 were erythroblastotic infants with intrauterine transfusions, Caesarian sections, and extremely complicated post-natal histories. Case 8 was obviously badly injured at birth. Nevertheless these babies survived. Each one shows some residual impairment (Table 2). Case 10, while presumably normal at birth, has had a problematical subsequent development.

GROUP III-3 ABNORMAL INFANTS. Two of these are already dead – (case 11 of congenital heart disease, case 13 of unknown causes) while the third, case 12, is in a State Hospital with an 'anticipated life span of 3 months to 3 years' because of absent cerebral hemispheres (hydranencephaly).

ACOUSTICAL ANALYSIS OF CRIES. The complete tape-recording of each infant's pain-stimulated cry behavior was converted (without editing) to a continuous sonagram, using RAYSCAN apparatus available through the courtesy of the Bioacoustic Laboratory, Stanford Research Institute. The filters were adjusted to display harmonic frequencies from 0-6000 Hz. No attempt to measure intensity levels was made. Since we were interested in expiratory components, only those sounds which resembled, visually and auditorily, what Lind (1965) and others have reported as expiratory cries were measured. In a typical sequence cries began after a brief delay following the pain-stimulus. The initial cry was usually long and accompanied by grimacing. Inspiratory gasps were heard and seen later, once the cry-cycle was 'cruising' (Truby and Lind 1965). These were not measured, but they helped in locating the expiratory sounds. On each sonagram we measured as many expiratory cries as possible; all other sounds and noises which could not be positively identified were ignored. A total of 356 cries from the thirteen cases were analyzed (Table 3).

We determined DURATION by ruler (9.75 cm = 1 sec), the presence of any visible sound on the sonagram serving to identify the onset of each cry. Termination was taken to be that point where the sonagram paper was again blank, i.e. no sound component was visible. PITCH was determined for each cry by locating the cry formants at three points in the sonagram, called initial, highest, and final pitch. In each instance the frequency-level of the topmost formant was measured, and this divided by the number of the formant to determine its fundamental tone. (We are well aware of the fact that subjective pitch depends on more than fundamental frequency of tone stimulus but will continue to use the term pitch to refer to tonal sound as MEASURED rather than as perceived.) Initial pitch was the very first tonal component of the cry which could be measured. Final pitch was the very last measurable tone component. Only when a cry did not begin or end with turbulence (a noise obscuring the formant structure) was there a correspondence between initial and final pitch with onset and termination of the cry-duration. Highest pitch refers to fundamental tone measurements of the peak or highest level attained in the course of each expiratory cry. When there was a shift in the fundamental tone, its topmost level was taken as highest pitch. Since no attempt was made to locate the point-in-time of the highest pitch, our term PITCH-PATTERN (see below) should not be confused with melody or intonation.

Results

A total of 356 cries were analyzed. Statistical description (Table 3) of the duration and pitch characteristics reveals several interesting findings.

1. Duration (length) of cries

Lind et al. (1965) called attention to the "super long (5.8 sec)" duration produced by a brain-damaged infant. Only among our questionably impaired infants, Group II, are there cries of comparable duration. Case 7 attained a maximum duration of 6.65 sec, and Case 8 of 4.5 sec. In

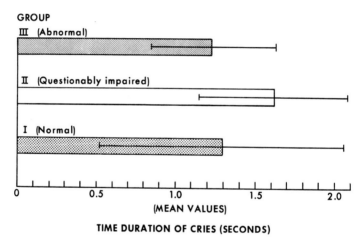

Fig. 1. Results of duration measurements of 356 cries from three clinical groups. There is no difference between cries from the normal and abnormal infants.

neither case can the presence of brain damage be ruled out. No unusual durations are found among normals, group I, where maximum length was 3.95 sec attained by Case 2, or among abnormals, group III, in which the longest cry was 3.75 sec, attained by Case 12. Results of duration measurements are illustrated graphically in figure 1 which shows that duration characteristics of the three groups overlap, and that ON THE BASIS OF DURATION ONLY ONE CANNOT PREDICT WHICH GROUP AN INFANT FITS INTO.

TABLE 3

Statistical description of infant cry patterns

Case No.	No. of cries analyzed	Cry durations (in sec)			Cry pitch patterns (in Hz)								
					Initial pitch			Highest pitch			Final pitch		
		Range	Mean	S.D.	Range	Mean	S.D.	Range	Mean	S.D.	Range	Mean	S.D.
Group I													
1	51	0.45–1.33	0.75	0.26	367–500	438	33	550–785	614	42	400–534	452	29
2	16	0.85–3.95	1.83	0.86	280–500	380	49	410–500	452	38	300–450	365	47
3	20	0.85–3.75	2.15	0.85	333–467	408	34	375–479	432	27	333–450	394	32
4	14	0.65–3.80	1.38	0.82	333–450	376	33	360–540	440	53	320–400	356	25
5	20	0.75–1.90	1.22	0.33	414–580	491	39	440–733	591	76	350–533	400	49
Group II													
6	22	0.75–3.85	1.20	0.65	460–1250	569	181	520–2875	1060	662	467–1600	884	373
7	25	1.00–6.65	2.02	1.07	217–600	435	80	425–642	519	61	300–600	376	67
8	39[a]	0.85–4.50	1.98	0.81	200–437	347	42	300–1667	421	208	250–950	346	105
9	20[a]	0.60–3.90	1.88	1.12	467–900	605	139	500–1350	743	224	300–833	525	145
10	15	0.16–1.95	1.04	0.37	400–500	449	27	422–550	459	32	400–560	431	41
Group III													
11	26[a]	0.75–2.3	1.41	0.46	240–900	514	177	380–1100	601	200	300–1100	557	237
12	68[a]	0.55–3.75	1.52	0.77	280–600	418	66	375–650	486	57	270–500	378	47
13	20	0.40–1.20	0.79	0.26	467–1333	838	261	428–1833	1162	374	360–1025	835	140

[a] From more than one recording session.

2. Pitch-pattern of cries

In regard to pitch, a potentially serviceable diagnostic criterion is quite apparent: CRIES OF EXCESSIVELY HIGH PITCH OCCUR ONLY AMONG THE QUESTIONABLY IMPAIRED AND THE ABNORMAL INFANTS. Each case in group I (the normals) shows ranges and means that correspond to all normative studies previously reported. No cry pitch is above 600 Hz at either onset or termination, and only two infants ever reach a level higher than 600 Hz throughout the entire expiratory cry.

However, several cases among group II (questionably impaired) and group III (abnormal) show extremely high pitch levels. Case 6, an intrauterine transfusion case with probably retarded mental development, shows mean initial pitch of 569 Hz, final pitch of 884 Hz and maximum pitch of 1060 Hz. Some of this infant's cries went as high as 3000 Hz. Case 9 has a mean initial pitch of 605 Hz and a mean maximum pitch of

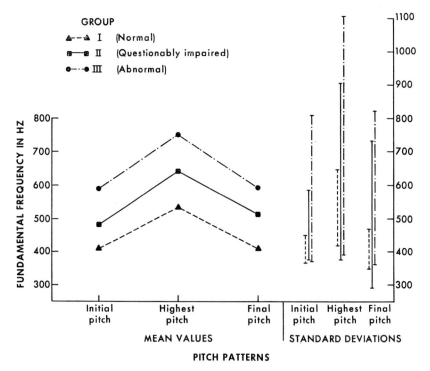

Fig. 2.   Results of fundamental tone measurements of 356 cries from three clinical groups. There is a marked difference in pitch pattern between normal (Group I) and abnormal (Group III) infants.

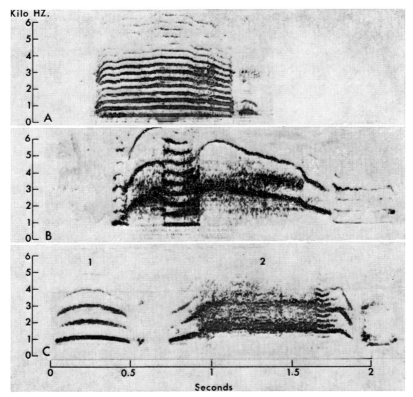

Fig. 3.   Sonagrams of cries from three infants. A: Normal infant (case 2) showing
typical configuration of the 'basic' cry. B: Questionably impaired infant (case 6)
showing an exceedingly high-pitched cry. C: Abnormal infant (case 13) showing very
high pitch without turbulence (cry 1) and with turbulence (cry 2).

743 Hz. This was a severely erythroblastotic girl with a one-minute Apgar
rating of 2, whose postnatal course was very problematical.

As for the abnormal infants, Case 13 shows a really extraordinary
pitch pattern; mean initial levels (838 Hz) are the highest recorded in our
entire series. Mean highest pitch is 1163 Hz, and final pitch 835 Hz.

Results of the pitch-pattern measurements are shown in figure 2. It
should be noted that at the low end of the fundamental frequency scale
(ordinate) the three groups overlap. Between 350 and 450 Hz one cannot
tell whether a cry belongs to a normal infant or one of the pathologicals.
Only when initial pitch is above 450 Hz, highest above 650 Hz, and final
above 465 Hz can a cry be identified as belonging to groups II or III.
When the initial pitch is above 585 Hz, the highest pitch above 900 Hz,

and the final pitch above 825 Hz can the cries be said to derive from the abnormal infants (see 'Standard Deviations', Fig. 2).

Figure 3 illustrates sonagrams of cries characteristic of three infants, one from each of the diagnostic groups.

Discussion

The structure of an acoustical signal is related to the function it serves in communication (Marler 1967), and it may be said that the function of a cry is to elicit those responses from the social environment which are most likely to meet the physiological requirements of the crying organism. We therefore would expect diseased infant cries to contain design-features capable of quickly evoking appropriately corrective measures, thereby assuring the survival of the child. High-pitched, screechy, irregular tones do in fact arouse and stimulate more urgency on the part of listeners than do low, soft, and regular patterns; fire-engines, whistles, and alarm signals of various kinds take advantage of this fact (Ostwald 1959). It is not surprising to find that human neonates produce yodel-like high-pitched 'shifts', which are auditorily inescapable. While the present analysis of 356 cries is based on only a small number of infants, and we did not attempt to match our cases in terms of sex, age, race, and other factors that could possibly influence the cry, the traditional clinical impression of a relationship between high-pitch and disease state is confirmed.

Sound-monitoring systems might thus have some value in the pediatric nursery, but we suggest that mechanical devices not be installed until they are capable of a greater degree of pattern-recognition. Pitch is not the only attribute used by the clinician, whose identification of abnormal cries is also based on recognizing irregular phonation, quavers, noises, anomalous intonation patterns, and other dimensions of the cry stimulus (Partanen et al. 1967). Had we relied only on a high-pass filter set at 700 Hz, two of the normal infants would have been incorrectly identified as diseased, while three of the questionable and abnormal cases could not have been spotted. The device would also have been confounded by inspiratory gasps, which are typically of higher pitch than the expiratory components of cry sounds.

The possibility of an infantile 'warning system' of impending or actual disease can be discussed more explicitly in connection with four cases. Infant 10 gave warning by way of 'respiratory problems' which were not however noticeable in the two acoustic dimensions of 15 cries studied.

Here an analysis of more cry material, especially in repeated tape-recordings, might have been productive. Case 11 is especially interesting in that the results of newborn examinations were completely normal, and it was only after the baby failed to grow and develop that her cardiac defect was discovered. But notes made during our tape-recording on the second day of life read: "difficult to stimulate crying. Repeated pinching was necessary. The nurse says this baby is going to be breast fed and hasn't learned to cry yet". Acoustic analysis shows a moderate elevation of pitch. In this case cry-anomalies seem to be the first indication of disease. Case 12, the hydranencephalic infant, was noted by ward personnel to utter a 'shrill' cry which led them to request the revealing neurologic consultation. By the time the infant was tape-recorded, cerebral pathology was already quite certain. We analyzed a total of 68 cries, some produced with the mouth closed, a phenomenon not observed in normal infants. Case 13 had such a remarkable cry that when first seen at 3 months, the resident was afraid the child was dying. Actually this infant lived for another 4 months, during which repeated clinical and laboratory study failed to disclose the cause of the problem. Post-mortem examination revealed some unusual infiltration of carbon particles throughout the lungs. The infant had obviously been neglected, and on one occasion when the child's screaming was being recorded his mother asked, "Isn't that the sound of a contented baby?" She had a background of severe mental illness.

Since even the normal physiology of infant vocalization is something of a mystery, all we can say about the cause of 'abnormal' cry sounds is that they presumably result from imbalances between subglottal respiratory pressure and the laryngeal tension mechanisms (Lieberman 1967). To what degree and in what manner there may be central nervous system control over the pattern of the neonate cry requires further research. In our opinion the infant cry reflects an innate, genetically-determined, species-specific pattern of organization. This would be consistent with the finding of abnormal cry patterns associated with chromosomal disorders like Down's Syndrome and Cri-du-Chat.[1] The likelihood that cooing and babbling are also determined by innate propensities for communicative development has been discussed by Lenneberg (1967). Psychoanalytic theory would suggest that anomalous vocalization in infancy reflects a disturbance in the development of age-appropriate ego control-mecha-

[1]   We have just completed an analysis of cries from a Trisomy 13-15 infant which also have atypical pitch patterns.

nisms (Spitz 1965). It therefore seems possible that more accurate definition of the pattern of structural and temporal characteristics of prelinguistic soundmaking might be useful in the early detection of pathology.

Summary

Auditory assessment of cry patterns has a traditional usefulness in clinical evaluation of the infant. Within the last decade acoustic studies have contributed more precise information about neonatal sound productions, specifically in regard to the properties of cries associated with different clinical states and disease conditions. The present study involves sonagraphic analysis of 356 expiratory cry utterances derived from 13 infants that on the basis of clinical data, behavioral development, and neurological status were classified as normal, impaired, or abnormal. Duration measurements showed no consistent differences between the three groups. Pitch measurements showed a marked increase of the fundamental tone only among infants rated as impaired or abnormal. It is postulated that this reflects a disorganization of innate adaptive mechanisms which assure that infants can elicit appropriate social responses from their environment. More thorough and detailed study of abnormalities in vocalization patterns within the first six months of life might be helpful in predicting results of subsequent language and intelligence tests, especially when there are early signs of neurological or developmental pathology.

28

CRIES OF A TRISOMY 13-15 INFANT*

(with P. Peltzman, M. Greenberg and J. Meyer)

(1970)

One adjuvant in diagnosis may be the vocal behavior of an infant. Characteristic cry sounds have already been described in two chromosome aberrations, the 'Cat-cry' syndrome (Luchsinger et al. 1967) and Down's syndrome (Fisichelli et al. 1966). Our purpose here is to describe cries from a trisomy 13-15 infant.

Patau and co-workers (1960) have described the multiple congenital anomalies caused by an additional chromosome in group D (13-15). The newborn infant exhibited cleft lip and palate, polydactyly, micropthalmia with hypoplasia of the optic nerves, simian palmar creases, retroflexible thumbs, and ventricular septal defect. The publication of further cases with additional anomalies (Snodgrass et al. 1966) clearly indicated that a new, specific, and easily recognizable clinical syndrome had been established.

Description of our case

The infant, a female weighing 3280 g, was cyanotic at birth (one-minute Apgar = 3). Physical examination revealed cardio-respiratory difficulties, an omphalocoele, and 6 toes bilaterally. There was no superficial evidence of cleft palate or cleft lip. Cardiac catheterization at three days of age revealed dextroposition of the heart and A-V shunting. Chromosomal analysis showed a trisomy 13-15 anomaly.

Tape-recording of cries was carried out on day 6. The infant was inside the incubator, with air-circulating motor in operation. An Electro-voice microphone (655 C) was placed approximately 4 cm in front of the infant's mouth. Recordings were made on an Ampex Tape Recorder,

* Reprinted from *Developmental Medicine and Child Neurology* 12: 472-77 (1970).

Model 601, with a speed of $7\frac{1}{2}$ inches per second. Since the infant emitted no spontaneous cries, vocalization was stimulated by pinching the skin of the right heel. At first the baby only moved, but did not cry. The onset of vocalization was atypical in that the initial cry did not have the long, drawn-out character usually heard when an infant is pain-stimulated.

Subjective analysis of cries

Nine identifiable cries were elicited. The attending nursery staff described these cries as "peculiar"; one staff doctor said they reminded him of Down's syndrome cries.

In listening to the tapes, we found a number of striking features in these cries. Firstly, each cry had what sounded like an unusually hard or abrupt onset, reminiscent of the beginning of a cough. Secondly there was a quavery or unsteady pitch to the cry. Thirdly, we heard a marked drop in pitch at the end of each vocalization. Finally, in several instances, we heard a raspy, snorting noise: it was impossible to be certain from the tape recording whether the infant produced this noise while inhaling, or whether this peculiar sound represented the very end of an expiratory cry that had fallen to an extremely low pitch.

Spectrographic analysis of cries

The cry recordings were converted to visible patterns by use of a Kay Sound Spectrograph (Sonagraph Model 6061), with filters set for wide-band analysis (see Fig. 1).

TABLE

Time and Frequency Measurements of Nine Cries

Cry no.	Time duration (in seconds)	Fundamental frequency (Hz)		
		At onset	At peak	At termination
1	.81	300	575	100
2	.72	380	525	120
3	1.02	400	615	150
4	1.03	320	590	180
5	1.68	380	615	200
6	.67	375	680	160
7	.15	200	405	160
8	.54	210	595	220
9	.99	355	565	250

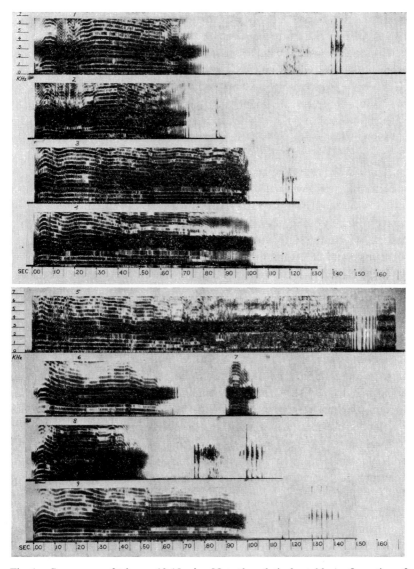

Fig. 1. Sonagrams of trisomy 13-15 cries. Note the relatively stable configuration of the first quaver, or microsegment, in each cry. The vertical striations at the end of cries (see for example Cry No. 1 between 0.7 and 0.8 sec.) denote a marked drop in the fundamental frequency. Good examples of click-like noises can be observed after Cry No. 1 (1.38-1.45 sec.) and after Cry No. 8 (0.75-1.15 sec.).

Three cries had durations in excess of 1 second, the longest being 1.68 sec. Five cries ranged between 0.5 and 1 second, while only one cry had a duration less than half a second (see Table). These figures generally correspond with measurements we reported previously for pain-induced cries from a group of infants who could not be differentiated on the basis of cry-duration (Ostwald et al. 1968). Wasz-Höckert and co-workers (1968) have reported that 60 pain cries in a normal 0-1 month-old population gave a mean duration of 2.6 seconds (s.d. = 1.5 second). However, these figures represent only initial pain-stimulated cries, which are usually considerably longer than subsequent cries in a series.

Unlike the relatively steady frequency pattern of normal six-day-old infant cries, the trisomy 13-15 cries showed a notable tonal instability or quaver. There were sequences consisting of a rise and fall in the harmonic pattern, which we elected to call 'microsegments'. As many as four micro-segments could be distinguished in some cries. In measuring the nine cries we found that only their initial microsegments had comparable durations, ranging from 0.10 to 0.18 seconds, while the duration of subsequent microsegments was much more variable.

The fundamental frequency of each cry was measured at its onset, its peak or maximum point, and its termination. The results are shown in the Table. A very striking feature of the frequency pattern of these cries was the unusually low final level at the end of each cry; for example, one cry terminated at 100 Hz and none remained at a level higher than 250 Hz. In our previous report of 356 cries from 13 normal and pathological cases, only two infants ever showed a final frequency level below 300 Hz (Ostwald et al. 1968). One of these, a female of 3700 g birth-weight with multiple birth injuries, went down to 250 Hz. The other infant, an anencephalic female of 3100 g birthweight, showed a final frequency of 270 Hz.

On the sonagrams, we also observed a series of click-like sounds, approximately 5 every 100 msec. near the end of several cries. These clicks corresponded with the raspy, snorting noise described above and might be similar to what has been described as "vocal fry" in the infant's cry (Wasz-Höckert et al. 1968).

Discussion

The question that concerns us is whether the cry of trisomy 13-15 has a certain uniqueness. If so, this might reflect differences in the neuro-motor patterning of vocal behavior in these neonates as contrasted with babies from other clinical categories. Such differences, besides their diagnostic value, could be important for further knowledge about possible genetic determinants of soundmaking and the biological basis for language development (Lenneberg 1967).

A single pain-cry elicited from a trisomy 13-15 infant appears in figure 33 of the 1968 monograph by Wasz-Höckert and colleagues. This is described as "a very long discontinuous signal – there are similarities with Down's syndrome cries." The cry under consideration has an extraordinary duration of 11.3 seconds, which is itself unusual enough to deserve discussion. No other cry of comparable duration is shown in the monograph, nor has our research group ever observed a cry signal of this length. The discontinuity referred to is a silent interval of about 5 seconds. One wonders what behavior the infant engaged in during this silent interval, for example whether it was apneic. Simultaneous recording of respiratory events along with vocal output would be necessary to answer this question (Bosma et al. 1965).

The quavering observed in our currently reported trisomy 13-15 cries can also be seen in the Wasz-Höckert cry described above. One notices it again in figure 28 in the Wasz-Höckert monograph: this is an 8-second pain cry in a baby with Down's syndrome. We have also observed quavering in the cries of short-gestation infants (Ostwald et al. 1967). It is therefore unlikely that the quavery pattern *per se* is in any way pathognomonic of a genetic anomaly. However, the association of quaver and low pitch could be a feature that typifies the trisomy condition we observed. Wasz-Höckert and co-workers state that it is possible to train observers to identify Down's syndrome cries by 5 minutes' work with a test tape. "The typical melody form is flat [...] the cries are of low pitch [...] the cry is tense and often only half-voice [...] periodically the tenseness is heightened (when attacks of glottal 'pressure' are superimposed on the phonation)." This latter descriptive comment about the Down's syndrome cry reminds us of the abrupt cough-like onset of our trisomy 13-15 cries. Our impression is that the consistent perturbation at the onset of our trisomy 13-15 cries might, by contrast with subsequently variable quavering, account for this cough-like behavior.

The acoustical properties of trisomy 13-15 and Down's syndrome cries stand in definite contrast to those of the 'Cat-cry' syndrome. Cries in the latter disease entity have an unusually high fundamental frequency (Luchsinger et al. 1967) and do not contain 'vocal fry' (Vuorenkoski et al. 1966). Down's syndrome, like trisomy 13-15, is a condition resulting from chromosome reduplication, whereas the 'Cat-cry' syndrome results from chromosomal deletion. Therefore it seems reasonable to expect similar cries from the trisomy anomaly group – Down's syndrome and trisomy 13-15 syndrome – while the 'Cat-cry' syndrome has, as its name indicates, a wholly unique cry sound.

Summary

Nine cries from a six-day-old trisomy 13-15 infant were analysed sonagraphically. They showed a generally low fundamental frequency pattern, with prominent quaver. The final position of the fundamental frequency at the end of the cries was much lower than that usually found in both normal and diseased infants without autosomal aberrations.

Trisomy 13-15 cries seem to bear a much greater resemblance to those of Down's syndrome than to those of the 'Cat-cry' syndrome. This is consistent with the similarity of the autosomal disorder involved in Down's and in trisomy 13-15 syndrome.

Further studies of abnormal cry phenomena should include respiratory and airflow measurements to reveal more accurate correlations between the acoustic structure and the concomitant physiologic events of crying.

29

ALTERNATIVE COMMUNICATION SYSTEMS FOR THE DEAF*

(1967)

Too little is known at the present time about the neurological basis of language-learning to permit any hard-and-fast recommendations about the best ways to habilitate congenitally deaf children. Yet the SPONTANEOUS compensatory behavior of these youngsters provides us with certain clues as to how one might procede, and since we live in an age of multi-media technology (McLuhan 1964) it seems appropriate to venture into this difficult field of education with renewed optimism and enthusiasm. The purpose of the following remarks is to stimulate interest and discuss possibilities in the development of alternative communication systems for members of the deaf population.

The problems of deafness handicap

Deafness imposes a drastic loss of input to one of the two sensory systems essential in distance communication. How the afflicted person compensates for this deficit depends on his age and the completeness of the sensory loss. The infant who is deaf – as a result of genetic, toxic, infectious, metabolic or other factors active during prelinguistic phases of development – can only compensate for the absence of auditory stimulation by making use of the other sensory modalities remaining at his disposal.

Vision, especially, serves the infant as a 'natural' alternative modality for contacting and interpreting events in his environment, a phylogenetic reminder of nonhuman primates and their dependence on facial ex-

---

* Expanded version of a paper presented at the New York State Psychiatric Institute Conference on Psychiatry and the Deaf, April 7, 1967.

pression and other visually perceived motor patterns for communication without language (Washburn and Hamburg 1968). Indeed, many deaf infants adapt themselves so perfectly on the basis of available visual information that considerable doubt may arise as to the actual presence of a severe auditory deficit. Only after the child fails to develop normal speech patterns does his inability to make use of sound-encoded information become obvious to others.

In schools for the deaf one invariably finds youngsters engaged in 'conversations' comprising only visual signs and gestures. Depending on the environmental responses to his signing, the child's exuberant interest in symbolic communication may flourish to such an extent that esoteric codes and mannerisms (so-called deafisms) become his exclusive means of 'talking' with parents and peers. Unfortunately this behavior, added to their primary inabilities in hearing and learning language, tends progressively to isolate deaf youngsters from the speaking society at large. With the passage of years, innate linguistic capacities atrophy to a point where learning new communication systems becomes an increasingly more laborious intellectual exercise (Lenneberg 1966). It is therefore of tremendous importance that physicians and educators emphasize the early application of every available method for enhancing communication with the deaf person, and that efforts continually be made to discover and develop the most effective alternatives to hearing.

In view of the fact that normal youngsters do not seem to suffer from 'Input-overload' during the critical formative years of language acquisition, it seems unnecessary to worry about overstimulating or confusing the deaf child (assuming he has no brain damage) by bombarding him with information. Lenneberg (1966) has suggested that word labels should be attached to various objects in the deaf child's environment – toys, furniture, clothing, etc. – so that the youngster can readily grasp the idea of word associations. The importance of early instruction in the use of the manual alphabet and gesture symbols has also been emphasized (Watson 1964). The child who can learn to recognize what people are saying by watching and interpreting their mouth-movements also has an advantage in communicating. In all of these instances, language seems to develop much better and quicker if some degree of sonic or vibratory experience can yet be made available for the deaf child (Whetnal 1956). Even a minimal auditory capacity may be enhanced sufficiently with modern electroacoustical aids to provide some language input for learning acceptable speech (Fry 1966), and it has also been possible in a few experimental situations to provide a deaf person with quasi-auditory experiences through direct excitation of the cochlear nerve mechanisms or with vibratory stimuli (Djourno and Eyries 1957).

When no sonic input whatsoever is available, several categories of information about his environment remain forever unknown to the deaf individual. First of all, he is unable to detect any of the movements in the environment that are inaccessible to touch or vision. People in other rooms, cars around corners, bells, thunder, music – in short, all the acoustical accompaniments of nature and social existence are totally lost. The deaf person's environment is circumscribed by two rings whose radii are the length of his arms and the distance of his field of vision. It seems quite likely that some of the awkwardness, postural peculiarity, and social anxiety clinically discernible among the deaf may be rooted in this primary loss of environmental information which, in hearing persons, helps establish appropriate responsiveness to spatial and territorial danger.

Next is the loss of vital information about how emotion is expressed and transmitted sonically. Cries, laughter, song, voice quality, and other tonal cues for emotional expression cannot be heard. Without the directive power of words and emotional sounds, the youngster is forced to rely exclusively on visual information about how people feel and what they expect from him. All too often the child has to be pushed or shoved to get his attention or get him to do something the parent wants. For the deaf individual, self-monitoring of vocalizations is difficult, since he gets no airborne feedback about laughing, cooing, babbling, and other sounds which are likely to be heard by others. In learning to speak, the deaf person's ability to produce intonation cues and vocal nuances of emotion remains severely limited. To the hearing world this lack of sound-transmitted emotional behavior may appear paradoxical; or annoying. Sometimes the deaf behavior even mimics mental illness (Rainer and Altshuler 1966).

Finally and most devastating of all is the loss of information about those finely-timed motor mechanisms that are required for speech (Liberman et al. 1962). The auditory system is uniquely capable of processing this sequential input of sound signals, which constitutes one of man's greatest achievements – his language code. Probably based on a binary contrast system of 'distinctive features' (Jakobson and Halle 1956), the phonemic patterning of the speech sounds cannot be appreciated through lip-reading alone since many significant articulations are produced behind the lips within the mouth and nasopharynx, while tone cues are of laryngeal origin. In any society dependent on verbal-linguistic interactions, deaf persons will be terribly disadvantaged unless they too can somehow learn to extract information from the articulated speech behavior of hearing people and thereby learn to reproduce understandable language symbols.

Possibilities for audio-visual translation

In the auditory sphere we deal primarily with time-bound stimuli. Speech is a sequential array of co-articulated acoustical patterns emanating in a time-patterned regularity from the respiratory, vocal, and oropharyngeal structures. By contrast, the visual sphere is a space world whose configurations may be grasped in an instant. It is the miracle of cortical integration that enables space-time patterns to coalesce, and the healthy human brain can perform really astounding feats of audiovisual synthesis (Luria 1966). Some persons quite consciously transform each heard sound into a visually experienced analogue, and the phenomena of synesthesia (Ostwald 1964c) surely suggest that there may potentially be a variety of satisfactory methods for intersensory transformations. Communal necessities force people to agree on using only a limited number of

LET'S TALK!

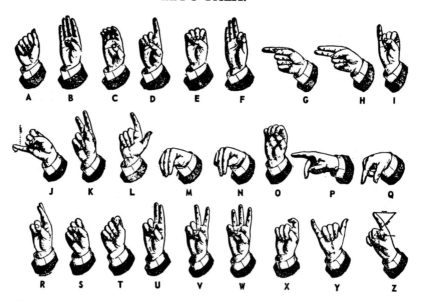

Fig. 1.   Manual Alphabet of the Deaf, showing finger-hand positions denoting each letter of the written alphabet.

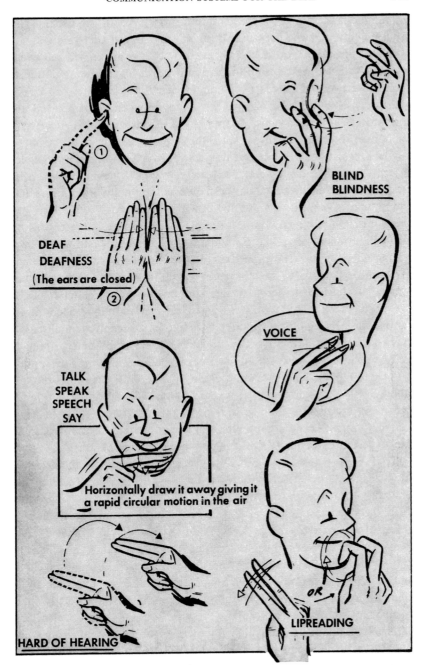

Fig. 2. Example of gestural signs used by the deaf for communication of concepts (reproduced, with the author's permission, from Watson (1964)).

communication systems, a specialization process which can exclude the deaf-handicapped who happen to be unable to adopt standard techniques.

ALPHABETS, while not necessarily easy to acquire, are considered to be absolutely indispensable transformation codes in most literate cultures. Our suggestion for alternative communication systems does not imply that we wish to do away with reading and writing. But deaf people long ago must have realized how disappointing the lexical alphabetical style of human interaction can be, since their speech handicap often makes digital itemization of actions, feelings, and abstractions almost impossible. When a language can neither be heard nor spoken, cognitive grasp of its phonology remains vague at best. Just as the totally blind individual never 'knows' what colors are, the deaf person cannot really appreciate what it is that phonetic notation is meant to represent. To learn this he has to use his fingers, like a child learning to count, and when deaf youngsters are not encouraged to do this or are forbidden to sign, irreparable damage to their cognitive skills may result. The MANUAL ALPHABET consists of specific finger positions denoting each letter of the written alphabet (see Fig. 1). It is easy to learn and should be encouraged among the deaf and those who try to help them. A good manualist also has command of a variety of analogue signs – a 'vocabulary' – which refers to words or ideas without the necessity of finger-spelling each sound-letter (see Fig. 2). The syntax of manual signing resembles somewhat the abbreviated forms used by children, or by adults speaking a foreign language. Translation from spoken into signed language requires a kind of facility often found among bilingual persons. Many of the best sign-language translators are the hearing offspring of deaf parents.

To dispense with written alphabets and move closer to a symbolization of primary motor speech patterns is an old dream which can now be actualized, thanks to modern electro-acoustics. The first important breakthrough was *Visible Speech*, a method of sound spectrography invented over twenty years ago (Potter et al. 1947). Visible speech preserves the sense of interconnectedness of the dynamic speech acts, showing words not the way they are transcribed by a printing machine but in terms of the way speech sounds are emitted in real time by a human speaker (see Fig. 3). Since no two speakers are built exactly alike or produce sounds in exactly the same way, the visible speech contains information about individuality of speech performances, much the way a sample of handwriting is more revealing of personality than the printed page.

Progress in deciphering visible speech is basically dependent on knowl-

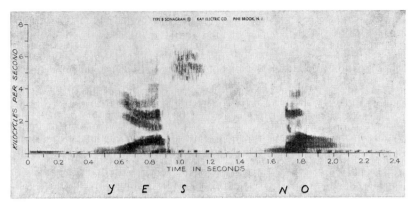

Fig. 3.   Sound spectrogram ('Visible Speech') showing contrasts in the vocalic and
consonantal structure of the words "yes" and "no".

edge about the acoustic cues essential for speech perception (Lane 1966).
Particularly striking are the visible analogues of vowel sounds. Being a
predominantly tonal event, each vowel consists of harmonic bands that
result from selective amplification and dampening of the laryngeal
fundamental. These bands, known as 'formants', appear as darkly-
shaded lines running horizontally and changing direction up or down
depending on the particular phonemic utterance produced.

Another striking visual contrast is provided by consonants with a
hissing character, (e.g., *s*, *ch*, and *sh*) because the acoustical structure is
essentially a shaped noise that shows up as mottled grey covering a wide
band of frequencies. The stop consonants (e.g., *p*, *t*, *k*) also provide an
excellent visual contrast because they are preceded by empty spaces
denoting the momentary cessation of air-flow required by the anticipated
release of sound. Voiced consonants (e.g., *b*, *d*, *g*) are preceded by characteristic densities near the low end of the frequency spectrum. Certain
paralinguistic voice qualities can also be visualized. Whisper, for example,
reduces the amplitude of vowel formants, because laryngeal tone is
absent. A harsh voice quality called rasp or 'vocal fry' exaggerates the
vertical striation pattern denoting glottalization. Nasality increases the
density of low-frequency resonance. Prosodic features that appear in
sonagrams include the rapidity or tempo of speech, its vocal pitch and
melodiousness, and information about rhythmicity or phrasing.

Today's speech analyzers permit a good deal of virtuosity in regard to
producing different kinds of visual displays (Flanagan 1965). The standard wide-band sonagraphic method is especially useful for analyzing
vowel formants. Narrow-band filtration gives better resolution of

harmonic patterns and thus provides a clearer picture of intonation. Logarithmic displays make the low-frequency components of speech signals more prominent. Total amplitude can be displayed along with magnification of selected portions of the signal. Topographic 'voiceprints' visualize fine detail of idiosyncratic resonance features through six-decibel intensity shadings. While traditionally the major research effort in acoustic phonetics has focussed on adult or 'standard' speech sounds, a more recent interest has been developing in the acoustic manifestations of organic and functional abnormalities (Lehiste 1965; Ostwald 1964b). We are currently engaged in a study of the very rudimentary cry behavior of infancy which may help yield understanding of relationships between prelinguistic soundmaking and emotive speech (Ostwald et al. 1968). As for direct application of visible speech to deaf education, there is still the problem of code-learning. Presentation of visible speech on a floures-cent screen is in essence presentation of a phonetic alphabet, albeit one that contains a great deal more information about how the speech was produced than does the standard alphabet. This overabundance of in-formation may be what makes the method so difficult to use, since communication implies a proper signal-to-noise ratio and the eye may be unable to ignore what the ear finds irrelevant. Nevertheless, good results with visible speech have been reported (Kopp and Kopp 1964).

CINERADIOGRAPHY (Truby 1959) offers another direct way to provide information about speech events, and now the need for code-learning is practically eliminated. X-rays penetrate the body surface to visualize entire mechanical sequences of articulations. Is this useful? A few minutes' contemplation of an X-ray movie will impress even unsophisti-cated viewers with the dramatic quality of speaking. Synchronized action of tongue, palate and pharynx is much more informative about speech physiology than the meager lip motions used in customary oral training of the deaf. X-ray films are usually made in the saggital plane; tomography is required for locating significant articulations in anterior-posterior projections. By watching an immediate playback of his flouroscoped speech motions, the student can correct his errors and practice more acceptable patterns. The big problem is that of radiation-exposure, which curtails the time and limits the practice sessions. The Bell Telephone Laboratories have recently come up with a solution to this problem – a computer-display of speech movements called VISIBLE ARTICULATION (Schroeder 1968). A resonator placed in front of the lips measures impedence changes of the vocal tract, from which calculations of arti-culation area are derived. The computer output displayed on a screen has remarkable resemblance to cineradiography, without any of the danger of radiation burns. Application of this method to deaf education remains for the future.

ELECTROMYOGRAPHY (MacNeilage and Sholes 1964) may also one day be a way to link the deaf person to the speaker's oropharyngeal musculature. At the present time, the pick-up leads are uncomfortable to wear, and due to interlarding of discharging fibers and confusing surface potentials, electromyograms do not delineate speech activity with sufficient clarity to justify an experiment in deaf education. This may also be said of today's ELECTROENCEPHALOGRAM, which reveals no direct information about higher brain function or speech. Our hope is that newer methods with averaged evoked potentials, which already are applied in audiometry, may be capable of describing perceptual events which the brain finds interesting (Callaway 1966), and that this information can ultimately be used to help the deaf.

A plea for more gadgets

Introduced early enough to the handicapped child and accepted by parents, physicians, and teachers, a prosthetic device comes to be part of the body image and is emotionally invested in the same way as are articles of clothing and toys. There is every reason to hope that our modern technology will invent and build practical electronic communication aids for the deaf. Indeed, some of this gadgetry is already available (Pickett 1967). Many years ago the late Norbert Wiener designed a hearing glove which breaks speech signals into frequency bands; the filtered output is used to activate tactile stimulators in the fingers of a glove-like contraption. The amount of information transmissible this way is of course quite limited. Available aids for telephonic communication include lights that go on when a call is made and translate the spoken message into a visible code. The SPEECH INDICATOR simply flashes "yes" (1 signal), "no, no" (2 signals) or "I don't get you" (3 signals). It can be adapted for deaf-blind communication by using tactile signals instead of light flashes.

One of the exciting hopes for the future is the VOICE-ACTIVATED TYPE-WRITER which would enable deaf people to read messages coming directly over telephone circuits. At the present, the art of automated pattern recognition has not progressed to a point where this fantasy can become reality (David and Selfridge 1962). Idiosyncratic rhythm, melody and voice quality in which phonetic symbols are embedded tend to confound the computer. A method for extracting this suprasegmental information from brief segments of recorded speech has been developed (Starkweather 1967). Teletype arrangements are already in use; vocal vicissitudes can be removed by having the speaker type out his message for immediate transmission to the deaf viewer. PICTURE-PHONES which will probably be available to the public in ten years give the additional possibility for seeing the speaker, which enables lip-reading and signing to be transmitted. This is an example of successful combination of several communication systems, and it should always be emphasized that these modalities and codes are not to be mutually exclusive but rather synthesized into whatever is the most useful way to overcome the handicap of deafness.

We have limited the above discussion to input-transducing devices for the deaf on the assumption that it is loss of input which handicaps these patients most drastically. In the wider context of communication disorders (Ruesch 1957), it seems pertinent to at least mention that output-transducers for the artificial synthesis of speech hold promise for patients who for a variety of reasons may be unable to speak. A great number of vocoder circuits have been tried within the last few years, mostly by computer simulation of the speech tract. With real-time computers one can now instantaneously adjust the phonetic and prosodic features of synthetic speech to conform with any desired model (Denes 1966). Thus the time may not be far off when a speech handicapped person can produce perfectly 'normal-sounding' speech simply by pushing buttons or moving a pen.

Perhaps a word of caution is in order here: we must be realists as well as optimists. No promises of simple solutions to complex problems in language translation have yet been fulfilled (Bar-Hillel 1964), and our wish to help a terribly disadvantaged population should not blind us to the unsolved and possibly unsolvable difficulties. But let us not be content either with simply applying standard education and treatment methods of milieu, social, personal, and pharmacologic assistance (though even this may be a costly and far-off goal). An era willing to risk going to the moon and capable of orbiting communication satellites may very well expect to create completely novel approaches to communication disorders, viz. alternative systems to provide artificial sensory inputs and synthetic motor outputs (Sterling 1967).

Summary

This paper reviews the kinds of spatial, interactional, and linguistic information lost to hearing-deprived patients. Substitutive input at an early age is essential to avoid atrophy of language capacity and prevent social isolation in childhood and adolescence. Traditional manual signs and lip-reading are helpful for communicating with the deaf but introduce new problems akin to those of bilingual subcultures. One of today's great hopes is the development of alternative communication systems which would enable the sequential, digital speech-language code to be instantaneously converted into visual patterns. Alphabets, visible speech, cineradiography, visible articulation, and other experimental possibilities for visualization of sounds have been discussed. While there are many serious problems of code-transformation involved, technical devices for automated speech analysis and speech synthesis should be utilized for training and rehabilitating individuals with severe communication disorders.

30

THE PSYCHIATRIST AND THE PATIENT WHO STUTTERS*

(1970)

Speech dysfluencies may occur at any time and under a variety of conditions, to any person who talks, but these are not considered pathological.
Stuttering is a disorder that persists, or intrudes itself predictably as one
speaks of certain things or to certain people. This condition becomes a
character trait when the afflicted person thinks of himself primarily in
terms of the speech problem, withdraws from communication because
of it, and comes to be labeled 'a stutterer'.

For centuries physicians have debated the relative importance of
organic vs functional determinants of stuttering (Diehl 1958). Three
psychiatrists in the United States contributed comprehensive formulations
of this syndrome during the past 15 years. Peter Glauber (1958) dealt
with the problem from a classic psychoanalytic point of view which
emphasizes the stutterer's pregenital fixations and consequent ego defenses. Dominick A. Barbara (1954) focused on characterological problems of stutterers, particularly their overvaluation of speech in social
discourse. Henry Freund (1966) gave an eclectic overview and called
attention to the stutterer's apparently unique inner language problems.
In the present paper, I will deal mainly with the practical aspects of
diagnosis and management, based on work with speech-handicapped
patients reported in more detail elsewhere (Ostwald 1969b). No matter
what theories and clinical experience he has, the psychiatrist faces certain
new problems when a patient who stutters seeks his help.

*   Reprinted from *The Journal of Nervous and Mental Disease* 150. 1: 317-24 (1970).

The psychiatrist

How many stuttering patients the psychiatrist sees, and at what ages or stages of complication, depends on demographic factors. These vary from one community to the next. Milder cases and even transient forms of speech dysfluency may have to be evaluated in areas where the psychiatrist cannot rely on speech pathologists and other therapists to help with the problem. Questions come up around such issues as progress in school, job qualifications, and Selective Service eligibility. Other aspects of learning and personality adjustment often will need to be considered in addition to the patient's speech functions. The overwhelming majority of stuttering patients show no physical evidence of disease (Luchsinger and Arnold 1965). Males exceed females approximately 5 to 1 in most caseloads. This confirms one's intuition that constitutional and learning factors influence speech acquisition. Recent studies have detected sexual differences in communication at 4 months, and it seems likely that they may be traced back to even earlier ages (Kagan 1968). Girls speak sooner and more fluently than boys. Almost all forms of speech and language disorder occur with greater frequency among males.

The physician who does routine electroencephalograms may find a somewhat higher incidence of atypical records among stuttering than among speech-fluent patients (Moravek and Langova 1962). Some authorities are prepared to postulate a "primary" or "central" language imbalance on the basis of these and other physiological test results (Weiss 1967). Theoretically this is justified, since, as we shall see, the stutterer has a number of other problems secondary to his communication disorder. But no one today can satisfactorily explain the neurophysiological basis of 'normal' speech behavior (Lenneberg 1967). Therefore, the physician should avoid telling patients that stuttering is an organic disease. He can limit himself to the explanation that dysrhythmias, perceptual distortions, and other manifestations of stuttering indicate a maturational delay and faulty learning (Beech and Francella 1968). One of the most remarkable aspects of this speech disorder is its evanescent nature, its ability to 'disappear' when the patient speaks to himself or with nonthreatening people, and its susceptibility to environmental control (Goldiamond 1965).

Let us turn now to the psychiatrist working in an urban setting replete with special schools and clinics staffed with speech therapists and psychologists. He is much more likely to be confronted only with more severe and complicated problems of stuttering. These are individuals whose problems do not respond to the usual techniques of education and speech therapy, or they are people in trouble for a variety of reasons, which may or may not be related to their speech difficulty. Under these circumstances it is seldom realistic to assume that "the speech defect is the problem itself, rather than the symptom of some underlying difficulty" (Sloane and MacAulay 1968). A much more comprehensive approach to the complicated life development of the stutterer is called for.

The problem of stuttering

Stuttering impedes the flow of speech. Normally one can slow down, speed up, stop, start, and repeat words at will, leaving the details of pronunciation and phrasing to unconscious mechanisms. In stuttering, the speaker loses this ability. His speech is alternately too redundant or too sparse. Redundancy manifests itself in an excessive repetition of speech sounds, syllables, words, or even parts of sentences. The patient cannot stop himself from repeating, nor can he go on without deliberately changing his mind about what he wants to say. This in turn leads to circumlocution, hesitation, and occasionally complete silence. Some stutterers interject nonverbal noises, or clichés such as "you know". Others plan in advance what they want to say in detail, hoping to avoid words that are lengthy, difficult to pronounce, or associated with anxiety. This destroys verve and spontaneity in verbal discourse. The overcontrolled stutterer makes speech seem condensed or telegraphic. It may be difficult to follow his ideas, which are not smoothly interconnected by the necessary filler words. On the other hand, he may get stuck on a single topic, fearing to branch out with difficult or new words.

The patient who stutters may be able to orate brilliantly from a prepared text. But unrehearsed dialogue that calls for flexibility and novelty in speaking poses a real challenge. In a group, the stutterer can then excuse himself from verbal participation and he remains silent. But when a demand for speech is very great, such as during job interviews, or classes in school, the stutterer reveals his symptom. The problem is especially severe if a time limit is put on speaking. For example, asking directions at a toll crossing or ordering tickets at a busy box office are conditions that make stutterers particularly uncomfortable.

Under stress, various motor automatisms are associated with stuttering. The patient grimaces, blinks his eyes, coughs, smacks his lips, clears his throat, clenches his fists, or snaps his fingers, Subjectively, he feels tense and apprehensive. A certain 'confusion' may be reported, but usually this refers to anxiety rather than a true loss of conceptual boundaries. Unlike the schizophrenic patient who withdraws or loses contact under the stress of an interpersonal crisis, stutterers usually hang on to the actuality of the immediate speech situation.

The initial contact with a psychiatrist

'Breaking the ice' is unusually difficult for patients who stutter. Many abhor the telephone and announce themselves in writing or ask another person to make the appointment. If he does call, the stutterer may try laboriously to spell out his rather obvious problem (e.g., "I a-a-am a st-st-stutterer"). Too often, the patient has already invested the psychiatrist with all kinds of real and fantasized powers. Prompt reassurance is called for. The psychiatrist should respond quickly, calmly, and matter-of-factly to the patient's initial 'confession' of disability and not try to prolong the telephone ordeal by asking for details. A meeting should be arranged as soon as possible, preferably within 24 hours, to offset the patient's initial dread of contact and his ambivalence regarding treatment. These patients hate themselves for speaking badly – a condition often equated with stupidity, helplessness, or even insanity. They avoid psychotherapy for this reason, plus the other fears that have arisen in speech situations at work, at school, or with friends.

Many adult stutterers are highly intelligent and gifted individuals who feel discouraged about the results of speech 'correction' in high school or college. These patients often have read widely about stuttering in the professional and lay literature. Many have developed some special techniques for dealing with their speech problem, including a style of speaking which is uniquely their own. It is essential for the psychiatrist to approach these efforts at self-healing and individuation with respect.

Diagnostic interviews

Disabled people regularly ask psychiatrists the following question: "Are you going to treat my disability (in this instance, speech problem) or my personality?" In my opinion there is only one way to answer this: "You cannot dichotomize – by treating one you also treat the other. Speech is a highly prized form of communication, but it is not the only one. Let's get better acquainted before we discuss treatment plans." The patient's response to this recommendation, his willingness to engage in further discussion, and his tolerance for the delay necessitated between the initial and later interviews, will often be of more diagnostic importance than any of the symptomatic manifestations revealed during the first consultation.

The stutterer's difficulty in verbal communication makes history-taking an ordeal. Both his speech tension and his desire to withhold embarrassing information may lead him away from topics which are of special interest to psychiatrists, such as interpersonal crises, marriage problems, 'unconscious' material, etc. Unless the psychiatrist indicates, in words and gestures, that he can tolerate circumstantiality and delay, the diagnostic interviews become nonproductive, to the patient's chagrin. He may try to drop hints suggestive of 'deeper' problems that have always been avoided in previous, more speech-centered, therapeutic encounters. When encouraged to do so, stutterers often reveal an uncanny awareness of somatic and psychic processes which are ordinarily held out of consciousness during speech. "My stuttering starts down here, in my guts", said one patient, pointing to his midabdominal region. Patients may mention appetite disorders, constipation, fatigability, sexual impotency, acne, and other manifestations of psychosomatic dyscontrol. Occasionally a communicative incompetency develops, to the extent that the patient blurts out material not usually revealed in initial interviews, e.g., homicidal or frankly sexual themes.

These early moments of self-revelation are used to plan an approach to treatment (Ostwald 1969a). The doctor asks himself: "Can I allow this patient to choose topics and themes for discussion, or should I be more directive in interviews?" His answer not only reflects diagnostic experience, but also indicates the level of personal tolerance for this patient's difficulties in communicating. Stuttering is a common symptom of children, and adults who stutter are displaying a form of 'infantile' behavior. Unless the psychiatrist is able to put up with a variety of primitive, preverbal expressions of affect – angry noisemaking, stubborn silences, magical thinking, pouting, and rage – he should encourage a symptom-reducing approach by referring the patient to a speech therapist. A good way to gauge diagnostic countertransference is by paying close attention to one's speech responses to the stuttering patient. Almost invariably the psychiatrist will find himself stuttering more often than he would with speech-fluent individuals. He must quickly try to understand which set of feelings and impulses toward the patient – frustration, impatience, uncertainty, overconcern, etc. – are being held in check.

Throughout the diagnostic period and while planning treatment, the psychiatrist is obligated to pay close attention to a number of typical problems that concern stutterers. First of all, there is the matter of scheduling interviews. The patient is in many ways a handicapped individual, for whom it is more difficult than for the normally speaking person to succeed in school and to obtain satisfactory employment. The psychiatrist should do nothing that might interfere with adjustments the patient has already managed to accomplish on his own or with a previous therapist's help. Interviews may have to be scheduled before or after working hours if the patient's vocational status is precarious or, as is often the case, he is not ready to discuss the matter of 'taking time off to see the doctor' with his employers or teachers. In avoiding a too noticeable break in daily routine, one spares the patient the additional pain of stigmatization as sick or deviant by fellow workers. Some patients stubbornly deny the severity of their disorder and do not seek help until told to do so by a boss or coworker. Scheduling interviews at times that are clearly inconvenient for the patient or his employer will simply add to the resistance.

Similarly, a realistic attitude must be taken toward money. If the patient cannot afford private care, he may be eligible for treatment in a mental health center or community clinic. Today many patients carry insurance policies or qualify for assistance through group programs at work. These plans usually require the patient himself to pay for part of the treatment. Since speaking is painful and psychotherapy requires speech, the patient is understandably reluctant to go to the additional trouble of 'putting out hard cash' in order to see a psychiatrist. In addition, this attitude reflects a long term conflict about money which – akin to the patient's speech itself – is alternately held back or squandered. If he can recognize that this ambivalence about maintenance and release of emotional controls is not his 'fault' but reflects earlier experiences in communicating with people, the patient may be able to develop a satisfactory treatment contract. On the other hand, when patients steadfastly regard themselves as either victims or villains, incapable of establishing good two-person relationships, further individual interviews should not be planned. These stutterers are better seen in groups, where the danger of a tense, rivalrous interaction with the doctor is lessened (Sadoff and Collins 1968).

The treatment

Whether a stutterer is seen in group or in individual psychotherapy, the psychiatrist will notice favorable responses to a number of treatment strategies. First of all, the patient appreciates a frank and realistic attitude to the matter of his speech handicap. Adult stutterers know from a long and painful series of past experiences that their symptoms are exceedingly noticeable whenever 'good speech' is a social requirement. It doesn't help matters to pretend that the patient speaks perfectly well. Nor will he feel good about a psychiatrist who repeatedly interrupts him by completing the blocked words or, worse yet, by making him write instead of talk. Without experience in the techniques of speech therapy and logopedics (Freund 1966; Luchsinger and Arnold 1965; Sloane and MacAulay 1968), psychiatrists should not try directly to influence the patient's fluency, articulation, or semantics. Rather, the emphasis has to be on reducing tension, improving morale, and lightening depressive affects and discouragement which burden the chronically handicapped person.

Psychotropic drugs, when indicated, will add immeasurably to the stutterer's sense of well-being, but they must be used with all the usual precautions in regard to toxicity, side effects, and addiction (Waskow 1966). In general, nonpsychotic stutterers respond well to drugs that have muscle-relaxing and mood-brightening effects. Phenothiazines sometimes produce a rapid worsening as extrapyramidal effects lessen the patient's control over his speech. Similarly, the use of psychotomimetics like marijuana and LSD can be extremely frightening to patients who stutter. Most will avoid these drugs like the plague. But occasionally one sees a speech-disturbed individual who claims to achieve a marvelous sense of freedom and fluency during a 'good trip'.

Crisis management is important in the treatment of stutterers. An emergency challenges entrenched patterns of reactivity and mobilizes untried defenses. Often it is during crisis – e.g., break-up of a love relationship, acute anxiety, fear of making a major decision – that the patient first seeks help. Insecure in his social behavior and handicapped in speaking, he fears the impending uncertainty of change. The psychotherapeutic relationship provides a continuous and dependable human contact, enabling realignments in affectionate ties to be made. Schizoid stutterers who lack companionship are treated to offset the transitory pain of a lonely depression. Compulsive stutterers can use therapy during an eruption of angry feelings that are too dangerous to express at home or in the work environment. Paranoid stutterers need therapy to combat the terror of slipping into a world of unacceptable fantasies.

Job problems are among the most important crises to be faced. Because of the chronic and often permanent speech handicap, there are certain vocations in which these patients cannot do well. While it is said that stutterers can become great orators, e.g., Demosthenes, Winston Churchill, these are obviously exceptions and not the rule. Stutterers are clearly most vulnerable in positions that require instantaneous and accurate verbal responsiveness, such as in a military headquarters, at the control of a telephone switchboard, or in running a sightseeing tour. Many patients will already have sought out a relatively comfortable vocational niche for themselves prior to consulting the psychiatrist. Others may have to be coaxed to seek and develop jobs where success is not bound up with exceptional speaking ability. The computer industry can presently absorb a large number of these patients, who may have unusual skills in mathematics, programming, and systems design. The psychiatrist should also encourage stutterers to seek avocational avenues for self-expression, e.g., writing, music, poetry, athletics, and art, which demand little speaking.

The intensive treatment of stuttering patients is best limited to periods of 2 or 3 months, during which serious problems in daily living, personal crises, and major emotional conflicts can be adequately aired. The patient usually needs at least this much time to discuss material which normal speakers can cover in 2 or 3 weeks. Persistent handicaps that cannot be influenced psychotherapeutically should be separated from remediable problems so that patient and therapist can use their energies realistically to gain fresh insights and to promote useful changes.

Specific psychotherapeutic tactics

Few stutterers are good candidates for long term psychoanalytic therapy, and in most instances the treatment is disappointing so far as the actual speech symptom is concerned (Glauber 1968). Not only are free-associative techniques extraordinarily taxing for stutterers, but these patients are likely to develop very highly charged transference reactions. There is a great deal of angry feeling when the psychiatrist is regarded as a pseudo-parent requesting fluent speech. Glauber interpreted this as a projection of the patient's own demand for continuity, a fundamental need, frustrated in infancy by his ambivalent "stuttering" mother (Glauber 1958).

While stutterers involved in psychotherapy for longer periods of time can usually bring out vivid screen memories and fantasies of Oedipal and pre-Oedipal traumatization, they tend to view these as the end point of psychological investigation rather than the beginning for more pains-taking work. On the basis of what he already knows about the patient's personal history, the psychiatrist can, at this point, direct attention to the way in which stuttering dramatizes the infantile emotional conflicts.

Careful observation of the speech-interrupting movements may enable patient and therapist to recognize elements of biting, swallowing, sucking, spitting, vomiting, licking, or gasping. Some patients respond very well if encouraged to make noises – to scream, rant, roar, or blather – which gives reality to their inhibited rage and dependency (Scott 1958). It is usually up to the psychiatrist to comment on these mock displays of sensuality and aggression, since the patient is unable to do so. One becomes the stutterer's 'mouthpiece', as it were, calmly designating these displays as appropriate to infancy but unnecessary in adult speech.

One of the most challenging aspects of the patient's care is knowing when to encourage greater activity outside of therapy and when to discourage it. Specific phobic avoidance maneuvers, such as not answering the telephone or refusing dinner invitations, have to be discussed in great detail. Concrete advice in terms of how to behave and how not to behave may have to be given, especially when a patient dares to brave some situation-specific fear for the first time. Analysis of the patient's progress since adolescence gives useful cues. For example, one stutterer abandons fire-setting, impulsive fighting, and a generally rowdy attitude at 16 to pursue a steady course of studies, achievement, and successful marriage. He can be expected to handle stress differently than a patient who at 35 still tortures animals and participates in masochistic sex orgies.

Heightened affectivity – euphoria, angriness, and abandonment of inhibitions – has a generally unchaining effect upon communication. Verbal output speeds up, becoming more dramatic and powerful not only among stutterers, but for normal speakers too. This gives the temporarily improved patient a sense of great relief. Occasionally he sees himself as 'cured', a judgment that may be shared by unsophisticated therapists. Psychiatric management should lay the groundwork for a more realistic self-appraisal, so that the patient does not become unduly upset when stuttering recurs under less favorable conditions. Dysfluency is as much a part of speech as stumbling is a part of walking. Any person who denies the possibility that these temporary upsets can happen either is forced to restrict his activity or cannot cope with the emergency when it arises.

In this respect it is often useful to treat stutterers in groups with speech-fluent persons. As the group members listen to each other, they learn that there is no such reality as perfect speech. One patient obscures a set of complicated problems behind a facade of verbal glibness; another candidly blurts out his private fears. Having had so much social difficulty, stutterers bring a catalytic accessibility to bear on the group. Their visual fantasies and held-back verbal ideas are already close to consciousness, whereas speech-fluent persons may have to be repeatedly interrupted and reminded to pay attention to themselves.

Whether he sees the patient in group or individual therapy, the psychiatrist has to be able to put up with the extraordinarily unpredictable pattern of stuttering behavior. On the one hand, he has to be extremely flexible, and quickly willing to change the topic of discussion, the level of analysis, or the pace of interaction as he notices the patient developing a disabling amount of tension. On the other hand, he must be firm and nonyielding in the face of a speech breakdown when it seems the patient is using his symptoms to avoid discussing troublesome topics. In this respect the psychiatrist's approach to the patient who stutters comes close to the way psychotic crises are managed psychotherapeutically in a hospital setting. To understand the stutterer's problem, one has to witness actual behavioral breakdowns instead of just listening to him describe fears or memories of breakdowns. The intense emotional reaction triggered off, or triggering off, a major episode of stuttering can happen quite suddenly. Brutten and Shoemaker (1967) have described the stutterer's painful uncertainty about when and how severely he will break down

With one leg shorter than the other, the individual *knows* he is going to limp. Even the phobic individual *knows* he will be afraid when the elevator door is closed. But with stuttering, even though patterns undoubtedly exist, they are more like cycles of complex wave forms than simple one-to-one relationships. Obviously, the sources of this difficulty are complex interactions of an unknown number of vaguely known factors.

A view to the future

Behind the riddle of stuttering lurks the question "How does the human brain transform mental elements into sequential language symbols?" Words we say are obviously not planned one at a time like beads strung on a chain. Rather, there is a deep structure of intended meaning which prefigures our spoken utterances (Chomsky 1967). Much of the planning about speech appears to go on during pauses, or silent intervals, that allow 'inner speech' to enter awareness.

A new approach to research in stuttering would consider this problem not as a 'speech disorder' but as a pause disorder (Goldman-Eisler 1968).

One would have to consider the phonetic and semantic manifestations as secondary to a deeper disturbance in the transformations between language competence and language performance. Such an approach seems entirely consistent with newer developments in behavior therapy emphasizing relaxation and selective introspection (Damsté et al. 1968). The stutterer learns, in effect, to preselect what he says without regard to earlier 'failures' in communication. He is urged to speak with a fuller awareness of his own body in the immediate social space. So long as there are no undesirable changes in total life adjustment, such techniques can be usefully incorporated into the psychiatric management of patients who stutter. Other useful methods, e.g., metronomes, masking noise, and delayed auditory feedback, are presently being investigated. They are based on the feedback model of stuttering (Sklar 1969), one of several dynamic concepts of speech behavior which hopefully will replace the old body-mind dualism.

Summary

This paper is about the practical clinical management of patients with severe and persistent speech fluency disturbances called stuttering. The fundamental causes of this symptomatic disorder are not known. There is evidence for constitutional and maturational factors, but little support for any specific epileptogenic or psychogenic etiology. The disorder is more frequent among males, and if it persists past adolescence patients may withdraw from social contacts or make undesirable personal adjustments requiring psychiatric attention.

Diagnostic evaluation sets the stage for a frank assessment of communicative skills and handicaps. Urgent crisis situations involving employment, marital difficulty, affective dyscontrol, and other transient maladjustments are handled as they come up. Symptom reduction often is best done by speech therapists. If psychotherapy is attempted, the focus should be on immediate breakdowns in behavior, similar to brief psychotic crises, in which infantile and preverbal processes are exposed. The primary goal of any therapy is to reduce the fear of stuttering. Group therapy helps with the stutterer's dependency, rigidity, and megalomanic defenses, especially in the sphere of speech behavior itself, which can never become 'perfect'. In this sense there is no 'cure' for stuttering, only a gradual shift in the direction of better rhythm, greater expressiveness, less redundancy, and calmer pausing in speech.

Conclusion: The Semiotic Process

HOW SOUNDS MAKE SENSE

(1971)

From the moment of birth, throughout a lifetime, and until death inter-
venes, the human organism is immersed in a sea of sounds. Some of these
sounds are picked up by the auditory receivers and used for self-orientation in space and time. Other sounds come in for a special form of information-processing, called linguistic, which also regulates the organization of speech. Still other sounds serve for the more direct communication
of moods, feelings and other aspects of human experience that are
relatively nonverbalizable.

MEANING is attributed to sounds – orienting, linguistic, or expressive –
only insofar as one recognizes a pattern and understands how this
pattern can be related to other aspects of human experience. Thus we
can say, for example that a person's hoarse voice 'means' that he has
cancer of the throat (this is diagnosis) or that the distant sound of
thunder 'means' that we better get prepared for some bad weather (this
is prognostication). If these imputations of meaningfulness turn out to
be correct (i.e., consensually validated) we say that they MAKE SENSE.
Indeed, the requirement that 'meanings should make sense' is basic to
any serious discussion of semiotic processes.

Throughout this book I have been saying various things about human
sounds, but the basic questions of meaning and of making sense have been
alluded to only tangentially, and even ignored altogether in those papers
that had to be edited to suit a particular format. Now in this concluding
article I want to pay particular attention to how sound makes sense. In
order to limit the topic I have selected that modality of sense-making
which is best dealt with in words, i.e., verbal behavior (speech and
language). It must not be assumed of course that this is the only way to
make sense. Mathematics, music, sculpting, engineering, pictorial rep-
resentations, cinema, architecture, pantomime – these are also meaningful

human activities. But an analysis of the semiotic processes involved would take us far afield, and indeed requires other approaches to semiotics than those discussed in the present volume.

The discussion will proceed by describing five essential functions – audition, cerebration, voice production, articulation, and socialization – without which it seems inconceivable that verbal-linguistic types of semiotic behavior as we know it could take place. Because each of these functions depends on specific physical structures (e.g., vocalization depends on the larynx; socialization depends on people), I have elected to delineate and describe these functions in terms of five systems – the receptor system, cortical system, phonatory system, oral system, and community system. It should be emphasized that semiotic processes are not the only functions that occupy these structural systems. For example, in addition to sense-making, the auditory system also is concerned with echo-location and orientation. In this respect each of the five systems discussed below are OPEN SYSTEMS (Von Bertalanffy 1968), with many simultaneous inputs, transformational activities, and outputs parallel to the semiotic processes.

Audition – The receptor system

The specialized processes of speech-sound perception which underlie verbal linguistic behavior depend ultimately on energy transferred from a moving source to a sensitive receiver. The medium for transmission is ordinarily air, containing gaseous, space-occupying particles. The energy of objects moving within this medium sets up waves of compression and decompression, travelling centrifugally at about 331.4 meters (1,087 feet) per second. Whatever stands in the way will be phasically subjected to pressure. If by virtue of its density, shape and flexibility an object responds with a to-and-fro vibration, ACOUSTICAL TRANSMISSION is said to take place between a source and a receiver of energy.

The receiving apparatus of the human ear has a conical drum stretched across the end of an inch-long auditory canal running from the ear pinna into the bone of the skull. This pressure-sensitive membrane responds to acoustical perturbations from various external sources by setting up a vibratory pattern of its own, which in turn is transmitted to three tiny bones fastened inside the ear. Thus what was originally a multidirectional movement of air-borne acoustical energy is now transformed into a linear flow of mechanical energy (Wever and Lawrence 1954). It must be pointed out that some autogenous influences are already at work during this pre-neurological stage of audition. Reverberations inside the auditory canal, the physical attributes of the drum itself, and vibratory events transmitted directly via the bones and tissue of the head all modify the incoming pressure waves. Of even greater importance for the personal shaping of input to the auditory system is the action of small striated middle-ear muscles. These muscles contract during general arousal when mesencephalic reticular substance is stimulated (Hugelin, et al. 1960) and during specific motor activities such as talking, swallowing, laughing, or moving the face and head (Salomon and Starr 1960). The net result of this feedback effect on middle-ear transmission is to dampen the excursion of the ear drum and bones, reducing the amplitude of inflowing acoustic vibrations.

At the oval window of the inner ear, mechanical vibrations from the ear bones are transmitted to a tapered, fluid-filled canal that lies coiled within the temporal bone. This COCHLEA is responsible for the most crucial step in auditory processing, viz., the transformation of mechanical-acoustic 'energy' into sensory-sonic 'information'. Each mechanical impulse at the oval window sets up a wave that travels the length of the cochlea, from its base to its apex. By means of a transducer mechanism of hair-cells and nerve fibers sandwiched between membranes stretched the length of the cochlear canal, vibratory events are converted to electrochemical processes in the cochlea nerve. This feat of acoustic-to-sonic energy transformation is accomplished in at least four phases. (1) The basilar membrane responds relatively more to weak than to strong impulses and performs a kind of frequency analysis on incoming vibrations. (2) A microphonic energy source intrinsic to the hair cells is modulated. (3) The electrochemical field between hair cells and their associated auditory nerve terminals undergoes some kind of modification. (4) A volley of signals goes towards the brainstem via afferent fibers of the auditory nerve.

Sonic barrages of the auditory nerve now undergo filtering and modulation at a number of way-stations along the auditory pathway. Each of these way-stations contains synaptic gates where certain signals can be held back while others are facilitated (Galin 1964). For example, some of the sonic information reaching the COCHLEAR NUCLEUS in one side of the brainstem crosses over to the auditory pathway of the opposite side. This enhances the binaural spatial location of energy sources in the acoustical environment such as people and loudspeakers. The precise tonal configuration of incoming sonic signal-events is also encoded in peripheral way-stations of the auditory systems (H. Davis 1961), assuring that frequency-cues upon which speech perception depends can be properly decoded when they reach the higher brain centers.

Sonic signals also reach the cerebellum for processing of information that is self-generated and proprioceptive. Self-protective reflexes – for example head and eye movements toward sound sources, generalized arousal, and the amplitude-reducing middle-ear muscle contractions mentioned earlier – are activated by the INFERIOR COLLICULI, another important bilateral way-station in the auditory system. Those sonic messages destined for cortical decoding of language must be further processed in the MEDIAL GENICULATE BODIES of the diencephalon. Here an important neuron linkage is made to the hypothalamus where emotional responses to sounds are evoked (Gellhorn and Loofbourrow 1963).

It is impossible, with the present state of knowledge in auditory physiology, to indicate precisely what the neural connections are between the receptor system and the higher brain areas that will be discussed in the next section as part of the cortical system. Investigators refer to the CORTICAL PROJECTIONS, thick fiber-tracts running bilaterally between the medial geniculate bodies of the brain-stem and the cortical brain areas (Neff 1961) which are predominantly concerned with processing auditory information. But it should be recognized that messages are transmitted in two directions between the cerebral cortex and the receptor system. Incoming (afferent) signals are screened and modulated before achieving conscious recognition. Presumably this is a cybernetic control which relies on the integrity of the neuronal apparatus for its transmission circuitry, and involves memory as part of the functional input (Desmedt 1960). Therefore at this level of the analysis of audition, one can no longer regard sounds as being merely sensations but has to regard them as perceptions. A great deal of information-processing has by now been accomplished, and the frequency components of the perceived sounds have already been analyzed to a very major extent. This allows the very specialized cortical activities of pattern-recognition and signal-interpretation to proceed (Uhr 1966). Also, as Green (1971) has recently emphasized, the sequential arrangement of sound has been accurately registered (temporal auditory acuity is about 1 to 2 milliseconds). We can now turn to the semiotic functions of the brain.

Cerebration – The cortical system

How the human brain may 'represent' an acoustical event after it has been processed by the receptor system is discussed at length in an excellent monograph by Whitfield (1967). He conceives of a group of ACTIVE

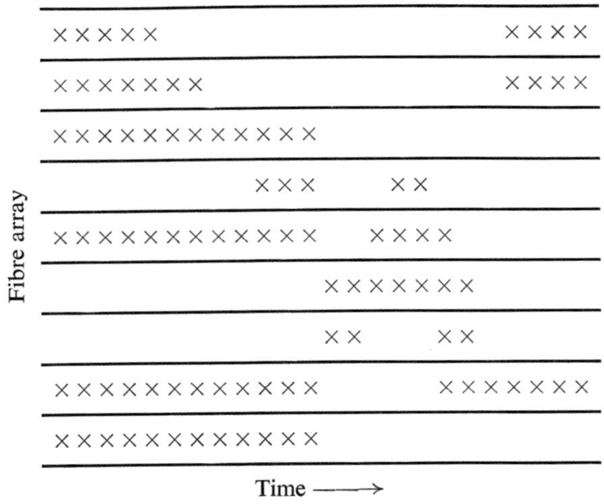

```
        ┌─────────────────────────────────────────────┐
        │ × × × × ×                        × × × ×      │
        ├─────────────────────────────────────────────┤
        │ × × × × × × ×                    × × × ×      │
        ├─────────────────────────────────────────────┤
        │ × × × × × × × × × × × ×                       │
        ├─────────────────────────────────────────────┤
   y    │            × × ×        × ×                   │
   a    ├─────────────────────────────────────────────┤
   r    │ × × × × × × × × × × × ×      × × × ×          │
   r    ├─────────────────────────────────────────────┤
   a    │                    × × × × × × ×             │
        ├─────────────────────────────────────────────┤
  e     │              × ×          × ×                │
  r     ├─────────────────────────────────────────────┤
  b     │ × × × × × × × × × × × ×      × × × × × × ×    │
  i     ├─────────────────────────────────────────────┤
  F     │ × × × × × × × × × × × × ×                     │
        └─────────────────────────────────────────────┘
                        Time ──────→
```

Fig. 1.

FIBRES in a total fibre array. In the course of time, different groups of fibres become active as the frequency structure of the signal changes. For example, using the symbol ' × ' to denote activity of a fibre, Figure 1 shows how blocks of active fibres might indicate the various frequency components of an incoming sound, while the width of each block (i.e., the number of active fibres) represents its intensity component. The arrangement of frequency-intensity patterning can change over time, as illustrated. This schematization of an auditory input is especially illuminating if we compare it with the output of a spectrograph machine that physically converts sounds into visible patterns.

Playback of these visible patterns reconverted into sounds has made it possible for investigators to demonstrate which of several different possible sensations a particular sound is responsible for (Liberman et al. 1967). Bands of continuous acoustical energy running horizontally across the spectrogram produce the sensation commonly identified as vowel-like. By changing the position of these energy-bands on the frequency scale one causes the listener to respond with various vowel sensations. (Later we shall see that these bands or 'formants' correspond directly to the steady-state vibratory activities of the vocal cords as amplified in speech. Acoustic cues for consonants are more complex; they reflect not only the type of muscle activity involved but also the place where speech is articulated.) Since consonants break up the vocalic flow of sound, they can serve as indicators simultaneously of the end of one speech segment and the beginning of the next. In other words, speech sound coming via the auditory system presents the brain with two kinds of information at the same time: (1) phonemes which are directly represented, or enciphered in sound (e.g., vowels and fricative consonants, especially in slow speech); and (2) phonemes that are indirectly referred to or 'encoded' in sound (e.g., most of the consonants).

Simultaneous transmission of two kinds of auditory information about language – one enciphered and the other encoded – is an important guarantee of perceptual efficiency. Since language is always heard against a background of other sounds, the auditory system alone cannot efficiently separate signal from noise. The feat of SIGNAL-DETECTION (Green, 1960) appears to be a specialized function of cortical organization, which cybernetically controls the flow of neuronal information across the gates and way-stations of the auditory system as mentioned in the preceding section. Inhibition of speech-irrelevant noises appears to be one of the physiological mechanisms involved, but it should not be assumed that this mechanism is limited only to the auditory perception of speech (Von Bekesy 1969). Knowledge of the social context in which linguistic behavior is expected to occur, visual awareness of a speaker and his mouth movements, and interest in finding out what is to be said – all of these contribute to the language experience. Accordingly, there has to be a DECODING FUNCTION linked specifically to the auditory perception of speech. The language decoder, when functioning properly under the auspices of memory, reimposes a segmental structure upon the auditory perceptions. The peculiarly rapid and undifferentiated sound we hear when listening to an unknown foreign language exemplifies speech perceptions which have not yet undergone this critical process of cortical decoding.

One of the most astonishing phenomena clearly to be observed at the level of language decoding is called CATEGORICAL PERCEPTION (Liberman, et al., 1967). Encoded phonemes are no longer distinguishable or perceivable on the basis of discrete differences in their acoustic-cue structure. Instead what happens is that recognition proceeds by way of quantal jumps from one category of speech sound to another, based on foreknowledge of what the expected phonetic patterns ought to be. This phenomenon is found at other levels of cognitive awareness as well. It reflects a characteristically human way of adaptation, by which one incorporates only certain portions of the environment and learns to get around without attending to all of the rest. Categorical perception saves us the trouble of having endlessly to make decisions on the basis of infinitesimal and unpredictable variations in the stimulus input. We devise 'plans' – not necessarily consciously – that allow a finite number of tests to be made on the available environmental resources (Miller et al. 1960). Once we 'jump to a conclusion' so to speak, it is possible to go to the next perceptual task.

I have alluded several times to MEMORY without explaining that there must be a long-term as well as a short-term memory store available for categorical perception. Long-term storage is stable, in the sense that prior information is more or less permanently available against which new information can be checked. When syllables are perceived, these have to be checked for phonetic structure. This takes a certain amount of time. Words arrive sequentially from the receptors, and there has to be a way for this information to be momentarily held up until further decoding and deciphering is no longer necessary (Peters 1969). Short-term memory does precisely that, and we try to exercise a degree of control over what gets admitted to short-term memory by focussing our attention on a particular kind of input.

It seems entirely possible that short-term or 'temporary' storage units are necessary at each level of speech perception – the phonetic, the syntactic, and the semantic (Norman 1969). Some of this briefly stored information has to be immediately discarded, so that new speech sequences can undergo processing. Occasionally a chunk of information lingers on, can be recalled for a while, and then only gradually 'fades away'. Then again there are items which seem to excite the long-term memory structures, which regularly pick this information up and hold on to it. This permanently stored data remains available for future retrieval, which can be done unconsciously – as when in a dream we hear a speech repeated – or consciously – as when we try to remember what somebody said.

This brings us then to the topic of CORTICAL SPECIALIZATION for language, which has long been one of the most hotly debated issues in regard to the activities of the brain. There is evidence that each of the two hemispheres of the brain conducts specialized semiotic functions in a somewhat independent fashion (Zangwill 1964). Verbal-intellectual processes tend to predominate on one side, in the so-called 'dominant' hemisphere, usually the left. The more non-verbal aspects of conscious thinking appear to be transacted in the opposite, or so-called 'non-dominant' hemisphere, usually the right, where schematization, interpretation of spatial relationships, and the appreciation of continuities and melodies are among the special functions (Kimura 1964).

Luria (1966) has described the dual nature of linguistic cerebration. On the one hand, segmental discontinuities of the incoming speech sound have to be integrated into 'simultaneities', while on the other hand, the brain has to manage a multitude of signals arriving at the same time, organizing these into time sequences of "successive" elements. A specialized part of the premotor cortex called Broca's area translates brain-encoded language information into a form capable of activating the voice-speech apparatus. To accomplish this, restructuring of information again takes place, in an opposite direction to that of auditory perception. Since intelligible speech can be produced at rates as high as 15 phonemes per second, there must be a kind of PARALLEL DISTRIBUTION of neuro-motor commands to the various output structures, i.e., larynx, throat, palate, tongue and lips. The Haskins model of speech production (Liberman et al. 1967) assumes that at least four conversions are efficiently made in an overlapping fashion between cortically engrammed phonemes and externally articulated speech sounds. These are represented by arrows in the following diagram:

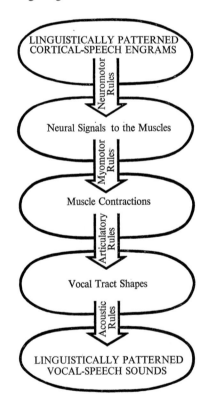

Voice production – The phonatory system

For more precise elucidation of the mechanisms involved in emitting patterned sound, we must next turn our attention to respiration. Vocalizations useful for social communication tend to be produced principally during expiration, requiring that the regular in-and-out breath rhythm be radically modified. Speech lowers the rate of breathing and reduces the inspiration/expiration time ratio to about one-quarter of the resting values, while it brings the tidal volume up 300 to 400 percent (Lenneberg 1967). Cohen (1970) has presented evidence for two possible brainstem control devices located in subsystems of the medullary RESPIRATORY CENTER. (1) An upper-pontine "pneumotaxic mechanism" inhibits inspiration. (2) A lower-pontine "apneustic mechanism" facilitates inspiration. During speech the first would have to be periodically activated, while the second is inhibited.

This generally dampening influence upon the Hering-Breuer reflex mechanism is most likely a cortical function. While only a limited number of loci in the motor and premotor cortex are known to activate respiratory movements, large portions of the medial and inferior brain surface known as the LIMBIC SYSTEM can inhibit breathing. (Here we can observe an example of how drastically the energetics of human behavior are affected by semiotic processes. As Plum (1970) has pointed out, breathing is the only autonomic function regulated entirely by skeletal muscle. Speech, which molds breathing in accordance with the dictates of linguistic intelligence, is therefore in many respects the finest instrument for harnessing the human emotions.)

The main power source for voice production comes from expiratory contraction of the chest cage and its contents. Diaphragmatic elevation exerts a major piston-like pressure from below, while the intercostal muscles push the thorax down and inwards from both sides. Air contained in the lungs is funneled into one central narrow pipe, the trachea. The resulting pressure builds up steadily, forcing bilaterally occluding vocal folds of the LARYNX to open up the passageway. As soon as sufficient air pressure has been released, the spring-like laryngeal valve closes again, and the process repeats itself. So long as there is a sustained expiratory push against the myoelastic larynx, vocal cords will vibrate at a steady rate, called the fundamental frequency of the voice. This is essentially the periodicity of air-puffs travelling away from the throat in all directions. Passive resonance of adjacent tissues and body structures will impart to the fundamental tone a series of overtones. In addition, the laryngeal muscles under cortico-bulbar control can give the voice a certain amount of oomph and coloration known as register (Van den Berg 1964).

Laryngeal vibration coupled to subglottal (chest) and supraglottal (head) resonance results in a complex acoustical wave form which carries, among other information, a precise analogue statement about the individuality of the soundmaker. One's unique VOICE QUALITY at any moment reflects the stable features of body size, the transient features of phonation, and the language-specific features of articulation which will be discussed shortly. Since the size and relative shapes of the body resonators change only gradually during the course of physical growth, it is possible with a certain degree of precision to identify individuals on the basis of their voice qualities. Gender is one dimension, for example, that often can be determined from vocal cues, since there are usually clear-cut physical differences between range, register, and timbre of male and female voices (Luchsinger and Arnold 1965).

Relatively low frequencies of the acoustical spectrum carry the personalized wave-forms which Trojan (1952) called "sound pictures" or ACTUEMES of the speaker. The effects of anger, excitement, depression, dishonesty, disgust and emotional expressiveness in general have all been detected within the first thousand-cycle band (Mahl 1964). This specialized vocal channel for broadcasting social signals is continually monitored and regulated by auditory-proprioceptive feedback. Whenever language is spoken, one hears and feels vocal aspects of self internally, as an unremitting flow of largely redundant information. Externally perceived voices of other people pass by in sharp contrast to this relatively stable and largely unconscious percept of one's own voice (Holzman and Rousey 1966). In the course of language acquisition and whenever speech is used for communication, the individual fashions his own voice into an instrument for social action, whereas his direct influence on the voices of others is negligible.

Voice is also instrumental in broadcasting many of the PROSODIC PARAMETERS which indicate the speech community an individual belongs to. Intonational cues are produced by directing the laryngeal fundamental tone upwards and downwards along the acoustic spectrum, or keeping it relatively uninflected at a steady monotone. Rhythmic phrasing, pausing, and other aspects of temporal order are controlled by a combination of respiratory and articulatory maneuvers (Peterson and Shoup 1966). Emphasis is placed on certain syllables, words and phrases by increasing the intensity of the voice and usually at the same time raising its pitch. Whether a vocal inflection or voice quality is phonemic rather than affective depends ultimately on the acoustical contrasts which are used by the particular community under consideration (Crystal 1970). Many languages in Asia, for example, use intonation cues to differentiate the semantic referents of words. Voice-quality too is used phonemically in some languages and affectively in others. For example, a form of glottalization that American listeners might describe as nonphonemic roughness or 'rasp' contributes to the differentiation among three vowels in the Vietnamese language (Jones and Thong 1957).

Articulation – The oral system

Phonated pulmonary air passes through the head, where it is expired via two apertures, the nose and the mouth. Each of these openings can be sealed independently, the nose by raising the soft palate and the mouth by closing the lips. When both valves are open the voice has a singing quality, enriched by resonance of the nasal turbinates and dentofacial sinuses (Kreshover 1970). There is a quasi-continuous acoustical output of FORMANTS which are the natural resonances of the vocal tract. Closing the velo-pharyngeal passageway to the nose denasalizes this output by changing the intensity and width of the formants.

Formants are easily visualized in wide-band sound spectrograms of speech, as dark structures running horizontally on the frequency spectrum. Three to four formants are typically seen within the 0-4000 Herz band, which is where most vocal resonance energy is located. The positioning of formants along the frequency spectrum and their placement relative to each other varies with the size of the mouth cavity, changed by contracting the tongue, peri-oral and mandibular muscles. For example, pursing the lips to articulate the word *who* results in a mouth cavity which casts formants at 300 Hz, 900 Hz, and 2500 Hz. By contrast, when the mouth is held in a more slit-like position to say *he*, formants appear at 300 Hz, 2500 Hz, and 3100 Hz. Some variability in distribution of formant positions among different speakers results from the fact that each person has a distinctive voice and articulates speech in his own way. Nevertheless, there is an obvious clustering of the formant frequencies in certain band-widths. The first formant (F_1) characteristically lies within the 200-1200 Hz band, the second formant (F_2) between 700 and 3500 Hz, and the third formant (F_3) between 1500 and 4000 Hz. This is due to the fact that all people normally have similarly constructed articulation equipment, with quite similar resonance properties. The other reason for the clustering of formant positions is allegiance to the rules of phonology, compelling speakers to articulate sounds in ways which promote phoneme perception. Unless a speaker moves his articulatory musculature into certain positions at certain moments, his formants will provide insufficient acoustical information for the transmission of language.

Whenever the articulation system is completely closed so that air cannot escape from the vocal tract, pulmonary expiration causes pressure to build up. Upon being released, there is a sudden aspiratory whoosh of air which plays an important role in indicating certain consonantal phonemes. For example, words like *pipe*, *toot* and *kick* depend very critically on briefly interrupting and restarting the vocal air-flow. In the case of *pipe* this segmenting activity is provided by closure of the lips, to form bilabial STOP CONSONANTS. For the word *toot*, stoppage of the vocal air-flow is accomplished by pushing the tip of the tongue against the upper gums. To say *kick* you must stop the air-flow by lifting the back of the tongue up against the hard palate. Obviously none of these articulatory maneuvers will have the proper air-stopping effect unless the nasal outflow is also blocked, by simultaneous closure of the velo-pharyngeal flap.

By forcing the vocal air stream across a persistent barrier, one produces another kind of phonemic sound effect, turbulence, which results in wide-band noises called FRICATIVES. For example, to articulate the word *fife* you must blow air though the narrow slit produced by holding the upper teeth against the lower lip. The word *soothe* depends on two fricative consonants, the first made by hissing when the upper and lower incisors are brought together, and the second when the tip of the tongue is pushed against the front teeth.

If the vocal resonances are now combined with the different interruptions and impedances of airflow, it is possible to produce various additional sounds that are phonemically distinctive (Flanagan 1965). The phoneme /l/ is indicated by allowing air to flow out of the sides of the mouth while touching the front of the maxilla with the tongue. The phoneme /m/ is indicated by closing the lips and letting vocalized air flow out through the nose only. DIPHTHONGS, GLIDES, AFFRICATIVES, and other sounds which depend on a combination of several articulatory maneuvers are especially impressive examples of the highly integrated neuromuscular skill of speech. Phoneticians are able to specify with considerable accuracy the place in the oropharyngeal cavity where sounds are articulated, the manner whereby the articulation is done, and the acoustical structure of the resulting sound (Fairbanks 1959).

Electromyography and other special techniques of study are necessary to elucidate the exact temporal order of muscular events within the oral apparatus (Ladefoged 1964). Cineradiography during speech shows the integrated patterns of articulatory motion in extraordinary detail. The crucial role of the massive tongue musculature within the mouth, the valving effect of the soft palate, and the interrelationships between jaw-motion, swallowing, and respiration become particularly impressive when viewed by X-ray. Most striking is the dynamic flow of coordinated events, many of which are invisible during ordinary conversation and thus come to consciousness only imperfectly through introspection. Especially when speech is rapid, the idealized oral positions described in articulatory-phonetics diagrams are not fully achieved, and some positions may even be totally skipped without making the acoustic output lose intelligibility. Single articulatory movements often merely hint at a particular feature for phoneme recognition. If discriminative cues are omitted entirely there usually is sufficient redundancy in the speaker's signal-output for the listener to figure out which words have been said. Thus at the motor output side of language behavior one observes the same probabilistics of information processing that pertain in the auditory receptor system (Pierce 1961). People are speakers and listeners simultaneously. Their experience with language as an instrumentality for acoustic symbolization protects against the loss of information whenever articulatory cues are incompletely perceived. Visual contact is an additional aid for linguistic communication. Intelligibility of speech improves when the listener can watch the speaker's lip movements and facial expressions.

Socialization – The community system

We have so far been concerned with the individual and the networks linking his ear, brain, and vocal-oral apparatus. Now we will focus on those aspects of semiotics that are generally considered to be part of socialization. The community provides not only opportunities for various patterns of semiotic behavior – chit-chats, debates, diatribes, sermons, etc. – it also regulates the intensity and variability of interpersonal expressiveness by way of the language-codes made available to its members. Any identifiable pattern of interpersonal conduct which employs language can be seen to represent a selected part of the verbal repertoire characterizing the collective habits of a SPEECH COMMUNITY. Such communities range in size from small clans to large nations. Geography has been one of the traditional factors in controlling their language. But throughout history, wars, invasions, commerce, migrations and other interpenetrations have occured between geographically isolated speech communities. In the twentieth century one sees the additional influence of mass media – recordings, films, and television – which bring about contact between speech communities and induce language change (Bright 1966).

While all members of a speech community are said to share at least one language, in reality different varieties of language coexist within any social system. No two people speak exactly alike, not even identical twins, and the uniquely personal use of language by an individual is called his IDIOLECT. When someone is exposed to a number of different speech communities in his lifetime, his idiolect may encompass additional varieties of language called DIALECTS. How language is used reflects a speaker's personal history, where he has lived and at what age, how he was educated, and with what groups he has been affiliated. Gumperz (1966) has distinguished the VERNACULAR as that variety of language used by all native-born speakers of a particular community. When it is written down, taught in schools, and formalized through dictionaries, grammar books, and rules of 'good' verbal manners, this variety comes to be known as the STANDARD LANGUAGE of a community. Such languages may of course go out of fashion or become historical artifacts, in which case they are said to belong to the more CLASSICAL varieties. Sometimes two speech communities interact in such ways as to produce a hybrid compromise of their languages. The resulting variety of speech is called PIDGIN LANGUAGE so long as its use is restricted to limited social functions, like commerce, administration or tourism. When all members of a community habitually use a pidgin language in their entire range of social functions it is called a CREOLE (Hymes 1968). Many societies also have languages of special status. These are used by only a segment of the population, for religious ceremonies or on formal occasions, and have to be specially taught at home or in private schools.

Every variety of language can undergo modification, in the direction of greater elaborateness and complexity, or towards simplification and uniformity (Fishman 1971). The crucial variable in this process of language change is TIME, since only a new crop of children can become native-born speakers of a community. But in addition there are various SOCIAL CONDITIONS which affect linguistic conformity or diversification, for example, poverty, lack of formal education, and malnutrition which reduces peoples' biological capacity for learning. On the other hand, employment puts people into new social roles, and industrialization exposes them to technological forms of communication. Thus one finds many overlapping varieties of language even within a single superficially homogeneous speech community. In the school room, on the playground, at church, in a hospital, at the supermarket, etc., distinctive styles of talk and behavior are observed. The speaker goes from one style of speech to another, depending on whether he is engaged in business, study, politics, love-making, partying or other customary social activities.

Obviously not all members of a speech community have equal opportunities to engage in code-switching. For example, a teen-ager from a Spanish speaking neighborhood, who goes to a racially integrated school, works weekends in a suburban supermarket, dates a Korean-American girl, and lives with a Jewish grandmother has much greater exposure to conflicting semiotic experiences than does a busy housewife who rarely goes out. The extent to which individuals become fully conversant with varieties of language depends very much on the 'Pygmalion' effect. When an intelligent and aggressive person is hurt by linguistic stigmatization, he may wish to adopt language varieties used by the more advantaged social groups. But his desire to continue to function comfortably among his own kinfolk can cause him to retain some competency with their forms of speech as well (Ferguson 1959). Some members of a speech community have a social and occupational role that demands an especially high degree of multilingual versatility. Actors, translators, language teachers, tourist guides, and psychotherapists belong to this subclass of the speech community (Bernstein 1969).

Summary

Of all the sounds that people hear and make, certain ones are selected and patterned in accordance with a basic human interest in 'making sense'. The foregoing discussion was designed to focus on five requirements for linguistic activity – (1) auditory perceiving of human sounds, (2) cortical processing of coded information, (3) voice production, (4) speech articulation, and (5) social exposure to languages.

I have divided these activities rather arbitrarily into the work of five 'systems', each of which might serve as a guide for future research. Once a field of semiotics has been 'approached' in this way, it remains for the individual reader to explore a given subject-area further, if this interests him or might lead to fruitful new investigations.

While I am aware that every approach to semiotics also entails some 'avoidances', it has been my hope to indicate, between the covers of this book, a sufficiently comprehensive approach, which could be pursued with enjoyment and confidence in the meaningfulness of human sounds.

BIBLIOGRAPHY

Abraham, K.
1942   *Selected Papers* (London: Hogarth Press).
Abse, D. W.
1959   "Hysteria", in: *American Handbook of Psychiatry*, S. Arieti (ed.), Vol. 1: 272-92 (New York).
Ackerknecht, E. H.
1955   *A Short History of Medicine* (New York: The Ronald Press Company).
Aldrich, C. A., C. Knop, and C. Sung
1945   "The Crying of Newly Born Babies: The Early Period at Home", *J. Pediat.* 27: 428-35.
Allen, D. W. and M. Houston
1959   "The Management of Hysteroid Acting-Out Patients in a Training Clinic", *Psychiatry* 22: 41-49.
Alvin, J.
1960   "Responses of Mentally Retarded Children to Music", in: *Music Therapy 1960*, E. Schneider (ed.) (Kansas: NAMT, Lawrence).
American Psychiatric Association
1968   *Diagnostic and Statistical Manual of Mental Disorders* (DSM II) (Washington, D.C.).
Andrews, G. C.
1947   *Diseases of the Skin* (Philadelphia).
Applebaum, R. M.
1968   "Infant Vocalization While Breast Feeding, and the Mother-Child Relationship", *La Leche League News* 10: 26-27.
Argelander, A.
1927   *Das Farbenhören und der synaesthetische Faktor in der Wahrnehmung* (Jena: Fischer).
Babbit, M.
1960   "The Revolution in Sound: Electronic Music", *University Princeton Magazine* 4: 4-8.
Barbara, D. A.
1954   *Stuttering: A Psychodynamic Approach to its Understanding and Treatment* (New York: Julian Press).
1958   *The Art of Listening* (Springfield: Thomas).
Bar-Hillel, Y.
1964   *Language and Information, Selected Essays on their Theory and Application* (Palo Alto: Addison-Wesley).

384

Barzun, J.
1956 *Berlioz and His Century* (New York: Noonday).
Bayley, N.
1932 *A Study of the Crying of Infants During Mental and Physical Tests, Pedagolog. Sem. and J. Genet. Psychol.* 40: 306-29.
1966 "The Two-Year Old: Is This a Critical Age for Development?" (Durham, North Carolina: Durham Education Improvement Program).
Bedichek, R.
1960 *The Sense of Smell* (New York).
Beech, H. R.
1959 "An Experimental Investigation of Sexual Symbolism in Anorexia Nervosa Employing a Subliminal Stimulation Technique", *Psychosom. Med.*, 21: 277-80.
Beech, H. R. and F. Francella
1968 *Research and Experiment in Stuttering* (Oxford: Pergamon Press).
Bell, F. R.
1960 "Why Cats Purr", *The Listener*, February, 4.
Bellak, L.
1952 *Manic-Depressive Psychosis and Allied Conditions* (New York).
Bellugi, U. and R. Brown
1964 *The Acquisition of Language* (= *Monograph No. 92 of the Society for Research in Child Development*).
Bender, L.
1938 *A Visual Motor Gestalt Test and its Clinical Use* (New York).
Beranek, L. L.
1954 *Acoustics* (New York: McGraw-Hill).
Berlyne, D. E.
1965 *Structure and Direction in Thinking* (New York: Wiley).
Bernstein, B.
1969 "Social Class, Speech Systems, and Psychotherapy", in: *Mental Health of the Poor*, F. Riessman, J. Cohen, and A. Pearl (eds.): 194-204 (Glencoe: The Free Press).
Bevan, W.
1955 "Sound-Precipitated Convulsions: 1947-1954", *Psychol. Bull.* 52: 473.
Birdwhistell, R. L.
1961 "Paralanguage – 25 Years after Sapir", in: *Lectures on Experimental Psychiatry*, H. Brosin (ed.) (Pittsburgh).
Bishop, J. P.
1956 "Auscultation before Laennec", *Tubercle* XXXVII: 213-15.
Black, J. W.
1951 "The Effect of Delayed Side-Tone Upon Vocal Rate and Intensity", *J. Speech and Hear. Dis.* 16: 56-60.
Bleuler, E.
1913 "Zur Theorie der Sekundärempfindungen", *Z. Psychol. Physiol. Sinnesorg.* 65: 1-39.
Bleuler, E. and K. Lehmann
1881 *Zwangmässige Lichtempfindungen durch Schall, und verwandte Erscheinungen auf dem Gebiete der anderen Sinnesempfindungen* (Leipzig: Fues's Verlag).
Bloomfield, L.
1933 *Language* (New York: Holt).
Boatman, M. J. and S. A. Szurek
1960 "A Clinical Study of Childhood Schizophrenia", in: *The Etiology of Schizophrenia* D. Jackson (ed.): 389-440 (New York).

Borland, L.
  n.d. Unpublished Study of Audio-Analgesia.
Bosma, J. F. and C. C. Smith
  1961 "Infant Cry: A Preliminary Study", *Logos* 4: 10-18.
Bosma, J. F., H. M. Truby and J. Lind
  1965 "Cry Motions of the Newborn Infant", *Acta Paediat. Scand.*, Suppl. 163: 61.
Bouliere, F.
  1954 *The Natural History of Mammals* (New York: Knopf).
Brain, R.
  1961 *Speech Disorders – Aphasia, and Agnosia* (Washington: Butterwords).
Bright, W. (ed.)
  1966 *Sociolinguistics* (The Hague: Mouton).
Broadbent, D. E.
  1957 "Effects of Noise on Behavior", in C. M. Harris (1957).
Brodbeck, A. J. and O. C. Irwin
  1946 "The Speech Behavior of Infants Without Families", *Child Develop.* 17: 145-46.
Brody, S.
  1956 *Patterns of Mothering* (New York: International Universities Press).
Brown, R.
  1958 *Words and Things* (Glencoe, Ill.: The Free Press).
Bruch, H.
  1961 "Conceptual Confusion in Eating Disorders", *J. Nerv. and Ment. Dis.* 133: 46-54.
Brunner-Orne, H.
  1958 "Englische Handglocken und ihre Verwendung in der psychiatrischen Klinik", In: *Musik in der Medizin*, H. R. Teirich (ed.): 98-103 (Stuttgart: Fischer).
Brutten, E. and D. Shoemaker
  1967 *The Modification of Stuttering* (New Jersey: Prentice-Hall).
Buehler, K.
  1934 *Die Sprachtheorie* (Jena: Fischer Verlag).
Bullowa, M., L. G. Jones, and A. R. Duckert
  1964 "The Acquisition of a Word", *Language and Speech* 7: 107-11.
Burris-Meyer, H. and V. Mallory
  1960 "Psycho-acoustics, Applied and Misapplied", *Journal of the Acoustical Society of America* 32: 1568-74.
Busnel, R. G., A. Moles, and M. Gilbert
  1962 "Un Cas de Langue Sifflée Utilisée dans les Pyrénées Françaises", *Logos* 5: 76-91.
Busnel, R. G., A. Moles, and B. Vallancien
  1962 "Sur l'Aspect Phonétique d'Une Langue Sifflée des Pyrénées Françaises", in: *Proceedings of the Fourth International Congress of Phonetic Sciences*, Helsinki, 1961 (The Hague: Mouton).
Cable, M.
  1959 "The Grand Seraglio", *Horizon* 1: 56.
Callaway, E.
  1966 "Averaged Evoked Response in Psychiatry", *J. Nerv. and Ment. Dis.* 143: 80-94.
Cameron, D. E.
  1956 "Psychic Driving", *Am. J. Psychiat.* 112: 502-09.
Cameron, J., N. Livson, and N. Bayley
  1967 "Infant Vocalizations and their Relationship to Mature Intelligence", *Science* 157: 331-33.

Caroll, J. B.
1955 *The Study of Language – A Survey of Linguistics and Related Disciplines in America* (Cambridge: Harvard University Press).

Chase, R. A., S. Sutton, and D. First
1959 "Bibliography: Delayed Auditory Feedback", *J. Speech and Hear. Res.* 2: 193-200.

Chase, R. A. et al.
1967 *Annual Report*. Neurocommunications Laboratory, Department of Psychiatry and Behavioral Sciences, The John Hopkins University School of Medicine, (Baltimore, Md.).

Chomsky, N.
1965 *Aspects of the Theory of Syntax* (Cambridge, Mass.: MIT Press).
1967 "The Formal Nature of Language", in: Lenneberg (1967): 397-442.

Chun, R. W. M., R. Pawsat, and F. M. Forster
1960 "Sound Localization in Infancy", *J. Nerv. and Ment. Dis.* 130: 472-76.

Classe, A.
1957 "The Whistled Language of La Gomera", *Scientific American* 196: 111.

Clynes, M.
1969 "Toward a Theory of Man: Precision of Essentic Form in Living Communication", in: *Information Processing in the Nervous System*, N. Leibovic and J. C. Eccles (eds.): 177-206 (New York: Springer).

Cohen, M. I.
1970 "How Respiratory Rhythm Originates: Evidence for Discharge Patterns of Brainstem Respiratory Neurones", in: *Breathing: Hering-Breuer Centenary Symposium*, R. Porter (ed.): 125-57 (London: Churchill).

Cooke, D.
1959 *The Language of Music* (London: Oxford University Press).

Cooper, L.
1970 "Empathy: A Developmental Model", *Journal of Nervous and Mental Disease* 151: 169-178.

Coriat, I.
1913a "Case of Synesthesia", *J. Abnorm. Psychol.* 8: 37-43.
1913b "Unusual Type of Synesthesia", *J. Abnorm. Psychol.* 8: 109-112.

Corso, J. F.
1959 "Age and Sex Differences in Pure Tone Thresholds", *Journal of the Acoustical Society of America* 31: 498.

Crosby, E.
1964 "Anatomical Considerations", in: *Research Potentials in Voice Physiology*, D. W. Brewer (ed.): 43-46 (New York: University Publishers).

Crystal, D.
1969 "Non-segmental Phonology in First-Language Acquisition", paper read at the *Second International Congress of Applied Linguistics* (Cambridge, England).
—1970 "Paralinguistics", to appear in: *Current Trends in Linguistics*, T. A. Sebeok (ed.), vol. 12: *Linguistics and Adjacent Arts and Sciences* (The Hague: Mouton).

Damsté, P., E. Zwaan, and T. Schoenaker
1968 "Learning Principles Applied to the Stuttering Problem", *Folia Phoniat.* 20: 327-41.

Darwin, C.
1955 *The Expression of the Emotions in Man and Animals* (New York: Philosophical Library).

David, E. E. Jr. and O. G. Selfridge
1962 "Eyes and Ears for Computers", *IRE Bulletin*, Jan. 8.

Davis, H.
  1961 "Peripheral Coding of Auditory Information", in: *Sensory Communication*, W. A. Rosenblith (ed.): 119-41 (Cambridge: MIT Press).
Davis, H. and S. H. Silverman
  1960 *Hearing and Deafness* (New York: Holt and Rinehart).
Delay, J., H.-P. Gerard, and P.-C. Racamier
  1951 "Les Synesthesies dans l'intoxication mescalinique", *Encephale* 40: 1-10.
Denes, P. B.
  1966 "The Elusive Process of Speech", *Bell Laboratories Record*: 255-59.
Desmedt, J. E.
  1960 "Neurophysiological Mechanisms Controlling Acoustic Input", in: *Neural Mechanisms of the Auditory and Vestibular Systems*, G. L. Rasmussen and W. F. Windel (eds.): 152-64 (Springfield: Thomas).
Deutsch, F.
  1952 "Analytic Posturology", *Psychoan. Quart.* 21: 196-214.
Dey, F. L.
  1970 "Auditory Fatigue and Predicted Permanent Hearing Defects from Rock-and-Roll Music", *New England Journal of Medicine* 282: 467-70.
Diehl, C. F.
  1958 *A Compendium of Research and Theory on Stuttering* (Springfield: Thomas).
Diethelm, O.
  1955 *Treatment in Psychiatry*[3] (Springfield, Ill.).
Diserens, C. M.
  1926 *The Influence of Music on Behaviour* (Princeton).
Dixon, N. F.
  1956 "Symbolic Associations Following Subliminal Stimulation", *Int. J. Psychoan.* 37: 159-70.
Djourno, A. and C. Eyries
  1957 "Prosthese auditive par excitation électrique à distance du nerf sensoriel à l'aide bien bobinage inclus à demeure", *Presse Medicale* 65: 1417.
Douthwaite, A. H. (ed.)
  1954 *French's Index of Differential Diagnosis*[7] (Baltimore: Williams and Wilkins).
Dunbar, F.
  1954 *Emotions and Bodily Changes*[4] (New York).
Egger, V.
  1904 *La Parole Intérieure* (Paris: Alean).
Ehrenzweig, A.
  1953 *The Psychoanalysis of Artistic Vision and Hearing* (New York: Julian Press).
Eimas, P. D., E. R. Siqueland, P. Jusczyk, and J. Vigorito
  1971 "Speech Perception in Infants", *Science* 171: 303-06.
Einstein, A.
  1938 *A Short History of Music* (New York: Knopf).
  1941 *Greatness in Music* (New York: Oxford Univ. Press).
Eisenson, J. (ed.)
  1958 *Stuttering – A Symposium* (New York: Harper).
  1966 "Developmental Patterns of Non-Verbal Children and Some Therapeutic Implications", *J. Neurol. Sci.* 3: 313-20.
Eldred, S. H. and D. B. Price
  1958 "A Linguistic Evaluation of Feeling States in Psychotherapy", *Psychiatry* 21: 115-21.
Engel, B. J. and S. P. Hansen
  1966 "Operant Conditioning of Heart Rate Slowing", *Journal of Neurophysiology* 3: 176-87.

Erikson, E. H.
  1959   "The Nature of Clinical Evidence", in *Evidence and Inference*, D. Levner
          (ed.): 73-95 (Glencoe, Ill.).
Fairbanks, G.
  1942   "An Acoustical Study of the Pitch of Infant Hunger Wails", *Child Develop.*
          13: 227-32.
  1959   *Voice and Articulation Drillbook* (New York: Harper and Row).
Farnsworth, P. R.
  1958   *The Social Psychology of Music* (New York: Dryden Press).
Feldman, S. S.
  1949   "Mannerisms of Speech" in: *Yearbook of Psychoanalysis* 5: 61-71.
  1959   *Mannerisms of Speech and Gestures in Everyday Life* (New York: International
          University Press).
Feldstein, S., C. Rogalski, and J. Jaffe
  1966   "Predictability and Disruption of Spontaneous Speech", *Language and
          Speech* 9: 137.
Fenichel, O.
  1945   *The Psychoanalytic Theory of Neurosis* (New York: Norton).
Ferenczi, S.
  1950a "Psychogenic Anomalies of Voice Production", in: *Further Contributions
          to the Theory and Technique of Psychoanalysis*: 105-09 (London: Hogarth
          Press).
  1950b "Embarassed Hands", in: *Further Contributions to the Theory and Practice
          of Psychoanalysis:* 315-316 (London).
Ferguson, C. A.
  1959   "Diglossia", *Word* 15: 325-40.
Fischer, C.
  1954   "Dreams and Perception", *J. Am. Psychoan. Assoc.* 2: 389-455.
Fischer, C. et al.
  1960   *Preconscious Stimulation in Dreams, Associations, and Images* (= *Psycho-
          logical Issues* 3) (New York: International Universities Press).
Fisher, S. and S. E. Cleveland
  1958   *Body Image and Personality* (Princeton).
Fishman, J. A.
  1971   *Sociolinguistics – A Brief Introduction* (Massachusetts: Newbury House).
Fisichelli, V. R. and S. Karelitz
  1963   "The Cry Latencies of Normal Infants and those with Brain Damage",
          J. Pediat. 62: 724-34.
Fisichelli, V. R., A. Haber, J. Davis, and S. Karelitz
  1966   "Audible Characteristics of the Cries of Normal Infants and those with
          Down's Syndrome", *Perceptual and Motor Skills* 23: 744-46.
Flanagan, P.
  1965   *Speech Analysis, Synthesis and Perception* (New York: Academic Press).
Flatau, T. S. and H. Gutzmann
  1906   "Die Stimme des Säuglings", *Arch. für Laryng. und Rhinol.* 18: 139-51.
Fleischer, O.
  1895   *Neumen-Studien* (Leipzig).
Fletcher, H.
  1953   *Speech and Hearing in Communication* (New York: Van Nostrand).
Flügel, J.
  1950   *The Psychology of Clothes* (London).
Fodor, J. A. and J. J. Katz (eds.)
  1964   *The Structure of Language – Readings in the Philosophy of Language* (New

Jersey: Prentice-Hall).

Foerster, H. (ed.)

1952 *Cybernetics, Transactions of the Eighth Conference, March 15-16, 1951* (Josiah Macy, Jr. Foundation).

Frank, J. D.

1961 *Persuasion and Healing* (Baltimore).

Frazer, J. G.

1959 *The New Golden Bough*, T. H. Gaster (ed.) (New York: Criterion Books).

Freedman, D. G.

1961 "The Differentiation of Identical and Fraternal Infant Twins on the Basis of Filmed Behavior", Second Int. Conf. Human Genetics, Rome.

Freud, S.

1891 *On Aphasia – A Critical Study* (Republished in English, New York: International Universities Press).

1925a "From the History of an Infantile Neurosis", in: *Collected Papers*, translated by A. and J. Strachey (London: Hogarth Press).

1925b "Mourning and Melancholia", in: *Collected Papers*, translated by A. and J. Strachey, Vol. 4: 152-70 (London: Hogarth Press).

1935 *Psychopathology of Everyday Life* (London: Benn). Also in: *The Complete Psychological Works of Sigmund Freud*, Vol. 6 (London, 1960).

1954 *The Interpretation of Dreams* (London: Allen and Unwin).

Freund, H.

1966 *Psychopathology and the Problem of Stuttering* (Springfield, Ill.: Thomas).

Friedman, S. M.

1960 "One Aspect of the Structure of Music", *J. Am. Psychoan. Assoc.* 8: 427-49.

Fry, D. B.

1955 "The Experimental Study of Speech", in: *Studies in Communication*: 147-167 (London: Martin Secker and Warburg).

1966 "The Development of the Phonological System in the Normal and the Deaf Child", in: *The Genesis of Language*, F. Smith and G. A. Miller (eds.): 187-206 (Cambridge, Mass.: MIT Press).

Furth, H.

1969 *Piaget and Knowledge* (New Jersey: Prentice-Hall).

Galambos, R.

1954 "Neural Mechanism of Audition", *Physiol. Review* 34: 497-528.

1956 "Suppression of Auditory Nerve Activity by Stimulation of Efferent Fibres to Cochlea", *J. Neurophysiol.* 19: 424-37.

Galin, D.

1964 "Effects of Conditioning on Auditory Signals", in: *Neurological Aspects of Auditory and Vestibular Disorders*, W. S. Fields and B. R. Alford (eds.): 61-76 (Springfield: Thomas).

Galton, F.

1883 *Inquiries into the Human Faculty* (London: Macmillan).

Gardiner, A.

1950 *Egyptian Grammar* (New York: Oxford University Press).

Gardiner, W.

1838 *The Music of Nature* (Boston: Wilkins and Carter).

Gardner, W. J. and J. C. R. Licklider

1959 "Auditory Analgesia in Dental Operations", *J. Am. Dent. Assn.* 59: 1144-49.

1960 "Suppression of Pain by Sound", *Science* 132: 32-33.

Gedda, L., A. Bianchi, and L. Bianchi-Neroni

1955 "La voce dei gemelli", *Acta Genet. Med. Roma* 4: 121-29.

Gedda, L., Fiori-Ratti, L., and G. Bruno

1960 "La voix chez les jumeaux monozygotiques", *Folia Phoniat.* 12: 81-94.
Gellhorn, E. and G. N. Loofbourrow
  1963 *Emotions and Emotional Disorders – A Neurophysiological Study* (New York: Harper and Row).
Geschwind, N.
  1970 "The Organization of Language and the Brain", *Science* 170: 940-44.
Gibson, E. J.
  1967 *Principles of Perceptual Learning and Development* (New York: Appleton-Century-Crofts).
Glauber, P.
  1958 "The Psychoanalysis of Stuttering", in: *Stuttering – A Symposium*, J. Eisenson (ed.): 71-120 (New York: Harper).
  1968 "Dysautomatization: A Disorder of the Preconscious Ego Functioning", *Int. J. Psychoanal.* 49: 89-99.
Goldfarb, W., P. Braunstein and I. Lorge
  1956 "A Study of Speech Patterns in a Group of Schizophrenic Children", *Am. J. Orthopsychiat.* 26: 544-55.
Goldiamond, I.
  1965 "Stuttering and Fluency as Manipulatable Operant Response Classes", in: *Research in Behavior Modification*, L. Grasner and L. Ullman (eds.) (New York: Holt, Rinehart, Winston).
Goldman-Eisler, F.
  1958 "Speech Analysis and Mental Processes", *Language and Speech* 1: 59-75.
  1964 "Discussion and Comments", in: *New Directions in the Study of Language*, E. Lenneberg (ed.) (Cambridge, Mass.: MIT Press).
  1968 *Psycholinguistics – Experiments in Spontaneous Speech* (New York: Academic Press).
Goldstein, K.
  1948 *Language and Language Disturbance* (New York: Grune and Stratton).
Goldstone, S.
  1962 "Psychophysics, Reality, and Hallucinations", in: West (1962).
Gould, L.
  1948 "Verbal Hallucinations and Activity of Vocal Musculature", *Am. J. Psychiat.* 105: 367.
Green, D. M.
  1960 "Psychoacoustics and Detection Theory", *Journal of the Acoustical Society of America* 32: 1189-1203. Also in: *Signal Detection and Recognition by Human Observers*, J. A. Swets (ed.): 58-94 (New York: Wiley, 1964).
  1971 "Temporal Auditory Acuity", *Psychol. Rev.* 78: 540-51.
Greenacre, P.
  1952a *Trauma, Growth and Personality* (New York: Norton).
  1952b "The Predisposition to Anxiety", in: Greenacre (1952a): 27-32.
  1952c "Pathological Weeping", in Greenacre (1952a): 120-31
Greenberg, J. H.
  1953 "Historical Linguistics and Unwritten Languages", in: *Anthropology Today*, A. Kroeber (ed.): 265-86 (Chicago: University of Chicago Press).
  1963 *Universals of Language* (Cambridge, Mass.: MIT).
Greene, W. A. Jr.
  1958 "Early Object Relations: Somatic, Affective, and Personal", *J. Nerv. Ment. Dis.* 126: 225-53.
Greenson, R. R.
  1954 "About the Sound *MM* . . .", *Psychoanal. Quart.* 23: 234-39.
  1967 *The Technique and Practice of Psychoanalysis*, V. I (New York: International

Universities Press).

Greenspoon, J.
1955 "The Reinforcing Effect of Two Spoken Sounds on the Frequency of Two Responses", *Amer. J. Psychol.* 68: 409-16.

Griffin, D. R.
1958 *Listening in the Dark – The Acoustic Orientation of Bats and Men* (New Haven: Yale University Press).

Grinker, R. R., P. C. Bucy, and A. L. Sahs
1960 *Neurology* (Springfield, Ill.).

Grinstein, A.
1972 *The Index of Psychoanalytic Writings*, 11 vols. (New York).

Grotjahn, M.
1957 *Beyond Laughter* (New York).

Grove's Dictionary of Music and Musicians
1954 E. Blom (ed.), 1: 1078 (London: McMillan).

Gruenberg, E. M., et al.
1968 *Diagnostic and Statistical Manual of Mental Disorders* (Washington, D.C.: American Psychiatric Association).

Grünewald, G.
1957 "Zur Schreib- und Sprech-Motorik der Konstitutionstypen", *Z. Psychother. Med. Psychol.* 7: 165-176.

Gumperz, J. J.
1966 "On the Ethnology of Linguistic Change", in: Bright (1966): 27-49.

Gutheil, E. A.
1951 "The Musicians – A New Group of Psychotherapists", *American Journal of Psychotherapy* V: 495-501.

Halle, M.
1959 "Questions of Linguistics", *Nuovo Cimento*, Supp. 2. 13: 494-517.

Harlow, H. F. and M. K. Harlow
1962 "Social Deprivation in Monkeys", *Scientific American* 207: 136-46

Harris, C. M. (ed.)
1957 *Handbook of Noise Control* (New York: McGraw-Hill).

Harris, H.
1962 *An Analysis of Singer's Formants and Their Relationship to Vowel Formants* (M. A. Thesis, Stanford University).

Helmholtz, H.
1885 *On the Sensations of Tone as a Physiological Basis for the Theory of Music* (New York: Dover, 1954).

Hess, E. H.
1959 "Imprinting", *Science* 130: 133-41.

Hiller, L. A. Jr.
1959 "Computer Music", *Scientific American*, December: 109-20.

Hilson, D.
1957 "Malformation of Ears as Sign of Malformation of Genito-Urinary Tract", *Brit. Med. J.* 2: 785-89.

Hippocrates
1950 *Medical Works*, translated by J. Chadwick and W. N. Mann (Springfield, Ill.: Thomas).

Hockett, C. F.
1958 *A Course in Modern Linguistics* (New York: The Macmillan Company).
1960 "The Origin of Speech", *Scientific American*, September: 89-96.

Hodeir, A.
1961 *Since Debussy: A View of Contemporary Music* (New York: Grove).

Hodgson, W.
1951 "Absolute Tempo: Its Existence, Extent, and Possible Explanation", *Mus. Teach. Nat. Assoc. Proc.* 43: 158-69.
Hoerman, H.
1971 *Psycholinguistics – An Introduction to Research and Theory*, translated from the German by H. H. Stern (New York: Springer).
Hollander, R.
1960 "Compulsive Cursing", *Psychiat. Quart.* 34: 599-622.
Holmes, T. H.
1950 *The Nose* (Springfield, Ill.)
Holzman, P. S. and C. Rousey
1966 "The Voice as a Percept", *J. Personality and Social Psychol.* 4: 79-86.
Holzman, P. S., C. Rousey, and C. Snyder
1966 "On Listening to One's Own Voice: Effects of Psychophysiological Responses and Free Associations", *Journal of Personal and Social Psychology* 4: 432-41.
Horowitz, M. J.
1970 *Psychosocial Function in Epilepsy; Rehabilitation after Surgical Treatment for Temporal Lobe Epilepsy* (Springfield, Ill.: Thomas).
Hubel, D. H., C. O. Henson, A. Rupert, and R. Galambos
1959 "'Attention' Units in the Auditory Cortex", *Science* 129: 1279-80.
Hug-Hellmuth, H.
1912 "Über Farbenhören: Ein Versuch das Phaenomen auf Grund der psycho-analytischen Methode zu erklären", *Imago* 1: 228-64.
Hugelin, A., S. Dumont, and N. Paillas
1960 "Tympanic Muscles and Control of Auditory Input During Arousal", *Science* 131: 1371-72.
Hurxtal, L. M. and N. Musulin
1953 *Clinical Endocrinology*, 2 vols. (Philadelphia).
Huysmans, J. K.
1885 *A Rebours* (Paris). Available in translation as *Against Nature* (Penguin).
Hymes, D.
1968 "Pidginization and Creolization of Languages: Their Social Contexts", *Social Science Research Council Items* 22: 13-18.
Illingworth, R. S.
1955 "Crying in Infants and Children", *Brit. Med. J.* 1: 75-78.
Innes, J. R.
1935 *Flash Spotters and Sound Rangers: How They Lived, Worked and Fought in the Great War* (London).
Irwin, O. C.
1947 "Infant Speech: Consonant Sounds According to Manner of Articulation", *J. Speech Disorders* 12: 397-401.
1948 "Infant Speech: Development of Vowel Sounds", *J. Speech Dis.* 13: 31-34.
Isakower, O.
1939 "On the Exceptional Position of the Auditory Sphere", *Int. J. Psychoanal.* 20: 340-48.
Jackson, J. H.
1958 *Selected Writings*, Vol. 1 (New York: Basic Books)
Jackson, L.
1958 "Non-Speaking Children: Seven Years Later", *Brit. J. Med. Psychol.* 31: 92–103.
Jaffe, J.
1958 "Language of the Dyad", *Psychiatry* 21: 249-58.
Jakobson, R., C. G. M. Fant, and M. Halle

1952   *Preliminaries to Speech Analysis – The Distinctive Features and Their Correlates* (Cambridge, Mass.: MIT).
Jakobson, R. and M. Halle
1956   *Fundamentals of Language* (The Hague: Mouton).
Jarcho, S.
1961   "Auenbrugger, Laennec, and John Keats – Some Notes on the Early History of Percussion and Auscultation", *Medical History* V: 167-72.
Jaspers, K.
1963   *General Psychopathology*[7], translated from the 7th German edition by J. Hoenig and M. W. Hamilton (Manchester: Manchester University Press).
Jones, E.
1951   *Essays in Applied Psychoanalysis* (London: Hogarth).
1951a "The Madonna's Conception through the Ear", in: Jones (1951).
Jones, R. B. Jr. and H. S. Thong
1957   *Introduction to Spoken Vietnamese* (New York: American Council of Learned Societies).
Jung, C. G.
1910   "The Association Method" in: *Psychology and Pedagogy* 1: 39-89 (Worcester, Mass.: Clark U.).
Kagan, J.
1968   "Continuity and Change in the First Year of Life", paper given at the 76th Annual Convention, Amer. Psychol. Assoc. San Francisco.
Kanner, L.
1957   *Child Psychiatry* (Springfield: Thomas).
Karelitz, S.
1960   *Infant Vocalizations*, part I: "The Infant Cry from Birth to Two Years of Age" (Phonograph Record Cl 2669 A).
Karelitz, S. and V. R. Fisichelli
1962   "The Cry Thresholds of Normal Infants and Those with Brain Damage", *J. Pediat.* 61: 679-85.
Karelitz, S., V. R. Fisichelli, J. Costa, R. Karelitz, and L. Rosenfeld
1964   "Relation of Crying Activity in Early Infancy to Speech and Intellectual Development at Age Three Years", *Child Develop.* 35: 769-77.
Karelitz, S., R. Karelitz, and L. S. Rosenfeld
1960   "Infants' Vocalizations and their Significance", in: *Mental Retardation – Proceedings of the First International Medical Conference, Bowman and Mautner* (ed.) (New York: Grune and Stratton).
Kevram, R.
1960   *Laennec – His Life and Times* (Oxford: Pergamom Press).
Kierkegaard, S.
1959   *Either/Or*, Vol. 1 (New York: Doubleday).
Kimura, D.
1964   "Left-Right Differences in the Perception of Melodies", *Quart. J. Exper. Psychol.* 16: 355-58.
King, L.
1967   "What is a Diagnosis?", *Journal of the American Medical Association* 202.8: 714-17.
Kinsky, G.
1930   *A History of Music in Pictures* (New York: Dutton).
Knapp, P. H.
1953   "The Ear, Listening and Hearing", *J. Am. Psychoanal. Assn.* 1: 672-89. Also in: *Yearbook of Psychoanalysis* 10: 177-92 (1954).
1956   "Sensory Impressions in Dreams", *Psychoan. Quart.* 25: 325-47.

Knapp, P. H. and S. J. Nemetz
1957 "Sources of Tension in Bronchial Asthma", *Psychosom. Med.* 19: 466-86.
Kohut, H.
1957 "Observations on the Psychological Functions of Music", *J. Amer. Psychol. Assoc.* 5: 389-407.
Kopp, G. A. and H. G. Kopp
1964 "An Investigation to Evaluate the Usefulness of the Visible Speech Cathode-Ray Tube Translator as a Supplement to the Oral Method of Teaching Speech to Deaf and Severely Deafened Children", VRA RD-526, A Final Report, *Wayne State Univ. Speech and Hearing Clinic* (Detroit, Michigan).
Kramer, E.
1964 "Personality Stereotypes in Voice: A Reconsideration of the Data", *Journal of Social Psychology* 62: 247-51.
Krapf, E. E.
1955 "The Choice of Language in Polyglot Psychoanalysis", *Psychoan. Quart.* 24: 343.
Kreshover, S. J.
1970 *Speech and the Dentofacial Complex: The State of the Art* (= *ASHA Report* 5) (Washington: American Speech and Hearing Association).
Kretschmer, E.
1925 *Physique and Character* (New York).
Kris, E.
1952a Psychoanalytic Explorations in Art (New York: International Univ. Press).
1952b "Laughter as an Expressive Process", in: Kris (1952a): 217-39.
Kryter, K. D.
1950 "The Effects of Noise on Man", *J. Speech and Hear. Dis.*, Monograph Supp. 1.
Kubie, L. S.
1958 "Some Theoretical Concepts Underlying the Relationship Between Individual and Group Therapies", *Int. J. Group Psychother.* 8: 3.
1961 "The Eagle and the Ostrich", *Arch. Gen. Psychiatry* 5: 109-19.
1965 "The Struggle Between Preconscious Insights and Psychonoxious Rewards in Psychotherapy", *Am. J. Psychother.* 19: 367.
Kubie, L. S. and S. G. Margolin
1944 "An Apparatus for the Use of Breath Sounds as an Hypnogogic Stimulus", *Am. J. Psychiat.* 100: 610.
Kucera, O.
1959 "On Teething", *J. Am. Psychoan. A.* 7: 284-91.
Kurtz, J. H.
1961 Tape-Recording of the Sounds of an Infant During the First 24 Hours of Life, *Langley Porter Neuropsychiatric Institute*.
Lacey, J. I.
1959 "Psychophysiological Approaches to the Evaluation of Psychotherapeutic Progress and Outcome", in: *Research in Psychotherapy*, E. A. Rubinstein and M. B. Parloff (eds.): 160-208 (Washington D.C.).
Ladefoged, P. (ed.)
1964 *Working Papers in Phonetics* (Los Angeles: University of California).
Laffal, J.
1965 *Pathological and Normal Language* (New York: Atherton).
Lane, H.
1966 "A Survey of the Acoustic and Discriminative Properties of Speech Sounds", *Center for Research on Language and Language Behavior* (Ann Arbor, Michigan: University of Michigan).
Langer, S. K.

1942 *Philosophy in a New Key* (New York: Mentor Books).

Lanyon, W. E. and W. N. Tavolga
1960 *Animal Sounds and Communication* (American Institute of Biological Science).

Lashley, K. S.
1951 "The Problem of Serial Order", in: *Cerebral Mechanisms in Behavior*, L. A. Jeffres (ed.) (New York: Wiley).

Lasswell, H.
1930 *Psychopathology and Politics* (Chicago).

Lear, J.
1959 "Music-Loving Spiders", *The New Scientist*, June.

Le Baron, G. I.
1962 "Ideomotor Signalling in Brief Psychotherapy", *Am. J. Clin. Hypnosis* 5: 81.

Lehiste, I.
1965 *Acoustic Characteristics of Dysarthric Speech* (New York: S. Karger).

Lehiste, I., R. S. Tikovsky, and R. P. Tikovsky
1961 "An Acoustic Description of Dysarthric Speech", *Journal of the Acoustical Society of America* 33: 1677.

Lenneberg, E. H.
1966 "The Natural History of Language", in: *The Genesis of Language*, F. Smith and G. A. Miller (eds.): 219-52 (Cambridge, Mass.: MIT Press).
1967 *Biological Foundations of Language* (New York: Wiley and Sons).

Lenneberg, E. H., F. G. Rebelsky, and I. A. Nichols
1965 "The Vocalizations of Infants Born to Deaf and Hearing Parents", *Vita Humana* 8, 23-37.

Levine, E. S.
1960 *The Psychology of Deafness* (New York: Columbia Univ. Press).

Levy, E. Z., G. E. Ruff, and V. H. Thaler
1959 "Studies in Human Isolation", *J. of Am. Med. Assn.* 169: 236-239.

Levy, K.
1958 "Silence in the Analytic Session", *Internat. J. Psycho-Anal.* 39: 50–58.

Lewin, B. D.
1946 "Sleep, the Mouth, and the Dream Screen", *Psychoan. Quart.* 15: 419-35.

Lewis, M. M.
1936 *Infant Speech – A Study of the Beginnings of Language* (New York: Harcourt Brace).

Liberman, A. M.
1957 "Some Results of Research on Speech Perception", *Journal of the Acoustical Society of America* 29: 117-23.
1970 "Some Characterics of Perception in the Speech Mode", in: *Perception and its Disorders*, D. A. Hamburg, K. H. Pribram, and A. J. Stunkard (eds.): 238-54 (Baltimore: Williams and Wilkins).

Liberman, A. M., F. S. Cooper, K. S. Harris, and P. F. MacNeilage
1962 "A Motor Theory of Speech Perception", in: *Proceedings of the Speech Communication Seminar* (Stockholm: Royal Institute of Technology).

Liberman, A. M., F. S. Cooper, D. P. Shankweiler, and M. Studdert-Kennedy
1967 "Perception and Speech Code", *Psychol. Rev.* 74: 431-61.

Licklider, J. C. R.
1959 "Three Auditory Theories", in: *Psychology: A Study of a Science*, vol. 1, S. Koch (ed.): 41-144 (New York: McGraw-Hill).

Licklider, J. C. R. and G. A. Miller
1951 "The Perception of Speech" in: *Handbook of Experimental Psychology*, Stevens (ed.): 1040-74 (New York: Wiley).

Lieberman, P.

1967 *Intonation, Perception, and Language* (Cambridge, Mass.: MIT Press).
Lilly, J. C.
1958 "Some Considerations Regarding Basic Mechanisms of Positive and Negative Types of Motivations", *Amer. J. Psychiat.* 115: 498-504.
Lind, J. A. (ed.)
1965 Newborn Infant Cry (=*Acta Paediatrica Scandinavia*, supplement 163) (Uppsala: Almquist and Wiksell).
Lind, J., O. Wasz-Höckert, V. Vuorenkoski, and E. Valanne
1965 "The Vocalization of a Newborn, Brain-Damaged Child", *Ann. Paediat. Fenn.* 11: 32-37.
Lind, J., O. Wasz-Höckert, V. Vuorenkoski, T. J. Partanen, K. Theorell, and E. Valanne
1966 "Vocal Response to Painful Stimuli in Newborn and Young Infant", *Ann. Paediat. Fenn.* 12: 55-63.
Lindsley, O. R.
1963 "Direct Measurement and Functional Definition of Vocal Hallucinatory Symptoms", *J. Nerv. Ment. Dis.* 136: 293.
Lorenz, K.
1952 *King Solomon's Ring* (New York).
Lowinsky, E. E.
1954 "Music in the Culture of the Renaissance", *J. Hist. Ideas* 15: 509-533.
Luchsinger, R.
1940 "Die Sprache und Stimme von ein- und zweieiigen Zwillingen in Beziehung zur Motorik und zum Erbcharakter", *Arch. Klaus-Stift. Vererb. Forsch.* 15: 461-527.
1961 "Die Sprachentwicklung von ein- und zweieiigen Zwillingen und die Vererbung von Sprachstörungen in den ersten drei Lebensjahren", *Folia Phoniat.* 13: 66-67.
Luchsinger, R. and G. E. Arnold
1959 *Lehrbuch der Stimm- und Sprachheilkunde*² (Wien).
1965 *Voice-Speech-Language, Clinical Communicology: Its Physiology and Pathology* (Belmont, California: Wadsworth).
Luchsinger, V. R., C. Dubois, F. Vassella, E. Joss, R. Gloor, and U. Wiesman
1967 "Spektralanalyse des Miauens bei Cri-du-Chat-Syndrom", *Folia phoniat.* 19: 27-33.
Luria, A. R.
1958 "Brain Disorders and Language Analysis", *Language and Speech* 1: 14-34.
1961 *The Role of Speech in the Regulation of Normal and Abnormal Behavior* (New York: Pergamom Press).
1966 *Human Brain and Psychological Processes*, translated by B. Haigh (New York: Harper and Row).
Lynch, J. J. and D. A. Paskewitz
1971 "On the Mechanism of the Feedback Control of Human Brain Wave Activity", *Journal of Nervous and Mental Diseases* 153: 205-17.
Lynip, A. W.
1951 "The Use of Magnetic Devices in the Collection and Analysis of the Preverbal Utterances of an Infant", *Genet. Psychol. Monogr.* 44: 221-62.
MacLean, P. D.
1949 "Psychosomatic Disease and the Visceral Brain", *Psychosom. Med.* 11: 338-53.
MacNeilage, P. F. and G. N. Sholes
1964 "An Electromyographic Study of the Tongue During Vowel Production", *J. of Speech and Hearing Research* 7: 209-32.
Mahl, G. F.

1956 "Disturbances and Silences in the Patient's Speech in Psychotherapy", *J. Abnorm. Soc. Psychol.* 53: 1-15.

1960 "Sensory Factors in the Control of Expressive Behavior", in *Proceedings of the 16th International Congress of Psychology* (Bonn, Germany).

1964 "Some Observations About Research on Vocal Behavior", in: *Disorders of Communication*, D. McK. Rioch and E. A. Weinstein (eds.): 466-83 (Baltimore: Williams and Wilkins Co.).

Mahl, G. F. and G. Schultze
1964 "Psychological Research in the Extra-Linguistic Area", in: Sebeok et al. (1964).

Mahler, M. and P. Elkisch
1953 "Some Observations on Disturbances of Ego – Case of Infantile Psychosis", *Psychoanal. Study Child* 8: 252-61.

Mahling, F.
1926 "Das Problem der *Audition Colorée*", *Arch. Ges. Psychol.* 57: 165-302.

Marler, P.
1967 "Animal Communication Signals", *Science* 157: 769-74.

Maurois, A.
1958 Quoted by R. Rodman, "Hush", *New York Times*, April, 6.

McAdam, D. W. and H. A. Whitaker
1971 "Language Production: Electroencephalographic Localization in the Normal Human Brain", *Science* 172: 499-502.

McCarthy, D.
1946 "Language Development in Children", in: *Manual of Child Psychology*, L. Carmichael (ed.): 492-630 (New York: Wiley).

1952 "Organismic Interpretation of Infant Vocalizations", *Child Develop.* 23: 272.

McDowell, F. (ed.)
1960 *Handbook of Neurologic Diagnostic Methods* (Baltimore).

McKellar, P.
1957 *Imagination and Thinking – A Psychological Analysis* (London: Cohen and West).

McKusick, V. A. and H. K. Wiskind
1959 "Felix Savart, Physician-Physicist", *Journal of Historical Medicine* 14: 411-23.

McLuhan, M.
1964 *Understanding Media: The Extension of Man* (New York: McGraw-Hill).

McNeill, D.
1966 "Developmental Psycholinguistics", in: The Genesis of Language, F. Smith and G. Miller (eds.) (Cambridge, Mass.: MIT Press).

1970 *The Acquisition of Language – The Study of Developmental Linguistics* (New York: Harper and Row).

McQuown, N. A.
1957 "Linguistic Transcription and Specification of Psychiatric Interview Materials", *Psychiatry* 20: 79-86.

Meares, A.
1960 *Shapes of Sanity* (Springfield, Ill.).

Meerloo, J. A. M.
1959 "Psychoanalysis as an Experiment in Communication", *Psychoanal. and Psychoanal. Review* 46: 2-16.

1961 "Rhythm in Babies and Adults", *Arch. Gen. Psychiatry* 5: 169-75.

Mehta, V.
1971 "John is Easy to Please", *New Yorker Magazine*, May, 8: 44-87.

Menninger, K.

1957   "Psychological Factors in the Choice of Medicine as a Profession, Part 2",
       Bull. Menninger Clin. 21: 96-106.
1963   *The Vital Balance: The Life Process in Mental Health and Illness* (New York:
       Viking Press).
Menninger-Lerchenthal, E.
1953   "Auenbrugger als Psychiater", *Wien Med. Wschr.* 103: 970-71.
Merrill, B. R.
1952   "Childhood Attitudes toward Flatulence and Their Possible Relation to
       Adult Character", in: *Yearbook of Psychoanalysis* 8: 213-24.
Meyer, L. B.
1957   *Emotion and Meaning in Music* (Chicago: Univ. Chicago Press).
Miller, G. A.
1967   *The Psychology of Communication* (New York: Basic Books).
Miller, G. A., E. Galanter, and K. H. Pribram
1960   *Plans and the Structure of Behavior* (New York: Holt, Rinehart and Winston).
Millet, J.
1892   *Audition Colorée* (Montpellier).
Milner, M.
1956   "The Communication of Primary Sensual Experience (The Yell of Joy)",
       Internat. J. Psycho-Analysis 37: 278-81.
Milner, B., C. Branch, and T. Rasmussen
1965   "Observations on Cerebral Dominance", in: *Disorders of Language: A
       CIBA Foundation*, A.V.S. DeReuck and M. O. O'Connor (eds.): 200-14
       (London: Churchill).
Mindel, E. D. and McC. Vernon
1971   *They Grow in Silence* (Silver Spring, Maryland: National Association of the
       Deaf).
Mitscherlich, M.
1961   "Psychologie und Therapie des Torticollis Spasticus", in: *Proceedings of
       the 3rd World Congress of Psychiatry* (Montreal).
Moravek, M. and J. Langova
1962   "Some Electrophysiological Findings Among Stutterers and Clutterers",
       Folia Phoniat. 14: 305-16.
Moser, H. M. et al.
1958   *Hand Signals: Finger-Spelling* (= Technical Note No. 49, Contract No.
       AF 19[604]-1577) (Air Force Cambridge Research Center).
Moses, P.
1954   *The Voice of Neurosis* (New York: Grune and Stratton).
Mysak, E. D.
1966   *Speech Pathology and Feedback Theory* (Springfield, Ill.: Thomas).
Neff, W. D.
1961   "Neural Mechanisms of Auditory Discrimination", in: *Sensory Communica-
       tion*, W. A. Rosenblith (ed.): 257-78 (Cambridge, Mass.: MIT Press).
Negus, V. E.
1949   *The Comparative Anatomy and Physiology of the Larynx* (New York: Grune
       and Stratton).
Neuburger, M.
1910   *History of Medicine* (London: Oxford University Press).
Newby, H. A.
1958   *Audiology – Principals and Practice* (New York: Appleton-Century-Crofts).
Norman, D. A.
1969   *Memory and Attention* (New York: Wiley).
Oberborbeck, F.

1961 "Musikerziehung", in: *Die Musik in Geschichte und Gegenwart*, F. Blume (ed.), vol. 9 (Bärenreiter, Kassel).

Obermayer, M. E.
1955 *Psychocutaneus Medicine* (Springfield, Ill.).

Olds, J.
1956 "Neurophysiology of Drive", *Psychiatric Research Reports (APA)* 6: 15-22.

Olson, H. F.
1957 *Acoustical Engineering* (Princeton, N.J.: Van Nostrand).

Osgood, C. E. and T. A. Sebeok
1954 *Psycholinguistics – A Survey of Theory and Research Problems* (Baltimore, Maryland: Waverly).

Osgood, C. E., G. J. Suci, and P. H. Tennenbaum
1957 *Measurement of Meaning* (Urbana: University of Illinois Press).

Osser, H., P. Ostwald, B. MacWhinney, and R. Casey
1973 "Glossolalic Speech from a Psycholinguistic Perspective", *J. Psycholing. Res.* 2: 9-19.

Ostwald, P. F.
1959 "When People Whistle", *Language and Speech* 2. 3: 137-45. Reprinted in this volume.

1960a "Human Sounds", in: *Psychological and Psychiatric Aspects of Speech and Hearing*, D. A. Barbara (ed.): 110-37 (Springfield, Ill.: Thomas). Reprinted in this volume.

1960b "The Sounds of Human Behavior – A Survey of the Literature", *Logos* 3. 1: 13-24. Reprinted in this volume.

1960c "A Method for the Objective Denotation of the Sound of the Human Voice", *Journal of Psychosomatic Research* 4: 301-05. Reprinted in this volume.

1960d "Sound, Music, and Human Behavior", in: *Music Therapy*, E. H. Schneider (ed.): 107-125 (Kansas: National Association for Music Therapy). Reprinted in this volume.

1960e "Visual Denotation of Human Sounds", *Archives of General Psychiatry* 3: 117-21. Reprinted in this volume.

1961a "The Sounds of Emotional Disturbance", *Archives of General Psychiatry* 5: 587-92. Reprinted in this volume.

1961b "Psychopathologic Mechanisms in Aversive Responses to Noise", in this volume. Abstract published in *Journal of the Acoustical Society of America* 33: 858.

1961c "Humming, Sound, and Symbol", *The Journal of Auditory Research* 3: 224-32. Reprinted in this volume.

1961d "Behavior Changes Produced by Selected Acoustic Stimuli", 3rd World Congress of Psychiatry (Montreal, Canada). Reprinted in this volume.

1963 *Soundmaking: The Acoustic Communication of Emotion* (Springfield: C. C. Thomas).

1964a "How the Patient Communicates about Disease with the Doctor", in: Sebeok et al. (1964): 11-34. Reprinted in this volume.

1964b "Acoustic Manifestations of Emotional Disturbance", *Disorders of Communication* XLII: *Research Publications, Proceedings of Association for Research in Nervous and Mental Disease*. Reprinted in this volume.

1964c "Color Hearing: A Missing Link Between Normal Perception and the Hallucination", *Arch. Gen. Psychiat.* 11: 40-47. Reprinted in this volume.

1967 "The Inner Speech of Psychotherapy", *Am. J. Psychother.* 21. 4: 757-66. Reprinted in this volume.

1968 "Symptoms, Diagnosis, and Concepts of Disease: Some Comments on the

Semiotics of Patient-Physician Communication", *Social Science Information* 7. 4: 95-106. Reprinted in this volume.

1969a "Inner Speech and Clinical Sensitivity", *Hospital and Community Psychiatry* 20: 34-38.

1969b *Psychiatric Evaluation and Treatment of Patients with Major Speech Handicaps* (= *California Mental Health Research Monograph* No. 10, Department of Mental Hygiene, Sacramento, Calif.).

1970 "Three Books About Stuttering", *American Journal of Psychiatry* 25: 331-34.

Ostwald, P. F., D. G. Freedman, and J. H. Kurtz

1962 "Vocalization of Infant Twins", *Folia Phoniat.* 14: 37-50. Reprinted in this volume.

Ostwald, P. F., R. Phibbs, and S. Fox

1968 "Diagnostic Use of Infant Cry", *Biol. neonat.* 13: 68: 82. Reprinted in this volume.

Ostwald, P. F., I. H. Slis, and L. F. Willems

1967 "Synthesis of Human Infant Cries", in: *Progress Report* 2: 109, Institute of Perception Research (Eindhoven: Holland).

Panconcelli-Calzia, G.

1954 "Leonardo da Vinci und die Frage vom Sprechenden und Weinenden Foetus im Maerchenmotiv vom 'Starken Knaben'", *Münchener Mediz. Wochenschr.* 96: 1456-58.

Parmelee, A. H.

1955 "Infant Speech Development: A Report of the Study of One Child by Magnetic Tape Recordings", *J. Pediat.* 46: 447-50.

Parrack, H. O.

1961 "Effects of Acoustic Energy", in: *Aero-Space Medicine*, H. G. Armstrong (ed.): 284-323 (Baltimore: Williams and Wilkins).

Partanen, J. J., O. Wasz-Höckert, V. Vuorenkoski, K. Theorell, E. H. Valanne, and J. Lind

1967 "Auditory Identification of Pain by Signals of Young Infants in Pathological Conditions and its Sound Spectrographic Basis", *Ann. Paediat. Fenn.* 13: 56-63.

Patau, K., E. Therman, D. W. Smith, S. L. Inhorn, and H. P. Wagner

1960 "Multiple Congenital Anomaly Caused by an Extra Autosome", *Lancet*, i: 790.

Pavlov, I. P.

1928 *Lectures on Conditioned Reflexes*, Vol. I (New York).

Penfield, W.

1968 "Memory and Perception", in: *Perception and its Disorders*, D. A. Hamburg, K. H. Pribram, and A. J. Stunkard (eds.): 108-22 (Baltimore: Williams and Wilkins).

Penfield, W. and L. Roberts

1959 *Speech and Brain Mechanisms* (Princeton, N.J.: Princeton University Press).

Peters, P. S.

1969 "On the Complexity of Language Processing by the Brain", in: *Information Processing in the Nervous System*, K. N. Leibovic (ed.): 51-83 (New York: Springer).

Peterson, A. and P. V. Brüel

1957 "Instruments for Noise Measurements", in: C. M. Harris (1957).

Peterson, G. E. and J. E. Shoup

1966 "The Elements of an Acoustic Phonetic Theory", *J. Speech and Hearing Research* 9: 68-99.

Pfister, O.

1912 "Die Ursache der Farbenbegleitung bei akustischen Wahrnehmungen und das Wesen anderer Synaesthesien", *Imago* 1: 265-75.

Pick, A.
1931 "Aphasie", in: *Handbuch der Normalen und Pathologischen Physiologie*, A. Bethe and G. von Bergmann (eds.), vol. 15. 2: 1416-1524 (Berlin: Springer).

Pickett, J. M.
1967 "Recent Research on Speech-Analyzing Aids for the Deaf", manuscript (Gallaudet College, Washington, D.C. 20002).

Pierce, J. R.
1961 *Symbols, Signals, and Noise* (New York: Harper).

Pierce, J. R., and E. E. David Jr.
1958 *Man's World of Sound* (New York: Doubleday).

Pike, K. L.
1967 *Language in Relation to a Unified Theory of the Structure of Human Behavior* (The Hague: Mouton).

Pittenger, R. E., C. F. Hockett, and J. J. Danehy
1960 *The First Five Minutes* (Ithaca, New York: Paul Martineau).

Pittenger, R. E. and H. L. Smith Jr.
1957 "A Basis for Some Contributions of Linguistics to Psychiatry", *Psychiatry* 20: 61-78.

Plato
1937 *Cratylos* in: *Dialogues of Plato*, translated by Jowett, Vol. 1: 173-229 (New York: Random House).

Plum, F.
1970 "Neurological Integration of Behavior and Metabolic Control of Breathing", in: *Breathing: Hering-Breuer Centenary Symposium*, R. Porter (ed.): 159-81 (London: Churchill).

Pollack, I.
1961 "Hearing", *Annu. Rev. Psychol.* 12: 335-62.

Potter, R. K., G. A. Kopp, and H. C. Green
1947 *Visible Speech* (New York: D. van Nostrand Co., Inc.).

Price, B.
1950 "Primary Biases in Twin Studies", *Amer. J. Hum. Genet.* 2: 293-352.

Rainer, J. D. and K. Z. Altshuler
1966 "Comprehensive Mental Health Services for the Deaf" (New York State Psychiatric Institute).

Rangell, L.
1954 "The Psychology of Poise – With a Special Elaboration on the Psychic Significance of the Snout or Peri-oral Region", *Int. J. Psychoan.* 35: 331-32.

Rapaport, D.
1946 *Diagnostic Psychological Testing*, Vol. II (Chicago: Year Book).
1960 *The Structure of Psychoanalytic Theory – A Systematizing Attempt* (New York: International Universities).

Redlich, F. C. and D. X. Freedman
1966 *The Theory and Practice of Psychiatry* (New York: Basic Books).

Reichard, G., R. Jakobson, and E. Werth
1949 "Language and Synesthesia", *Word* 5: 224-33.

Révész, G.
1954 *Introduction to the Psychology of Music* (Norman, Oklahoma: University of Oklahoma Press).
1956 *The Origins and Prehistory of Language* (London: Longmans, Green).

Rimbaud, A.
1948 "Voyelles", in: *Oeuvres Complètes*, Henri Kaeser (ed.), vol. 2 (Lausanne,

Switzerland).

Ringel, R. L. and D. D. Kluppel
  1964   "Neonatal Crying: A Normative Study", *Folia phoniat.* 16: 44-58.
Rinkel, M.
  1966   *Biological Treatment of Mental Illness* (New York: Page and Co.).
Rioch, D. McK.
  1961   "Dimensions of Human Behavior", in: *Lectures on Experimental Psychiatry*,
           H. Brosin (ed.): 341-61.
Robertson, J. P. S. and S. J. Shamsie
  1959   "A Systematic Examination of Gibberish in a Multilingual Schizophrenic
           Patient", *Language and Speech* 2: 1-8.
Rockwell, D. and P. Ostwald
  1968   "Amphetamine Use and Abuse in Psychiatric Patients", *Archives of General
           Psychiatry* 18: 612-16.
Roman, K. G.
  1959   "Handwriting and Speech", *Logos* 2: 29-39.
Roose, L. J.
  1960   "The Influence of Psychosomatic Research on the Psychoanalytic Process",
           J. Amer. Psychoan. Assn. 8: 317-34.
Rosen, C.
  1971   "Art Has its Reasons", *The New York Review*, June 17: 32-38.
Rosen, V. H.
  1969   "Sign Phenomena and their Relationship to Unconscious Meaning", *Inter-
           national Journal of Psycho-analysis* 50: 197-207.
Rudmose, H. W. et al.
  1948   "Voice Measurements with an Audio Spectrometer", *J. Acoust. Soc. Amer.*
           20: 503-12.
Ruesch, J.
  1955   "Nonverbal Language and Therapy", *Psychiatry* 18: 323-30.
  1957   *Disturbed Communication* (New York: W. W. Norton).
Ruesch, J. and G. Bateson
  1951   *Communication – The Social Matrix of Psychiatry* (New York: Norton).
Ruesch, J. and W. Kees
  1956   *Nonverbal Communication* (Berkeley and Los Angeles: University of California
           Press).
Rümke, H. C.
  1961   "Problems of Nosology and Nomenclature in the Mental Disorders", in:
           Field Studies in the Mental Disorders, J. Zubin (ed.): 73-84 (New York).
Rush, J.
  1867   *The Philosophy of the Human Voice*[6] (Philadelphia).
Sachs, C.
  1940   *The History of Musical Instruments* (New York: Norton).
  1953   *Rhythm and Tempo* (New York: Norton).
Sadoff, R. and D. Collins
  1968   "Passive Dependency in Stutterers", *Amer. J. Psychiatry* 124: 8.
Salk, L.
  1960   "The Effects of the Normal Heartbeat Sound of the Newborn Infant",
           World Fed. Mental Health/AM 13/16, TS. E/3 (Edinburgh, Scotland).
Salomon, G. and A. Starr
  1960   "Electromyography of Middle Ear Muscles in Man During Motor Activities",
           Acta Neurol. Scandinavia 39: 161-68.
Sapir, E.
  1949   *Selected Writings*, D. Mandelbaum (ed.) (Berkeley: University of California

Press).
Saul, L. J.
1948   "Feminine Significance of the Nose", *Psychoan. Quart.* 17: 51-57.
Schilder, P.
1950   *The Image and Appearance of the Human Body* (New York).
Schilling, R.
1929   "Über Inneres Sprechen", *Z. Psychol.* 3: 204.
Schroeder, M. R.
1968   "Determination of the Geometry of the Human Vocal Tract by Acoustic Measurements", *J. Acoust. Soc. Am.*
Schullian, D. M. and M. Schoen (eds.)
1948   *Music and Medicine* (New York: Schumann).
Schumann, H. J.
1959   *Träume der Blinden* (Basel).
Scott, W. C. M.
1955   "A Note on Blathering", *Int. J. Psychoanal.* 36: 2-4.
1958   "Noise, Speech, and Technique", *Int. J. Psychoanal.* 39: 1-4.
Scriabin. A.
1913   *Poem of Fire: "Prometheus".*
Searl, M. N.
1936   "The Psychology of Screaming", *Int. J. Psycho-Anal.* 14: 193-205.
Searles, H. F.
1960   *The Nonhuman Environment* (New York: Int. Univ. Press).
Sebeok, T. A., A. Hayes, and M. C. Bateson (eds.)
1964   *Approaches to Semiotics* (The Hague: Mouton).
Sedláčková, E.
1964   "Analyse acoustique de la voix de nouveaux-nés", *Folia phoniat.* 16: 44-58.
Semmes, J.
1966   "Science and Inner Experience", *Science* 154: 754-56.
Shands, H. C.
1967   "Outline of a General Theory of Human Communication: Implications of Normal and Pathological Schizogenesis", in: *Communication Concepts and Perspectives*, L. Thayer (ed.) (Washington D.C.: Spartan Books). Also published in *Social Science Information* 7. 4: 55-94.
1970   *Semiotic Approaches to Psychiatry* (The Hague: Mouton).
Shannon, C. A. and W. Weaver
1949   *The Mathematical Theory of Communication* (Urbana: University of Illinois Press).
Shapiro, J.
1966   "An Introduction to Inner Speech", Discussion Paper #74, *Arkansas Rehabilitation Research and Training Center* (Fayetteville, Ark.).
Shatin, L.
1957   "The Influence of Rhythmic Drumbeat Stimuli upon the Pulse Rate and General Activity of Long-Term Schizophrenics", *J. Ment. Sci.* 103: 172-188.
Shaw, R. F.
1938   *Finger Painting* (Boston).
Sheldon, W. H.
1940   *The Varieties of Human Physique* (New York).
Sheppard, W. C. and H. L. Lane
1965   "Development of the Prosodic Features of Infants' Vocalizing", Report from Center for Research on Language and Language Behavior (Ann Arbor, Mich.).
Sherman, M.

1927   "The Differentiation of Emotional Responses in Infants", *Comp. Psychol.* 7: 335-51.

Sherwin, A. C.
   1953   "Reactions to Music of Autistic (Schizophrenic) Children", *Amer. J. Psychiat.* 109: 823-31.
   1958   "A Consideration of the Therapeutic Use of Music in Psychiatric Illness", *J. Nerv. and Ment. Dis.* 127: 84-90.

Siegel, S.
   1956   *Nonparametric Statistics for the Behavioral Sciences* (New York: McGraw-Hill).

Silbermann, R. M.
   1971   *CHAM* (Amsterdam: Excerpta Medica).

Skinner, B. F.
   1957   *Verbal Behavior* (New York: Appleton-Century-Crofts).

Sklar, B.
   1969   "A Feedback Model of the Stuttering Problem – An Engineer's View", *J. Speech Hearing Dis.* 34: 226-30.

Slater, E., A. W. Beard, and E. Glithero
   1963   "The Schizophrenic Psychoses of Epilepsy (Psychiatric Aspects)", *Brit. J. Psychiat* 109: 95-150.

Sloane, H. and B. MacAulay
   1968   *Operant Procedures in Remedial Speech and Language Training* (New York: Houghton-Mifflin).

Smith, K. and J. O. Sines
   1960   "Demonstration of a Peculiar Odor in the Sweat of Schizophrenic Patients", *Arch. Gen. Psychiatry* 2: 184-88.

Snodgrass, G. J. A. I., L. J. Butler, and N. E. France
   1966   "The 'D' (13-15) Trisomy Syndrome: an Analysis of 7 Examples", *Arch. Dis. Childh.* 41: 250.

Sontag, L. W. and Wallace, R. F.
   1935   "The Response of the Human Foetus to Sound Stimuli", *Child Development* 6: 253-58.

Spitta, P.
   1951   Johann Sebastian Bach – His Work and Influence on the Music of Germany (translated by Bell and Fuller-Maitland), vol. 1 (New York: Dover).

Spitz, R. A.
   1945   "Hospitalism: An Inquiry into the Genesis of Psychiatric Conditions in Early Childhood", *Psychoanal. Stud. Child.* 1: 53-74.
   1957   *No and Yes* (New York: International Universities Press).
   1965   *The First Year of Life* (New York: International Universities Press).

Spoerri, T.
   1964   *Sprachphänomene und Psychose* (Basel: S. Karger).

Stanislavski, C.
   1949   *Building a Character* (New York).

Starkweather, J. A.
   1956   "The Communication Value of Content-free Speech", *Amer. J. Psychol.* 69: 121-23.
   1961   "Vocal Communication of Personality and Human Feelings", *J. of Communication* 11: 63-72.
   1967   "Vocal Behavior as an Informant Channel of Speaker Status", in: *Research in Verbal Behavior and Some Neurophysiological Implications*, K. and S. Salzinger (eds.) (New York: Academic Press).

Steer, M. D. and T. D. Hanley
   1957   "Instruments of Diagnosis, Therapy, and Research", in: *Handbook of Speech Pathology*, L. Travis (ed.).
Sterba, R.
   1946   "Toward the Problem of the Musical Process", *Psychoan. Rev.* 33: 37-43.
Sterling, T. D.
   1967   "A New Direction in Rehabilitation through Advanced Instrumentation and Computation", *JAMA* 200: 145-49.
Stetson, R. H.
   1951   *Motor Phonetics*² (Amsterdam: North Holland Pub. Co.).
Stevens, S. S. (ed.)
   1951   *Handbook of Experimental Psychology* (New York: Wiley).
   1956   "Calculation of the Loudness of Complex Noise", *Journal of the Acoustical Society of America* 28: 807-32.
Stewart, A. et al.
   1954   "Excessive Infant Crying (Colic) in Relation to Parent Behavior", *Amer. J. Psychiatry* 110: 687-94.
Stovkis, R.
   1958   "Psychosomatische Gedanken über Musik", in: *Musik in der Medizin*, H. R. Teirich (ed.): 43-54 (Stuttgart: Fischer).
Strauss, H.
   1959   "Epileptic Disorders", in: *American Handbook of Psychiatry*, S. Arieti (ed.): 1109-43 (New York).
Strawinsky, I.
   1947   *Poetics of Music in the Form of Six Easy Lessons* (New York: Vintage).
Strawinsky, I. and R. Craft
   1959   *Conversations with Igor Strawinsky* (Garden City, New York: Doubleday).
Sullivan, H. S.
   1953   *Interpersonal Theory of Psychiatry* (New York: Norton).
   1954   *The Psychiatric Interview* (New York: Norton).
Tanner, W. P.
   1958   "What is Masking?", *Journal of the Acoustical Society of America* 30: 919-21.
Teirich, H. R.
   1958   *Musik in der Medizin* (Stuttgart: Fischer).
Tembrock, G.
   1959   *Tierstimmen – Eine Einführung in die Bioakustik* (Wittenberg Lutherstadt: Ziemsen).
Thompson, E. T. and A. C. Hayden (eds.)
   1961   *Standard Nomenclature of Diseases and Operations*⁵ (New York: McGraw-Hill).
Thorek, M.
   1946   *The Face in Health and Disease* (Philadelphia).
Tilly, M.
   1948   "Music Therapy", unpublished, Med. Lib. Assoc. (San Francisco).
Trager, G. L.
   1958   "Paralanguage: A First Approximation", *Studies in Linguistics* 13: 1-12.
Trojan, F.
   1952   "Der Ausdruck der Sprechstimme – Eine Phonetische Lautstilistik", *Wiener Beiträge zur Hals-, Nasen-, und Ohrenheilkunde*, vol. 1 (Wien-Düsseldorf: W. Mandrich).
   1959   "Die Ausdruckstheorie der Sprechstimme (Literatur seit 1945)", *Phonetica* 4: 121-50.
   1960   "Die Stimme des Hypnotiseurs", *Folia Phoniat.* 12: 137-44.

Truax, C. and D. Wargo
    1966 "Psychotherapeutic Encounters that Change Behavior: For Better or for Worse", *Am. J. Psychother.* 20. 3: 499-520.
Truby, H. M.
    1959 "Acoustico-Cineradiographic Analysis Considerations with Especial Reference to Certain Consonantal Complexes", *Acta Radiologica*, Supplementum 182 (Stockholm).
    1960 "Some Aspects of Acoustical and Cineradiographic Analysis of Newborn-Infant and Adult Phonation and Associated Vocal-Tract Activity", *J. Acoust. Soc. Am.* 32: 1518.
Truby, H. M. and J. Lind
    1965 "Cry Sounds of the Newborn Infant", in: *Newborn Infant Cry* (= *Acta Paediat.* Suppl. 163) (Uppsala).
Turnbull, R. B.
    1951 *Radio and Television Sound Effects* (New York: Rinehart).
Uhlich, E.
    1957 "Synesthesie und Geschlecht", *Z. Exp. Angewa. Psychol.* 4: 31-57.
Uhr, L. M. (ed.)
    1966 *Pattern Recognition* (New York: Wiley).
United States Army
    1950 *Atmospheric Physics and Sounds Propagation* (DPA Project 3-99-04-022).
United States Bureau of the Census
    1959 *Statistical Abstract of the United States: 1959* (Washington D.C.).
Van den Berg, J.
    1964 "Physical Aspects of Voice Production", in: *Research Potentials in Voice Physiology*, D. W. Brewer (ed.): 63-101 (New York: University Publishers).
Van der Heide, C.
    1941 "A Case of Pollakiuria Nervosa", *Psychoan. Quart.* 10: 267-383.
Vetter, H.
    1969 *Language Behavior and Psychopathology* (Chicago, Ill.: Rand McNally).
Von Békésy, G.
    1960 *Experiments in Hearing* (New York: McGraw-Hill).
    1969 "Similarities of Inhibition in the Different Sense Organs", *American Psychologist* 24: 707-19.
Von Bertalanffy, L.
    1968 *General System Theory* (New York: Braziller).
Von Gierke, H.
    1957 "Aircraft Noise Sources", in: C. M. Harris (1957).
Vuorenkoski, V., J. Lind, T. J. Partanen, J. Lejeune, J. Lafourcade and O. Wasz-Höckert
    1966 "Spectrographic Analysis of Cries from Children with Maladie du Cri du Chat", *Ann. Paediat. Fenn.* 12: 174-80.
Vygotsky, L. S.
    1962 *Thought and Language* (Cambridge, Mass.: MIT Press).
Waddington, C. H.
    1969 "A Matter of Life and Death", *New York Review of Books* 12: 29-34.
Wartenberg, R.
    1947 "The Babinsky Reflex After Fifty Years", *J. Am. Med. Assoc.* 135: 763-67.
Washburn, S. and D. A. Hamburg
    1968 "Aggressive Behavior in Old World Monkeys and Apes", in: *Primates: Studies in Adaptation and Variability*, P. Jay (ed.) (New York: Rinehart and Winston).
Waskow, I.

1966 "The Effects of Drugs on Speech: A Review", *Psychopharm. Bull.* 3: 1–20.

Wasz-Höckert, O., J. Lind, V. Vuorenkoski, T. Partanen, and E. Valanne
1968 "The Infant Cry – A Spectrographic and Auditory Analysis", *Clinics in Developmental Medicine* 29 (London: Spastics International Medical Publications with Heinemann).

Wasz-Höckert, W., T. Partanen, V. Vuorenkoski, E. Valanne, and K. Michelsson
1964 "Effect of Training on Ability to Identify Preverbal Vocalizations", *Develop. Med. Child Neurol.* 6: 393-96.

Waterman, J. I.
1970 *Perspectives in Linguistics* (Chicago, Ill.: University of Chicago).

Watson, D. O.
1964 *Talk with your Hands* (Menasha, Wisconsin: George Banta).

Weinstein, E. A. and R. L. Kahn
1955 *Denial of Illness – Symbolic and Psychological Aspects* (Springfield: Thomas).

Weir, R.
1966 "Development of Phonology in the Child", in: *The Genesis of Language*, Smith and Miller (eds.) (Cambridge, Mass.: MIT Press).

Weiss, D.
1967 "Cluttering", *Folia Phoniat.* 19: 233-63.

Welch, B. L. and A. S. Welch
1970 *Physiological Effects of Noise* (New York: Plenum).

Welleck, A.
1931 "Zur Geschichte und Kritik der Synaesthesie-Forschung", *Arch. Ges. Psychol.* 79: 325-84.

Wellesz, E. (ed.)
1957 *Ancient and Oriental Music* (London: Oxford University Press).

Wells, F.
1919 "Symbolism and Synaesthesia", *Amer. J. Insan.* 75: 481-88.

Wentworth, H. and S. B. Flexner
1960 *Dictionary of American Slang* (New York: Crowell).

Werner, H.
1948 *Comparative Psychology of Mental Development* (New York: International Universities Press).

Werner, H. and B. Kaplan
1963 *Symbol Formation* (New York: Wiley).

Wessel, F. T.
1955 *The Affektenlehre in the 18th Century* (Ph.D. Thesis, Indiana University).

West, L. (ed.)
1962 *Hallucinations* (New York: Grune and Stratton).

West, R.
1957 *The Pathology of Speech and the Rationale of its Rehabilitation* (New York).

Wever, E. G. and M. Lawrence
1954 *Physiological Acoustics* (New Jersey: Princeton).

Whetnal, E.
1956 "The Development of Usable (Residual) Hearing in the Deaf Child", *J. Laryngol. and Otol.* 70: 630-47.

Whitfield, I. C.
1967 *The Auditory Pathway* (Baltimore: Williams and Wilkins).

Wilmer, H.
1951 "An Auditory Sound Association Technique", *Science* 14: 621-22.
1967 "Television: Technical and Artistic Aspects of Videotaping in Psychiatric Teaching", *J. Nerv. Ment. Dis.* 144: 207.

Winitz, H.

1969   *Articulatory Acquisition and Behavior* (New York: Appleton-Century-Crofts).
Witzleben, H.
   1958   "On Loneliness", *Psychiatry* 21: 37-43.
Wolff, C.
   1952   *The Hand in Psychological Diagnosis* (New York).
Wolff, P.
   1967   "The Role of Biological Rhythms in Early Psychological Development",
          Bull. Menn. Clinic 31: 197-218.
Wood, C. C., W. R. Goff, and R. S. Day
   1971   "Auditory Evoked Potentials During Speech Perception", *Science* 173:
          1248-51.
Zangwill, O. L.
   1964   "Current Status of Cerebral Dominance", *Association for Research in Nervous
          and Mental Disease, Disorders of Communication* 42: 103-13 (Baltimore:
          Williams and Wilkins).
Zipf, G. K.
   1959   *Human Behavior and the Principle of Least Effort* (Cambridge, Mass.).

AUTHOR INDEX

SUBJECT INDEX

Electronic
  communication, 26-27
  music, 26, 199
  (also see Mass media, Telephone)
Embolophrasias, 233, 255
  (also see Hesitation phenomena)
Emotion, 197, 203
Emotional
  behavior, 167, 171
  disturbance, 109-134
  expression, 67, 71-72, 111, 150, 167, 240
Empathy, 225
Engrams, 163, 219, 374
Epilepsy, 144, 152, 161, 240, 288
Excitement, 66, 133, 150, 162

Facial expression, 239-241, 262
  (also see Kinesics)
Falsetto voice, 55
Fantasy, 70, 302
Fear, 22, 45, 66, 134, 239, 365
  (also see Anxiety)
Feedback, 279
  (also see Auditory feedback)
Flatus, 24, 28, 50, 168, 183, 229
"Flat" voice, 106, 113
Foot behavior, 242-243
  (also see Kinesics)
Four-letter words, 161, 184
Frustration, 203
Fugue, 186

Gestalt principles, 188, 198
Gestures, 346
  (also see Hand signs)
Gilles de la Tourette Syndrome, 141
Glossolalia, 272
Grammar, 7, 78, 83, 85, 161
Graphology, 242
Group
  dynamics, 63
  therapy, 153, 361-362, 364-365
Growth disturbances, 238
Guido d'Arezzo, 24, 46, 204

Hair, 239
Hallucinations, 52, 174, 182, 210, 218-219, 272-273
Hand signs, 28, 241-242, 348-349
  (also see Kinesics)
Harmony, 163, 199
Healing, 206
  (also see Psychotherapy)

Hearing, 113-114
  (also see Auditory perception, Listening)
Hearing aids, 346, 353
Heart murmurs, 230
Heartbeat, 28, 168, 180
Hemispheric specialization, 373
  (also see Brain mechanisms)
Hesitation phenomena, 40, 169, 250-251, 272, 358
History, 22-25, 45-47, 58-60, 70, 78-79, 176, 201, 228-232
Hoarseness, 367
  (also see Rasp)
"Hollow" voice, 105, 113, 128
Human sounds, 20-42, 177-179, 244-259
Humming, 17, 18, 45, 50, 69-76, 169, 234, 249, 251
Hunger cry, 248
  (also see Baby cry)
Hyperacusis, 65, 153
Hypnosis, 160, 165, 273
Hysteria, 100-101, 162, 199, 240, 253, 282
  (also see Neurosis)

Idiolect, 380
Illusion, 171-172, 182
Imitation, 33
Immature personality, 172
Imprinting, 44, 84
Improvisation, 274
Inappropriate affect, 149
Infancy, 18, 54, 71, 153, 168, 183, 248, 323, 325
  deafness in, 346
  reflex patterns during, 243
Infant vocalizations, 55, 75-76, 84, 112, 117, 248, 325, 340
  (also see Baby cry)
Information
  processing, 157, 161, 370
  theory, 49, 81, 133, 165, 372
Inner speech, 79, 86, 226, 270-279, 356, 365
  dialogues, 225, 266-267
Intensity of sound, 163-164, 178
  (also see Acoustics)
Interpersonal relationships, 66-67, 265-266
Interpretation, 157, 225, 303
  (also see Semiotics)
Interviews, 260-269, 361
  initial interview, 359

418   SUBJECT INDEX

Intonation, 149-252-254, 303, 377
  (also see Speech melody)
Intra-uterine environment, 180
  crying in utero, 54, 229
  (also see Prenatal development)

Jargon, 233
Joy, 203

Kinesics, 8, 226, 233, 241-243, 362
  (also see Nonverbal behavior)

Language, 6, 7, 19
  acquisition, 218, 284, 346
  change, 380
  code, 232, 234, 347
  communal, 379
  competence, 276
  deficit in deafness, 347-348
  development, 83-86, 152
  medical, 237-238
  non-human, 249-250
  origins of, 78, 216, 247-248
  psychiatric, 291-300
Larynx, 48, 178, 375
  (also see Voice)
Laughter, 149, 168, 184, 246-247
Life cycle, 183-184, 367
Linguistics, 7, 43, 77-90, 252
Listening, 49-53, 63-66, 157, 189, 203
  (also see Auditory perception)
Localization of sounds, 183
Loudness, 178, 194
  (also see Intensity of sound)
Love, 73-74

Magical beliefs, 61-62, 360
Manic-depressive psychosis, 115
Masking, 72, 161, 166
Mass media, 380
  (also see Electronic communication)
Meaning, 32, 161, 166, 181, 367
  (also see Semantics)
Medical
  education, 306
  practice of, 8, 17, 226, 228, 336
  research, 228-235
Meditation, 276
Melody, 186
  (also see Music)
Memory, 17, 218, 373
Mental retardation, 123, 249-251, 285, 293

Mimicry, 22
Monotony, 127-128
  (also see "Flat" voice)
Mood music, 193
Moods, 186
Mother-child relationship, 17, 55, 60, 73, 109, 133, 203, 247-248, 284
Motor
  automatisms, 358
  control of soundmaking, 186, 205-206
  patterning of speech, 48, 84, 347, 379
  theory of speech perception, 273, 374
Mourning, 187
Music, 21-27, 50, 62, 67, 69-70, 73, 79, 158, 160, 162, 163-165, 367
  critics, 205
  elements of, 185-186, 204
  emotion and, 197-200
  human behavior and, 176-190
  lessons, 201-209
  social functions of, 164
  teaching, 199, 201
  therapy, 158, 164-165, 188-189, 191, 199, 206-208
Musical
  expression, 185-186
  ideas, 187-189
  instruments, 21, 23-27, 45-47, 59, 165, 186-187, 206, 229
  language, 198
  notation, 42, 102, 109-110, 232, 234, 317
  organization of sound, 204
  styles, 193-195
  symbols, 186
  thinking, 52, 88
Musicology, 17, 20, 43, 109, 210
Mutism, 55-56
Mysticism, 22
Myths, 62, 109, 167, 170, 218

Nasality, 144, 351
Neonatalogy, 325-338, 343, 345
Neophasia, 272
Neurolinguistics, 86-89
Neurological tests, 241-243
Neurophysiology, 48, 89, 95, 163, 357, 370
Neurosis, 99-101, 116, 125-126, 130-131, 138, 162, 233, 240, 295-296
Noise, 20, 25, 53, 67, 123-124, 158, 160, 165, 167, 196, 208, 232
  aversive responses to, 170-175